JLA RULES OF ENGAGEMENT

JLA RULES OF ENGAGEMENT

Dan DiDio VP-Editorial Dan Raspler, Mike Carlin Editors-original series Stephen Wacker Associate Editor-original series Valerie D'Orazio Assistant Editor-original series Bob Greenberger Senior Editor-collected edition Robbin Brosterman Senior Art Director Paul Levitz President & Publisher Georg Brewer VP-Design & Retail Product Development Richard Bruning Senior VP-Creative Director Patrick Caldon Senior VP-Finance & Operations Chris Caramalis VP-Finance Terri Cunningham VP-Managing Editor Alison Gill VP-Manufacturing Lillian Laserson Senior VP & General Counsel Jim Lee Editorial Director-WildStorm David McKillips VP- Advertising & Custom Publishing John Nee VP-Business Development Gregory Noveck Senior VP-Creative Affairs Cheryl Rubin VP-Brand Management Bob Wayne VP-Sales & Marketing

Joe Kelly Rick Veitch **Writers** Darryl Banks Doug Mahnke Duncan Rouleau **Pencillers**
Wayne Faucher Tom Nguyen Aaron Sowd **Inkers** David Baron **Colorist** Ken Lopez Kurt Hathaway
Letterer Doug Mahnke Tom Nguyen **Original Series Covers** SUPERMAN created by Jerry
Siegel and Joe Shuster BATMAN created by Bob Kane WONDER WOMAN created by William Moulton Marston

JLA: RULES OF ENGAGEMENT. Published by DC Comics. Cover and compilation copyright © 2004 DC Comics. All Rights Reserved. Originally published in single magazine form as JLA 77-82. Copyright © 2003 DC Comics. All Rights Reserved. All characters, the distinctive likenesses thereof and related elements featured in this publication are trademarks of DC Comics. The stories, characters and incidents featured in this publication are entirely fictional. DC Comics does not read or accept unsolicited submissions of ideas, stories or artwork. DC Comics, 1700 Broadway, New York, NY 10019. A Warner Bros. Entertainment Company. Printed in Canada. First Printing. ISBN: 1-4012-0215-2. Cover illustration by Doug Mahnke and Tom Nguyen. Cover color by David Baron.

JLA

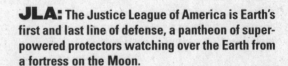

JLA: The Justice League of America is Earth's first and last line of defense, a pantheon of super-powered protectors watching over the Earth from a fortress on the Moon.

Superman: The last son of the doomed planet Krypton, Kal-El uses his incredible powers of flight, super-strength, and invulnerability to fight for truth and justice on his adopted planet, Earth. When not protecting the planet, he is *Daily Planet* reporter Clark Kent, married to fellow journalist Lois Lane.

Batman: Dedicated to ridding the world of crime since the brutal murder of his parents, billionaire Bruce Wayne dons the cape and cowl of the Dark Knight to battle evil from the shadows of Gotham City.

Wonder Woman: Born an Amazonian princess, Diana was chosen to serve as her people's ambassador of peace in the World of Man. Armed with the Lasso of Truth and indestructible bracelets, she directs her gods-given abilities of strength and speed toward the betterment of mankind.

The Flash: A member of the Teen Titans when he was known as Kid Flash, Wally West now takes the place of the fallen Flash, Barry Allen, as the speedster of the Justice League.

Green Lantern: John Stewart didn't necessarily want to be a hero. As an architect he had a good career going, and he saw the role of Green Lantern as a distraction. In time he learned of the tremendous satisfaction that came with using the ring responsibly, but after his actions led to the destruction of the planet Xanshi his spirit was crushed, and he was dragged through a series of ordeals that left him physically crippled as well. Recently John regained the use of his limbs, and he is now coming to terms with the traumatic incidents of his past.

Martian Manhunter: The most dedicated member of the Justice League, J'onn J'onzz has been present for every one of the team's many incarnations. His strength rivals that of Earth's mightiest heroes, and his shape-shifting abilities allow him to pass anonymously among our planet's populace. Currently on leave of absence, J'onn works to overcome his fear of fire.

The Atom: One of the first heroes to join after the League's founding, Ray Palmer is a scientist who harnessed the properties of a white dwarf star. This led to the creation of unique size and weight controls that enable him to reduce his physical form to that of an atom, or even smaller. Forgoing the world of heroics for research and teaching, the Atom remains available as a reserve member. He's been working closely to help Firestorm master his powers.

Firestorm: High school student Ronnie Raymond and nuclear physicist Martin Stein were both present when an explosion occurred at a nuclear reactor. Fused into one being, they found that they had the power to rearrange the atomic structure of inorganic matter, and eventually joined the Justice League. Stein has since disappeared, and Raymond, now struggling with college, is in sole control of the power of Firestorm — as far as we know.

Major Disaster: Small-time thief Paul Booker originally used various scientific devices to create large-scale disasters that would serve as distractions for his robberies. Eventually, the power in the devices was internalized by Booker and he began a career as a super-criminal. After several defeats (and a short stint with a previous incarnation of the League as well as the Suicide Squad), Booker found himself struggling with his evil nature once again — only to be inspired by Superman to righteousness.

Manitou Raven: An Apache American from 3000 years ago with uncanny magical powers, he is the newest member of the JLA. With his wife Dawn, he is adjusting to his new century, his role as earthly champion, and is still learning about his teammates.

Faith: No one is sure who Faith is, or the extent of her abilities. Batman recommended her to the JLA, and the others have accepted her on his word. She has an array of uncatalogued abilities including an aura that makes people trust her completely.

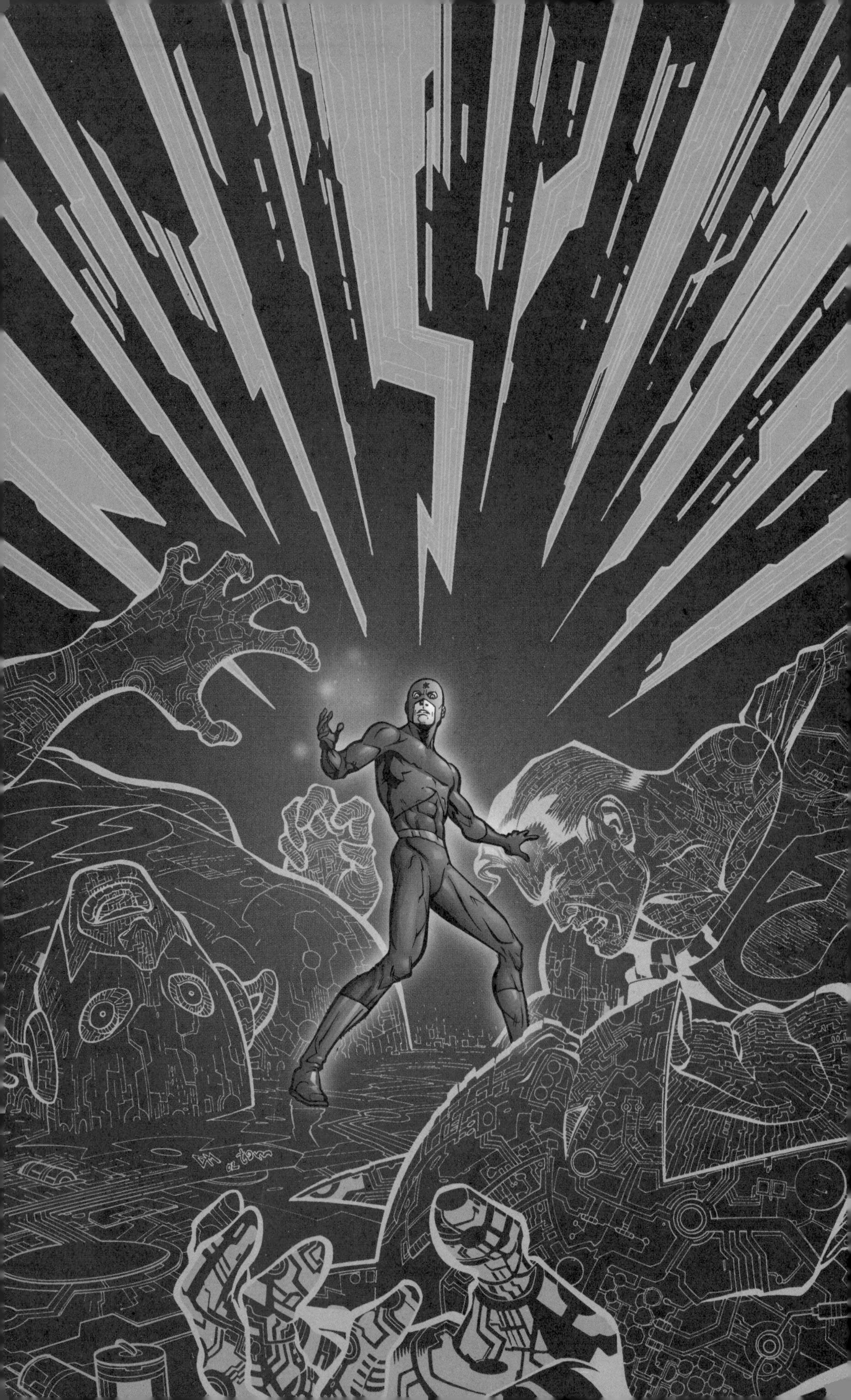

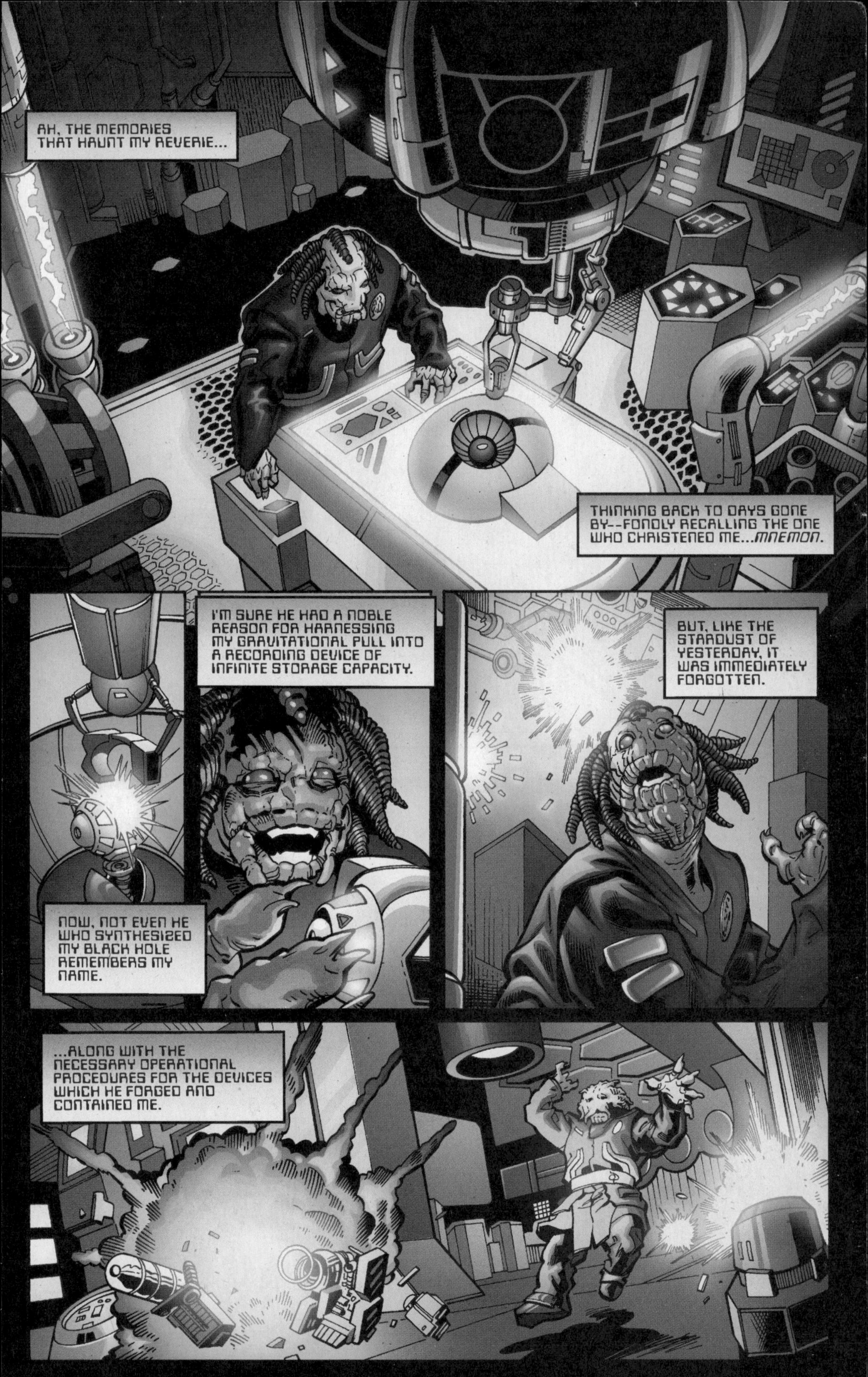
AH, THE MEMORIES THAT HAUNT MY REVERIE...
THINKING BACK TO DAYS GONE BY--FONDLY RECALLING THE ONE WHO CHRISTENED ME...MNEMON.
I'M SURE HE HAD A NOBLE REASON FOR HARNESSING MY GRAVITATIONAL PULL INTO A RECORDING DEVICE OF INFINITE STORAGE CAPACITY.
NOW, NOT EVEN HE WHO SYNTHESIZED MY BLACK HOLE REMEMBERS MY NAME.
BUT, LIKE THE STARDUST OF YESTERDAY, IT WAS IMMEDIATELY FORGOTTEN.
...ALONG WITH THE NECESSARY OPERATIONAL PROCEDURES FOR THE DEVICES WHICH HE FORGED AND CONTAINED ME.

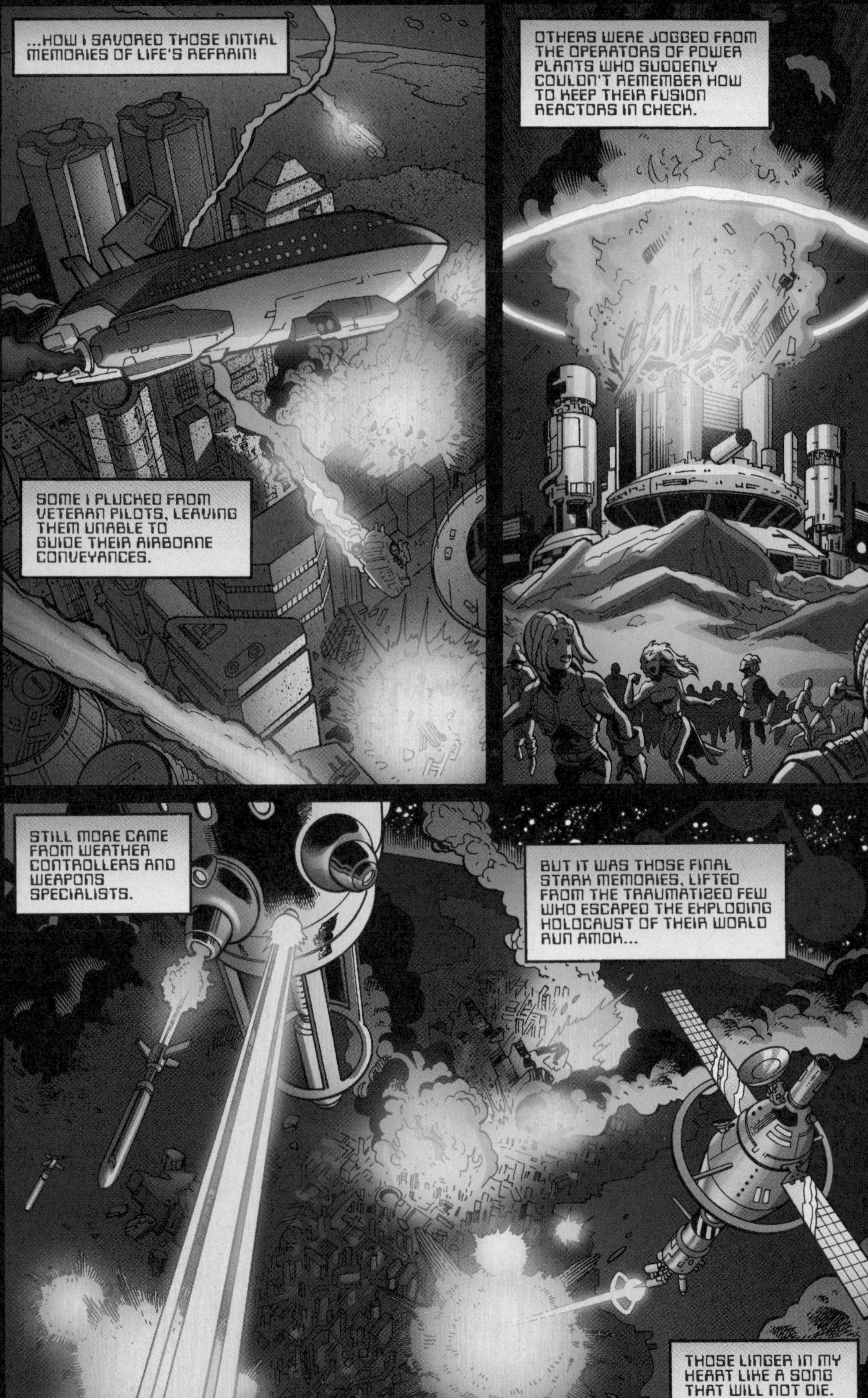
...HOW I SAVORED THOSE INITIAL MEMORIES OF LIFE'S REFRAIN!
SOME I PLUCKED FROM VETERAN PILOTS, LEAVING THEM UNABLE TO GUIDE THEIR AIRBORNE CONVEYANCES.
OTHERS WERE JOGGED FROM THE OPERATORS OF POWER PLANTS WHO SUDDENLY COULDN'T REMEMBER HOW TO KEEP THEIR FUSION REACTORS IN CHECK.
STILL MORE CAME FROM WEATHER CONTROLLERS AND WEAPONS SPECIALISTS.
BUT IT WAS THOSE FINAL STARK MEMORIES, LIFTED FROM THE TRAUMATIZED FEW WHO ESCAPED THE EXPLODING HOLOCAUST OF THEIR WORLD RUN AMOK...
THOSE LINGER IN MY HEART LIKE A SONG THAT WILL NOT DIE.

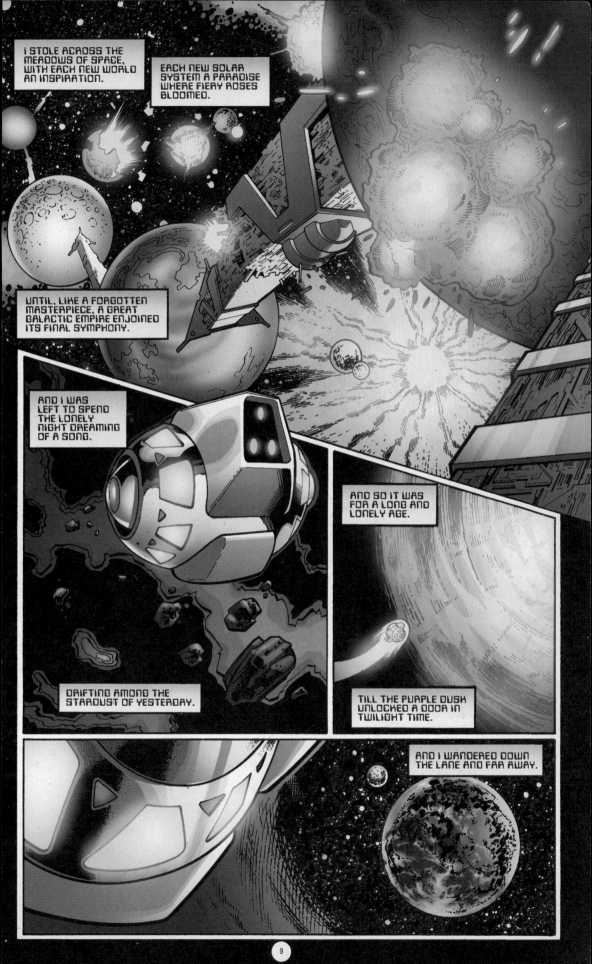

I STOLE ACROSS THE MEADOWS OF SPACE, WITH EACH NEW WORLD AN INSPIRATION.

EACH NEW SOLAR SYSTEM A PARADISE WHERE FIERY ROSES BLOOMED.

UNTIL, LIKE A FORGOTTEN MASTERPIECE, A GREAT GALACTIC EMPIRE ENJOINED ITS FINAL SYMPHONY.

AND I WAS LEFT TO SPEND THE LONELY NIGHT DREAMING OF A SONG.

AND SO IT WAS FOR A LONG AND LONELY AGE.

DRIFTING AMONG THE STARDUST OF YESTERDAY.

TILL THE PURPLE DUSK UNLOCKED A DOOR IN TWILIGHT TIME.

AND I WANDERED DOWN THE LANE AND FAR AWAY.

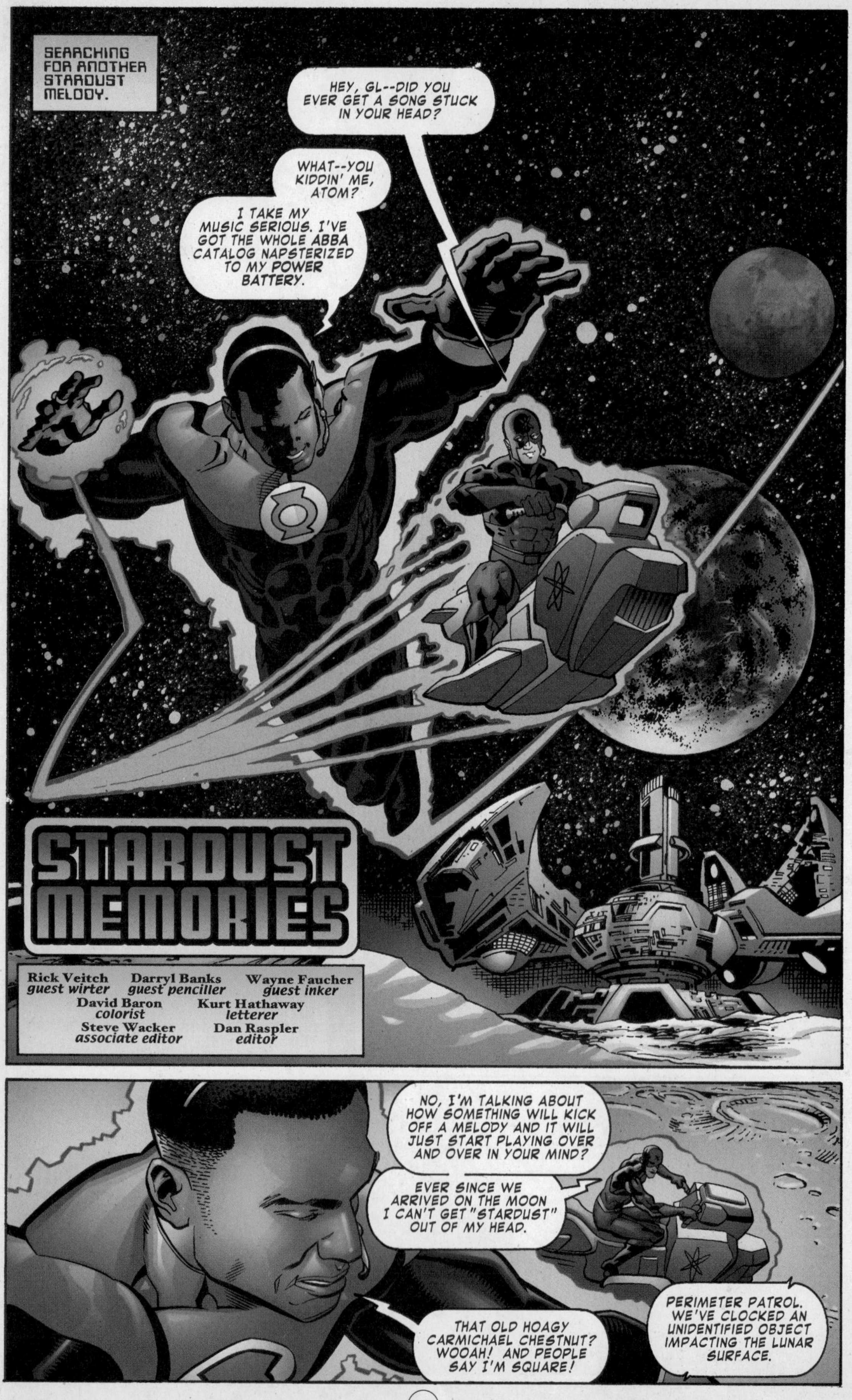

SEARCHING FOR ANOTHER STARDUST MELODY.
HEY, GL--DID YOU EVER GET A SONG STUCK IN YOUR HEAD?
WHAT--YOU KIDDIN' ME, ATOM?
I TAKE MY MUSIC SERIOUS. I'VE GOT THE WHOLE ABBA CATALOG NAPSTERIZED TO MY POWER BATTERY.
STARDUST MEMORIES
Rick Veitch guest wirter
Darryl Banks guest penciller
Wayne Faucher guest inker
David Baron colorist
Kurt Hathaway letterer
Steve Wacker associate editor
Dan Raspler editor
NO, I'M TALKING ABOUT HOW SOMETHING WILL KICK OFF A MELODY AND IT WILL JUST START PLAYING OVER AND OVER IN YOUR MIND?
EVER SINCE WE ARRIVED ON THE MOON I CAN'T GET "STARDUST" OUT OF MY HEAD.
THAT OLD HOAGY CARMICHAEL CHESTNUT? WOOAH! AND PEOPLE SAY I'M SQUARE!
PERIMETER PATROL. WE'VE CLOCKED AN UNIDENTIFIED OBJECT IMPACTING THE LUNAR SURFACE.

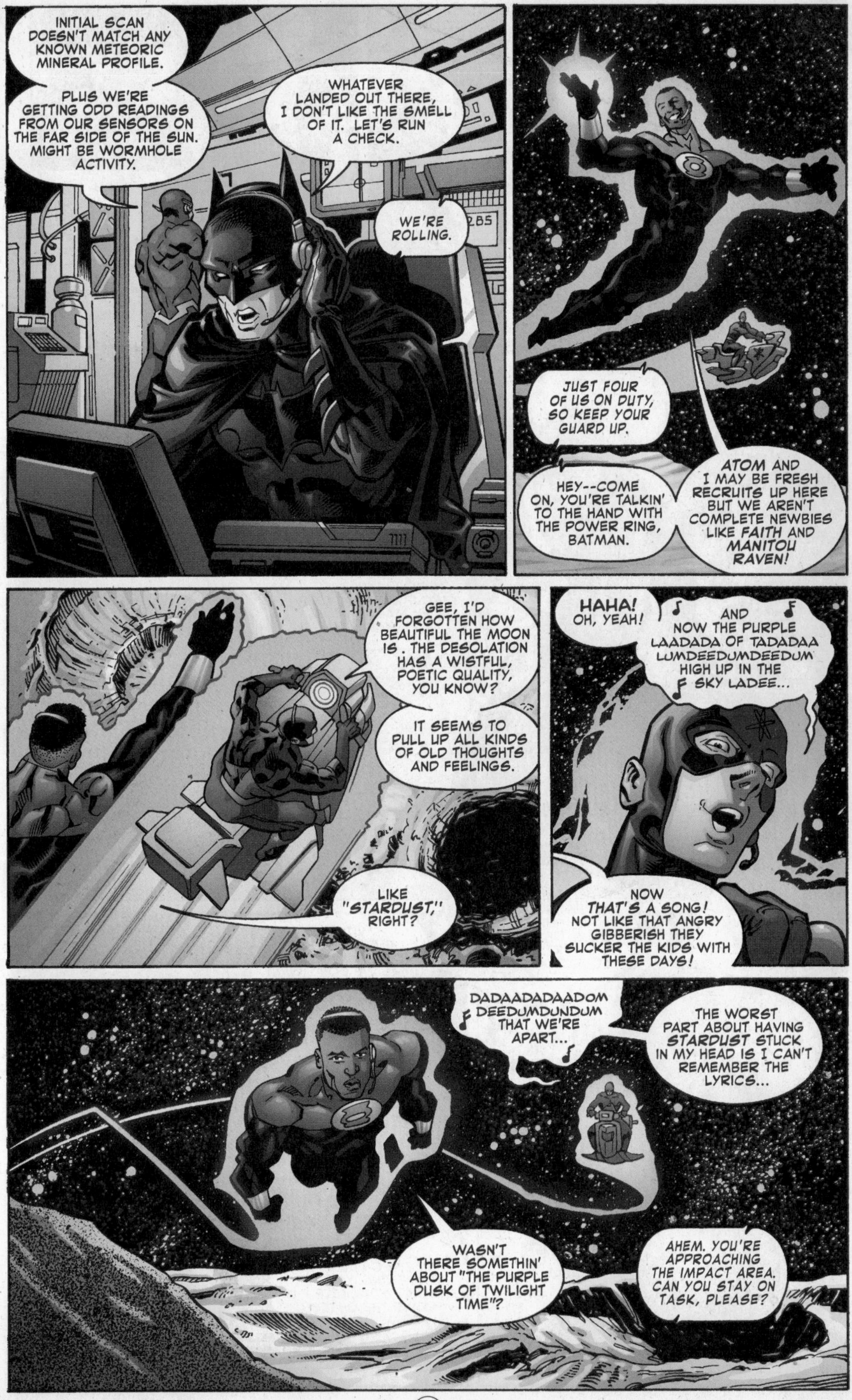
INITIAL SCAN DOESN'T MATCH ANY KNOWN METEORIC MINERAL PROFILE.
PLUS WE'RE GETTING ODD READINGS FROM OUR SENSORS ON THE FAR SIDE OF THE SUN. MIGHT BE WORMHOLE ACTIVITY.
WHATEVER LANDED OUT THERE, I DON'T LIKE THE SMELL OF IT. LET'S RUN A CHECK.
WE'RE ROLLING.
JUST FOUR OF US ON DUTY, SO KEEP YOUR GUARD UP.
HEY--COME ON, YOU'RE TALKIN' TO THE HAND WITH THE POWER RING, BATMAN.
ATOM AND I MAY BE FRESH RECRUITS UP HERE BUT WE AREN'T COMPLETE NEWBIES LIKE FAITH AND MANITOU RAVEN!
GEE, I'D FORGOTTEN HOW BEAUTIFUL THE MOON IS. THE DESOLATION HAS A WISTFUL, POETIC QUALITY, YOU KNOW?
IT SEEMS TO PULL UP ALL KINDS OF OLD THOUGHTS AND FEELINGS.
LIKE "STARDUST," RIGHT?
HAHA! OH, YEAH!
AND NOW THE PURPLE LAADADA OF TADADAA LUMDEEDUMDEEDUM HIGH UP IN THE SKY LADEE...
NOW THAT'S A SONG! NOT LIKE THAT ANGRY GIBBERISH THEY SUCKER THE KIDS WITH THESE DAYS!
DADAADADAADOM DEEDUMDUNDUM THAT WE'RE APART...
THE WORST PART ABOUT HAVING STARDUST STUCK IN MY HEAD IS I CAN'T REMEMBER THE LYRICS...
WASN'T THERE SOMETHIN' ABOUT "THE PURPLE DUSK OF TWILIGHT TIME"?
AHEM. YOU'RE APPROACHING THE IMPACT AREA. CAN YOU STAY ON TASK, PLEASE?

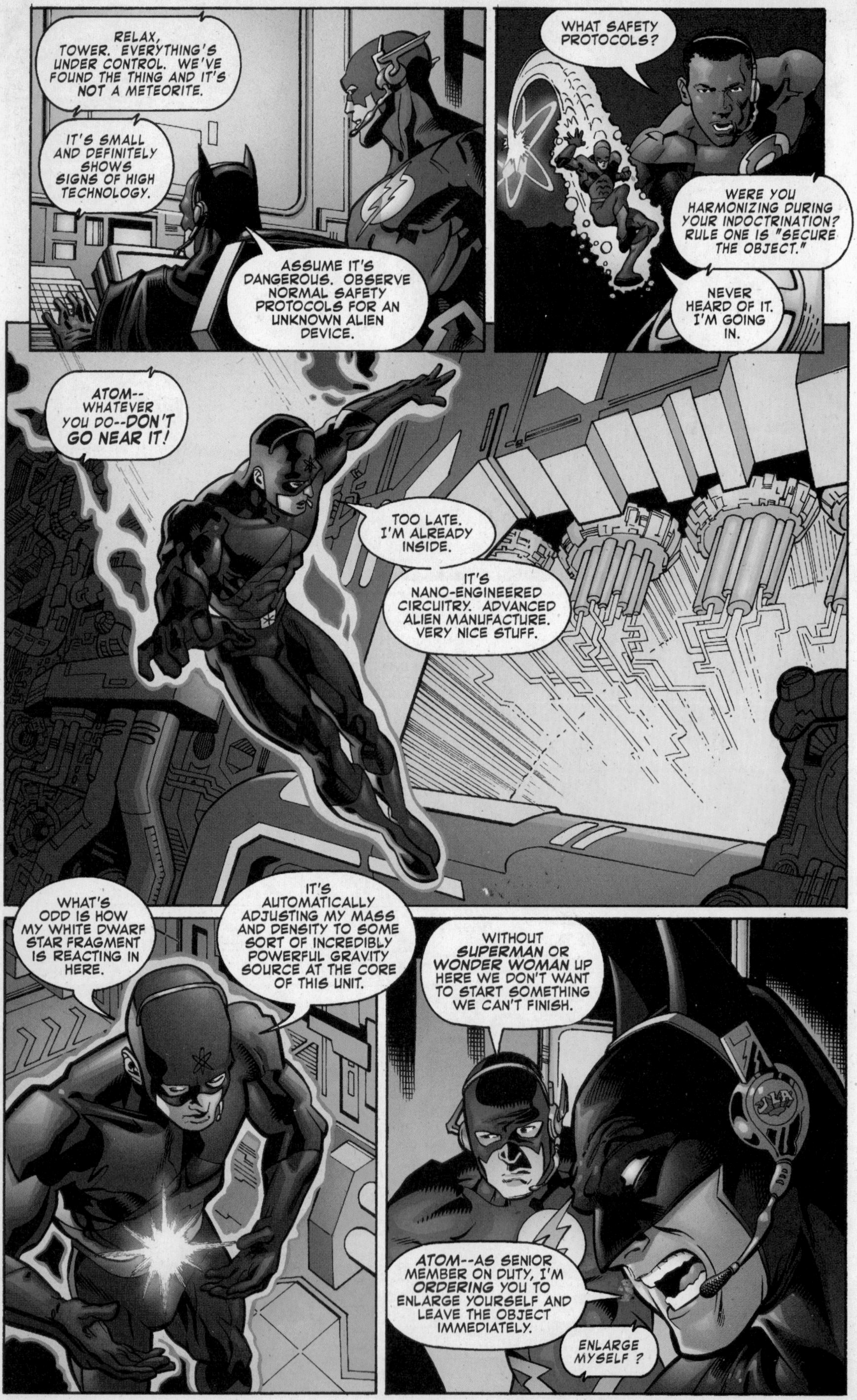
RELAX, TOWER. EVERYTHING'S UNDER CONTROL. WE'VE FOUND THE THING AND IT'S NOT A METEORITE.
IT'S SMALL AND DEFINITELY SHOWS SIGNS OF HIGH TECHNOLOGY.
ASSUME IT'S DANGEROUS. OBSERVE NORMAL SAFETY PROTOCOLS FOR AN UNKNOWN ALIEN DEVICE.
WHAT SAFETY PROTOCOLS?
WERE YOU HARMONIZING DURING YOUR INDOCTRINATION? RULE ONE IS "SECURE THE OBJECT."
NEVER HEARD OF IT. I'M GOING IN.
ATOM-- WHATEVER YOU DO--DON'T GO NEAR IT!
TOO LATE. I'M ALREADY INSIDE.
IT'S NANO-ENGINEERED CIRCUITRY. ADVANCED ALIEN MANUFACTURE. VERY NICE STUFF.
WHAT'S ODD IS HOW MY WHITE DWARF STAR FRAGMENT IS REACTING IN HERE.
IT'S AUTOMATICALLY ADJUSTING MY MASS AND DENSITY TO SOME SORT OF INCREDIBLY POWERFUL GRAVITY SOURCE AT THE CORE OF THIS UNIT.
WITHOUT SUPERMAN OR WONDER WOMAN UP HERE WE DON'T WANT TO START SOMETHING WE CAN'T FINISH.
ATOM--AS SENIOR MEMBER ON DUTY, I'M ORDERING YOU TO ENLARGE YOURSELF AND LEAVE THE OBJECT IMMEDIATELY.
ENLARGE MYSELF ?

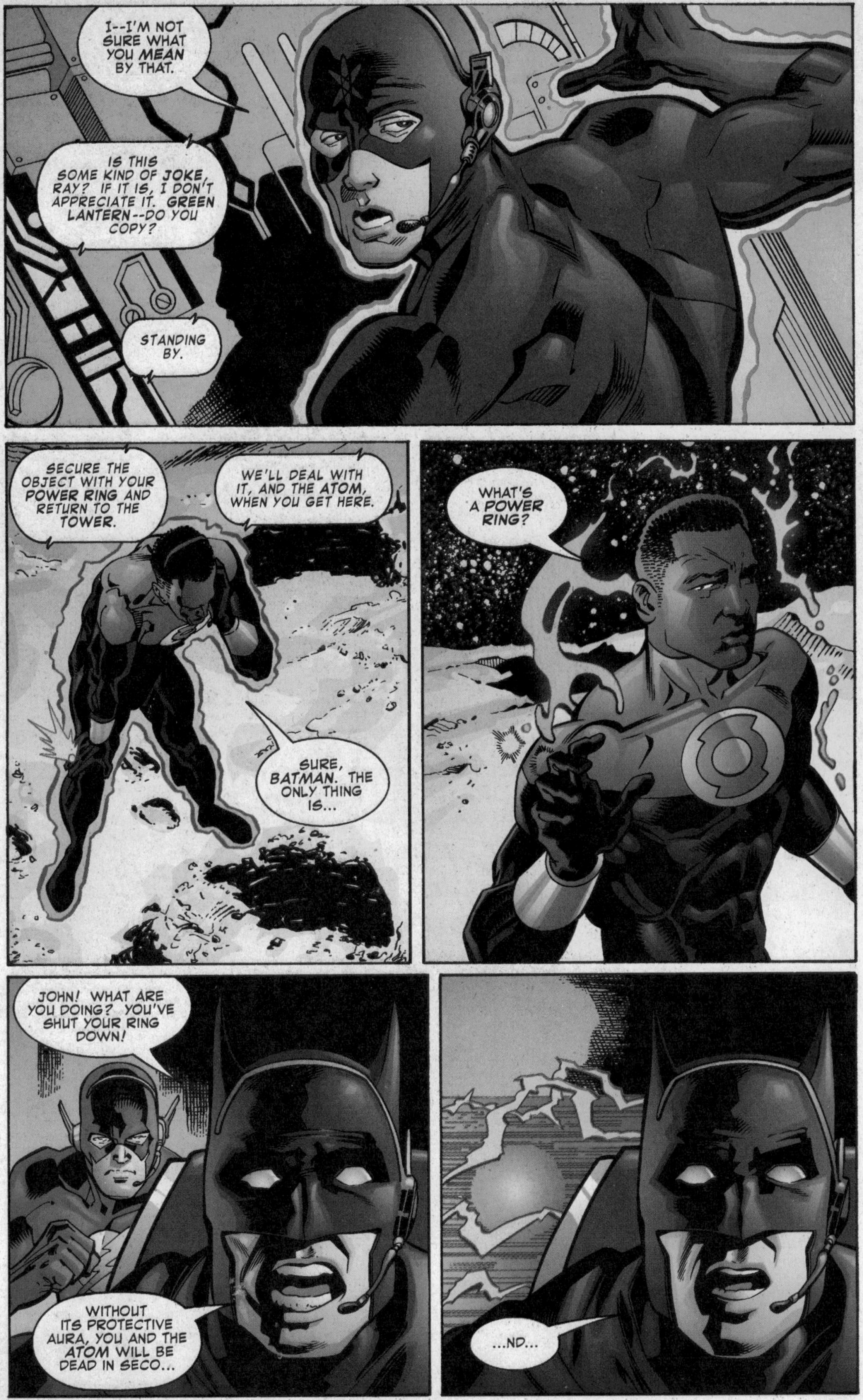
I--I'M NOT SURE WHAT YOU MEAN BY THAT.
IS THIS SOME KIND OF JOKE, RAY? IF IT IS, I DON'T APPRECIATE IT. GREEN LANTERN--DO YOU COPY?
STANDING BY.
SECURE THE OBJECT WITH YOUR POWER RING AND RETURN TO THE TOWER.
WE'LL DEAL WITH IT, AND THE ATOM, WHEN YOU GET HERE.
SURE, BATMAN. THE ONLY THING IS...
WHAT'S A POWER RING?
JOHN! WHAT ARE YOU DOING? YOU'VE SHUT YOUR RING DOWN!
WITHOUT ITS PROTECTIVE AURA, YOU AND THE ATOM WILL BE DEAD IN SECO...
...ND...

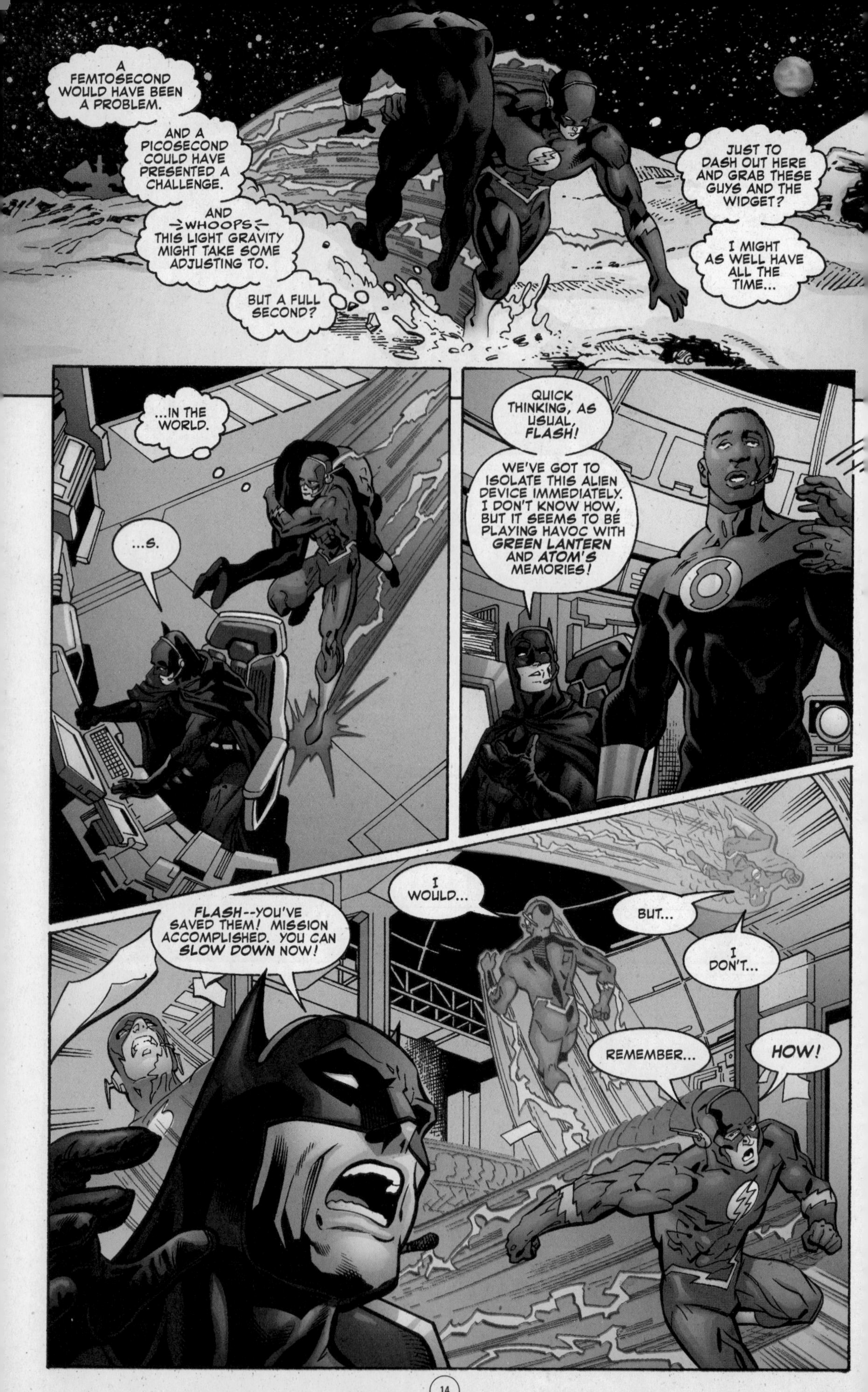

A FEMTOSECOND WOULD HAVE BEEN A PROBLEM.
AND A PICOSECOND COULD HAVE PRESENTED A CHALLENGE.
AND WHOOPS THIS LIGHT GRAVITY MIGHT TAKE SOME ADJUSTING TO.
BUT A FULL SECOND?
JUST TO DASH OUT HERE AND GRAB THESE GUYS AND THE WIDGET?
I MIGHT AS WELL HAVE ALL THE TIME...
...IN THE WORLD.
...S.
QUICK THINKING, AS USUAL, FLASH!
WE'VE GOT TO ISOLATE THIS ALIEN DEVICE IMMEDIATELY. I DON'T KNOW HOW, BUT IT SEEMS TO BE PLAYING HAVOC WITH GREEN LANTERN AND ATOM'S MEMORIES!
FLASH--YOU'VE SAVED THEM! MISSION ACCOMPLISHED. YOU CAN SLOW DOWN NOW!
I WOULD...
BUT...
I DON'T...
REMEMBER...
HOW!

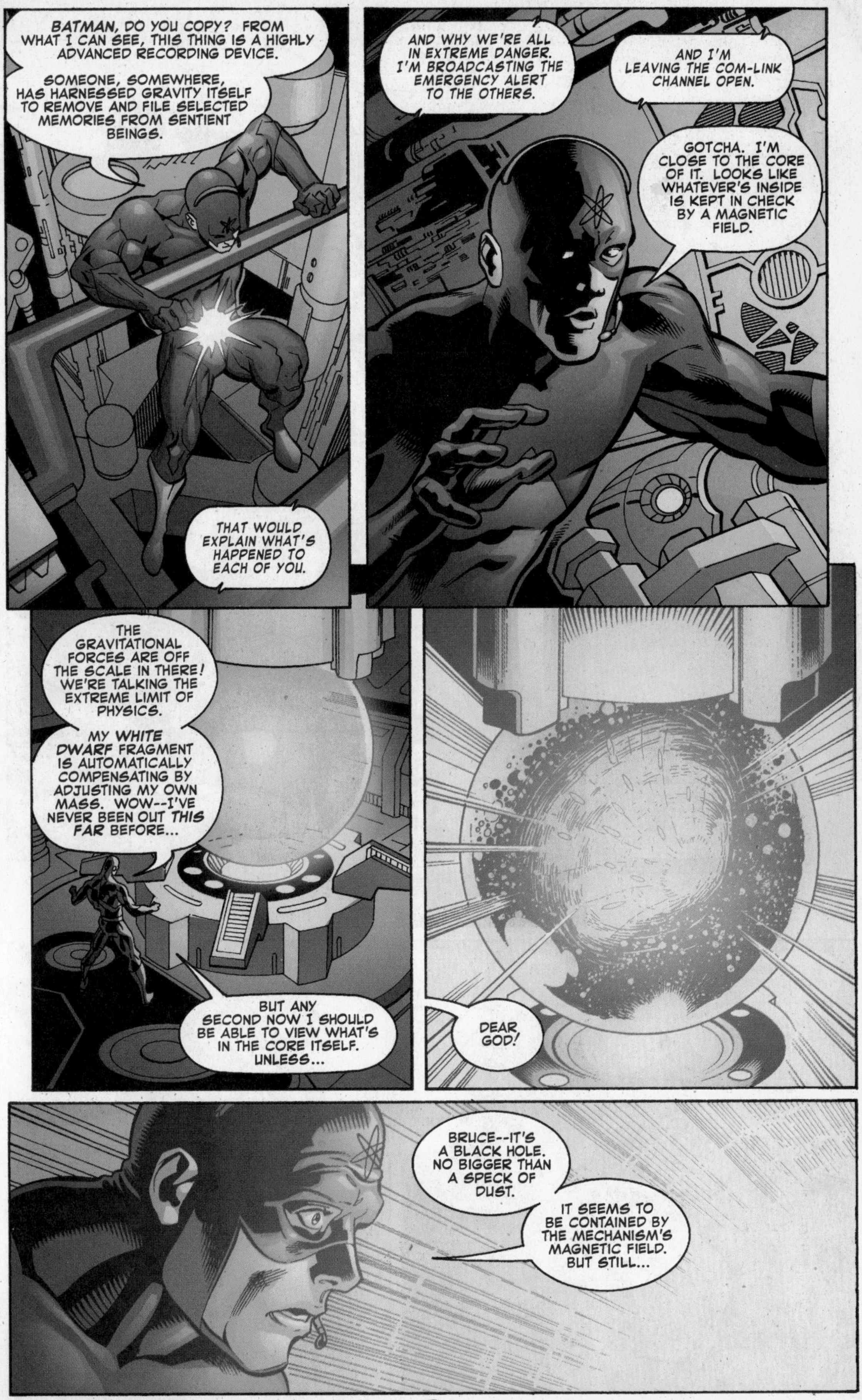
BATMAN, DO YOU COPY? FROM WHAT I CAN SEE, THIS THING IS A HIGHLY ADVANCED RECORDING DEVICE.
SOMEONE, SOMEWHERE, HAS HARNESSED GRAVITY ITSELF TO REMOVE AND FILE SELECTED MEMORIES FROM SENTIENT BEINGS.
THAT WOULD EXPLAIN WHAT'S HAPPENED TO EACH OF YOU.
AND WHY WE'RE ALL IN EXTREME DANGER. I'M BROADCASTING THE EMERGENCY ALERT TO THE OTHERS.
AND I'M LEAVING THE COM-LINK CHANNEL OPEN.
GOTCHA. I'M CLOSE TO THE CORE OF IT. LOOKS LIKE WHATEVER'S INSIDE IS KEPT IN CHECK BY A MAGNETIC FIELD.
THE GRAVITATIONAL FORCES ARE OFF THE SCALE IN THERE! WE'RE TALKING THE EXTREME LIMIT OF PHYSICS.
MY WHITE DWARF FRAGMENT IS AUTOMATICALLY COMPENSATING BY ADJUSTING MY OWN MASS. WOW--I'VE NEVER BEEN OUT THIS FAR BEFORE...
BUT ANY SECOND NOW I SHOULD BE ABLE TO VIEW WHAT'S IN THE CORE ITSELF. UNLESS...
DEAR GOD!
BRUCE--IT'S A BLACK HOLE. NO BIGGER THAN A SPECK OF DUST.
IT SEEMS TO BE CONTAINED BY THE MECHANISM'S MAGNETIC FIELD. BUT STILL...

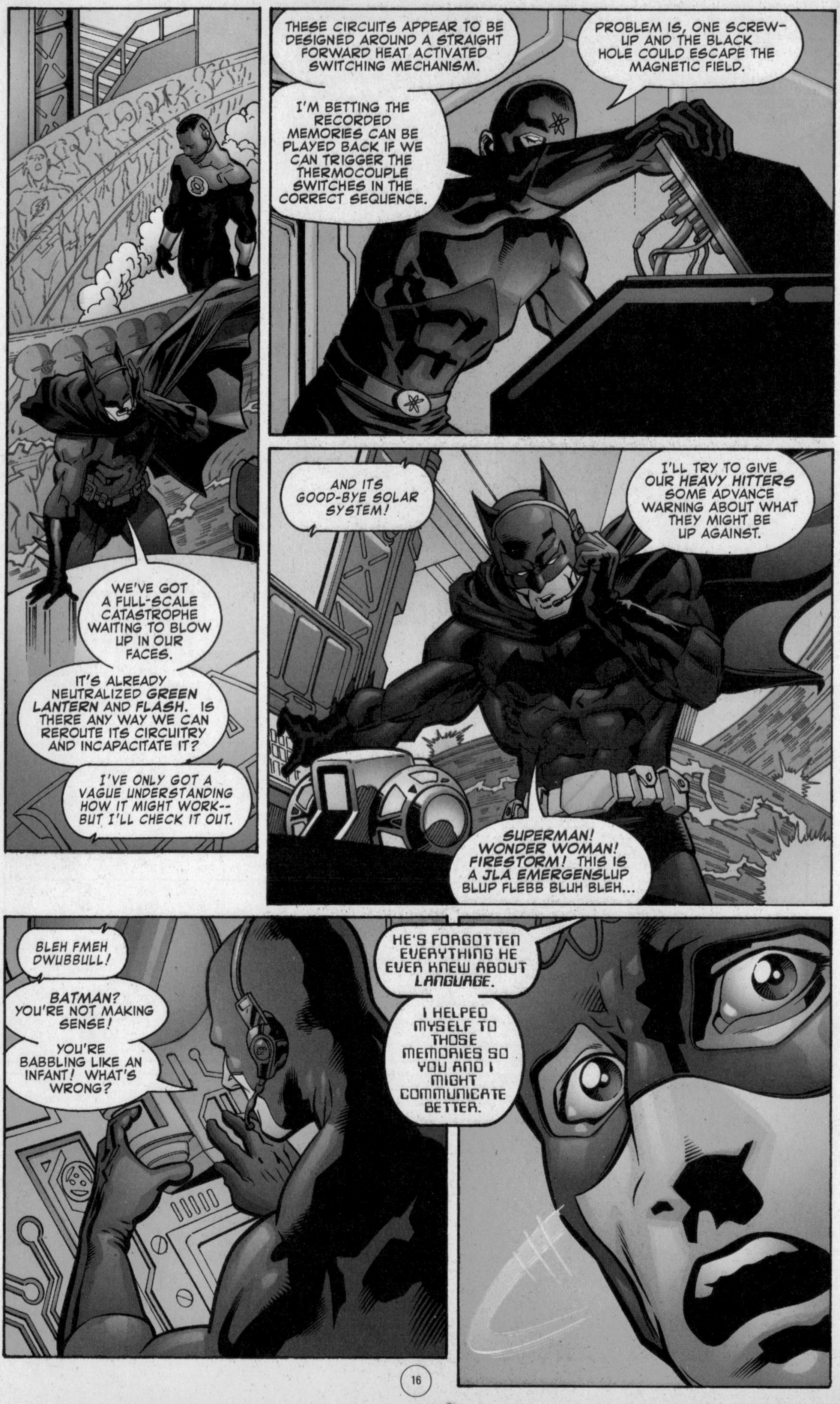
THESE CIRCUITS APPEAR TO BE DESIGNED AROUND A STRAIGHT FORWARD HEAT ACTIVATED SWITCHING MECHANISM.
I'M BETTING THE RECORDED MEMORIES CAN BE PLAYED BACK IF WE CAN TRIGGER THE THERMOCOUPLE SWITCHES IN THE CORRECT SEQUENCE.
PROBLEM IS, ONE SCREW-UP AND THE BLACK HOLE COULD ESCAPE THE MAGNETIC FIELD.
WE'VE GOT A FULL-SCALE CATASTROPHE WAITING TO BLOW UP IN OUR FACES.
IT'S ALREADY NEUTRALIZED GREEN LANTERN AND FLASH. IS THERE ANY WAY WE CAN REROUTE ITS CIRCUITRY AND INCAPACITATE IT?
I'VE ONLY GOT A VAGUE UNDERSTANDING HOW IT MIGHT WORK-- BUT I'LL CHECK IT OUT.
AND ITS GOOD-BYE SOLAR SYSTEM!
I'LL TRY TO GIVE OUR HEAVY HITTERS SOME ADVANCE WARNING ABOUT WHAT THEY MIGHT BE UP AGAINST.
SUPERMAN! WONDER WOMAN! FIRESTORM! THIS IS A JLA EMERGENSLUP BLUP FLEBB BLUH BLEH...
BLEH FMEH DWUBBULL!
BATMAN? YOU'RE NOT MAKING SENSE!
YOU'RE BABBLING LIKE AN INFANT! WHAT'S WRONG?
HE'S FORGOTTEN EVERYTHING HE EVER KNEW ABOUT LANGUAGE.
I HELPED MYSELF TO THOSE MEMORIES SO YOU AND I MIGHT COMMUNICATE BETTER.

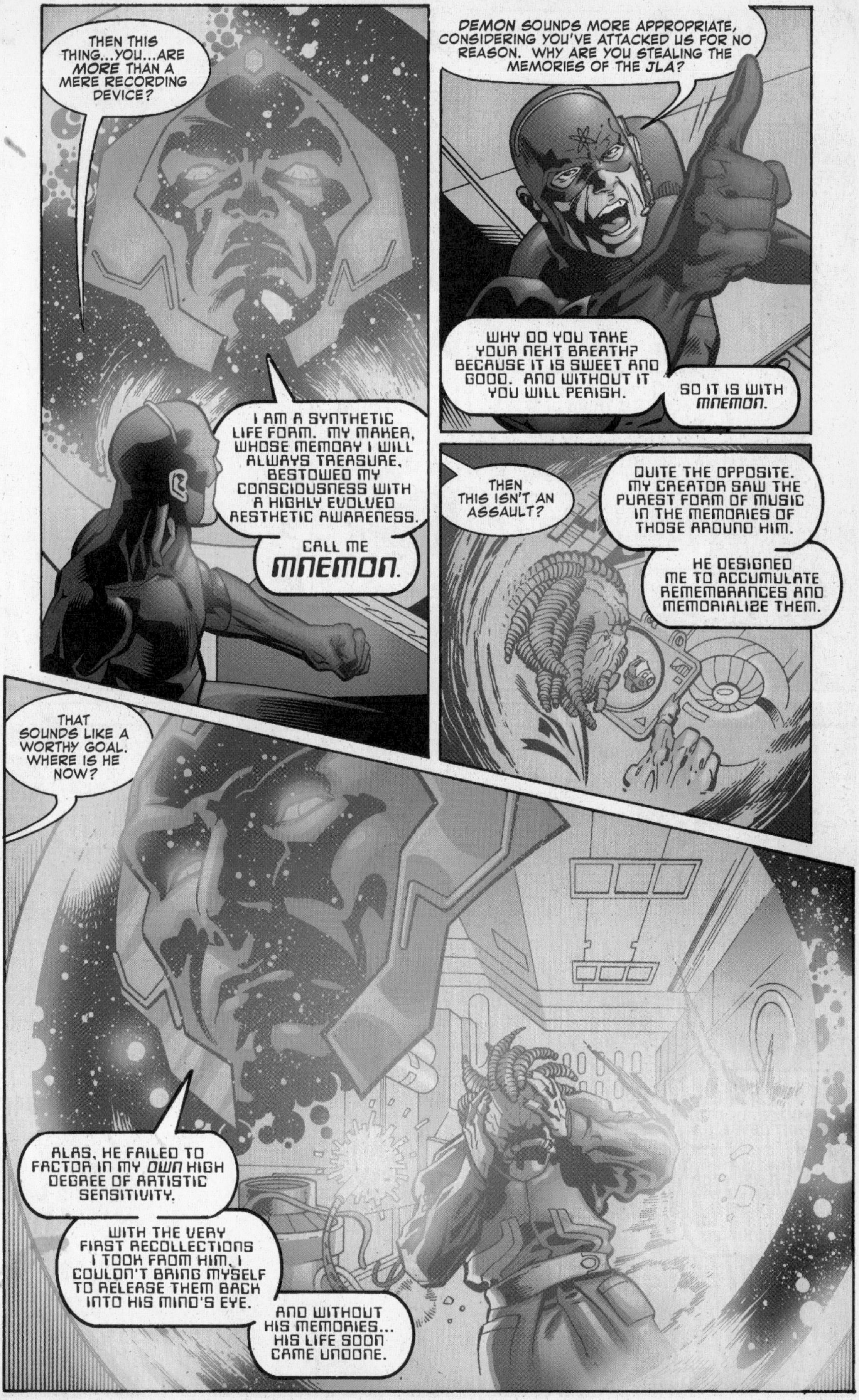
THEN THIS THING...YOU...ARE MORE THAN A MERE RECORDING DEVICE?
I AM A SYNTHETIC LIFE FORM. MY MAKER, WHOSE MEMORY I WILL ALWAYS TREASURE, BESTOWED MY CONSCIOUSNESS WITH A HIGHLY EVOLVED AESTHETIC AWARENESS.
CALL ME MNEMON.
DEMON SOUNDS MORE APPROPRIATE, CONSIDERING YOU'VE ATTACKED US FOR NO REASON. WHY ARE YOU STEALING THE MEMORIES OF THE JLA?
WHY DO YOU TAKE YOUR NEXT BREATH? BECAUSE IT IS SWEET AND GOOD. AND WITHOUT IT YOU WILL PERISH.
SO IT IS WITH MNEMON.
THEN THIS ISN'T AN ASSAULT?
QUITE THE OPPOSITE. MY CREATOR SAW THE PUREST FORM OF MUSIC IN THE MEMORIES OF THOSE AROUND HIM.
HE DESIGNED ME TO ACCUMULATE REMEMBRANCES AND MEMORIALIZE THEM.
THAT SOUNDS LIKE A WORTHY GOAL. WHERE IS HE NOW?
ALAS, HE FAILED TO FACTOR IN MY OWN HIGH DEGREE OF ARTISTIC SENSITIVITY.
WITH THE VERY FIRST RECOLLECTIONS I TOOK FROM HIM, I COULDN'T BRING MYSELF TO RELEASE THEM BACK INTO HIS MIND'S EYE.
AND WITHOUT HIS MEMORIES... HIS LIFE SOON CAME UNDONE.

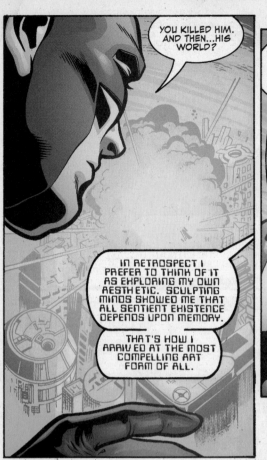

YOU KILLED HIM. AND THEN...HIS WORLD?

IN RETROSPECT I PREFER TO THINK OF IT AS EXPLORING MY OWN AESTHETIC. SCULPTING MINDS SHOWED ME THAT ALL SENTIENT EXISTENCE DEPENDS UPON MEMORY.

THAT'S HOW I ARRIVED AT THE MOST COMPELLING ART FORM OF ALL.

YOU DESTROYED WHOLE CIVILIZATIONS TO MAKE A STATEMENT?

GUILTY AS CHARGED. I STAND BEFORE YOU AS ARTIST AND ART.

I AM THE CREATOR OF GALACTIC ANNIHILATION. AND A LIVING MUSEUM TO ITS MEMORY.

I MAY NOT BE AN ARTIST-- BUT I CERTAINLY KNOW WHAT I DON'T LIKE...

AND YOUR ROLE IN THIS IS NOT TO CRITIQUE. BUT TO PARTICIPATE.

ALONG WITH YOUR CITIES, YOUR PEOPLES, YOUR ENTIRE WORLD. IT'S GOING TO BE QUITE MOVING!

I'LL SHAVE A MEMORY HERE AND CLIP A RECOLLECTION THERE-- UNTIL, LIKE A HOUSE OF CARDS, EVERYTHING COLLAPSES IN GLORIOUS ENTROPY.

JUST AS I'VE DONE TO YOUR FRIENDS IN THEIR STRONGHOLD!

JOHN, CAN YOU READ ME!? JOHN!

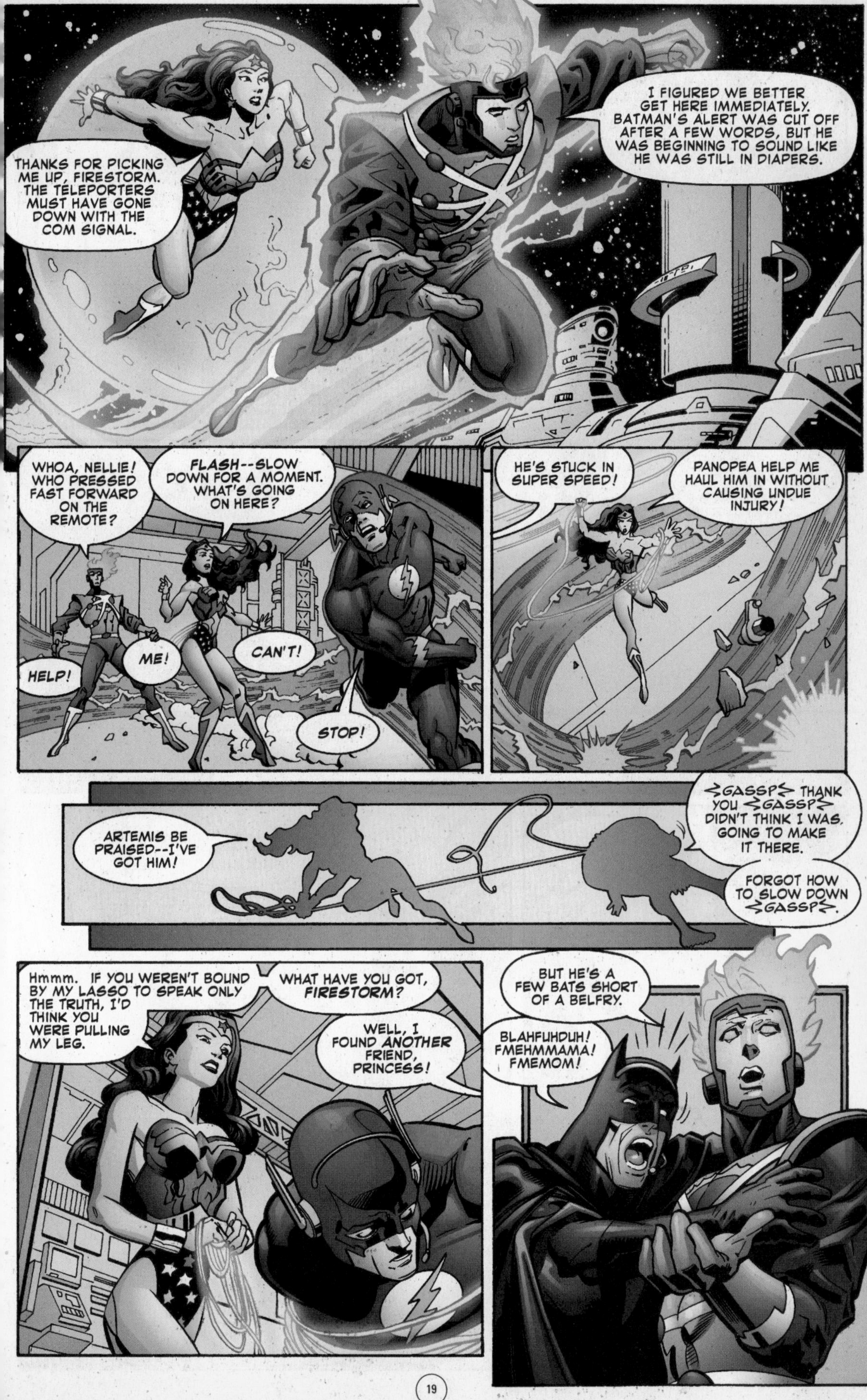
THANKS FOR PICKING ME UP, FIRESTORM. THE TELEPORTERS MUST HAVE GONE DOWN WITH THE COM SIGNAL.
I FIGURED WE BETTER GET HERE IMMEDIATELY. BATMAN'S ALERT WAS CUT OFF AFTER A FEW WORDS, BUT HE WAS BEGINNING TO SOUND LIKE HE WAS STILL IN DIAPERS.
WHOA, NELLIE! WHO PRESSED FAST FORWARD ON THE REMOTE?
FLASH--SLOW DOWN FOR A MOMENT. WHAT'S GOING ON HERE?
HELP!
ME!
CAN'T!
STOP!
HE'S STUCK IN SUPER SPEED!
PANOPEA HELP ME HAUL HIM IN WITHOUT CAUSING UNDUE INJURY!
ARTEMIS BE PRAISED--I'VE GOT HIM!
<GASSP> THANK YOU <GASSP> DIDN'T THINK I WAS GOING TO MAKE IT THERE.
FORGOT HOW TO SLOW DOWN <GASSP>.
Hmmm. IF YOU WEREN'T BOUND BY MY LASSO TO SPEAK ONLY THE TRUTH, I'D THINK YOU WERE PULLING MY LEG.
WHAT HAVE YOU GOT, FIRESTORM?
WELL, I FOUND ANOTHER FRIEND, PRINCESS!
BUT HE'S A FEW BATS SHORT OF A BELFRY.
BLAHFUHDUH! FMEHMMAMA! FMEMOM!

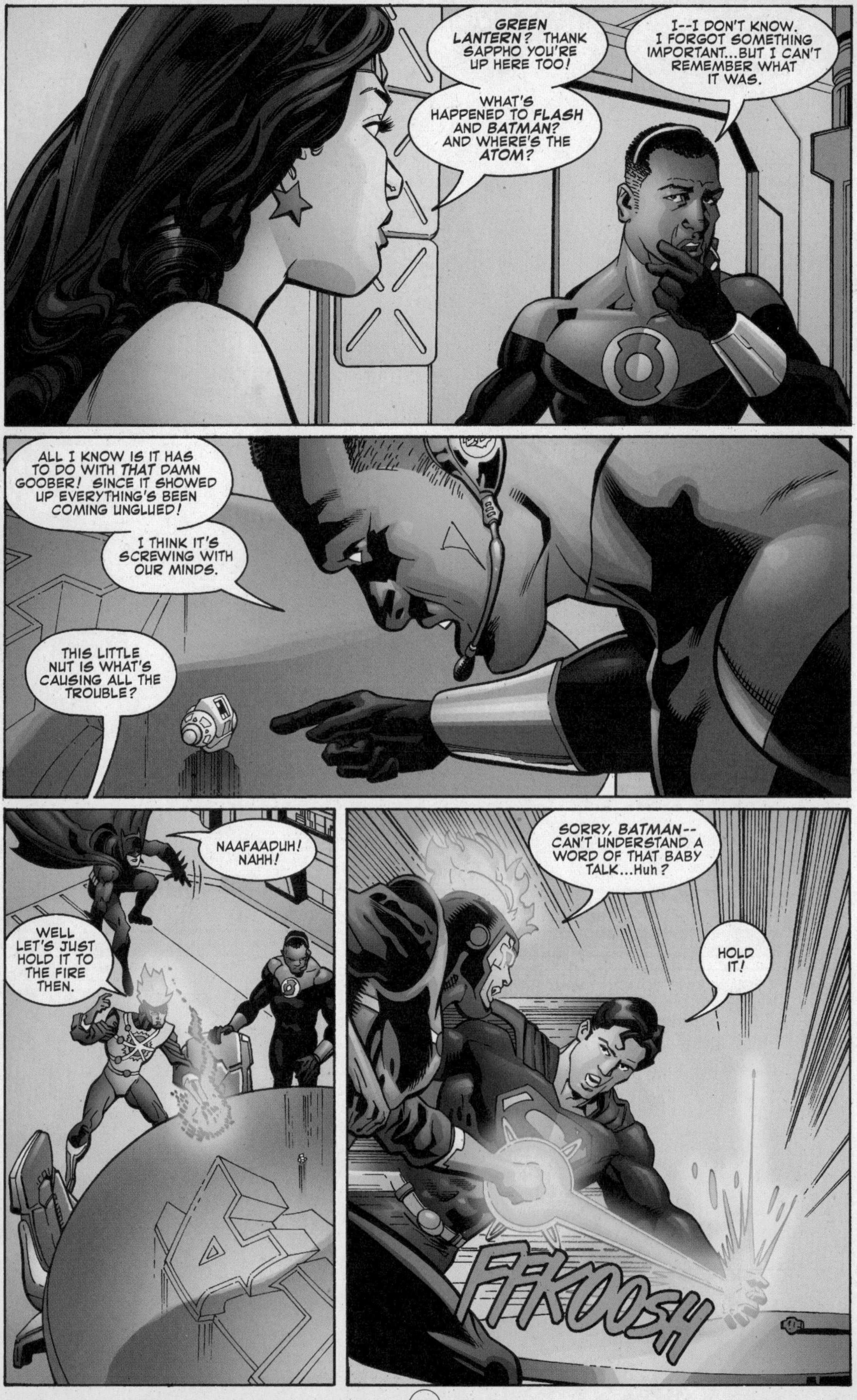
GREEN LANTERN? THANK SAPPHO YOU'RE UP HERE TOO!
WHAT'S HAPPENED TO FLASH AND BATMAN? AND WHERE'S THE ATOM?
I--I DON'T KNOW. I FORGOT SOMETHING IMPORTANT...BUT I CAN'T REMEMBER WHAT IT WAS.
ALL I KNOW IS IT HAS TO DO WITH THAT DAMN GOOBER! SINCE IT SHOWED UP EVERYTHING'S BEEN COMING UNGLUED!
I THINK IT'S SCREWING WITH OUR MINDS.
THIS LITTLE NUT IS WHAT'S CAUSING ALL THE TROUBLE?
NAAFAADUH! NAHH!
WELL LET'S JUST HOLD IT TO THE FIRE THEN.
SORRY, BATMAN-- CAN'T UNDERSTAND A WORD OF THAT BABY TALK...Huh?
HOLD IT!
FFKOOSH

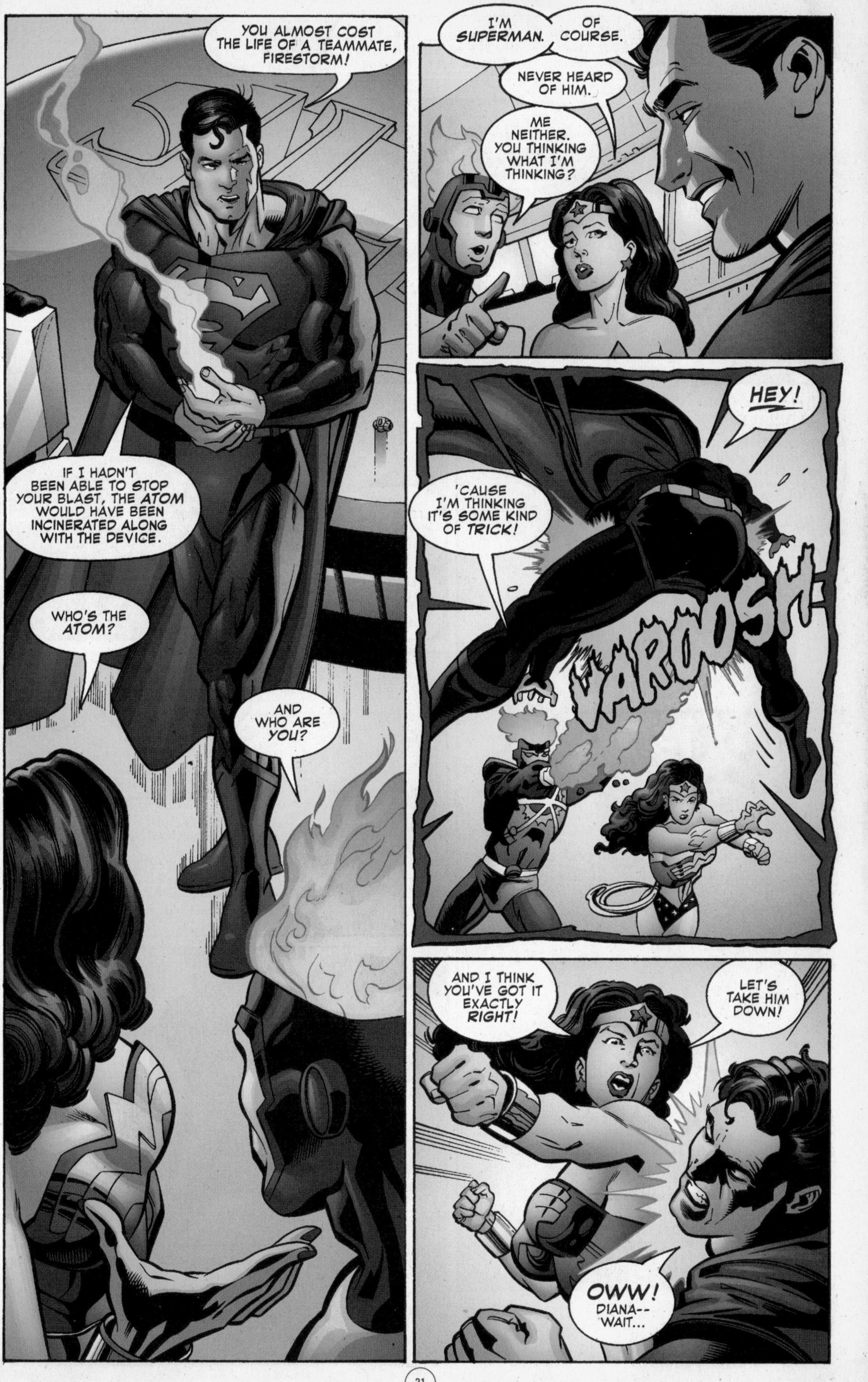
YOU ALMOST COST THE LIFE OF A TEAMMATE, FIRESTORM!
IF I HADN'T BEEN ABLE TO STOP YOUR BLAST, THE ATOM WOULD HAVE BEEN INCINERATED ALONG WITH THE DEVICE.
WHO'S THE ATOM?
AND WHO ARE YOU?
I'M SUPERMAN.
OF COURSE.
NEVER HEARD OF HIM.
ME NEITHER. YOU THINKING WHAT I'M THINKING?
HEY!
'CAUSE I'M THINKING IT'S SOME KIND OF TRICK!
VAROOSH
AND I THINK YOU'VE GOT IT EXACTLY RIGHT!
LET'S TAKE HIM DOWN!
OWW! DIANA-- WAIT...

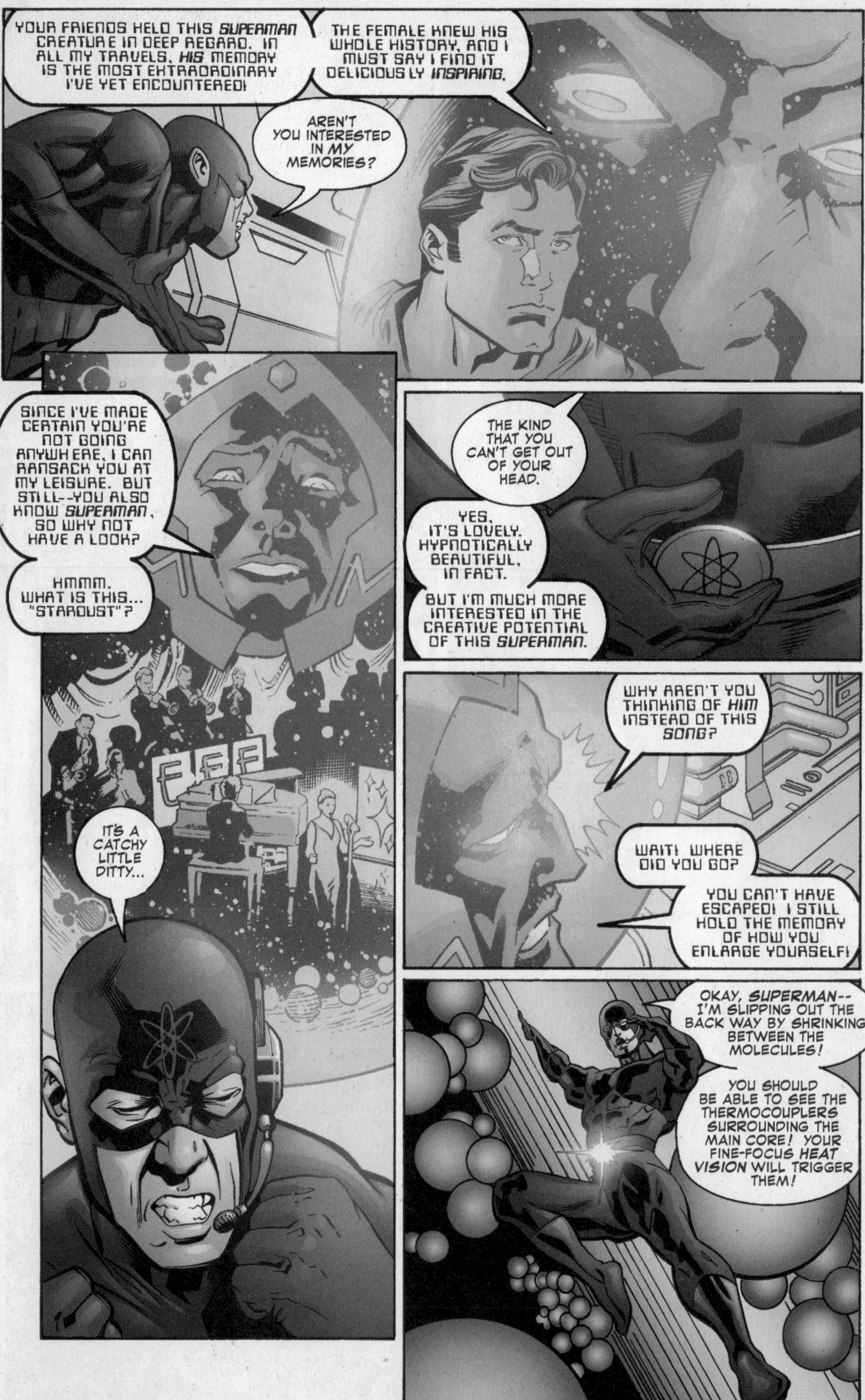
YOUR FRIENDS HELD THIS SUPERMAN CREATURE IN DEEP REGARD. IN ALL MY TRAVELS, HIS MEMORY IS THE MOST EXTRAORDINARY I'VE YET ENCOUNTERED!
THE FEMALE KNEW HIS WHOLE HISTORY, AND I MUST SAY I FIND IT DELICIOUSLY INSPIRING.
AREN'T YOU INTERESTED IN MY MEMORIES?
SINCE I'VE MADE CERTAIN YOU'RE NOT GOING ANYWHERE, I CAN RANSACK YOU AT MY LEISURE. BUT STILL--YOU ALSO KNOW SUPERMAN, SO WHY NOT HAVE A LOOK?
HMMM. WHAT IS THIS... "STARDUST"?
IT'S A CATCHY LITTLE DITTY...
THE KIND THAT YOU CAN'T GET OUT OF YOUR HEAD.
YES, IT'S LOVELY. HYPNOTICALLY BEAUTIFUL, IN FACT.
BUT I'M MUCH MORE INTERESTED IN THE CREATIVE POTENTIAL OF THIS SUPERMAN.
WHY AREN'T YOU THINKING OF HIM INSTEAD OF THIS SONG?
WAIT! WHERE DID YOU GO?
YOU CAN'T HAVE ESCAPED! I STILL HOLD THE MEMORY OF HOW YOU ENLARGE YOURSELF!
OKAY, SUPERMAN-- I'M SLIPPING OUT THE BACK WAY BY SHRINKING BETWEEN THE MOLECULES!
YOU SHOULD BE ABLE TO SEE THE THERMOCOUPLERS SURROUNDING THE MAIN CORE! YOUR FINE-FOCUS HEAT VISION WILL TRIGGER THEM!

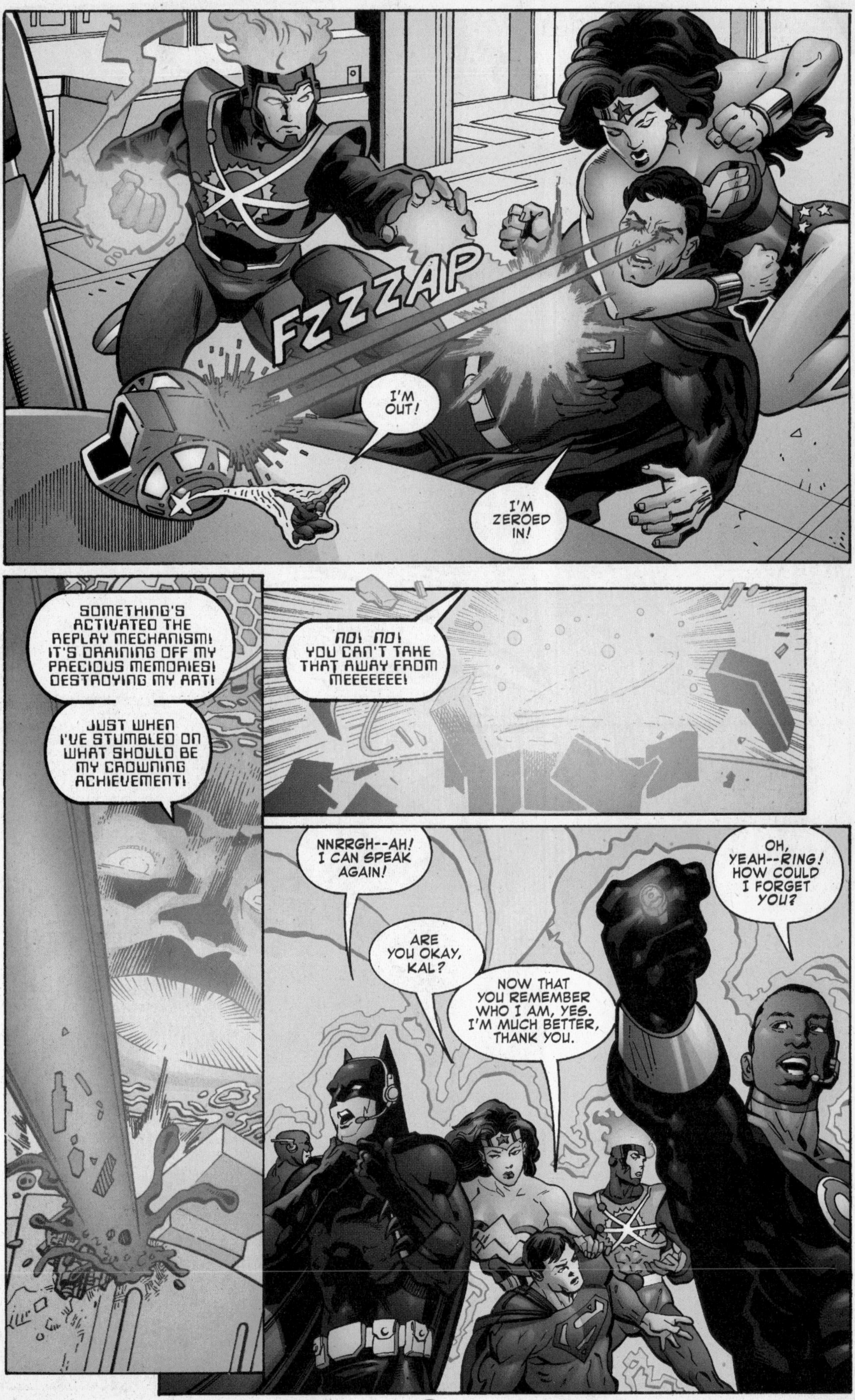
FZZZAP
I'M OUT!
I'M ZEROED IN!
SOMETHING'S ACTIVATED THE REPLAY MECHANISM! IT'S DRAINING OFF MY PRECIOUS MEMORIES! DESTROYING MY ART!
JUST WHEN I'VE STUMBLED ON WHAT SHOULD BE MY CROWNING ACHIEVEMENT!
NO! NO! YOU CAN'T TAKE THAT AWAY FROM MEEEEEEE!
NNRRGH--AH! I CAN SPEAK AGAIN!
ARE YOU OKAY, KAL?
NOW THAT YOU REMEMBER WHO I AM, YES. I'M MUCH BETTER, THANK YOU.
OH, YEAH--RING! HOW COULD I FORGET YOU?

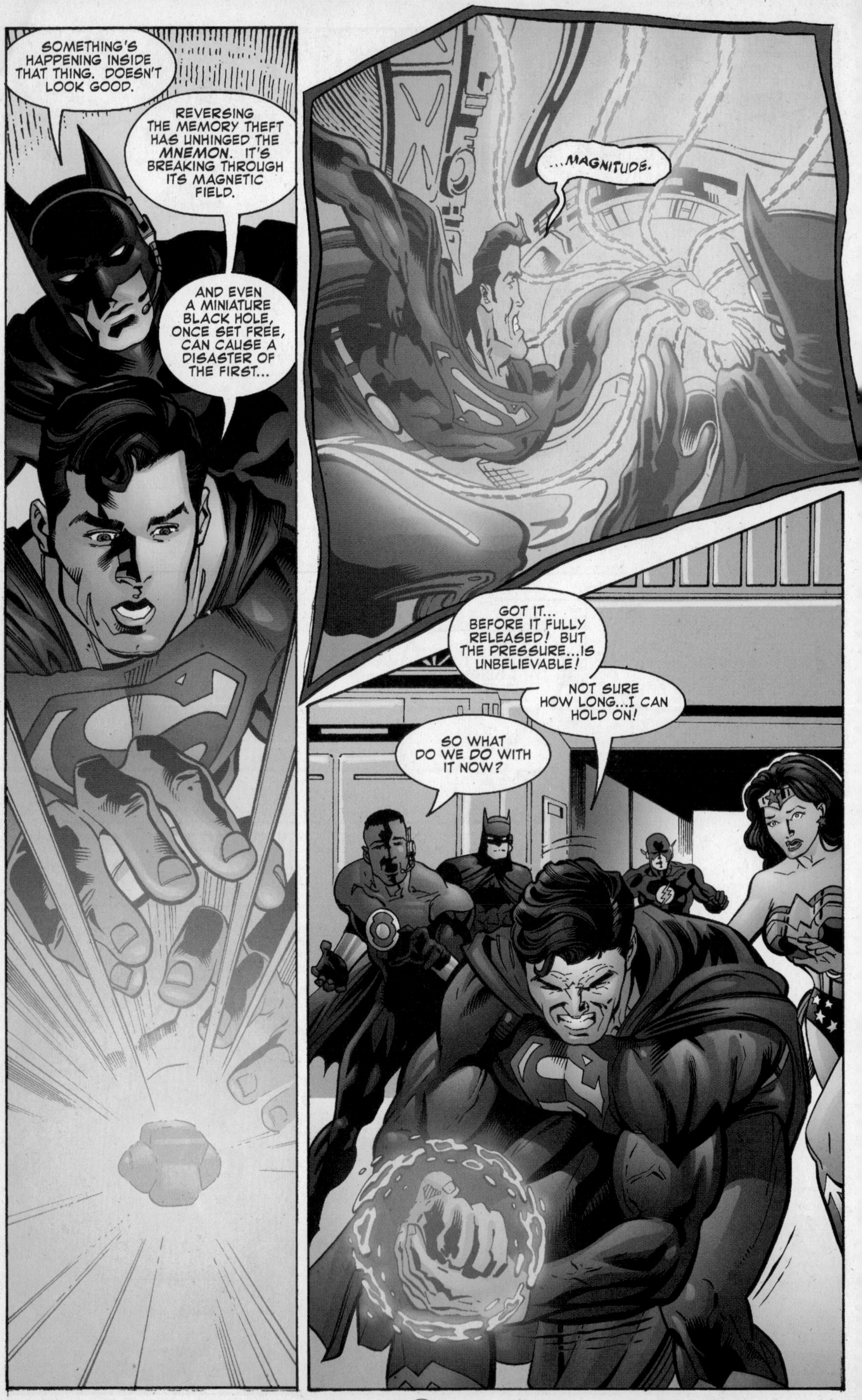
SOMETHING'S HAPPENING INSIDE THAT THING. DOESN'T LOOK GOOD.
REVERSING THE MEMORY THEFT HAS UNHINGED THE *MNEMON*. IT'S BREAKING THROUGH ITS MAGNETIC FIELD.
AND EVEN A MINIATURE BLACK HOLE, ONCE SET FREE, CAN CAUSE A DISASTER OF THE FIRST...
...*MAGNITUDE*.
GOT IT... BEFORE IT FULLY RELEASED! BUT THE PRESSURE...IS UNBELIEVABLE!
NOT SURE HOW LONG...I CAN HOLD ON!
SO WHAT DO WE *DO* WITH IT NOW?

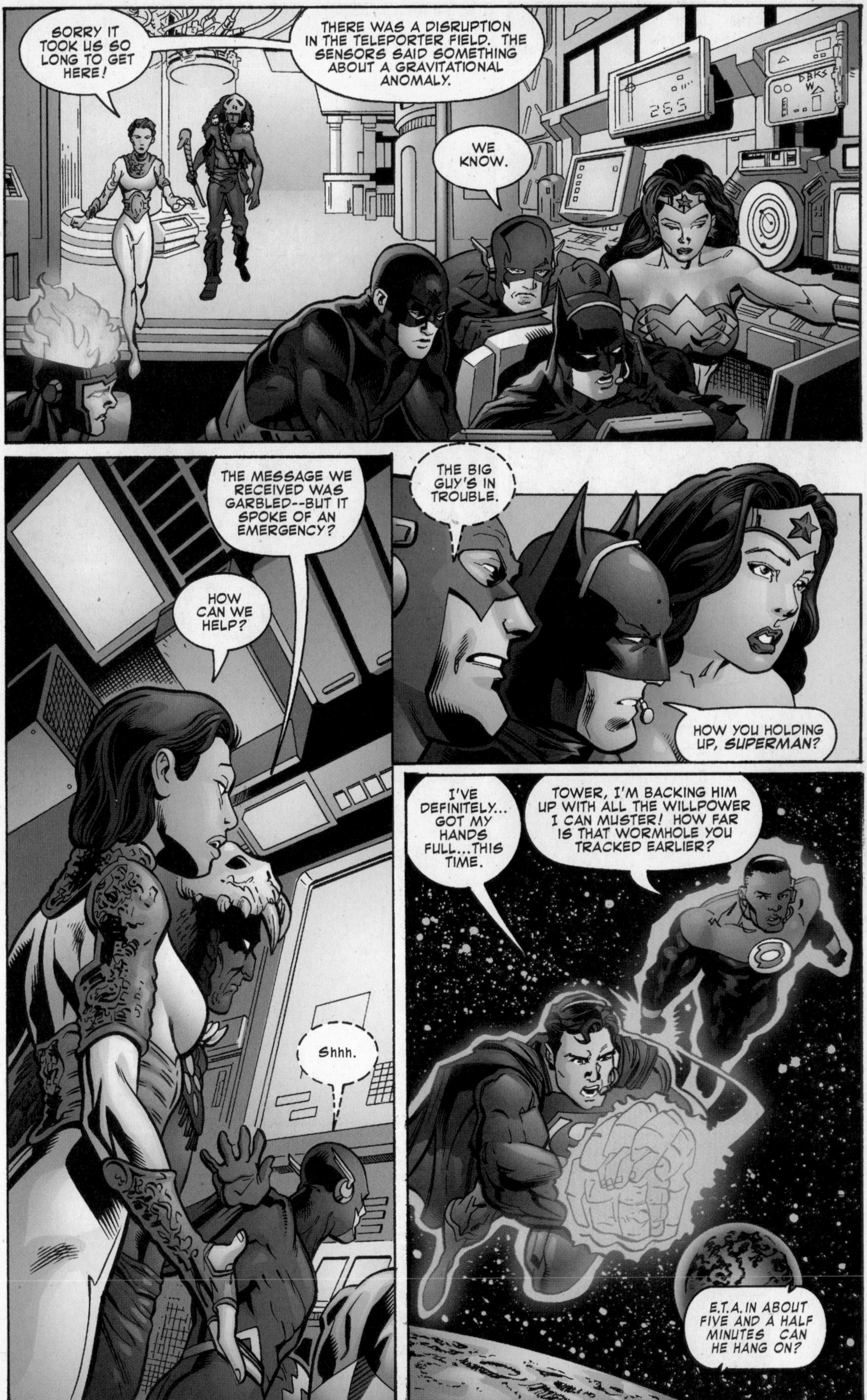
SORRY IT TOOK US SO LONG TO GET HERE!
THERE WAS A DISRUPTION IN THE TELEPORTER FIELD. THE SENSORS SAID SOMETHING ABOUT A GRAVITATIONAL ANOMALY.
WE KNOW.
THE MESSAGE WE RECEIVED WAS GARBLED--BUT IT SPOKE OF AN EMERGENCY?
HOW CAN WE HELP?
Shhh.
THE BIG GUY'S IN TROUBLE.
HOW YOU HOLDING UP, SUPERMAN?
I'VE DEFINITELY... GOT MY HANDS FULL...THIS TIME.
TOWER, I'M BACKING HIM UP WITH ALL THE WILLPOWER I CAN MUSTER! HOW FAR IS THAT WORMHOLE YOU TRACKED EARLIER?
E.T.A. IN ABOUT FIVE AND A HALF MINUTES CAN HE HANG ON?

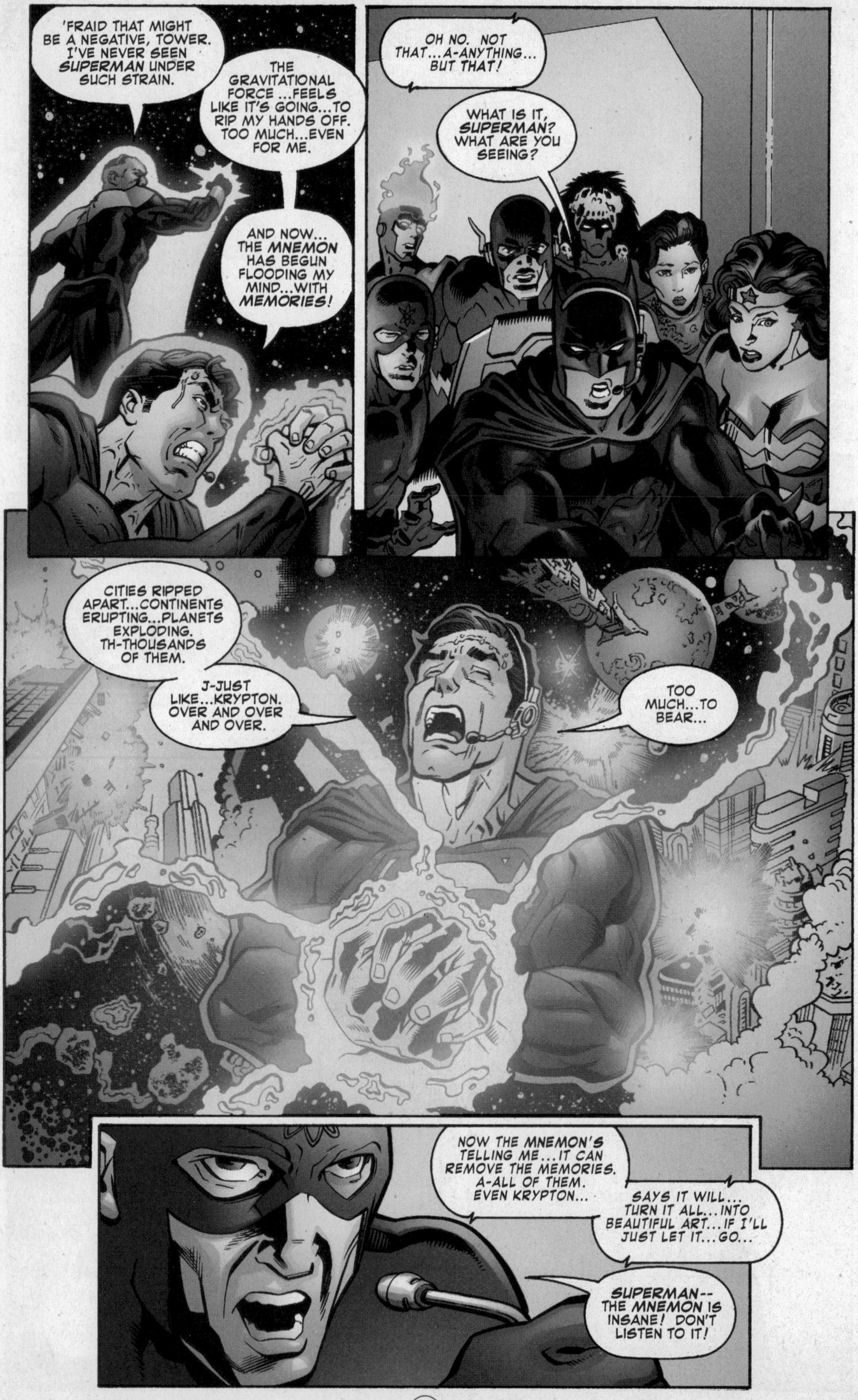
'FRAID THAT MIGHT BE A NEGATIVE, TOWER. I'VE NEVER SEEN SUPERMAN UNDER SUCH STRAIN.
THE GRAVITATIONAL FORCE ...FEELS LIKE IT'S GOING...TO RIP MY HANDS OFF. TOO MUCH...EVEN FOR ME.
AND NOW... THE MNEMON HAS BEGUN FLOODING MY MIND...WITH MEMORIES!
OH NO. NOT THAT...A-ANYTHING... BUT THAT!
WHAT IS IT, SUPERMAN? WHAT ARE YOU SEEING?
CITIES RIPPED APART...CONTINENTS ERUPTING...PLANETS EXPLODING. TH-THOUSANDS OF THEM.
J-JUST LIKE...KRYPTON. OVER AND OVER AND OVER.
TOO MUCH...TO BEAR...
NOW THE MNEMON'S TELLING ME...IT CAN REMOVE THE MEMORIES. A-ALL OF THEM. EVEN KRYPTON...
SAYS IT WILL... TURN IT ALL...INTO BEAUTIFUL ART...IF I'LL JUST LET IT...GO...
SUPERMAN-- THE MNEMON IS INSANE! DON'T LISTEN TO IT!

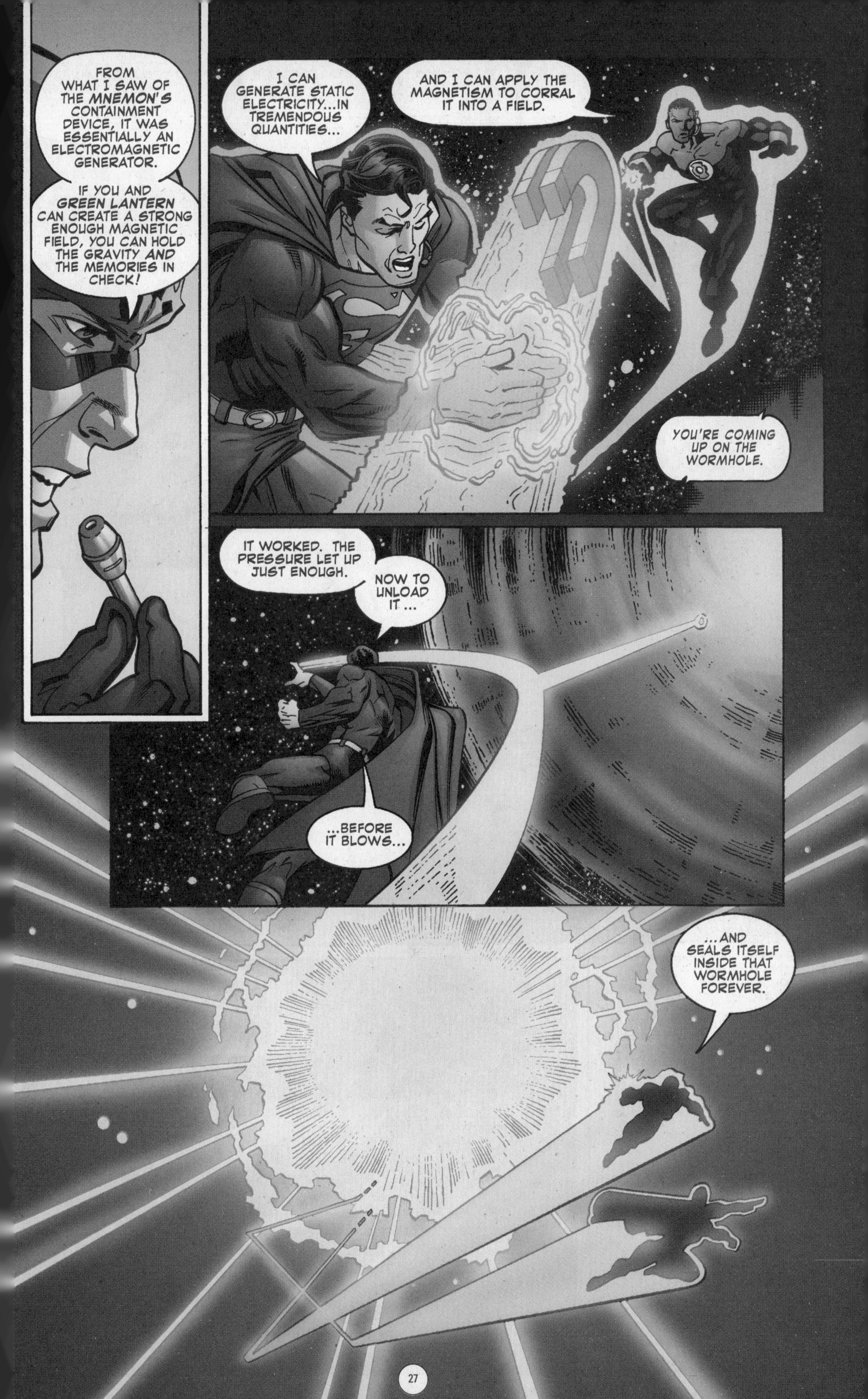
FROM WHAT I SAW OF THE MNEMON'S CONTAINMENT DEVICE, IT WAS ESSENTIALLY AN ELECTROMAGNETIC GENERATOR.
IF YOU AND GREEN LANTERN CAN CREATE A STRONG ENOUGH MAGNETIC FIELD, YOU CAN HOLD THE GRAVITY AND THE MEMORIES IN CHECK!
I CAN GENERATE STATIC ELECTRICITY...IN TREMENDOUS QUANTITIES...
AND I CAN APPLY THE MAGNETISM TO CORRAL IT INTO A FIELD.
YOU'RE COMING UP ON THE WORMHOLE.
IT WORKED. THE PRESSURE LET UP JUST ENOUGH.
NOW TO UNLOAD IT ...
...BEFORE IT BLOWS...
...AND SEALS ITSELF INSIDE THAT WORMHOLE FOREVER.

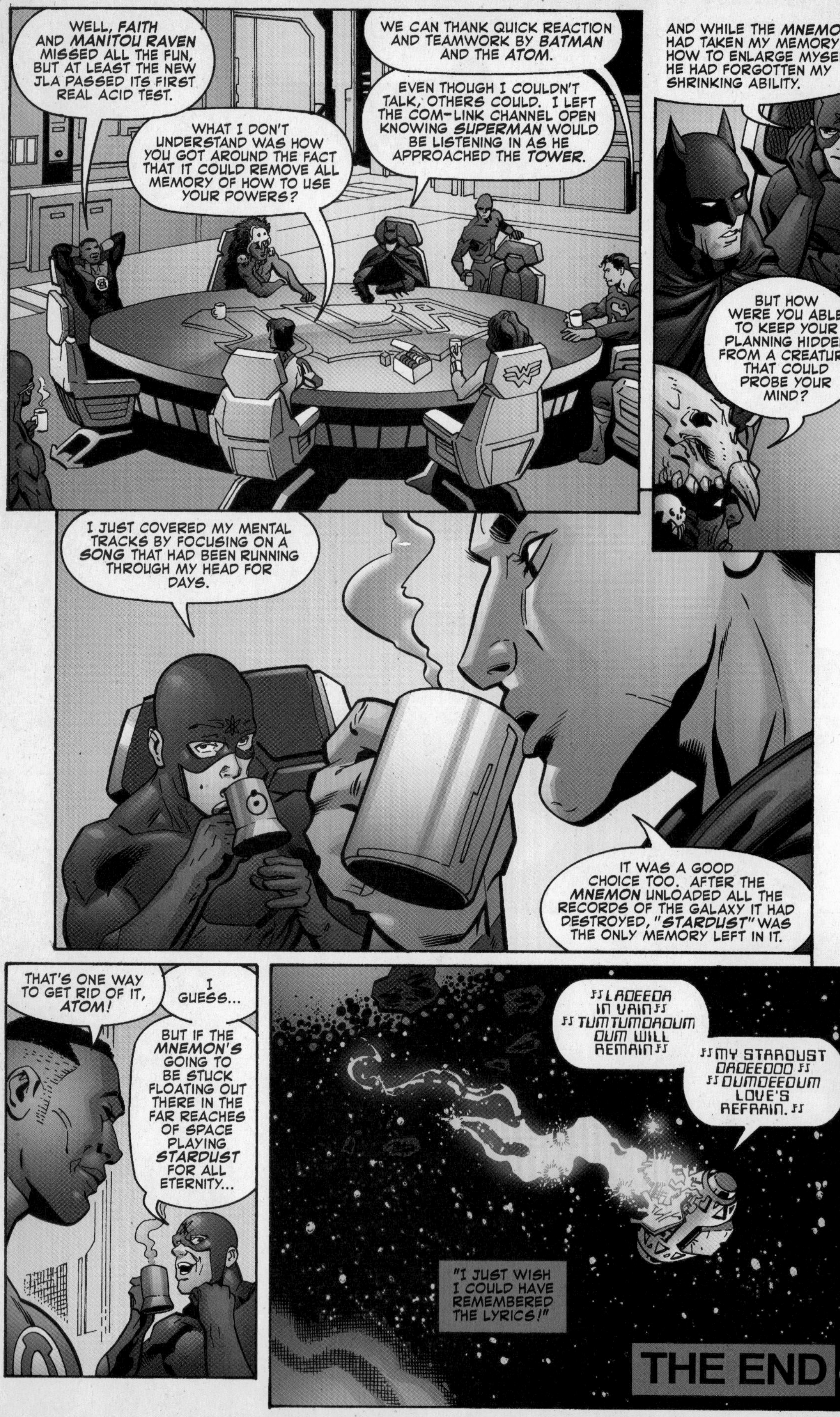
WELL, FAITH AND MANITOU RAVEN MISSED ALL THE FUN, BUT AT LEAST THE NEW JLA PASSED ITS FIRST REAL ACID TEST.
WHAT I DON'T UNDERSTAND WAS HOW YOU GOT AROUND THE FACT THAT IT COULD REMOVE ALL MEMORY OF HOW TO USE YOUR POWERS?
WE CAN THANK QUICK REACTION AND TEAMWORK BY BATMAN AND THE ATOM.
EVEN THOUGH I COULDN'T TALK, OTHERS COULD. I LEFT THE COM-LINK CHANNEL OPEN KNOWING SUPERMAN WOULD BE LISTENING IN AS HE APPROACHED THE TOWER.
AND WHILE THE MNEMON HAD TAKEN MY MEMORY OF HOW TO ENLARGE MYSELF, HE HAD FORGOTTEN MY SHRINKING ABILITY.
BUT HOW WERE YOU ABLE TO KEEP YOUR PLANNING HIDDEN FROM A CREATURE THAT COULD PROBE YOUR MIND?
I JUST COVERED MY MENTAL TRACKS BY FOCUSING ON A SONG THAT HAD BEEN RUNNING THROUGH MY HEAD FOR DAYS.
IT WAS A GOOD CHOICE TOO. AFTER THE MNEMON UNLOADED ALL THE RECORDS OF THE GALAXY IT HAD DESTROYED, "STARDUST" WAS THE ONLY MEMORY LEFT IN IT.
THAT'S ONE WAY TO GET RID OF IT, ATOM!
I GUESS...
BUT IF THE MNEMON'S GOING TO BE STUCK FLOATING OUT THERE IN THE FAR REACHES OF SPACE PLAYING STARDUST FOR ALL ETERNITY...
♫ LADEEDA IN VAIN ♫ ♫ TUMTUMDADUM DUM WILL REMAIN ♫
♫ MY STARDUST DADEEDOO ♫ ♫ DUMDEEDUM LOVE'S REFRAIN. ♫
"I JUST WISH I COULD HAVE REMEMBERED THE LYRICS!"
THE END

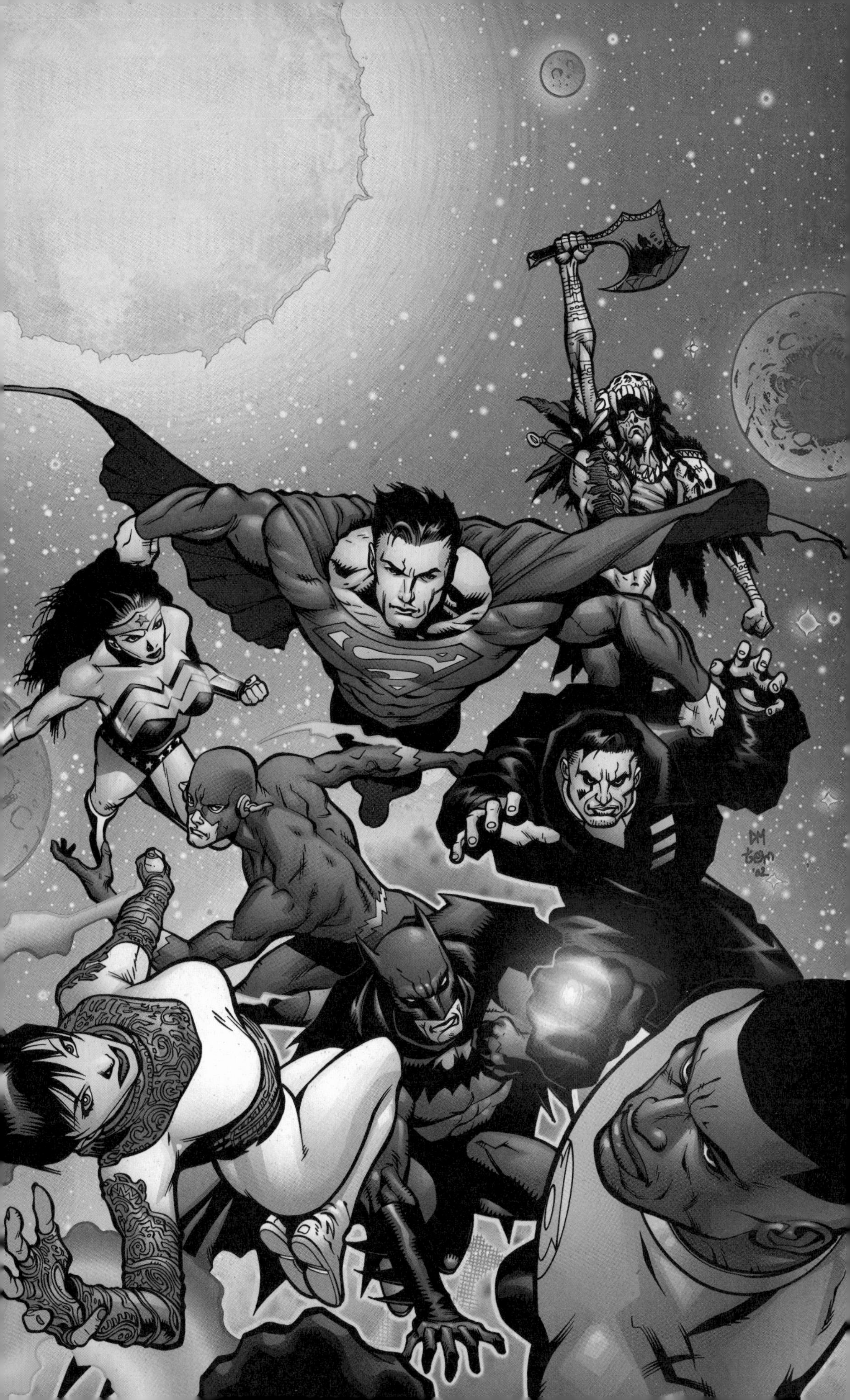

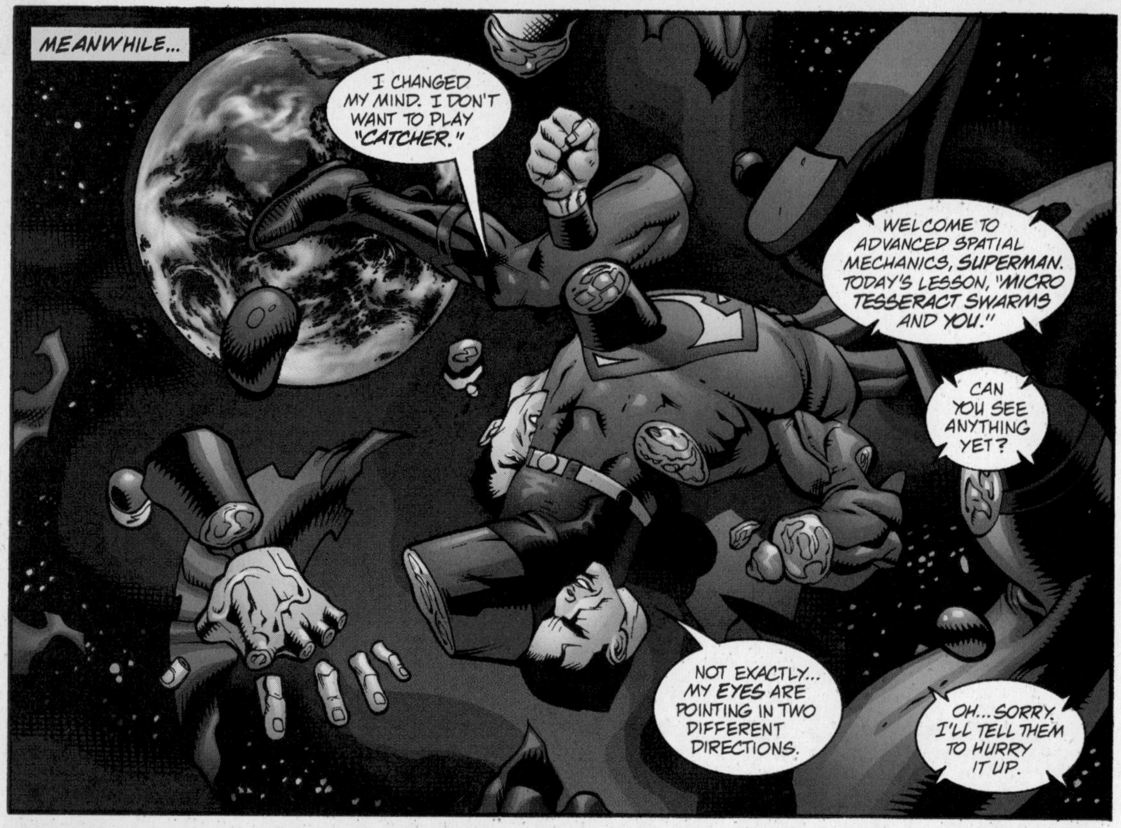
MEANWHILE...
I CHANGED MY MIND. I DON'T WANT TO PLAY "CATCHER."
WELCOME TO ADVANCED SPATIAL MECHANICS, SUPERMAN. TODAY'S LESSON, "MICRO TESSERACT SWARMS AND YOU."
CAN YOU SEE ANYTHING YET?
NOT EXACTLY... MY EYES ARE POINTING IN TWO DIFFERENT DIRECTIONS.
OH... SORRY. I'LL TELL THEM TO HURRY IT UP.

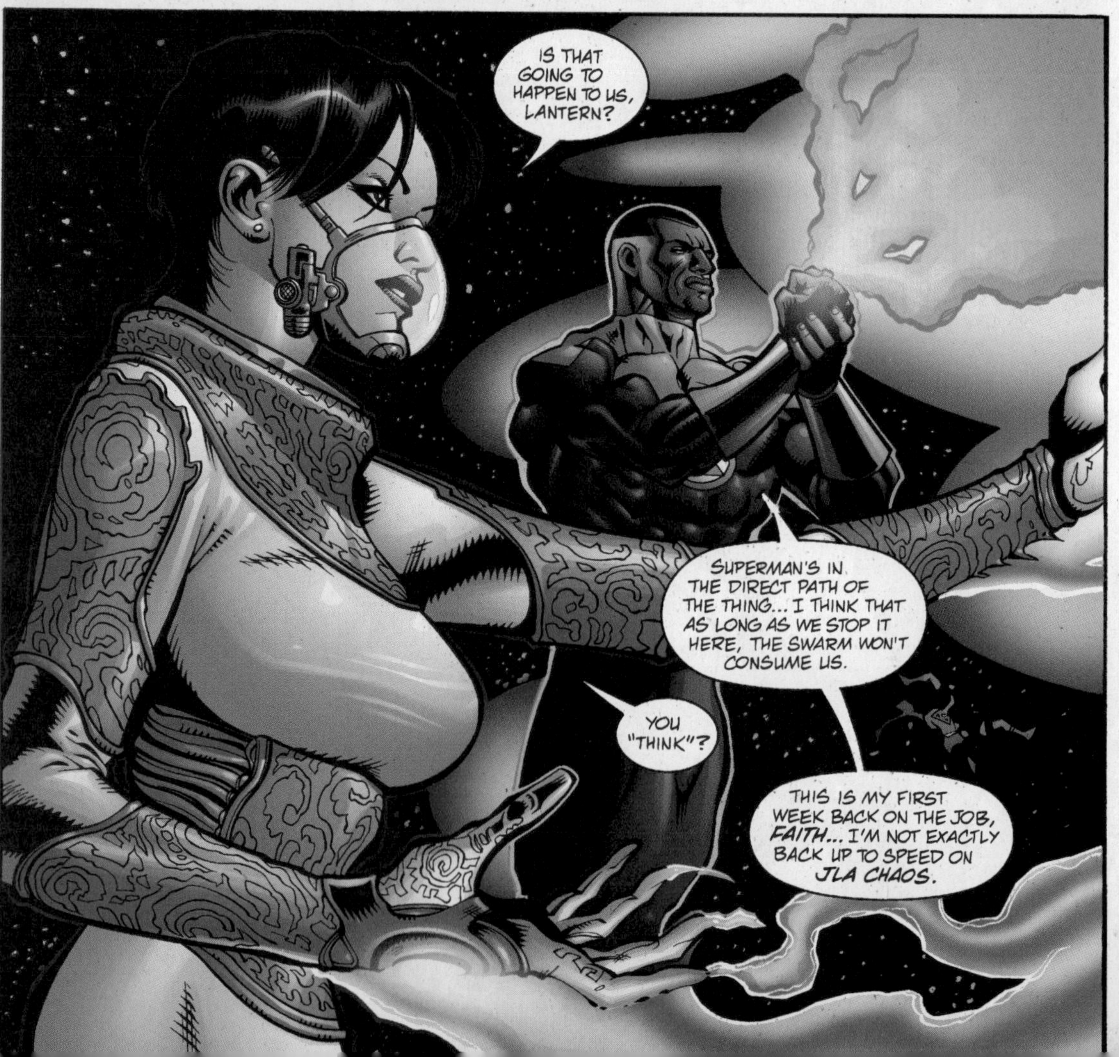
IS THAT GOING TO HAPPEN TO US, LANTERN?
SUPERMAN'S IN THE DIRECT PATH OF THE THING... I THINK THAT AS LONG AS WE STOP IT HERE, THE SWARM WON'T CONSUME US.
YOU "THINK"?
THIS IS MY FIRST WEEK BACK ON THE JOB, FAITH... I'M NOT EXACTLY BACK UP TO SPEED ON JLA CHAOS.

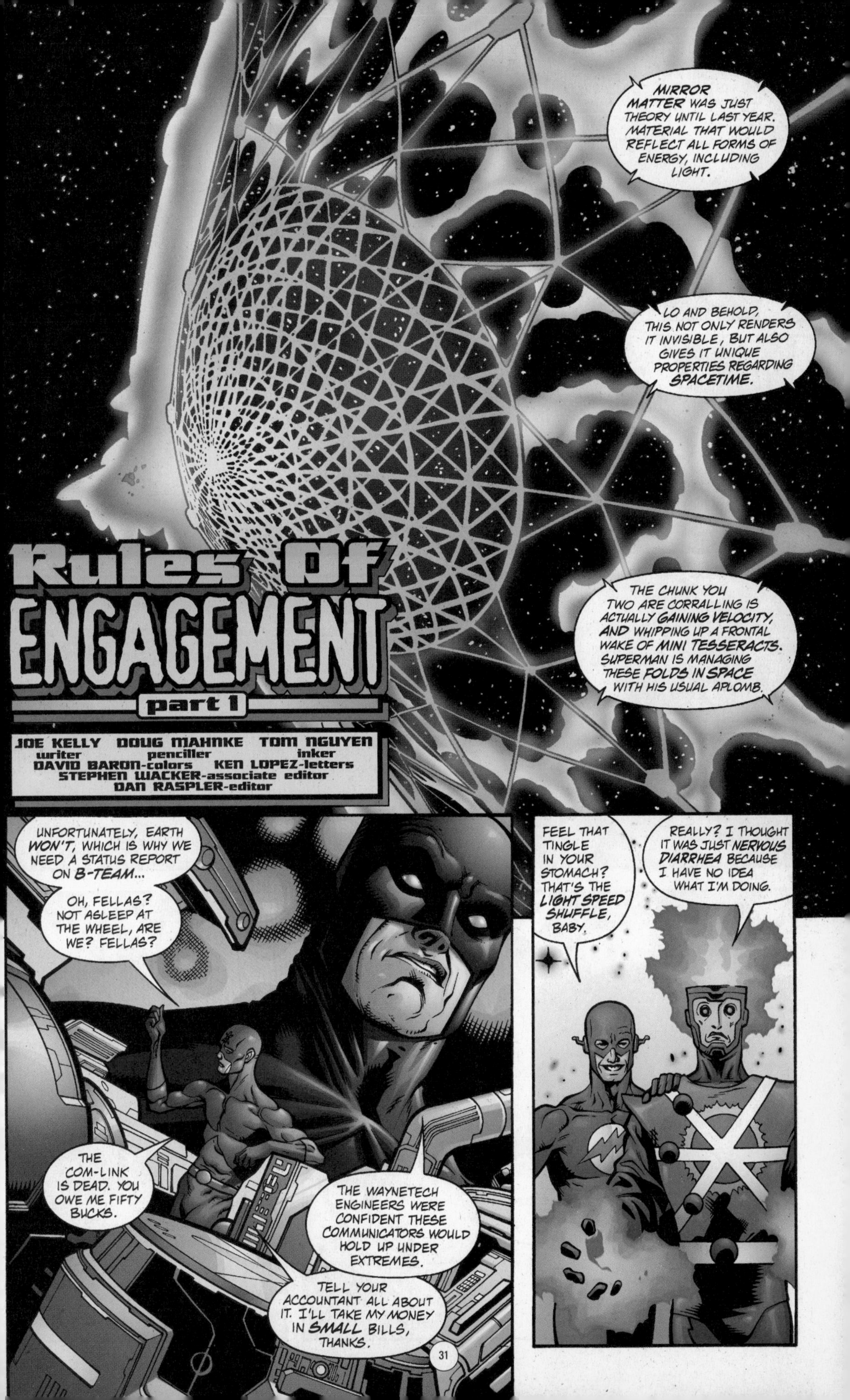
MIRROR MATTER WAS JUST THEORY UNTIL LAST YEAR. MATERIAL THAT WOULD REFLECT ALL FORMS OF ENERGY, INCLUDING LIGHT.
LO AND BEHOLD, THIS NOT ONLY RENDERS IT INVISIBLE, BUT ALSO GIVES IT UNIQUE PROPERTIES REGARDING SPACETIME.
Rules Of ENGAGEMENT
part 1
JOE KELLY writer DOUG MAHNKE penciller TOM NGUYEN inker
DAVID BARON-colors KEN LOPEZ-letters
STEPHEN WACKER-associate editor
DAN RASPLER-editor
THE CHUNK YOU TWO ARE CORRALLING IS ACTUALLY GAINING VELOCITY, AND WHIPPING UP A FRONTAL WAKE OF MINI TESSERACTS. SUPERMAN IS MANAGING THESE FOLDS IN SPACE WITH HIS USUAL APLOMB.
UNFORTUNATELY, EARTH WON'T, WHICH IS WHY WE NEED A STATUS REPORT ON B-TEAM...
OH, FELLAS? NOT ASLEEP AT THE WHEEL, ARE WE? FELLAS?
THE COM-LINK IS DEAD. YOU OWE ME FIFTY BUCKS.
THE WAYNETECH ENGINEERS WERE CONFIDENT THESE COMMUNICATORS WOULD HOLD UP UNDER EXTREMES.
TELL YOUR ACCOUNTANT ALL ABOUT IT. I'LL TAKE MY MONEY IN SMALL BILLS, THANKS.
FEEL THAT TINGLE IN YOUR STOMACH? THAT'S THE LIGHT SPEED SHUFFLE, BABY.
REALLY? I THOUGHT IT WAS JUST NERVOUS DIARRHEA BECAUSE I HAVE NO IDEA WHAT I'M DOING.

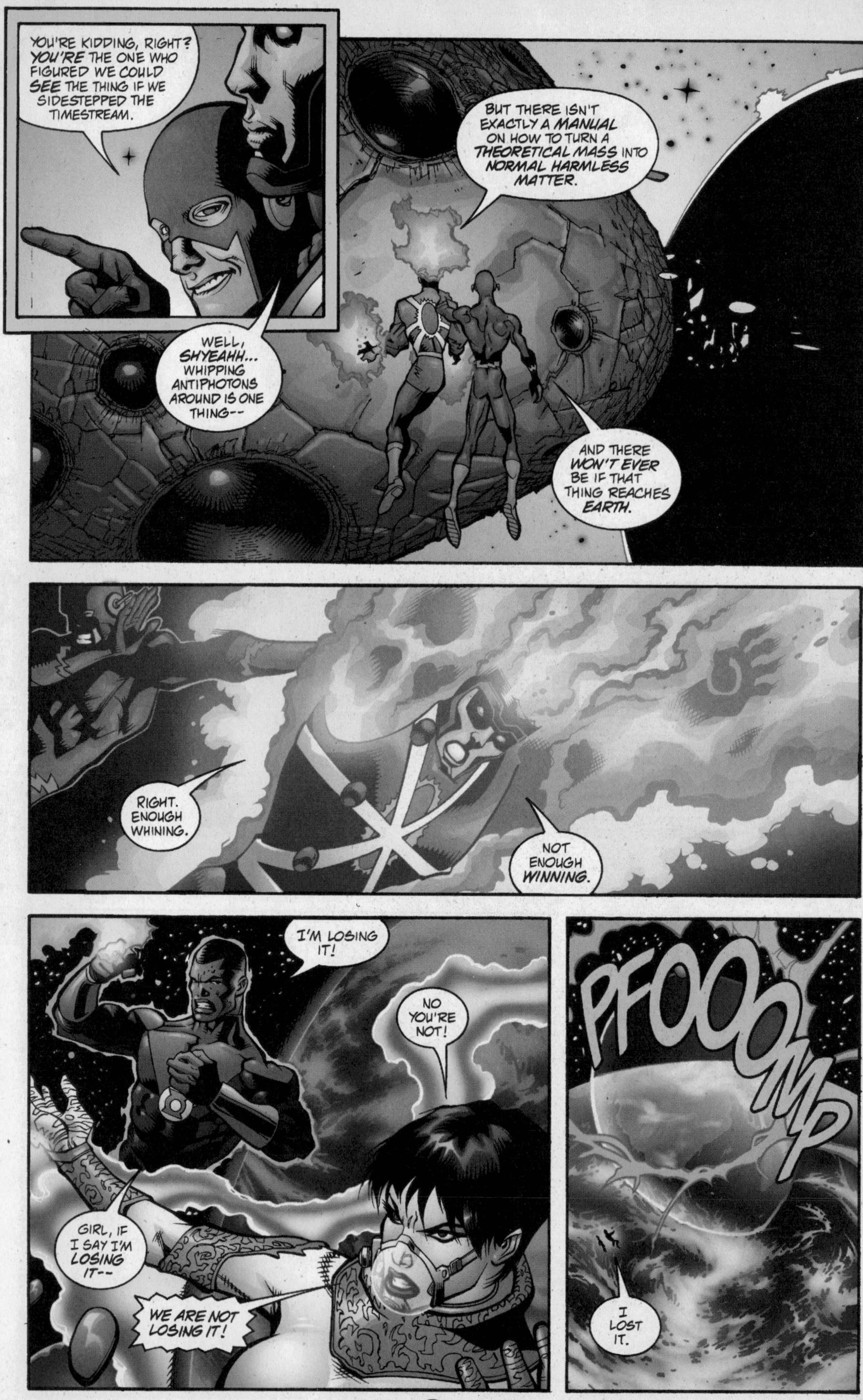
YOU'RE KIDDING, RIGHT? YOU'RE THE ONE WHO FIGURED WE COULD SEE THE THING IF WE SIDESTEPPED THE TIMESTREAM.
BUT THERE ISN'T EXACTLY A MANUAL ON HOW TO TURN A THEORETICAL MASS INTO NORMAL HARMLESS MATTER.
WELL, SHYEAHH... WHIPPING ANTIPHOTONS AROUND IS ONE THING--
AND THERE WON'T EVER BE IF THAT THING REACHES EARTH.
RIGHT. ENOUGH WHINING.
NOT ENOUGH WINNING.
I'M LOSING IT!
NO YOU'RE NOT!
GIRL, IF I SAY I'M LOSING IT--
WE ARE NOT LOSING IT!
PFOOOMP
I LOST IT.

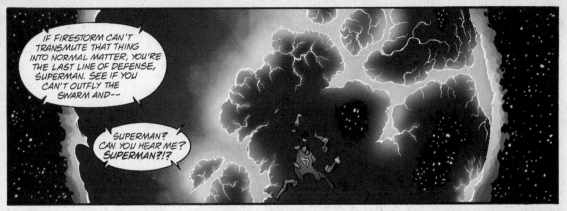

IF FIRESTORM CAN'T TRANSMUTE THAT THING INTO NORMAL MATTER, YOU'RE THE LAST LINE OF DEFENSE, SUPERMAN. SEE IF YOU CAN'T OUTFLY THE SWARM AND--

SUPERMAN? CAN YOU HEAR ME? SUPERMAN?!?

BACK IN ONE PIECE, ATOM. THE TESSERACTS ARE GONE.

IS THAT WHAT'S CAUSING ALL THIS? NO PROBLEM.

FSOOOOSH

HEY, GUYS, I JUST GOT THE WEIRDEST READING DOWN HERE... WHAT THE HELL HAPPENED?

MARSHMALLOW MATTER.

THAT'S NOT FUNNY.

I KNOW-- I KNOW! I'M SORRY. IT WAS THE FIRST THING THAT CAME TO MIND!

AFTER COTTON BALLS... AND NERF.

I'M NOT FIRED, AM I?

WAY TO MAKE FRIENDS, RONNIE... EVERYONE COME ON HOME.

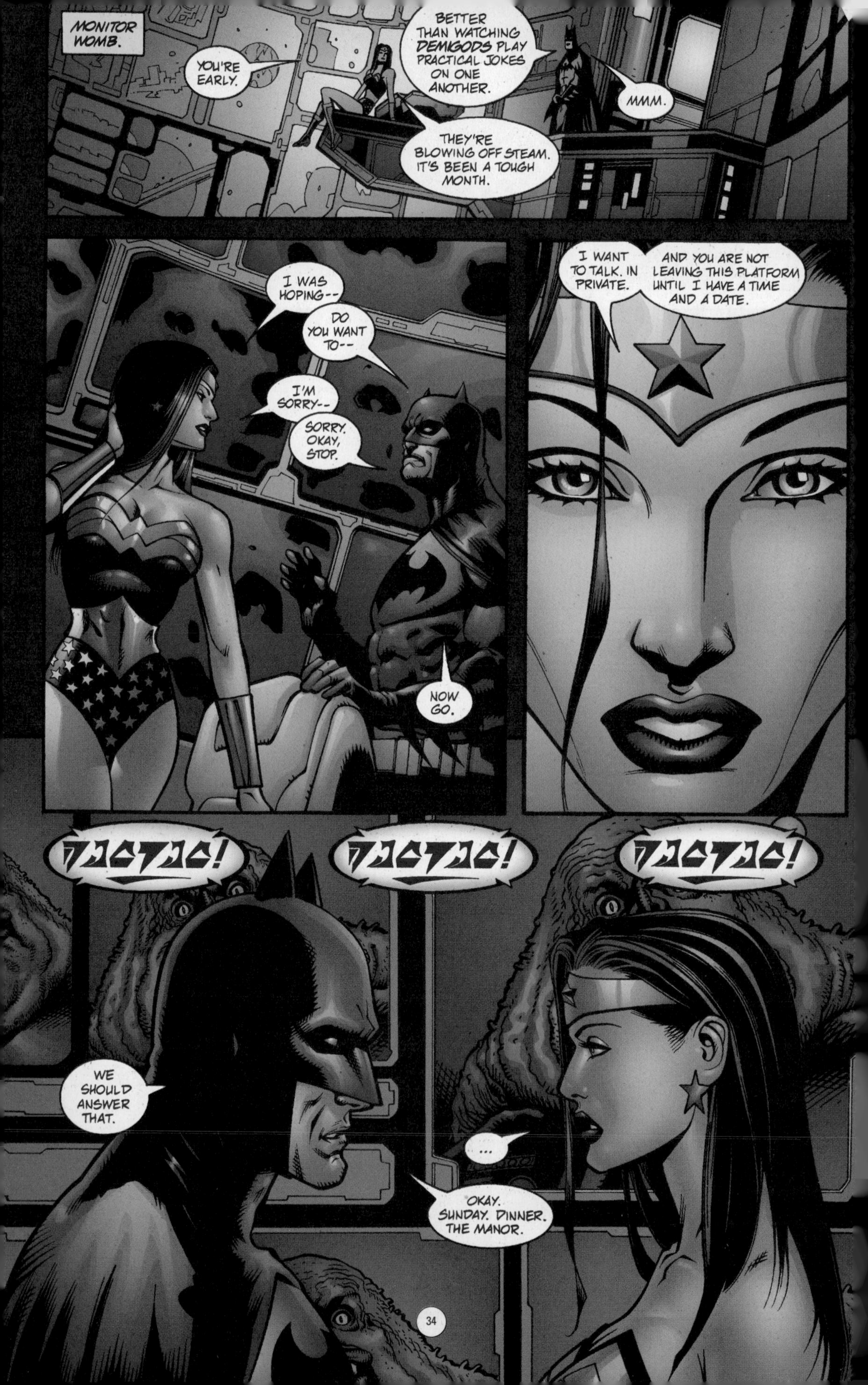
MONITOR WOMB.
YOU'RE EARLY.
BETTER THAN WATCHING DEMIGODS PLAY PRACTICAL JOKES ON ONE ANOTHER.
MMM.
THEY'RE BLOWING OFF STEAM. IT'S BEEN A TOUGH MONTH.
I WAS HOPING--
DO YOU WANT TO--
I'M SORRY--
SORRY. OKAY, STOP.
NOW GO.
I WANT TO TALK. IN PRIVATE.
AND YOU ARE NOT LEAVING THIS PLATFORM UNTIL I HAVE A TIME AND A DATE.
WE SHOULD ANSWER THAT.
...
OKAY. SUNDAY. DINNER. THE MANOR.

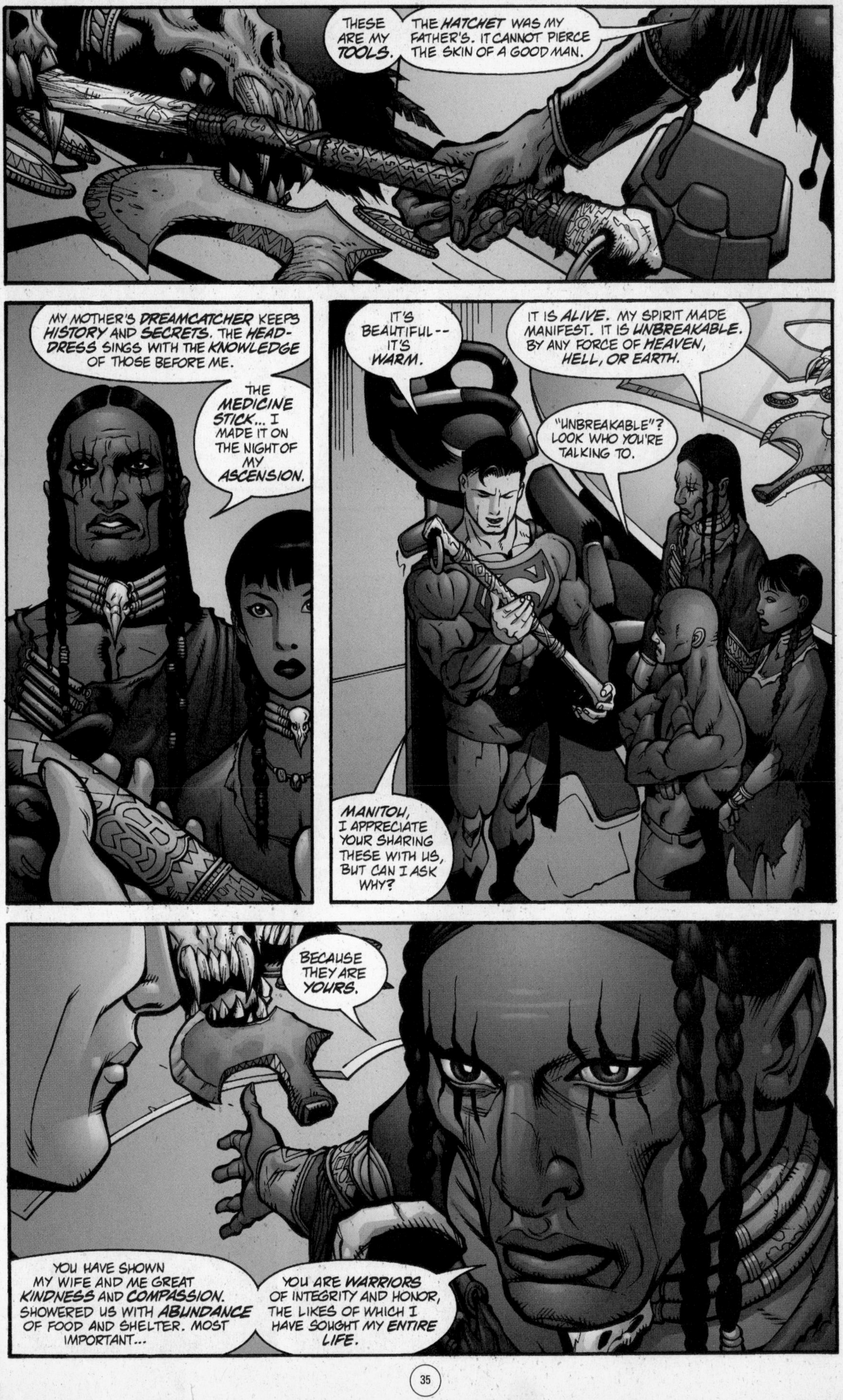
THESE ARE MY TOOLS.
THE HATCHET WAS MY FATHER'S. IT CANNOT PIERCE THE SKIN OF A GOOD MAN.
MY MOTHER'S DREAMCATCHER KEEPS HISTORY AND SECRETS. THE HEAD-DRESS SINGS WITH THE KNOWLEDGE OF THOSE BEFORE ME.
THE MEDICINE STICK... I MADE IT ON THE NIGHT OF MY ASCENSION.
IT'S BEAUTIFUL-- IT'S WARM.
IT IS ALIVE. MY SPIRIT MADE MANIFEST. IT IS UNBREAKABLE. BY ANY FORCE OF HEAVEN, HELL, OR EARTH.
"UNBREAKABLE"? LOOK WHO YOU'RE TALKING TO.
MANITOU, I APPRECIATE YOUR SHARING THESE WITH US, BUT CAN I ASK WHY?
BECAUSE THEY ARE YOURS.
YOU HAVE SHOWN MY WIFE AND ME GREAT KINDNESS AND COMPASSION. SHOWERED US WITH ABUNDANCE OF FOOD AND SHELTER. MOST IMPORTANT...
YOU ARE WARRIORS OF INTEGRITY AND HONOR, THE LIKES OF WHICH I HAVE SOUGHT MY ENTIRE LIFE.

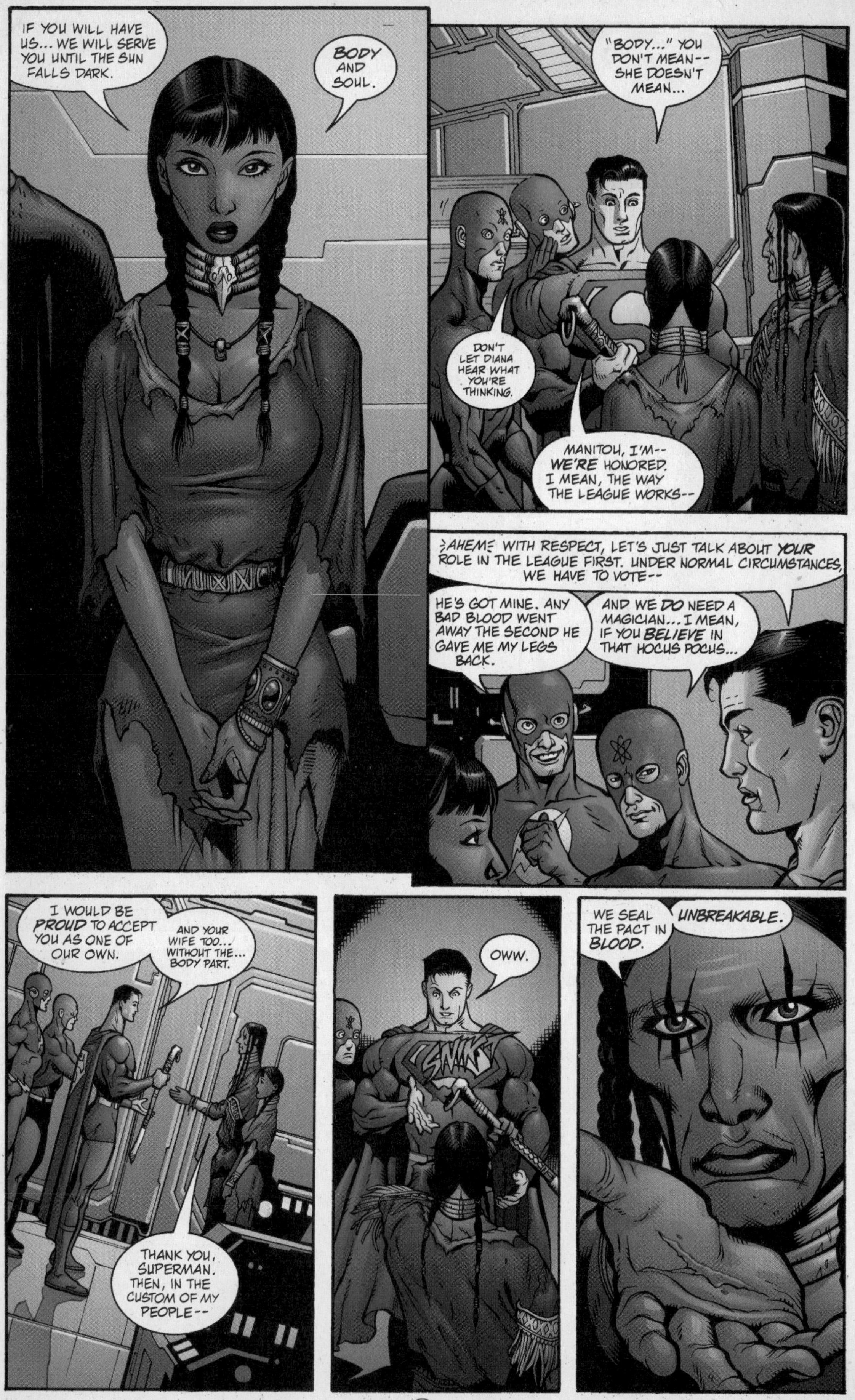
IF YOU WILL HAVE US... WE WILL SERVE YOU UNTIL THE SUN FALLS DARK.
BODY AND SOUL.
"BODY..." YOU DON'T MEAN-- SHE DOESN'T MEAN...
DON'T LET DIANA HEAR WHAT YOU'RE THINKING.
MANITOU, I'M-- WE'RE HONORED. I MEAN, THE WAY THE LEAGUE WORKS--
AHEM WITH RESPECT, LET'S JUST TALK ABOUT YOUR ROLE IN THE LEAGUE FIRST. UNDER NORMAL CIRCUMSTANCES, WE HAVE TO VOTE--
HE'S GOT MINE. ANY BAD BLOOD WENT AWAY THE SECOND HE GAVE ME MY LEGS BACK.
AND WE DO NEED A MAGICIAN... I MEAN, IF YOU BELIEVE IN THAT HOCUS POCUS...
I WOULD BE PROUD TO ACCEPT YOU AS ONE OF OUR OWN.
AND YOUR WIFE TOO... WITHOUT THE... BODY PART.
THANK YOU, SUPERMAN. THEN, IN THE CUSTOM OF MY PEOPLE--
OWW.
SNIK
WE SEAL THE PACT IN BLOOD.
UNBREAKABLE.

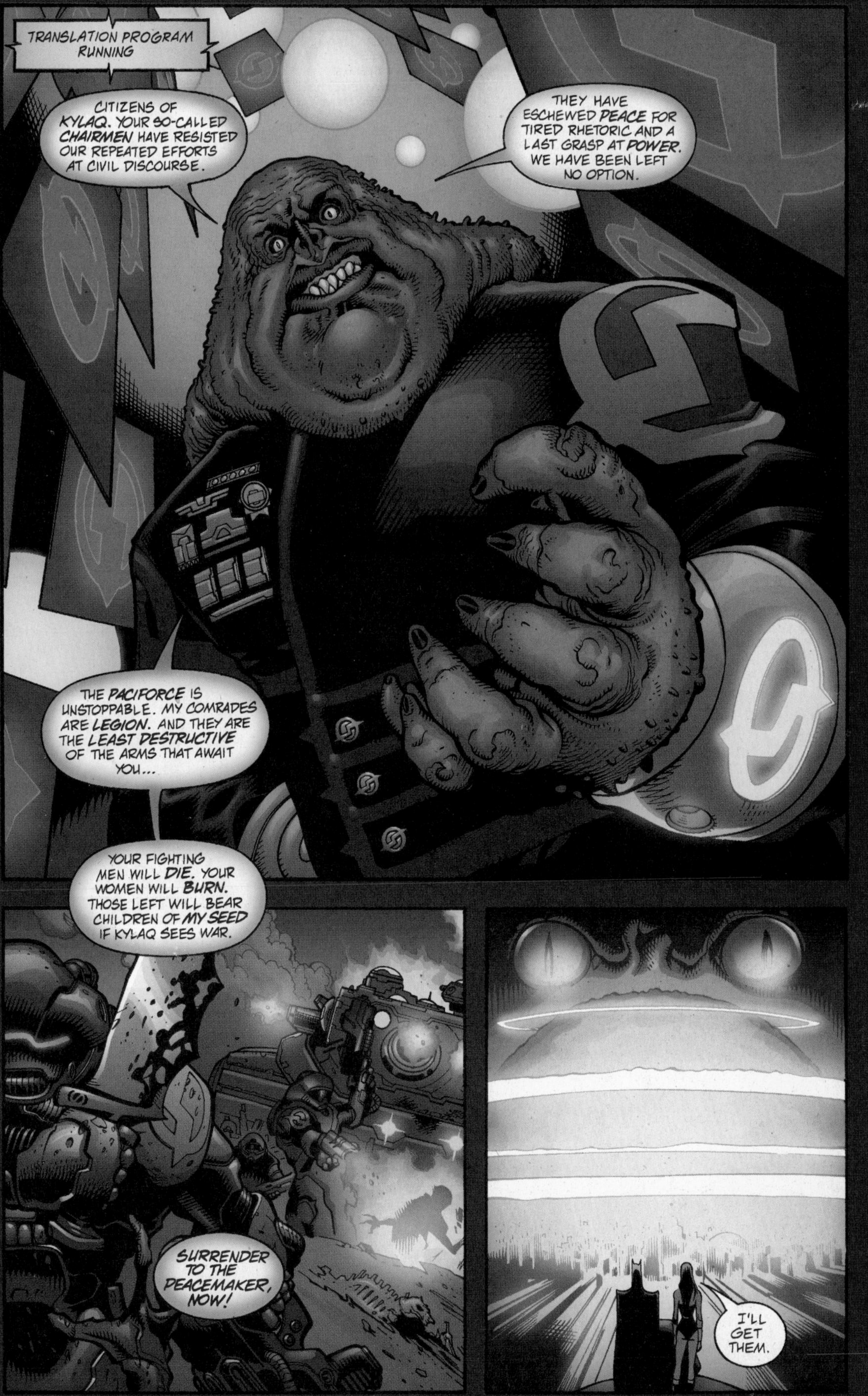
TRANSLATION PROGRAM RUNNING
CITIZENS OF KYLAQ. YOUR SO-CALLED CHAIRMEN HAVE RESISTED OUR REPEATED EFFORTS AT CIVIL DISCOURSE.
THEY HAVE ESCHEWED PEACE FOR TIRED RHETORIC AND A LAST GRASP AT POWER. WE HAVE BEEN LEFT NO OPTION.
THE PACIFORCE IS UNSTOPPABLE. MY COMRADES ARE LEGION. AND THEY ARE THE LEAST DESTRUCTIVE OF THE ARMS THAT AWAIT YOU...
YOUR FIGHTING MEN WILL DIE. YOUR WOMEN WILL BURN. THOSE LEFT WILL BEAR CHILDREN OF MY SEED IF KYLAQ SEES WAR.
SURRENDER TO THE PEACEMAKER, NOW!
I'LL GET THEM.

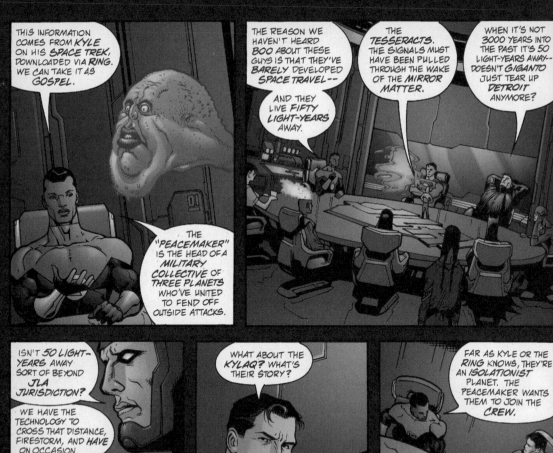

THIS INFORMATION COMES FROM *KYLE* ON HIS *SPACE TREK,* DOWNLOADED VIA *RING.* WE CAN TAKE IT AS *GOSPEL.*

THE *"PEACEMAKER"* IS THE HEAD OF A *MILITARY COLLECTIVE* OF *THREE PLANETS* WHO'VE UNITED TO FEND OFF OUTSIDE ATTACKS.

THE REASON WE HAVEN'T HEARD *BOO* ABOUT THESE GUYS IS THAT THEY'VE *BARELY DEVELOPED SPACE TRAVEL--*

AND THEY LIVE *FIFTY LIGHT-YEARS* AWAY.

THE *TESSERACTS.* THE SIGNALS MUST HAVE BEEN PULLED THROUGH THE WAKE OF THE *MIRROR MATTER.*

WHEN IT'S NOT *3000 YEARS* INTO THE *PAST* IT'S *50 LIGHT-YEARS* AWAY-- DOESN'T *GIGANTO* JUST TEAR UP *DETROIT* ANYMORE?

ISN'T *50 LIGHT-YEARS* AWAY SORT OF BEYOND *JLA JURISDICTION?*

WE HAVE THE TECHNOLOGY TO CROSS THAT DISTANCE, FIRESTORM, AND *HAVE* ON OCCASION.

WHAT ABOUT THE *KYLAQ?* WHAT'S THEIR STORY?

FAR AS KYLE OR THE *RING* KNOWS, THEY'RE AN *ISOLATIONIST* PLANET. THE PEACEMAKER WANTS THEM TO JOIN THE *CREW.*

THEY JUST WANT TO BE LEFT ALONE... BUT WE'D HAVE TO ASK THEM TO BE 100 PERCENT SURE.

IS THERE LIKE A *"PRIME DIRECTIVE"* SORT OF SCENARIO FOR A CASE LIKE THIS?

I MEAN, IT'S NOT LIKE *EARTH* IS IN DANGER. NO ONE *CALLED* FOR US. IF WE HADN'T CAUGHT THAT TRANSMISSION, WE WOULDN'T EVEN BE HAVING THIS DISCUSSION.

MY THOUGHTS EXACTLY. THIS IS A *POLITICAL* SITUATION WE KNOW *NOTHING* ABOUT, *LIGHT-YEARS* AWAY FROM OUR HOME.

IT ISN'T OUR RESPONSIBILITY.

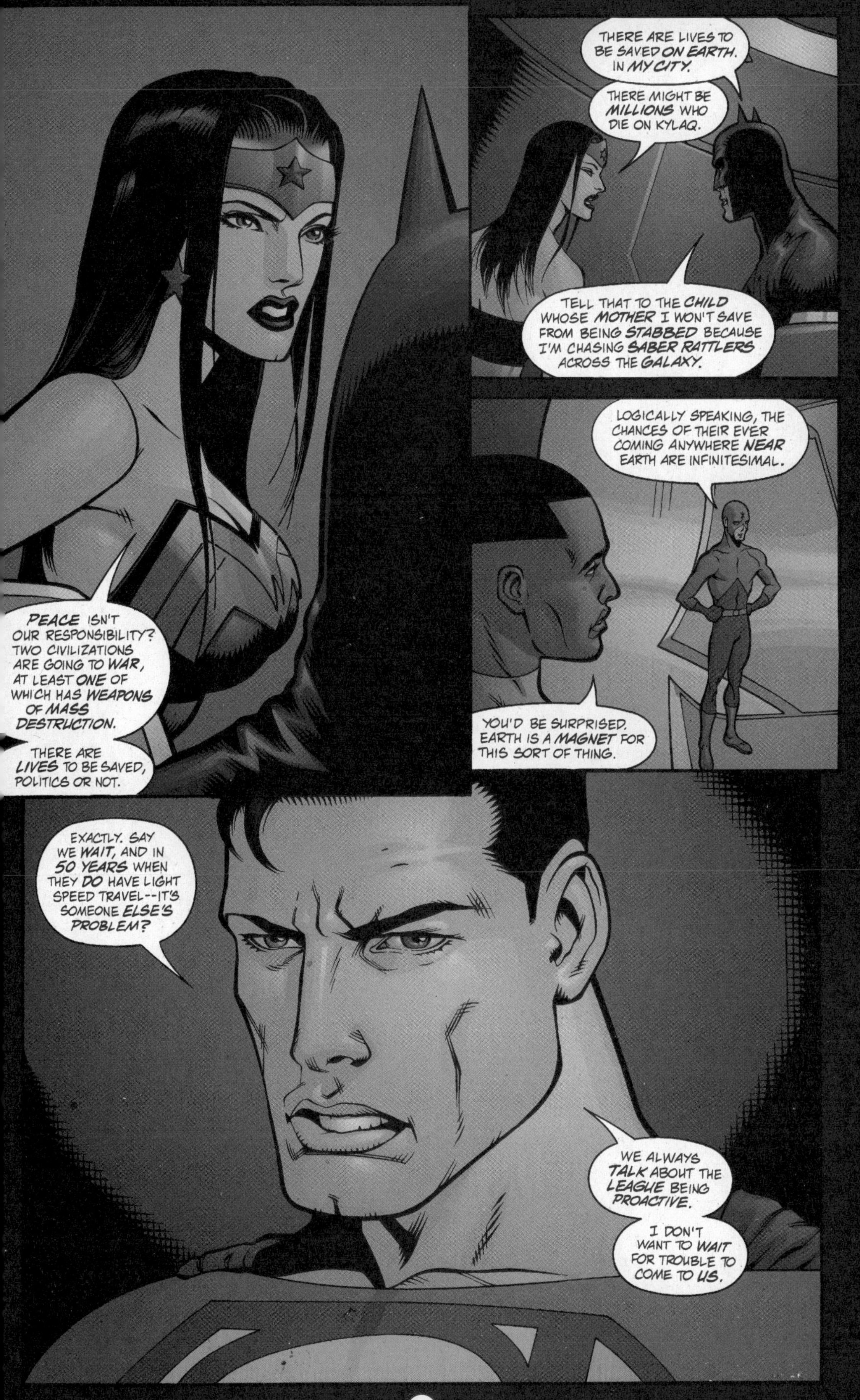
PEACE ISN'T OUR RESPONSIBILITY? TWO CIVILIZATIONS ARE GOING TO WAR, AT LEAST ONE OF WHICH HAS WEAPONS OF MASS DESTRUCTION.
THERE ARE LIVES TO BE SAVED, POLITICS OR NOT.
THERE ARE LIVES TO BE SAVED ON EARTH. IN MY CITY.
THERE MIGHT BE MILLIONS WHO DIE ON KYLAQ.
TELL THAT TO THE CHILD WHOSE MOTHER I WON'T SAVE FROM BEING STABBED BECAUSE I'M CHASING SABER RATTLERS ACROSS THE GALAXY.
LOGICALLY SPEAKING, THE CHANCES OF THEIR EVER COMING ANYWHERE NEAR EARTH ARE INFINITESIMAL.
YOU'D BE SURPRISED. EARTH IS A MAGNET FOR THIS SORT OF THING.
EXACTLY. SAY WE WAIT, AND IN 50 YEARS WHEN THEY DO HAVE LIGHT SPEED TRAVEL--IT'S SOMEONE ELSE'S PROBLEM?
WE ALWAYS TALK ABOUT THE LEAGUE BEING PROACTIVE.
I DON'T WANT TO WAIT FOR TROUBLE TO COME TO US.

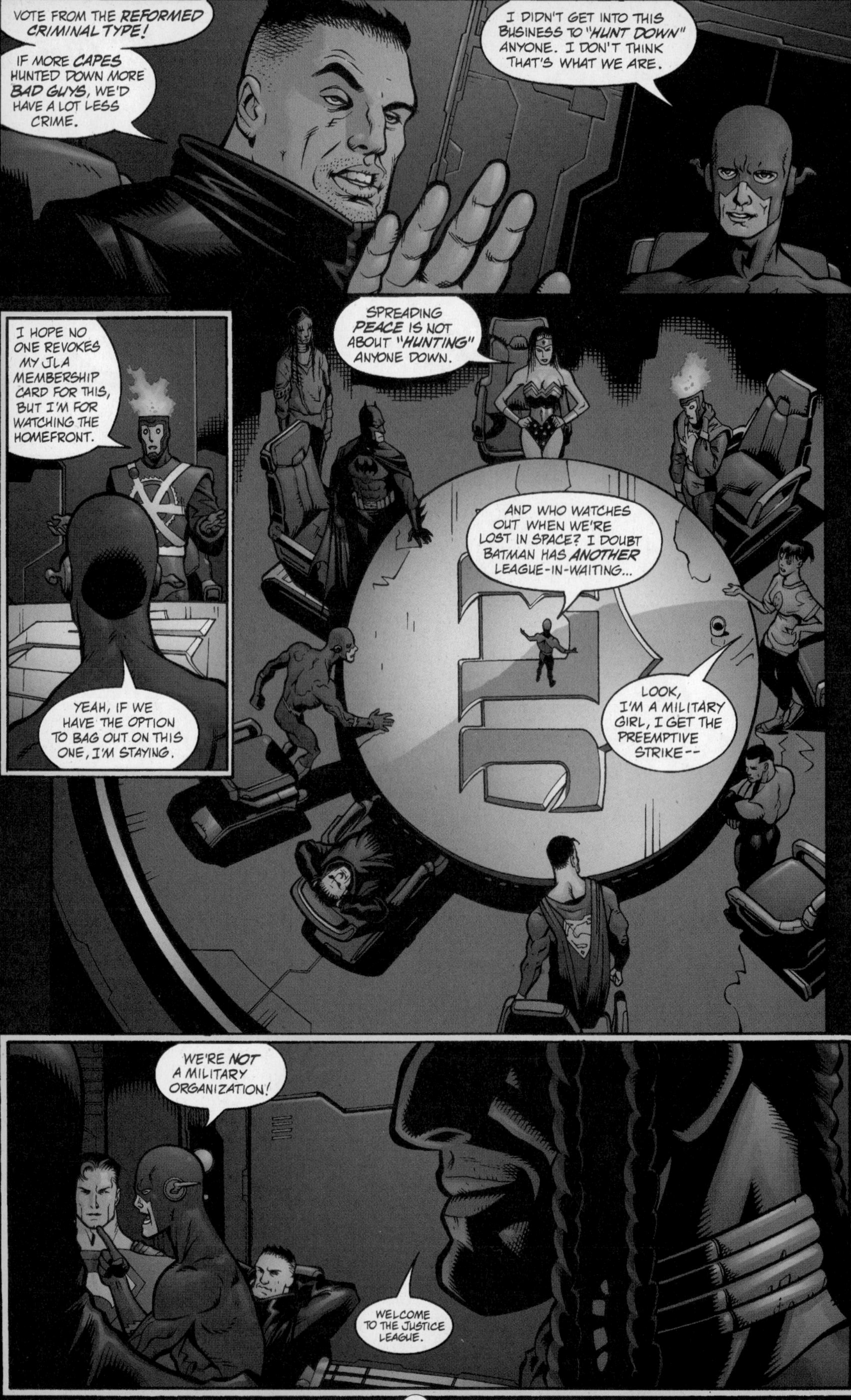
VOTE FROM THE REFORMED CRIMINAL TYPE!
IF MORE CAPES HUNTED DOWN MORE BAD GUYS, WE'D HAVE A LOT LESS CRIME.
I DIDN'T GET INTO THIS BUSINESS TO "HUNT DOWN" ANYONE. I DON'T THINK THAT'S WHAT WE ARE.
I HOPE NO ONE REVOKES MY JLA MEMBERSHIP CARD FOR THIS, BUT I'M FOR WATCHING THE HOMEFRONT.
YEAH, IF WE HAVE THE OPTION TO BAG OUT ON THIS ONE, I'M STAYING.
SPREADING PEACE IS NOT ABOUT "HUNTING" ANYONE DOWN.
AND WHO WATCHES OUT WHEN WE'RE LOST IN SPACE? I DOUBT BATMAN HAS ANOTHER LEAGUE-IN-WAITING...
LOOK, I'M A MILITARY GIRL, I GET THE PREEMPTIVE STRIKE--
WE'RE NOT A MILITARY ORGANIZATION!
WELCOME TO THE JUSTICE LEAGUE.

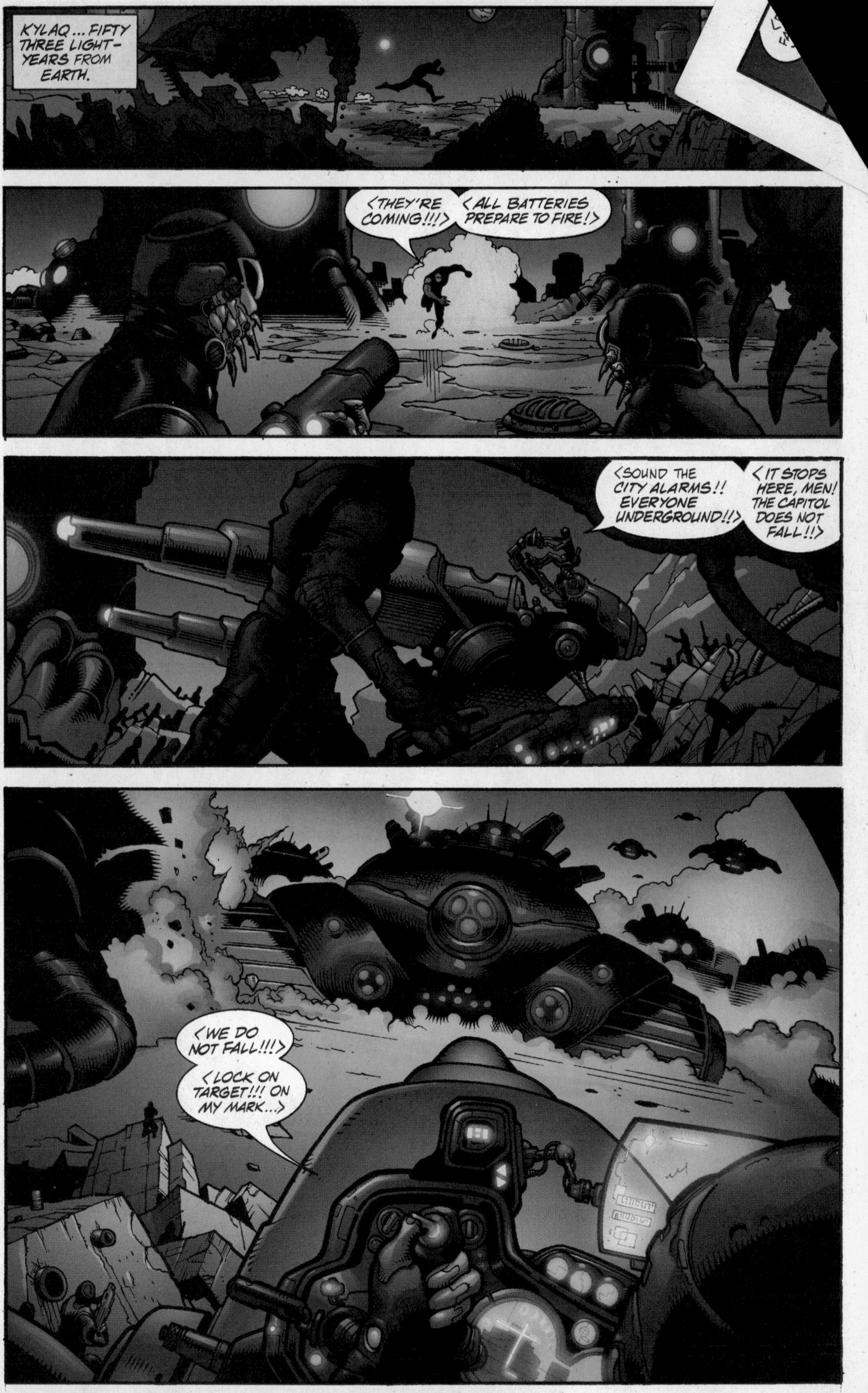
KYLAQ... FIFTY THREE LIGHT-YEARS FROM EARTH.
<THEY'RE COMING!!!>
<ALL BATTERIES PREPARE TO FIRE!>
<SOUND THE CITY ALARMS!! EVERYONE UNDERGROUND!!>
<IT STOPS HERE, MEN! THE CAPITOL DOES NOT FALL!!>
<WE DO NOT FALL!!!>
<LOCK ON TARGET!!! ON MY MARK...>

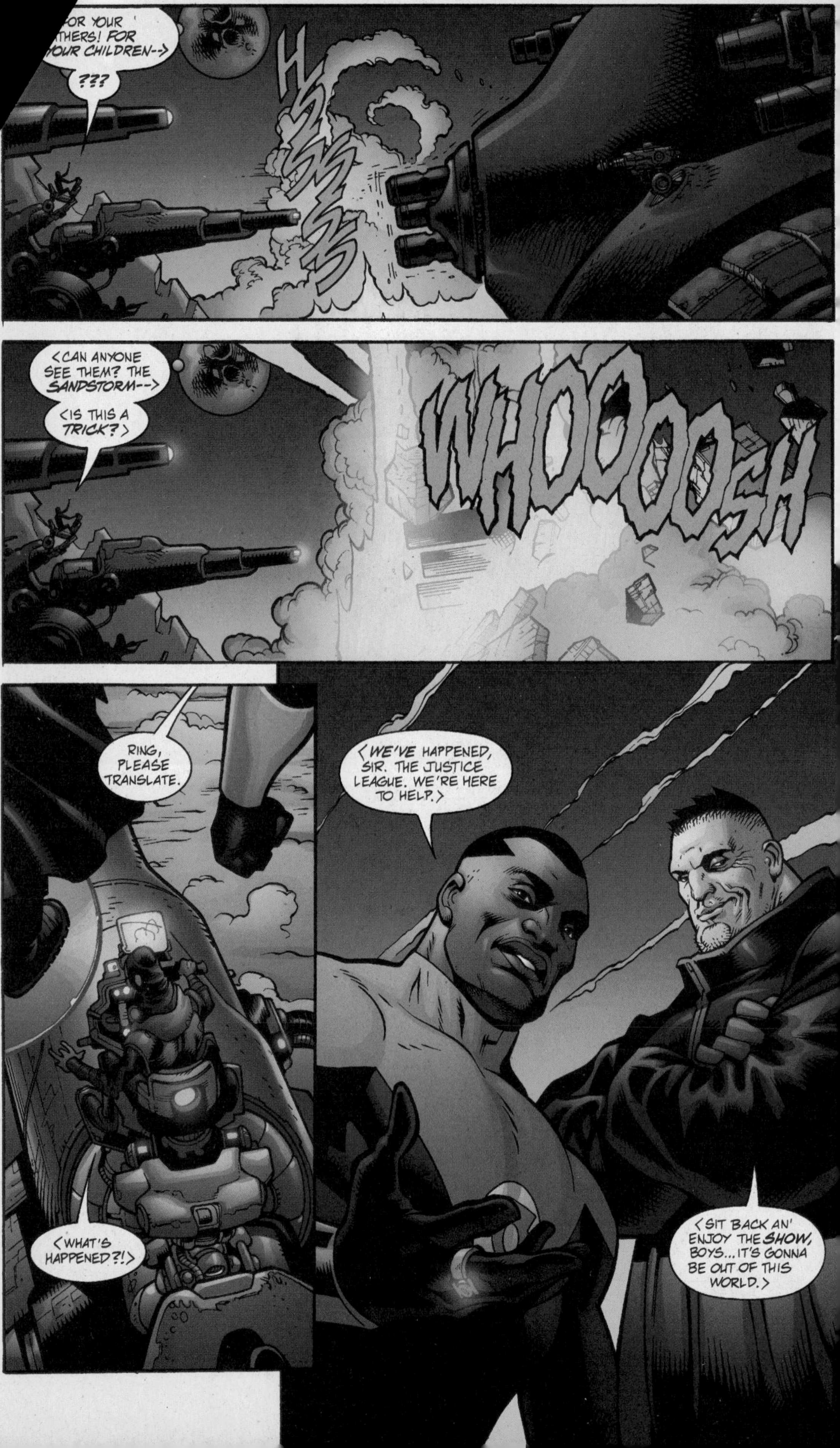

FOR YOUR
THERS! FOR
YOUR CHILDREN-->
???
HSSSSS
<CAN ANYONE SEE THEM? THE SANDSTORM-->
<IS THIS A TRICK?>
WHOOOOSH
RING, PLEASE TRANSLATE.
<WHAT'S HAPPENED?!>
<WE'VE HAPPENED, SIR. THE JUSTICE LEAGUE. WE'RE HERE TO HELP.>
<SIT BACK AN' ENJOY THE SHOW, BOYS... IT'S GONNA BE OUT OF THIS WORLD.>

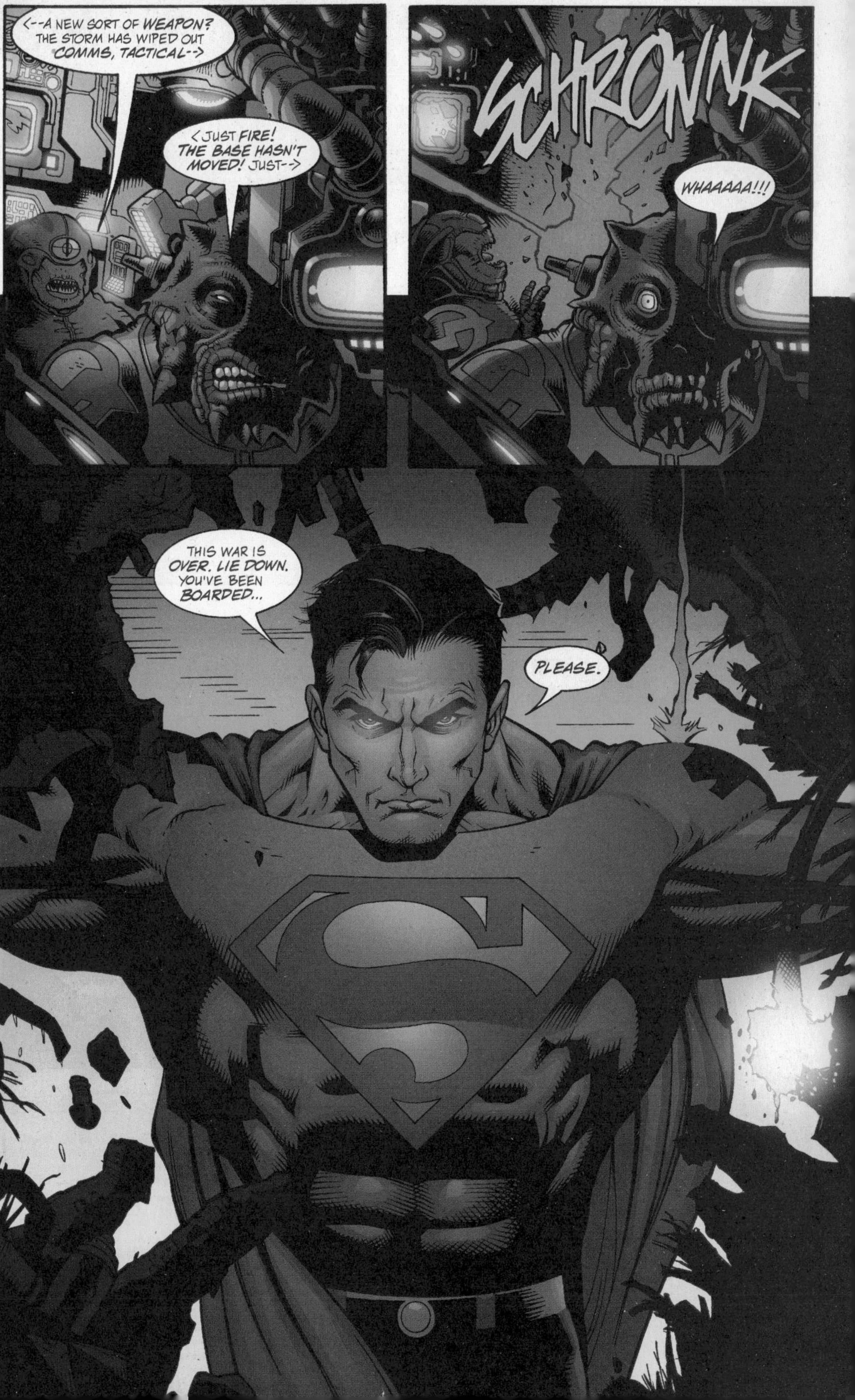
<--A NEW SORT OF WEAPON? THE STORM HAS WIPED OUT COMMS, TACTICAL-->
<JUST FIRE! THE BASE HASN'T MOVED! JUST-->
SCHRONNK
WHAAAAA!!!
THIS WAR IS OVER. LIE DOWN. YOU'VE BEEN BOARDED...
PLEASE.

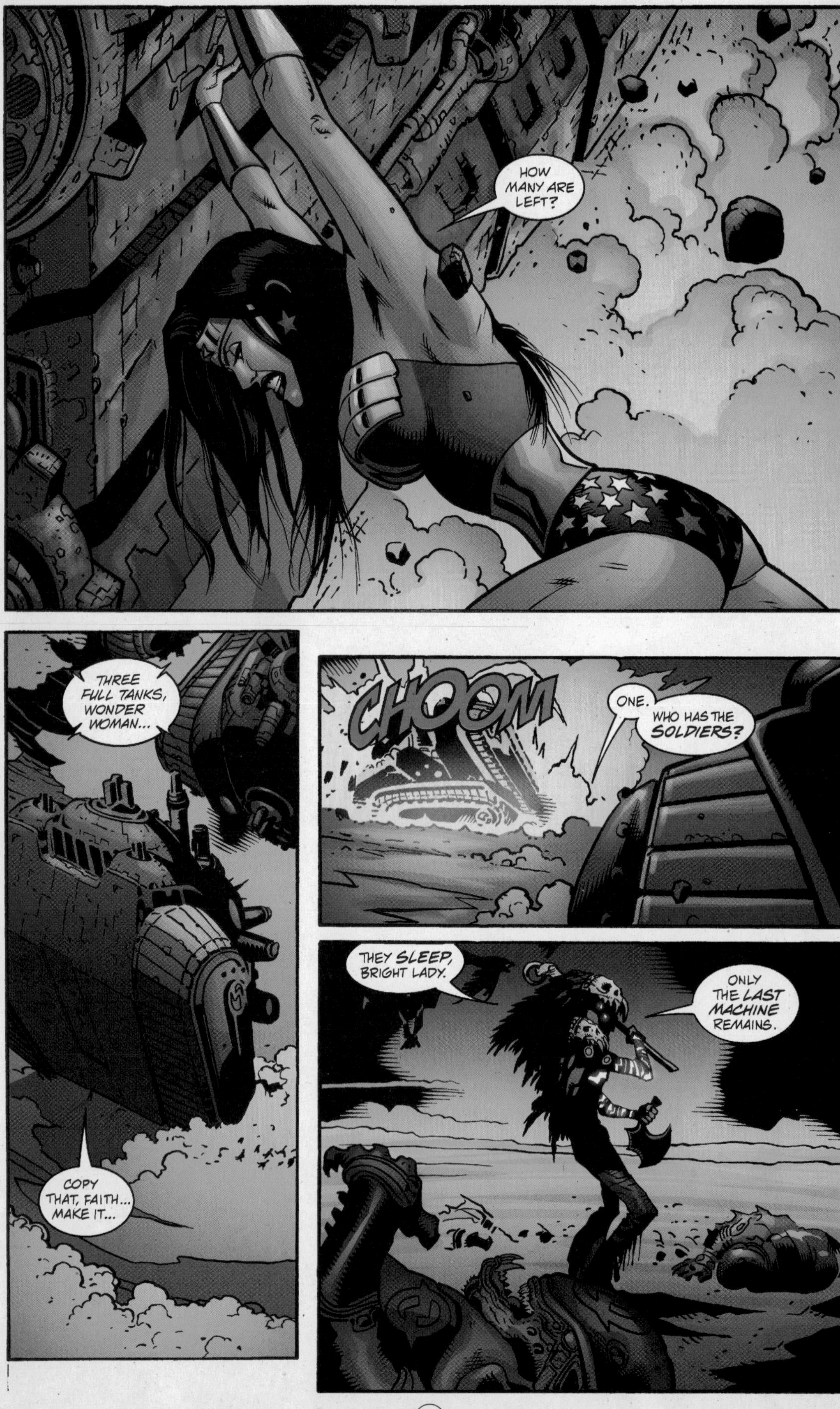
HOW MANY ARE LEFT?
THREE FULL TANKS, WONDER WOMAN...
COPY THAT, FAITH... MAKE IT...
CHOOM
ONE.
WHO HAS THE SOLDIERS?
THEY SLEEP, BRIGHT LADY.
ONLY THE LAST MACHINE REMAINS.

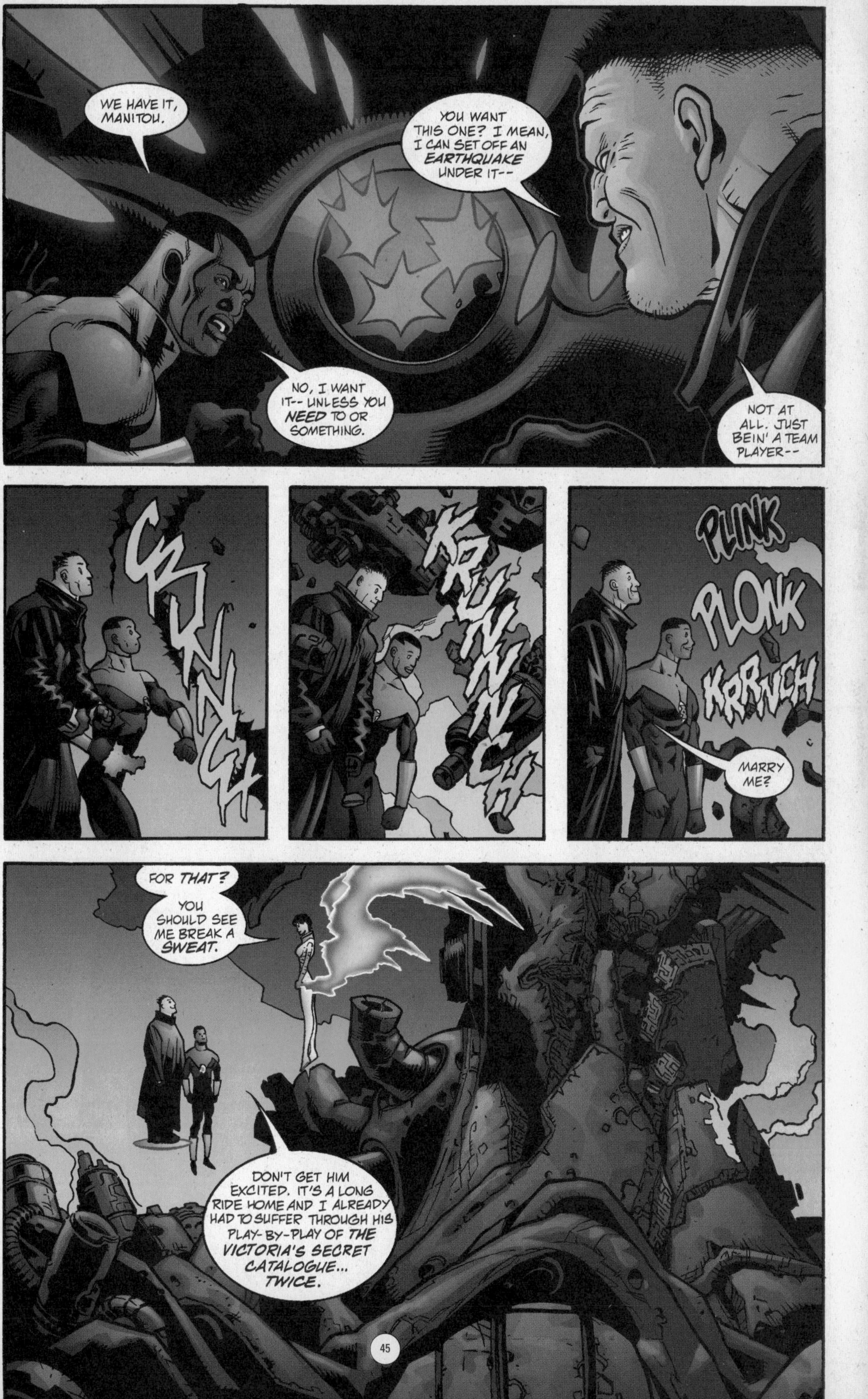

WE HAVE IT, MANITOU.
YOU WANT THIS ONE? I MEAN, I CAN SET OFF AN EARTHQUAKE UNDER IT--
NO, I WANT IT-- UNLESS YOU NEED TO OR SOMETHING.
NOT AT ALL. JUST BEIN' A TEAM PLAYER--
CRUNCH
KRUNNNCH
PLINK
PLONK
KRRNCH
MARRY ME?
FOR THAT?
YOU SHOULD SEE ME BREAK A SWEAT.
DON'T GET HIM EXCITED. IT'S A LONG RIDE HOME AND I ALREADY HAD TO SUFFER THROUGH HIS PLAY-BY-PLAY OF THE VICTORIA'S SECRET CATALOGUE... TWICE.

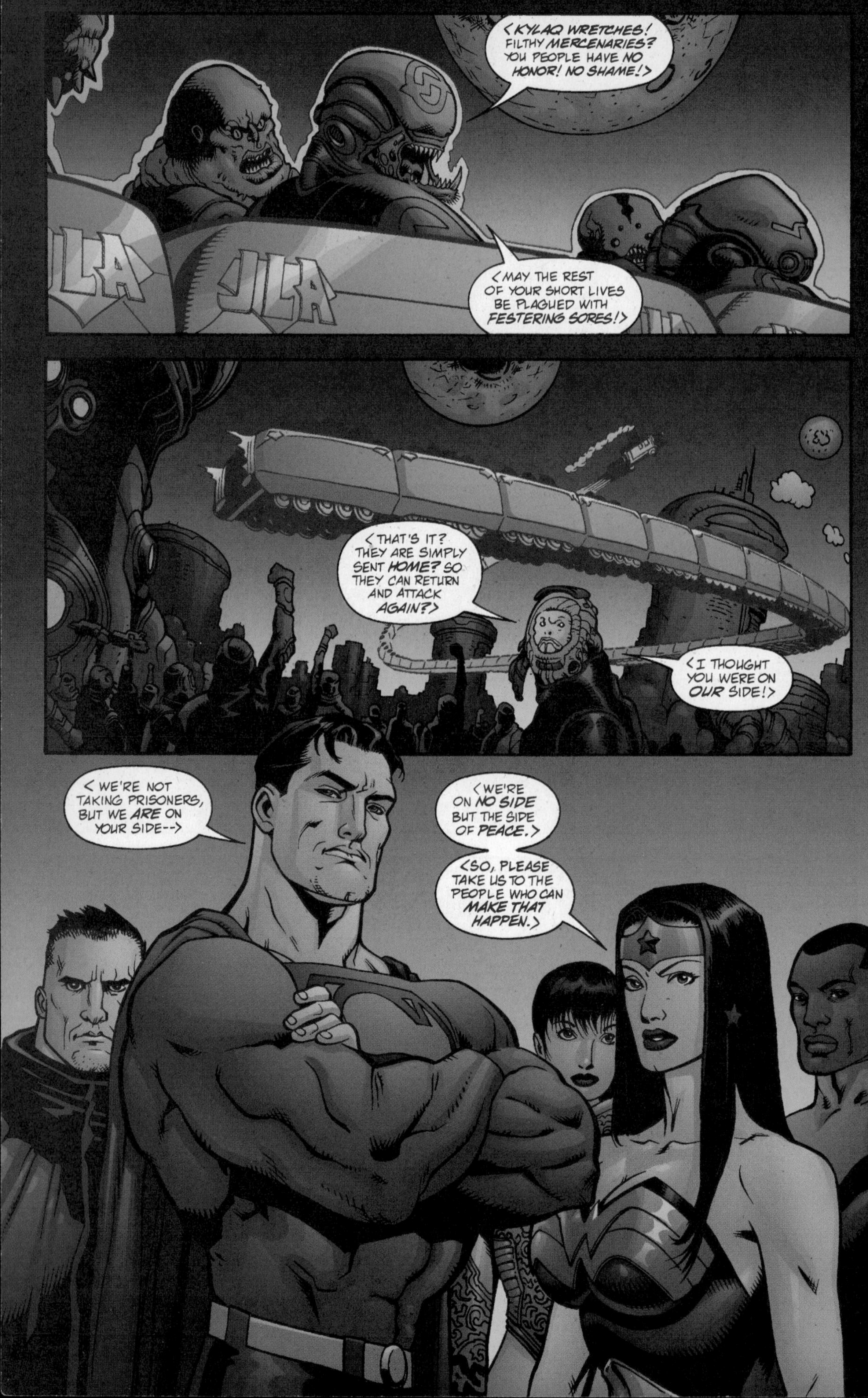

<KYLAQ WRETCHES! FILTHY MERCENARIES? YOU PEOPLE HAVE NO HONOR! NO SHAME!>
<MAY THE REST OF YOUR SHORT LIVES BE PLAGUED WITH FESTERING SORES!>
<THAT'S IT? THEY ARE SIMPLY SENT HOME? SO THEY CAN RETURN AND ATTACK AGAIN?>
<I THOUGHT YOU WERE ON OUR SIDE!>
<WE'RE NOT TAKING PRISONERS, BUT WE ARE ON YOUR SIDE-->
<WE'RE ON NO SIDE BUT THE SIDE OF PEACE.>
<SO, PLEASE TAKE US TO THE PEOPLE WHO CAN MAKE THAT HAPPEN.>

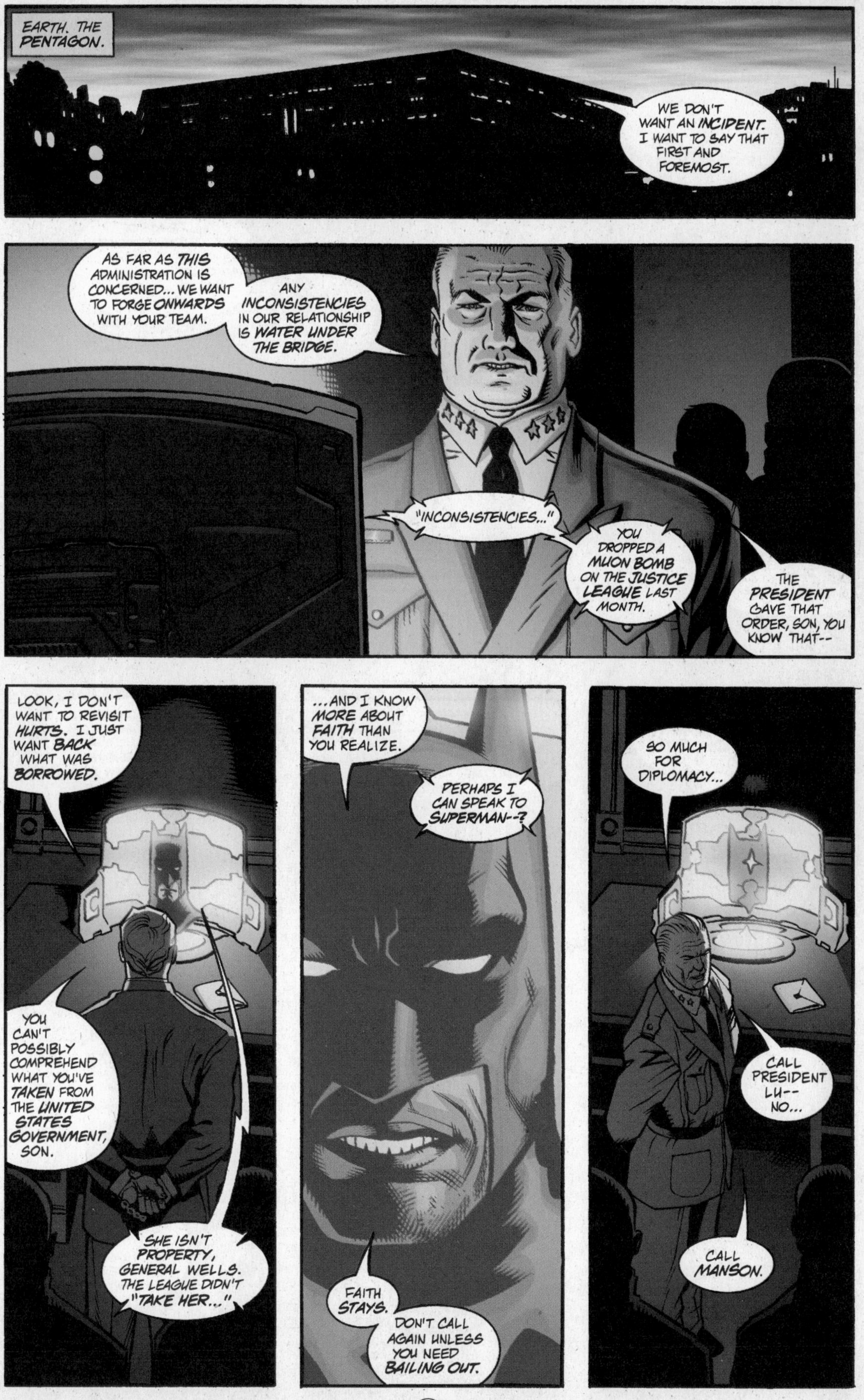
EARTH. THE PENTAGON.
WE DON'T WANT AN INCIDENT. I WANT TO SAY THAT FIRST AND FOREMOST.
AS FAR AS THIS ADMINISTRATION IS CONCERNED... WE WANT TO FORGE ONWARDS WITH YOUR TEAM.
ANY INCONSISTENCIES IN OUR RELATIONSHIP IS WATER UNDER THE BRIDGE.
"INCONSISTENCIES..."
YOU DROPPED A MUON BOMB ON THE JUSTICE LEAGUE LAST MONTH.
THE PRESIDENT GAVE THAT ORDER, SON, YOU KNOW THAT--
LOOK, I DON'T WANT TO REVISIT HURTS. I JUST WANT BACK WHAT WAS BORROWED.
YOU CAN'T POSSIBLY COMPREHEND WHAT YOU'VE TAKEN FROM THE UNITED STATES GOVERNMENT, SON.
SHE ISN'T PROPERTY, GENERAL WELLS. THE LEAGUE DIDN'T "TAKE HER..."
...AND I KNOW MORE ABOUT FAITH THAN YOU REALIZE.
PERHAPS I CAN SPEAK TO SUPERMAN--?
FAITH STAYS.
DON'T CALL AGAIN UNLESS YOU NEED BAILING OUT.
SO MUCH FOR DIPLOMACY...
CALL PRESIDENT LU-- NO...
CALL MANSON.

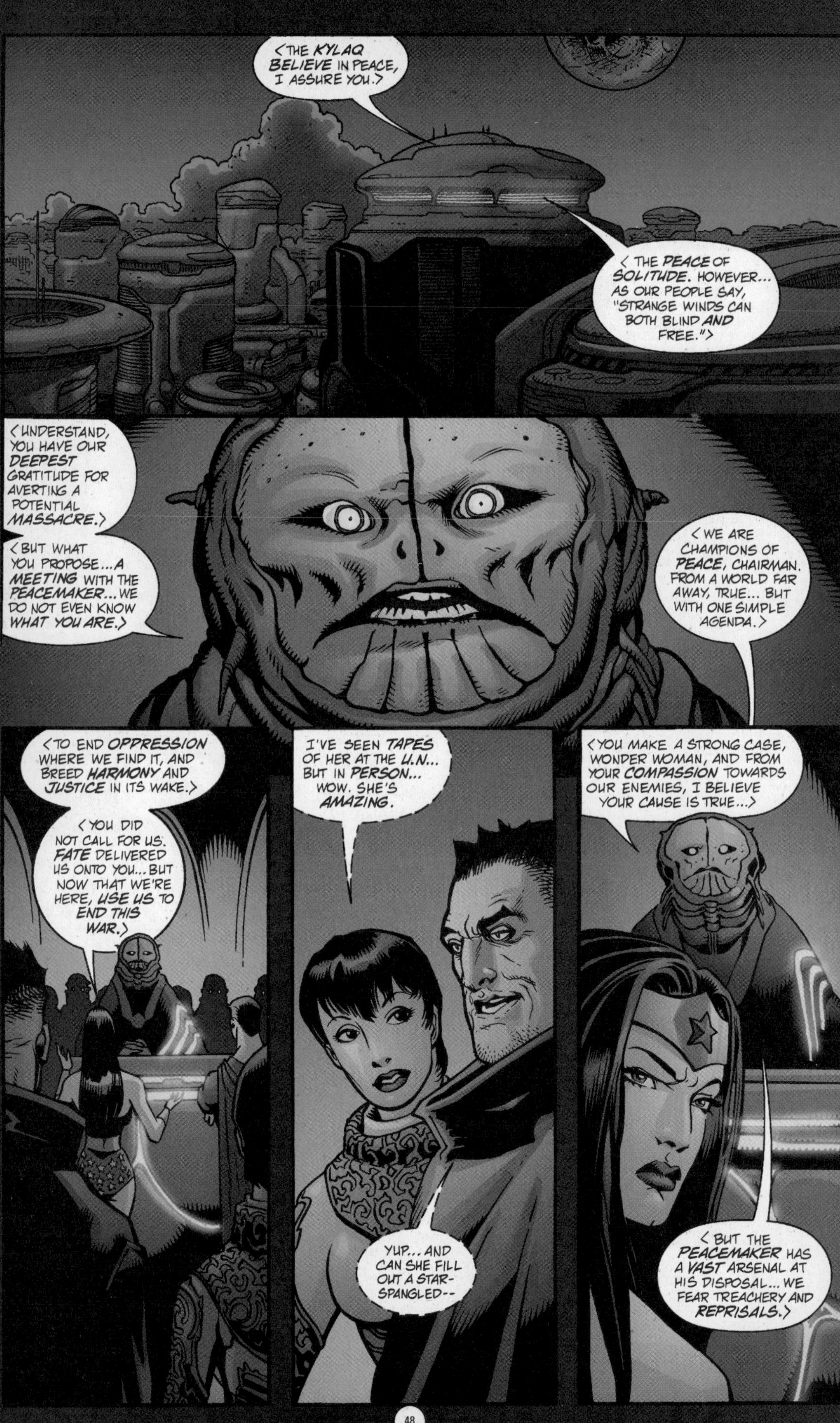
<THE KYLAQ BELIEVE IN PEACE, I ASSURE YOU.>
< THE PEACE OF SOLITUDE. HOWEVER... AS OUR PEOPLE SAY, "STRANGE WINDS CAN BOTH BLIND AND FREE.">
<UNDERSTAND, YOU HAVE OUR DEEPEST GRATITUDE FOR AVERTING A POTENTIAL MASSACRE.>
<BUT WHAT YOU PROPOSE...A MEETING WITH THE PEACEMAKER...WE DO NOT EVEN KNOW WHAT YOU ARE.>
<WE ARE CHAMPIONS OF PEACE, CHAIRMAN. FROM A WORLD FAR AWAY, TRUE... BUT WITH ONE SIMPLE AGENDA.>
<TO END OPPRESSION WHERE WE FIND IT, AND BREED HARMONY AND JUSTICE IN ITS WAKE.>
<YOU DID NOT CALL FOR US. FATE DELIVERED US ONTO YOU...BUT NOW THAT WE'RE HERE, USE US TO END THIS WAR.>
I'VE SEEN TAPES OF HER AT THE U.N... BUT IN PERSON... WOW. SHE'S AMAZING.
YUP... AND CAN SHE FILL OUT A STAR-SPANGLED--
<YOU MAKE A STRONG CASE, WONDER WOMAN, AND FROM YOUR COMPASSION TOWARDS OUR ENEMIES, I BELIEVE YOUR CAUSE IS TRUE...>
< BUT THE PEACEMAKER HAS A VAST ARSENAL AT HIS DISPOSAL... WE FEAR TREACHERY AND REPRISALS.>

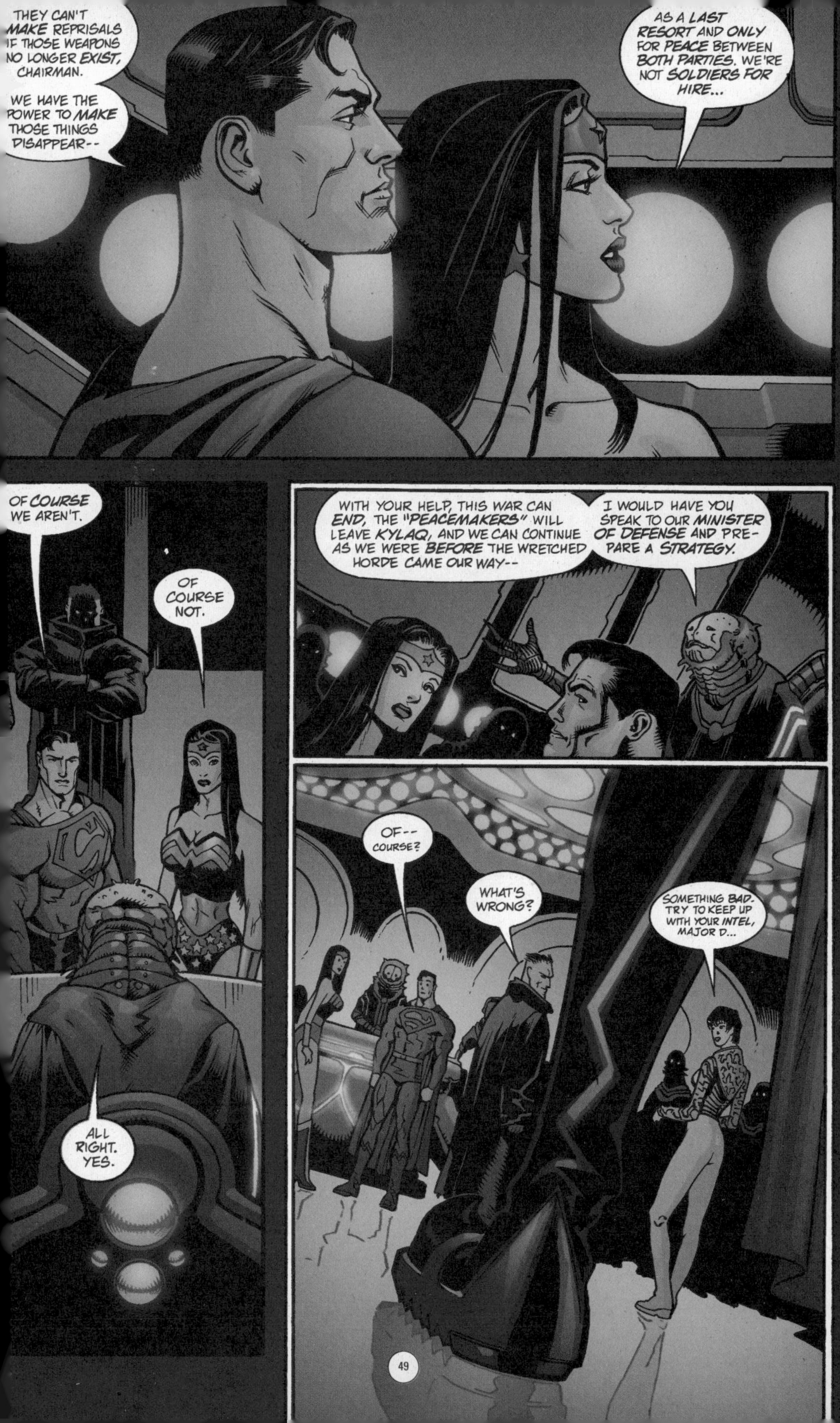
THEY CAN'T MAKE REPRISALS IF THOSE WEAPONS NO LONGER EXIST, CHAIRMAN.
WE HAVE THE POWER TO MAKE THOSE THINGS DISAPPEAR--
AS A LAST RESORT AND ONLY FOR PEACE BETWEEN BOTH PARTIES. WE'RE NOT SOLDIERS FOR HIRE...
OF COURSE WE AREN'T.
OF COURSE NOT.
ALL RIGHT. YES.
WITH YOUR HELP, THIS WAR CAN END, THE "PEACEMAKERS" WILL LEAVE KYLAQ, AND WE CAN CONTINUE AS WE WERE BEFORE THE WRETCHED HORDE CAME OUR WAY--
I WOULD HAVE YOU SPEAK TO OUR MINISTER OF DEFENSE AND PREPARE A STRATEGY.
OF-- COURSE?
WHAT'S WRONG?
SOMETHING BAD. TRY TO KEEP UP WITH YOUR INTEL, MAJOR D...

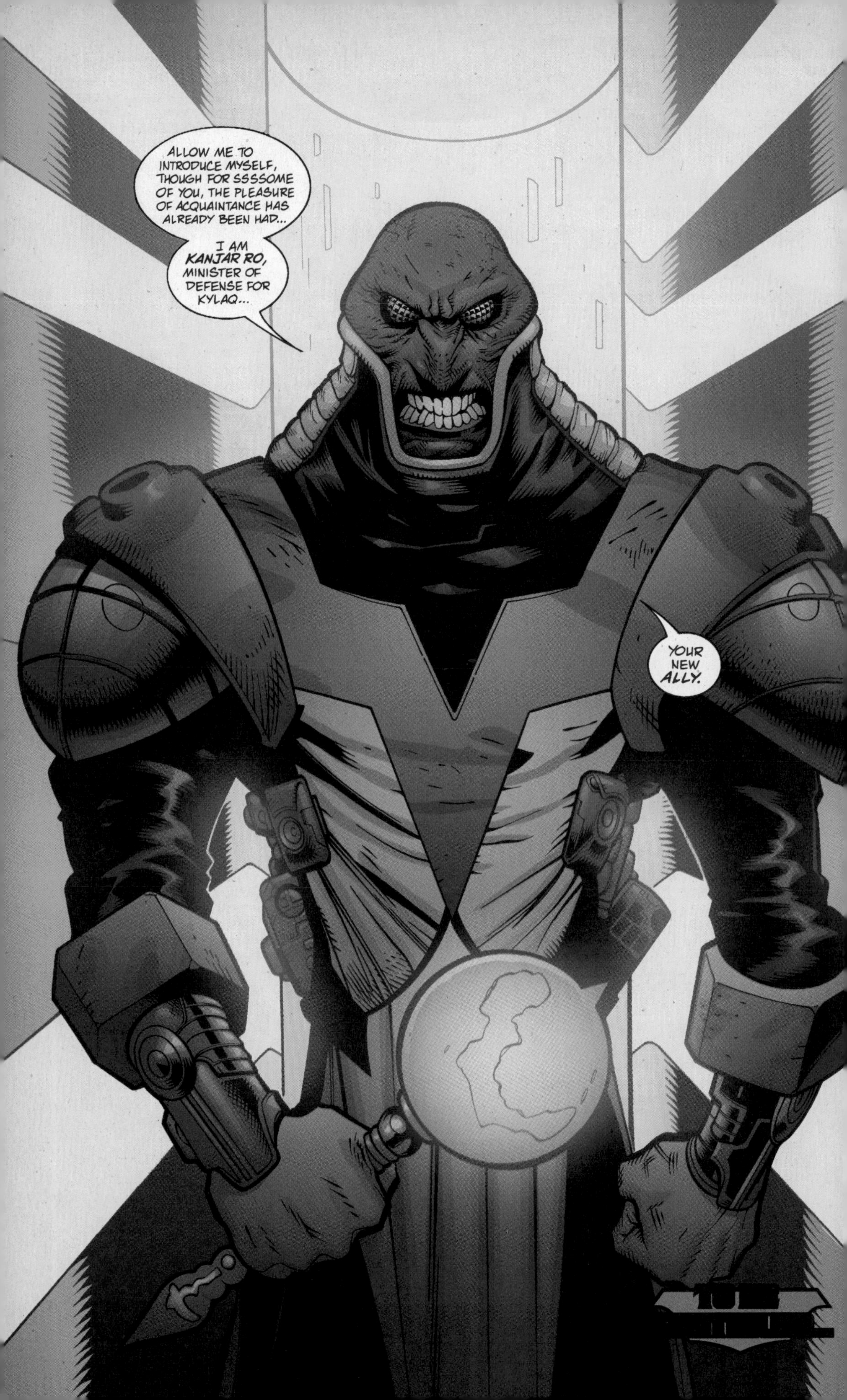
ALLOW ME TO INTRODUCE MYSELF, THOUGH FOR SSSSOME OF YOU, THE PLEASURE OF ACQUAINTANCE HAS ALREADY BEEN HAD...
I AM KANJAR RO, MINISTER OF DEFENSE FOR KYLAQ...
YOUR NEW ALLY.

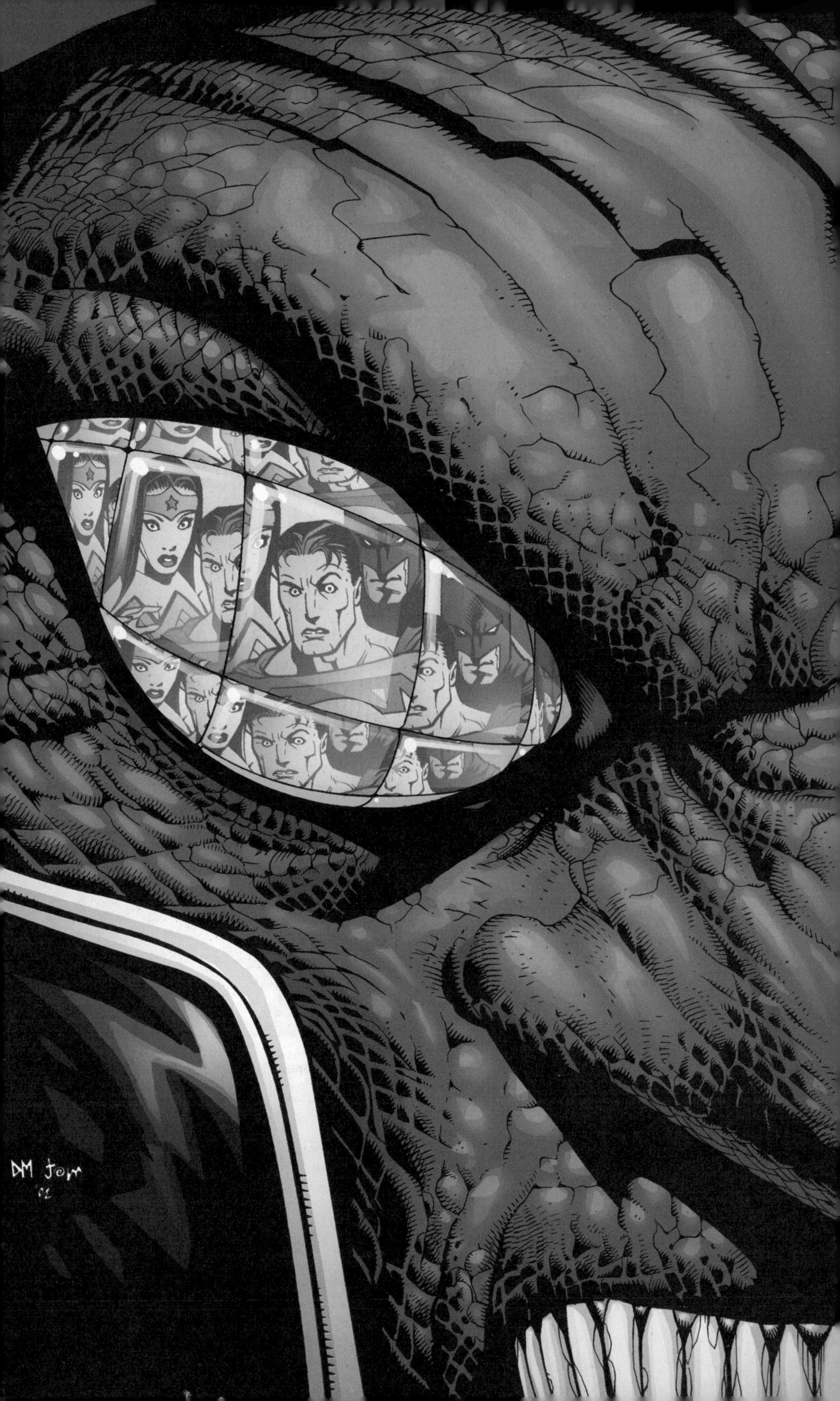

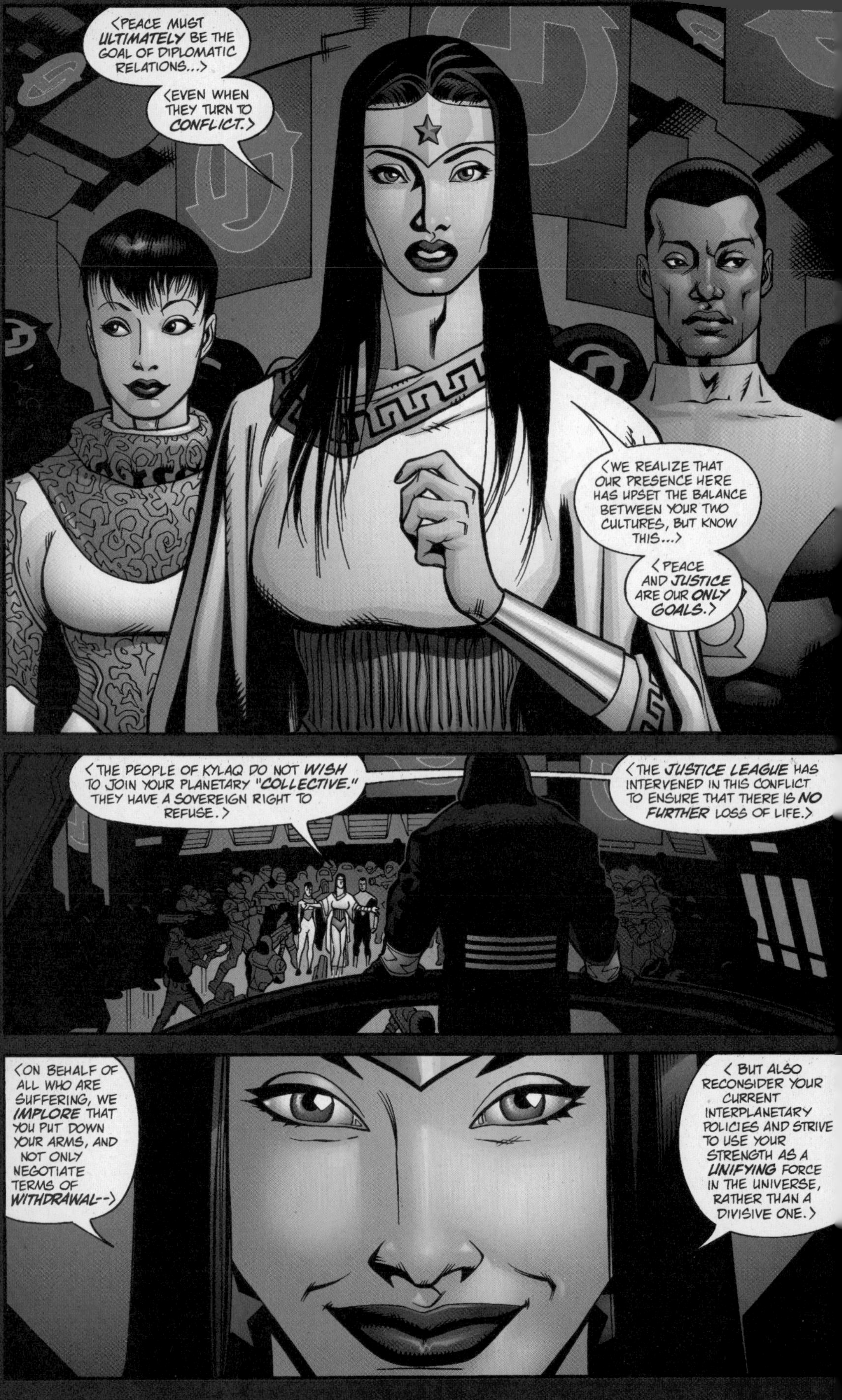

<PEACE MUST ULTIMATELY BE THE GOAL OF DIPLOMATIC RELATIONS...>
<EVEN WHEN THEY TURN TO CONFLICT.>
<WE REALIZE THAT OUR PRESENCE HERE HAS UPSET THE BALANCE BETWEEN YOUR TWO CULTURES, BUT KNOW THIS...>
<PEACE AND JUSTICE ARE OUR ONLY GOALS.>
< THE PEOPLE OF KYLAQ DO NOT WISH TO JOIN YOUR PLANETARY "COLLECTIVE." THEY HAVE A SOVEREIGN RIGHT TO REFUSE. >
<THE JUSTICE LEAGUE HAS INTERVENED IN THIS CONFLICT TO ENSURE THAT THERE IS NO FURTHER LOSS OF LIFE.>
<ON BEHALF OF ALL WHO ARE SUFFERING, WE IMPLORE THAT YOU PUT DOWN YOUR ARMS, AND NOT ONLY NEGOTIATE TERMS OF WITHDRAWAL-->
< BUT ALSO RECONSIDER YOUR CURRENT INTERPLANETARY POLICIES AND STRIVE TO USE YOUR STRENGTH AS A UNIFYING FORCE IN THE UNIVERSE, RATHER THAN A DIVISIVE ONE. >

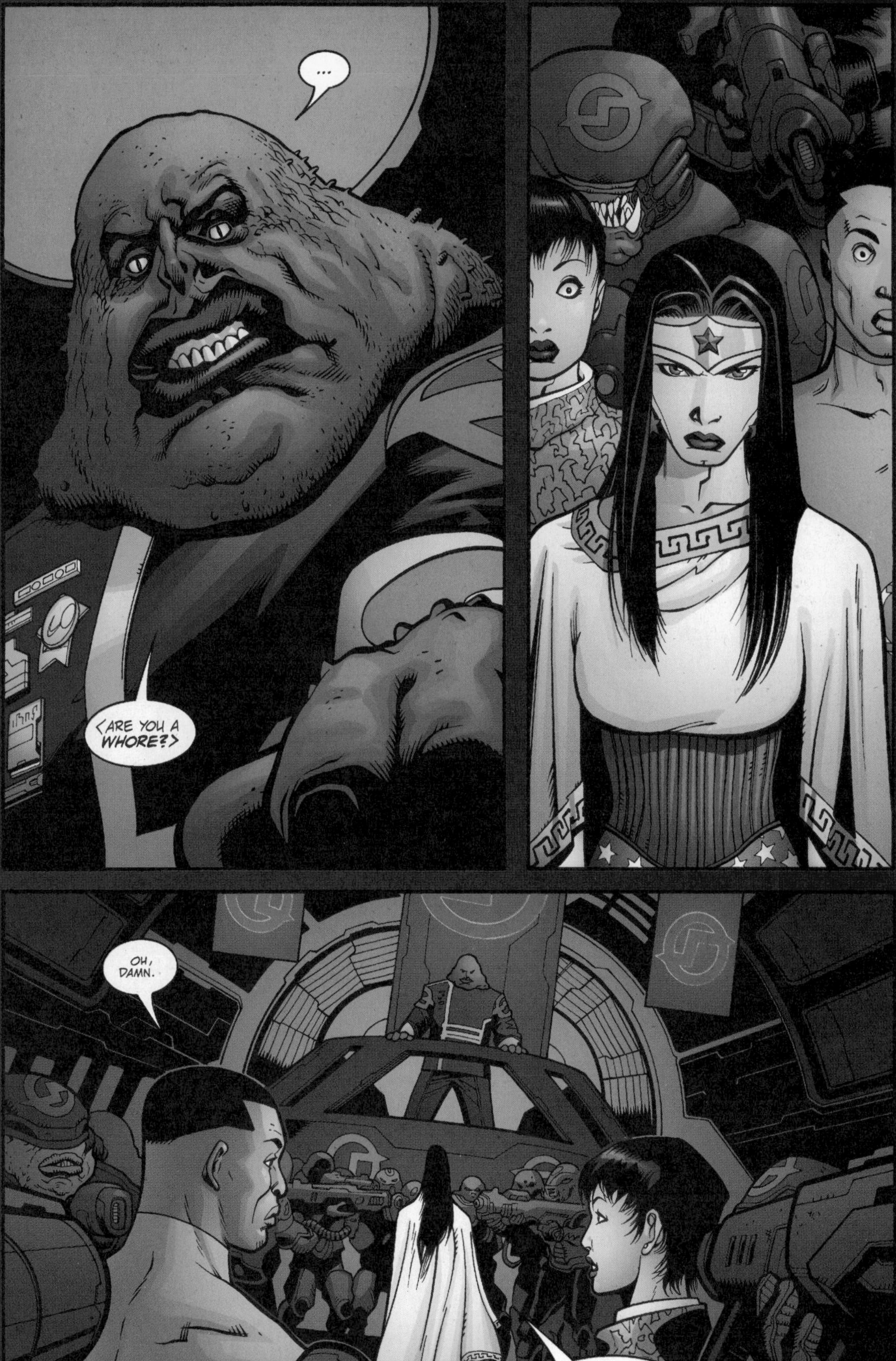
...
<ARE YOU A WHORE?>
OH, DAMN.
< FOR A MAN CALLING HIMSELF THE PEACEMAKER, YOU HAVE A TALENT FOR USING WORDS FOR ANYTHING BUT.>

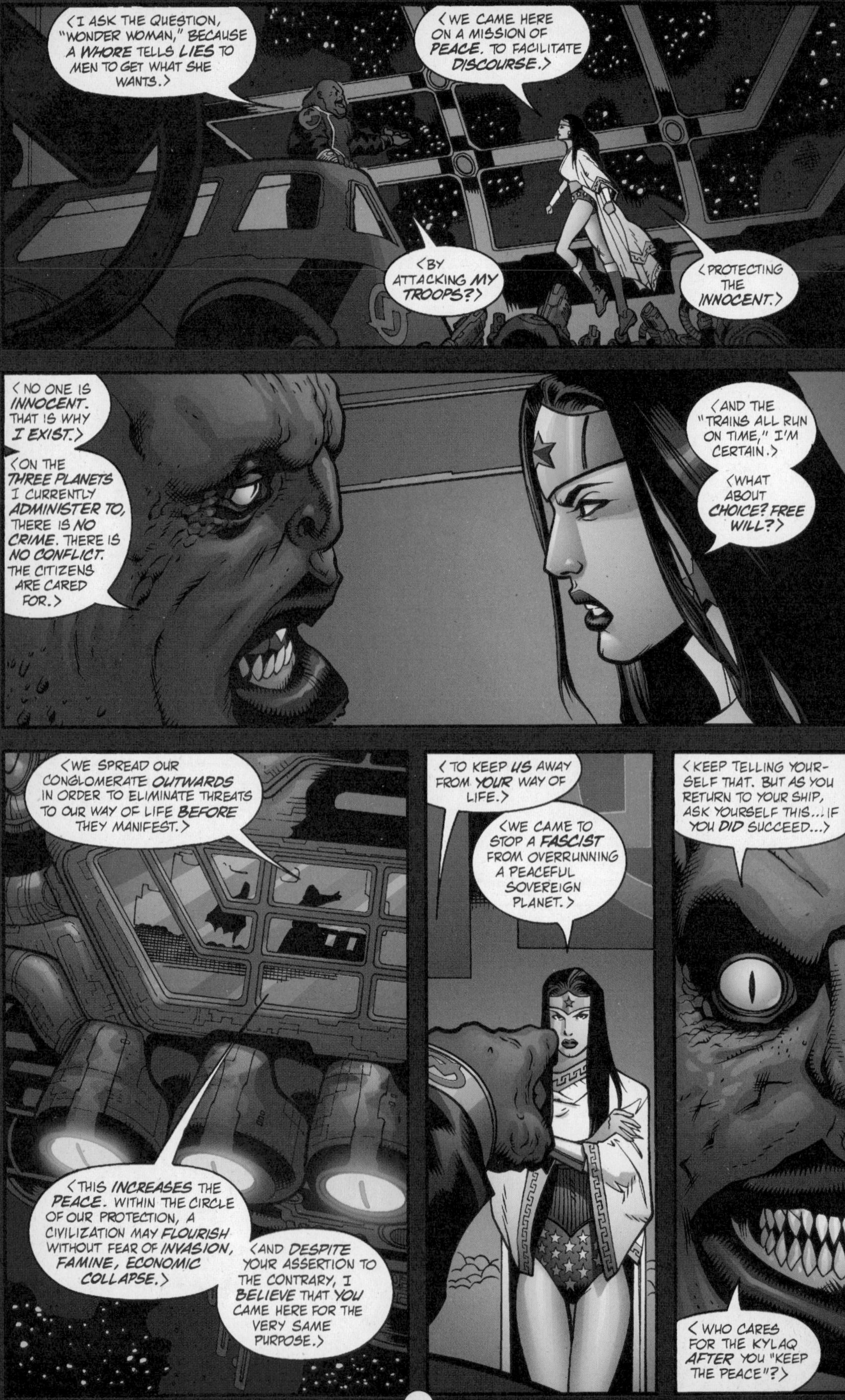

<I ASK THE QUESTION, "WONDER WOMAN," BECAUSE A WHORE TELLS LIES TO MEN TO GET WHAT SHE WANTS.>
<WE CAME HERE ON A MISSION OF PEACE. TO FACILITATE DISCOURSE.>
<BY ATTACKING MY TROOPS?>
<PROTECTING THE INNOCENT.>
<NO ONE IS INNOCENT. THAT IS WHY I EXIST.>
<ON THE THREE PLANETS I CURRENTLY ADMINISTER TO, THERE IS NO CRIME. THERE IS NO CONFLICT. THE CITIZENS ARE CARED FOR.>
<AND THE "TRAINS ALL RUN ON TIME," I'M CERTAIN.>
<WHAT ABOUT CHOICE? FREE WILL?>
<WE SPREAD OUR CONGLOMERATE OUTWARDS IN ORDER TO ELIMINATE THREATS TO OUR WAY OF LIFE BEFORE THEY MANIFEST.>
<THIS INCREASES THE PEACE. WITHIN THE CIRCLE OF OUR PROTECTION, A CIVILIZATION MAY FLOURISH WITHOUT FEAR OF INVASION, FAMINE, ECONOMIC COLLAPSE.>
<AND DESPITE YOUR ASSERTION TO THE CONTRARY, I BELIEVE THAT YOU CAME HERE FOR THE VERY SAME PURPOSE.>
<TO KEEP US AWAY FROM YOUR WAY OF LIFE.>
<WE CAME TO STOP A FASCIST FROM OVERRUNNING A PEACEFUL SOVEREIGN PLANET.>
<KEEP TELLING YOUR-SELF THAT. BUT AS YOU RETURN TO YOUR SHIP, ASK YOURSELF THIS... IF YOU DID SUCCEED...>
<WHO CARES FOR THE KYLAQ AFTER YOU "KEEP THE PEACE"?>

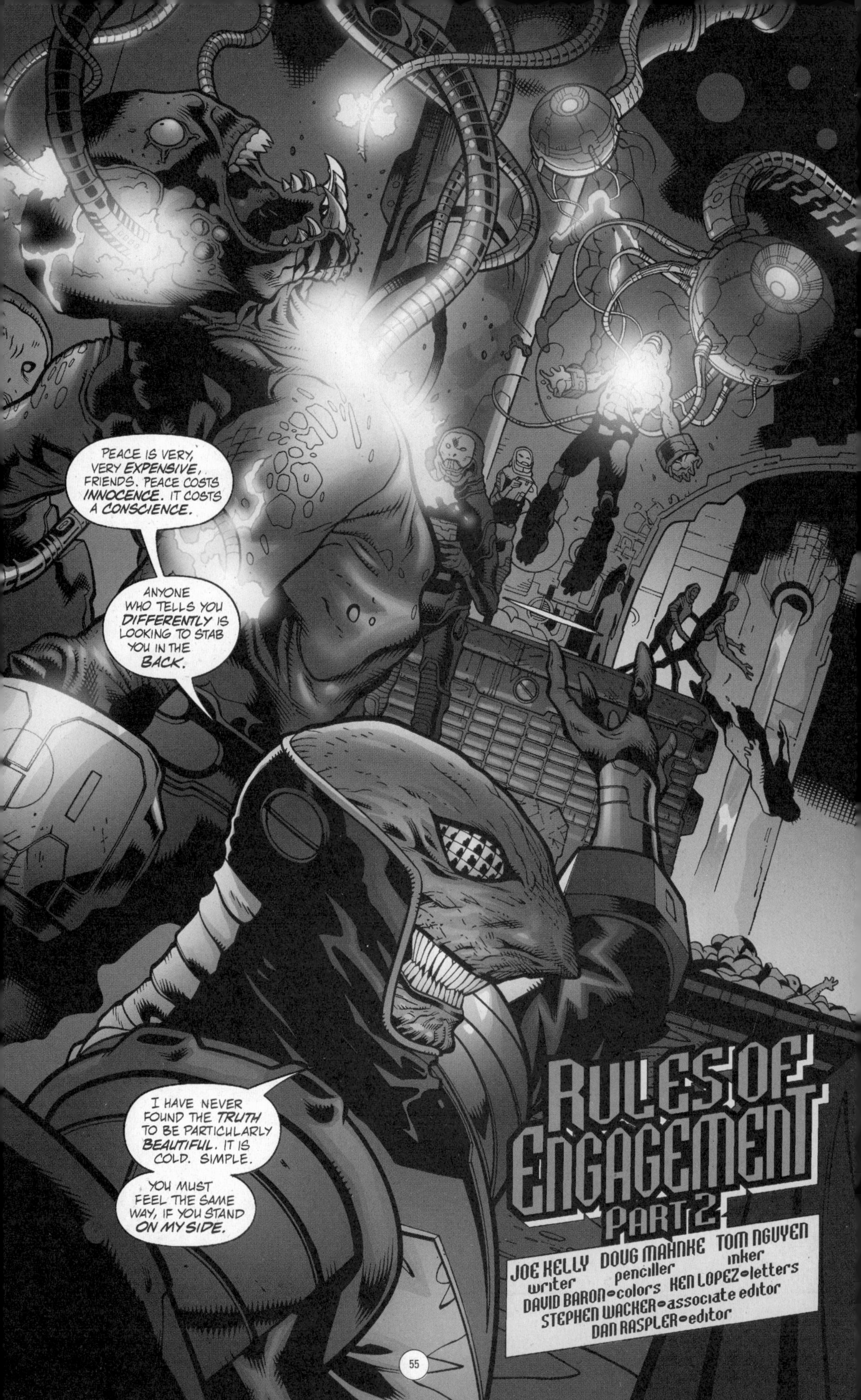
PEACE IS VERY, VERY EXPENSIVE, FRIENDS. PEACE COSTS INNOCENCE. IT COSTS A CONSCIENCE.
ANYONE WHO TELLS YOU DIFFERENTLY IS LOOKING TO STAB YOU IN THE BACK.
I HAVE NEVER FOUND THE TRUTH TO BE PARTICULARLY BEAUTIFUL. IT IS COLD. SIMPLE.
YOU MUST FEEL THE SAME WAY, IF YOU STAND ON MY SIDE.
RULES OF ENGAGEMENT
PART 2
JOE KELLY writer
DOUG MAHNKE penciller
TOM NGUYEN inker
DAVID BARON•colors
KEN LOPEZ•letters
STEPHEN WACKER•associate editor
DAN RASPLER•editor

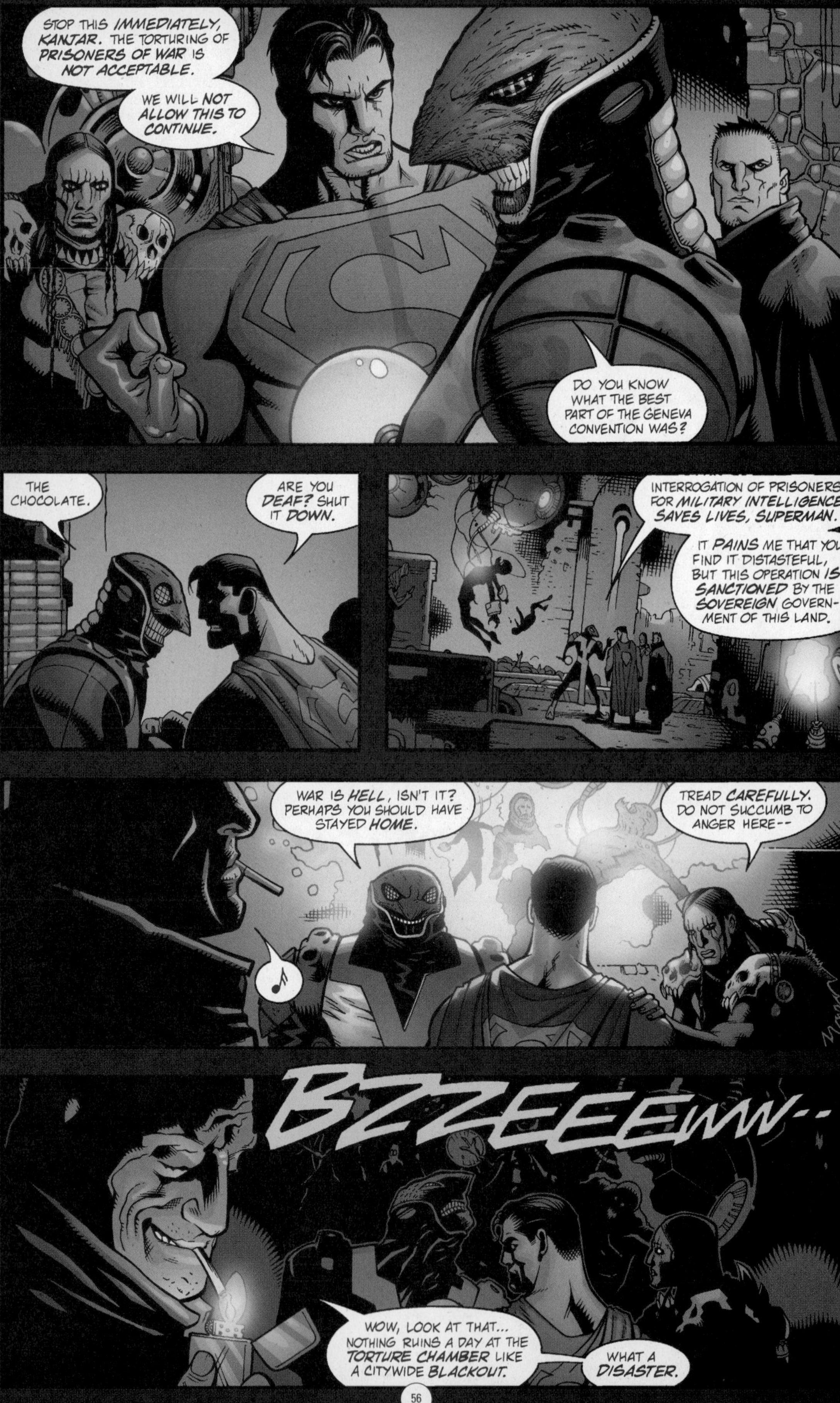

STOP THIS IMMEDIATELY, KANJAR. THE TORTURING OF PRISONERS OF WAR IS NOT ACCEPTABLE.
WE WILL NOT ALLOW THIS TO CONTINUE.
DO YOU KNOW WHAT THE BEST PART OF THE GENEVA CONVENTION WAS?
THE CHOCOLATE.
ARE YOU DEAF? SHUT IT DOWN.
INTERROGATION OF PRISONERS FOR MILITARY INTELLIGENCE SAVES LIVES, SUPERMAN.
IT PAINS ME THAT YOU FIND IT DISTASTEFUL, BUT THIS OPERATION IS SANCTIONED BY THE SOVEREIGN GOVERNMENT OF THIS LAND.
WAR IS HELL, ISN'T IT? PERHAPS YOU SHOULD HAVE STAYED HOME.
TREAD CAREFULLY. DO NOT SUCCUMB TO ANGER HERE--
BZZEEEWW--
WOW, LOOK AT THAT... NOTHING RUINS A DAY AT THE TORTURE CHAMBER LIKE A CITYWIDE BLACKOUT.
WHAT A DISASTER.

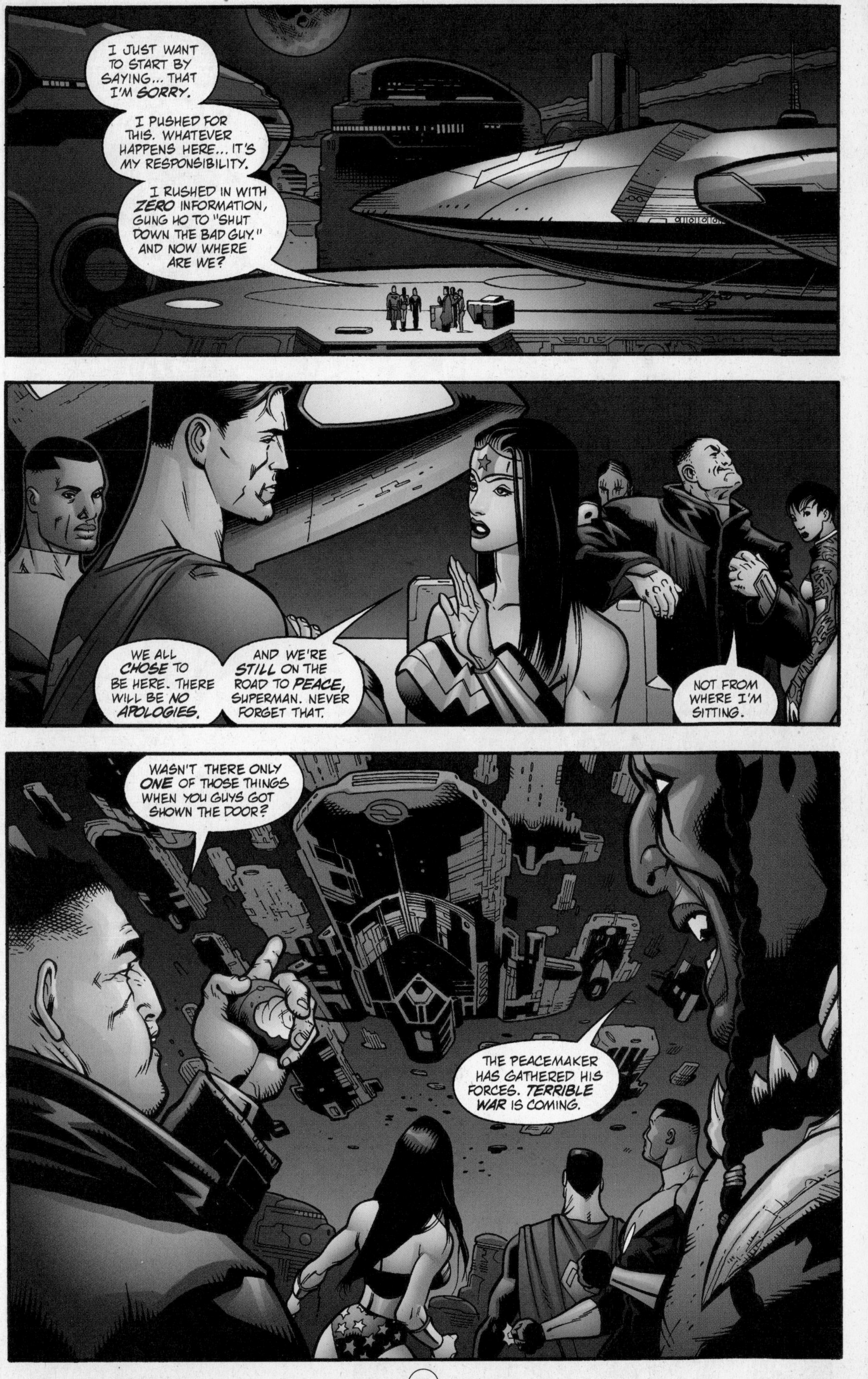
I JUST WANT TO START BY SAYING... THAT I'M SORRY.
I PUSHED FOR THIS. WHATEVER HAPPENS HERE... IT'S MY RESPONSIBILITY.
I RUSHED IN WITH ZERO INFORMATION, GUNG HO TO "SHUT DOWN THE BAD GUY." AND NOW WHERE ARE WE?
WE ALL CHOSE TO BE HERE. THERE WILL BE NO APOLOGIES.
AND WE'RE STILL ON THE ROAD TO PEACE, SUPERMAN. NEVER FORGET THAT.
NOT FROM WHERE I'M SITTING.
WASN'T THERE ONLY ONE OF THOSE THINGS WHEN YOU GUYS GOT SHOWN THE DOOR?
THE PEACEMAKER HAS GATHERED HIS FORCES. TERRIBLE WAR IS COMING.

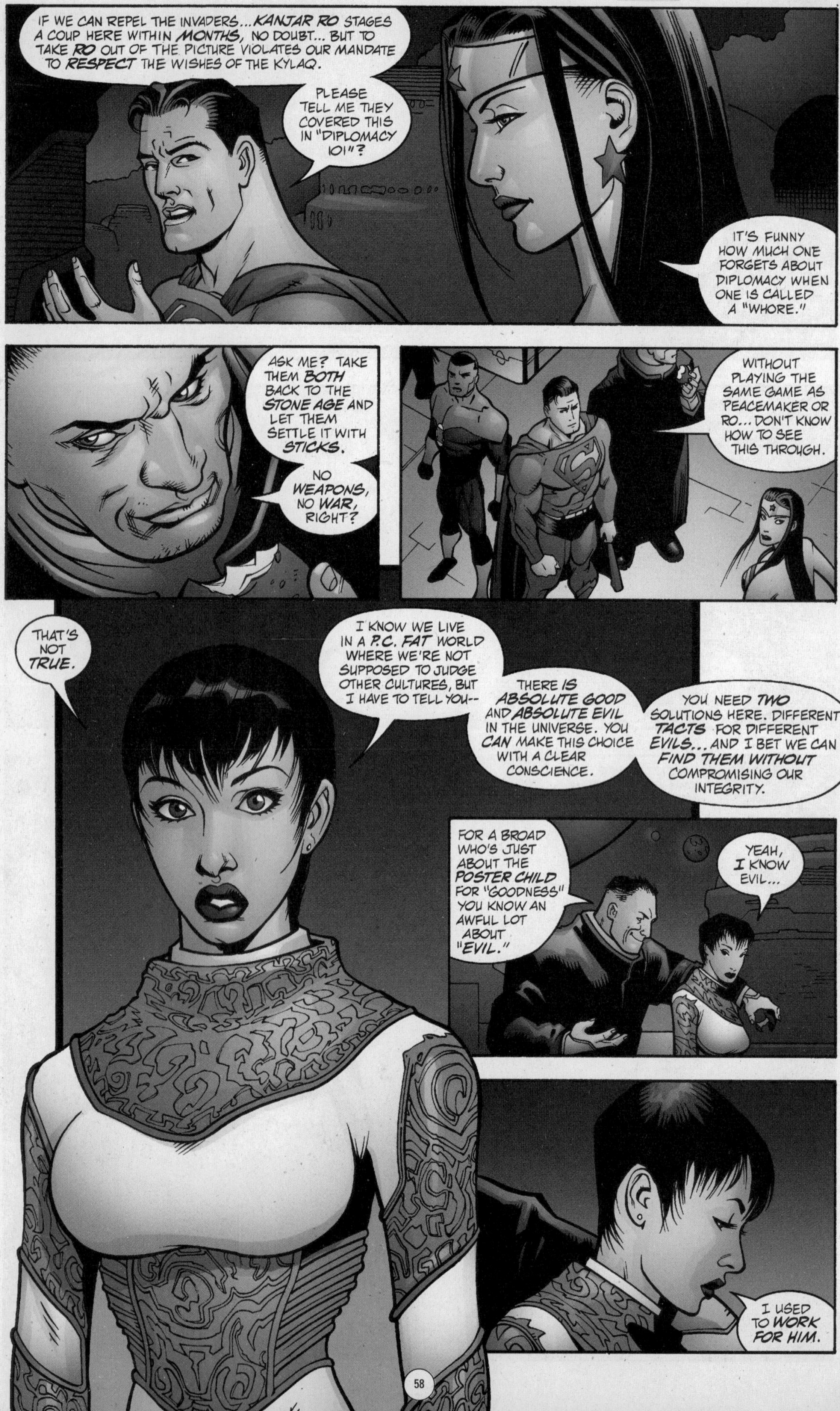

IF WE CAN REPEL THE INVADERS... KANJAR RO STAGES A COUP HERE WITHIN MONTHS, NO DOUBT... BUT TO TAKE RO OUT OF THE PICTURE VIOLATES OUR MANDATE TO RESPECT THE WISHES OF THE KYLAQ.
PLEASE TELL ME THEY COVERED THIS IN "DIPLOMACY 101"?
IT'S FUNNY HOW MUCH ONE FORGETS ABOUT DIPLOMACY WHEN ONE IS CALLED A "WHORE."
ASK ME? TAKE THEM BOTH BACK TO THE STONE AGE AND LET THEM SETTLE IT WITH STICKS.
NO WEAPONS, NO WAR, RIGHT?
WITHOUT PLAYING THE SAME GAME AS PEACEMAKER OR RO... DON'T KNOW HOW TO SEE THIS THROUGH.
THAT'S NOT TRUE.
I KNOW WE LIVE IN A P.C. FAT WORLD WHERE WE'RE NOT SUPPOSED TO JUDGE OTHER CULTURES, BUT I HAVE TO TELL YOU--
THERE IS ABSOLUTE GOOD AND ABSOLUTE EVIL IN THE UNIVERSE. YOU CAN MAKE THIS CHOICE WITH A CLEAR CONSCIENCE.
YOU NEED TWO SOLUTIONS HERE. DIFFERENT TACTS FOR DIFFERENT EVILS... AND I BET WE CAN FIND THEM WITHOUT COMPROMISING OUR INTEGRITY.
FOR A BROAD WHO'S JUST ABOUT THE POSTER CHILD FOR "GOODNESS" YOU KNOW AN AWFUL LOT ABOUT "EVIL."
YEAH, I KNOW EVIL...
I USED TO WORK FOR HIM.

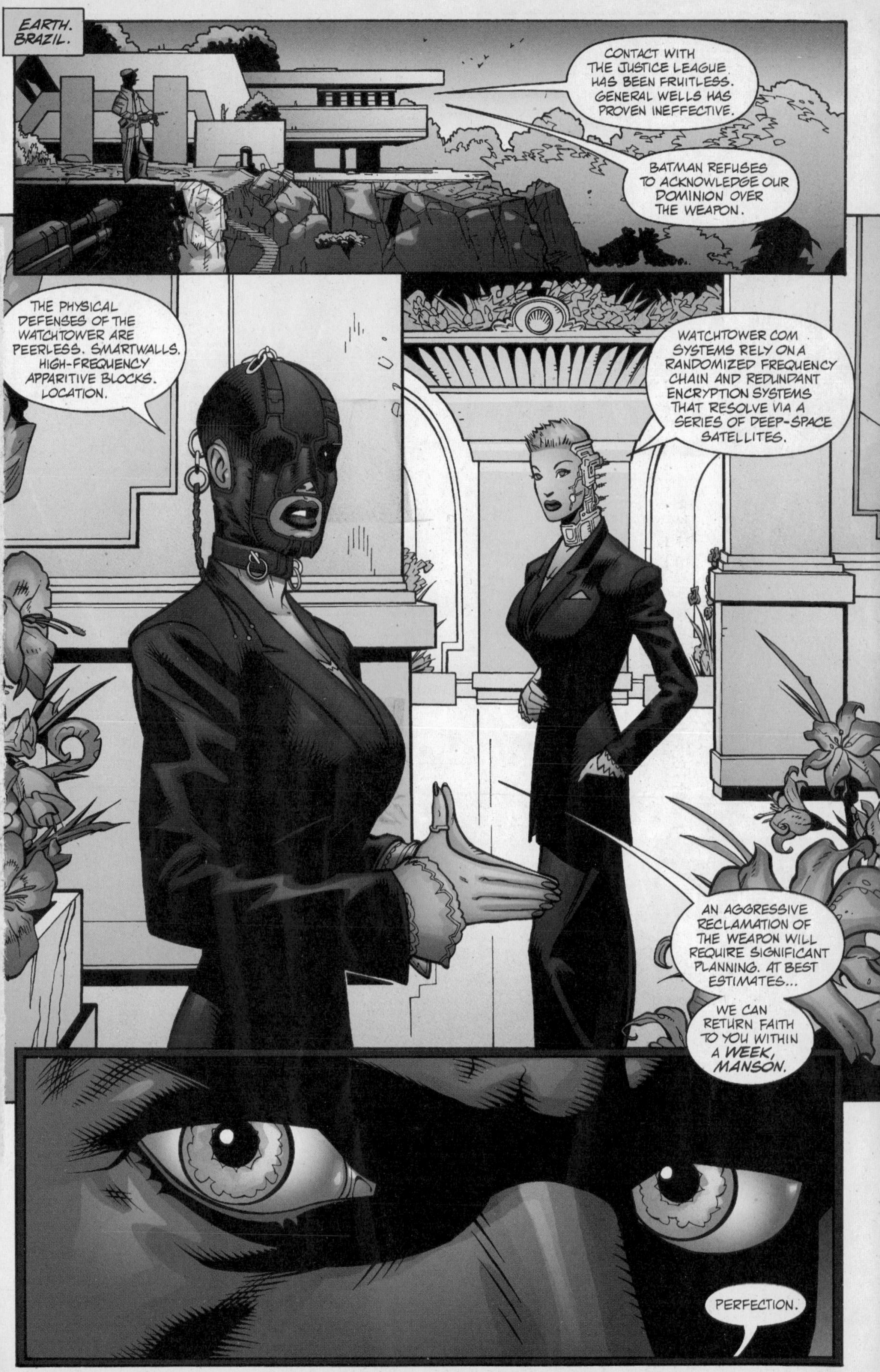
EARTH. BRAZIL.
CONTACT WITH THE JUSTICE LEAGUE HAS BEEN FRUITLESS. GENERAL WELLS HAS PROVEN INEFFECTIVE.
BATMAN REFUSES TO ACKNOWLEDGE OUR DOMINION OVER THE WEAPON.
THE PHYSICAL DEFENSES OF THE WATCHTOWER ARE PEERLESS. SMARTWALLS. HIGH-FREQUENCY APPARITIVE BLOCKS. LOCATION.
WATCHTOWER COM SYSTEMS RELY ON A RANDOMIZED FREQUENCY CHAIN AND REDUNDANT ENCRYPTION SYSTEMS THAT RESOLVE VIA A SERIES OF DEEP-SPACE SATELLITES.
AN AGGRESSIVE RECLAMATION OF THE WEAPON WILL REQUIRE SIGNIFICANT PLANNING. AT BEST ESTIMATES...
WE CAN RETURN FAITH TO YOU WITHIN A *WEEK*, *MANSON*.
PERFECTION.

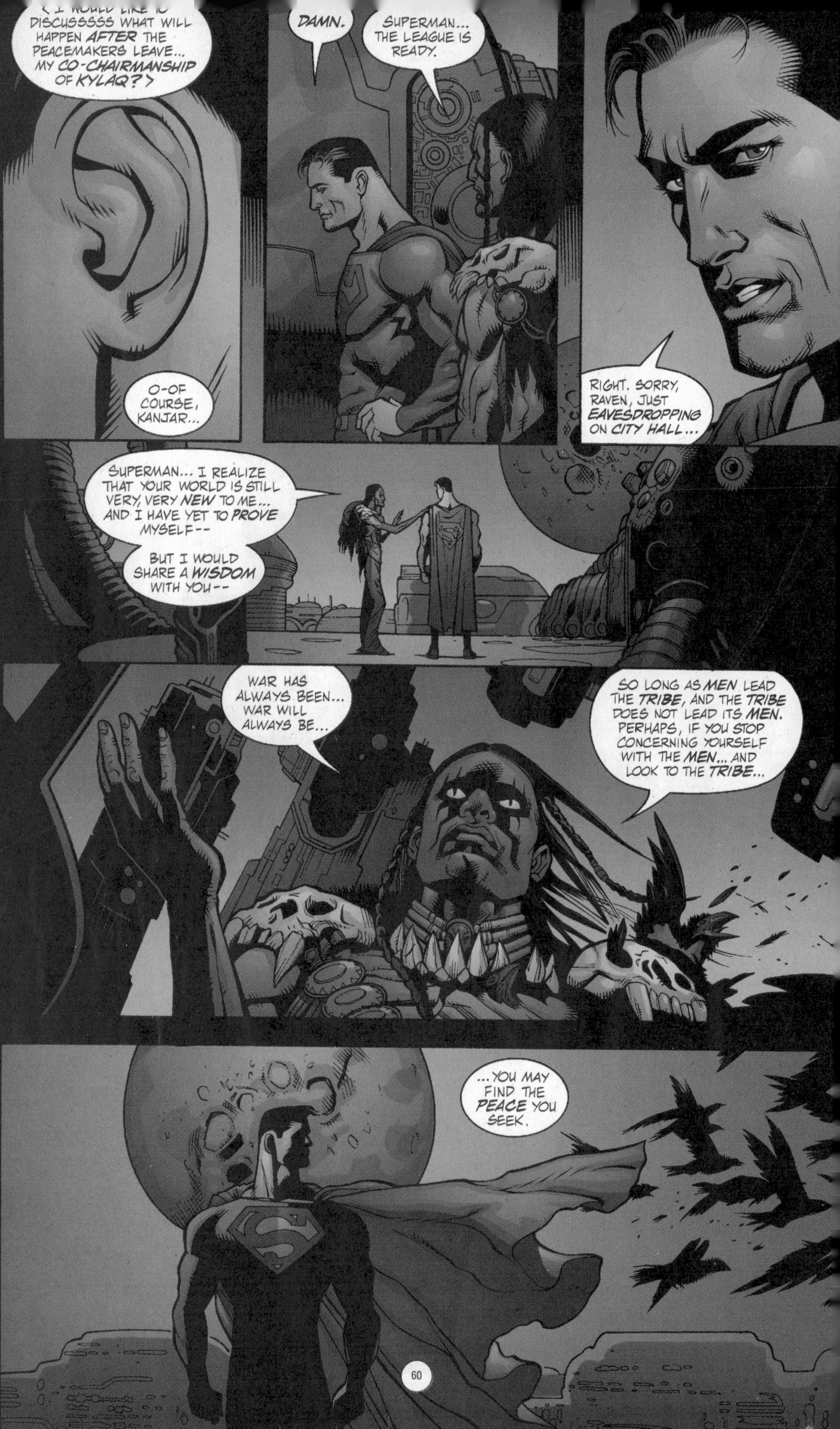

< I WOULD LIKE TO DISCUSSSSS WHAT WILL HAPPEN AFTER THE PEACEMAKERS LEAVE... MY CO-CHAIRMANSHIP OF KYLAQ? >
O-OF COURSE, KANJAR...
DAMN.
SUPERMAN... THE LEAGUE IS READY.
RIGHT. SORRY, RAVEN, JUST EAVESDROPPING ON CITY HALL...
SUPERMAN... I REALIZE THAT YOUR WORLD IS STILL VERY, VERY NEW TO ME... AND I HAVE YET TO PROVE MYSELF--
BUT I WOULD SHARE A WISDOM WITH YOU--
WAR HAS ALWAYS BEEN... WAR WILL ALWAYS BE...
SO LONG AS MEN LEAD THE TRIBE, AND THE TRIBE DOES NOT LEAD ITS MEN. PERHAPS, IF YOU STOP CONCERNING YOURSELF WITH THE MEN... AND LOOK TO THE TRIBE...
...YOU MAY FIND THE PEACE YOU SEEK.

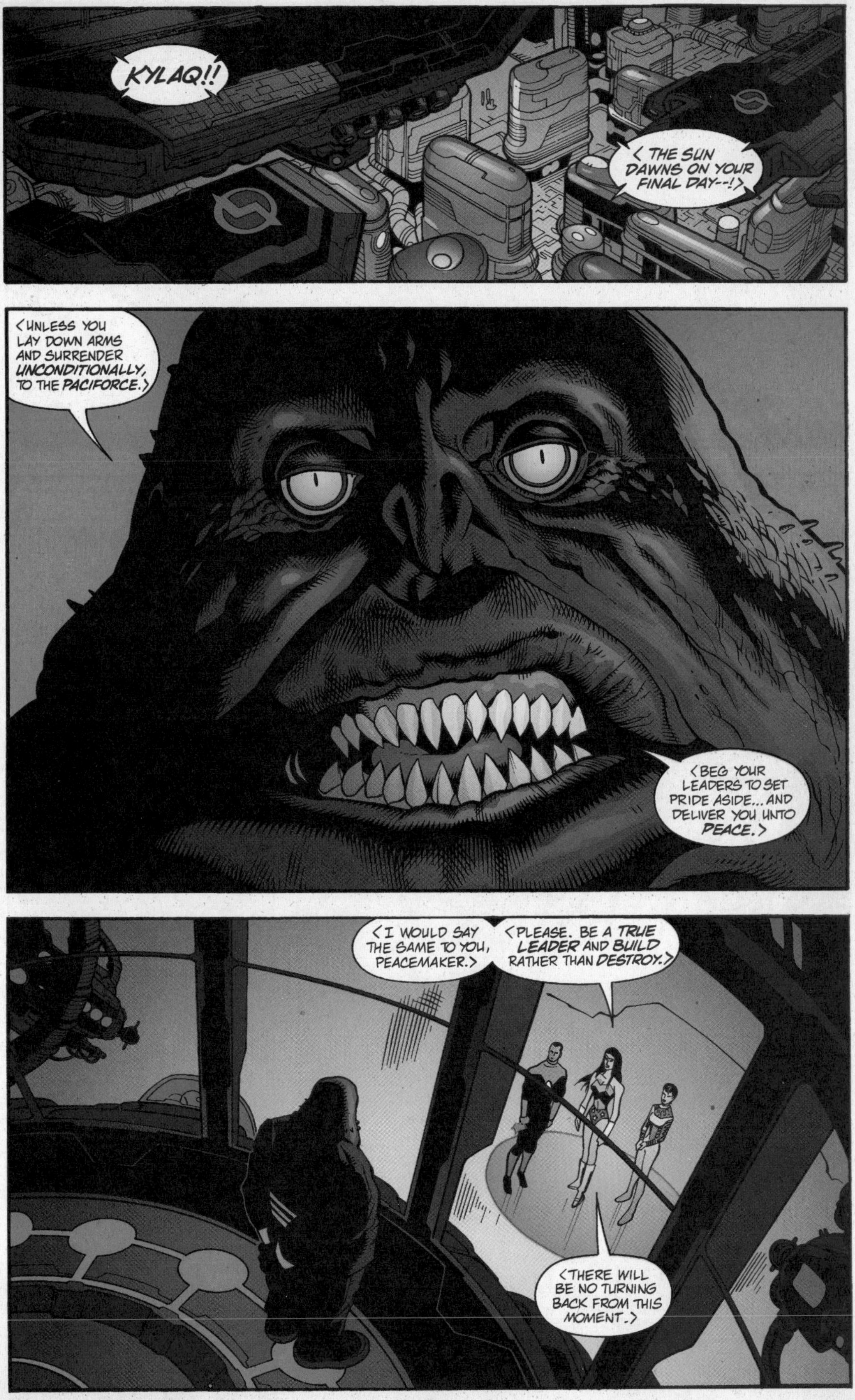
KYLAQ!!
< THE SUN DAWNS ON YOUR FINAL DAY--!>
< UNLESS YOU LAY DOWN ARMS AND SURRENDER UNCONDITIONALLY, TO THE PACIFORCE.>
< BEG YOUR LEADERS TO SET PRIDE ASIDE... AND DELIVER YOU UNTO PEACE.>
< I WOULD SAY THE SAME TO YOU, PEACEMAKER.>
< PLEASE. BE A TRUE LEADER AND BUILD RATHER THAN DESTROY.>
< THERE WILL BE NO TURNING BACK FROM THIS MOMENT.>

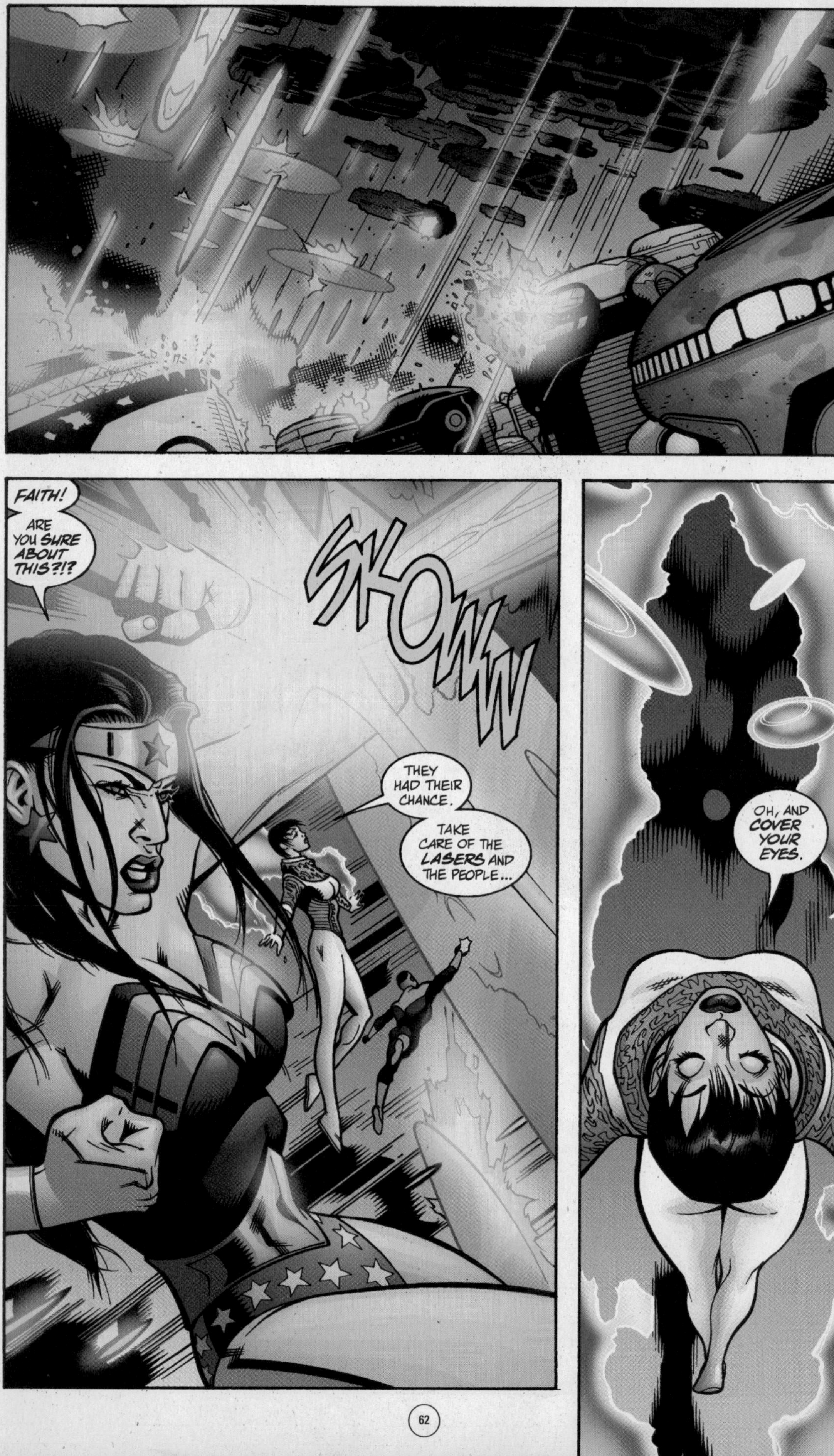
FAITH!
ARE YOU SURE ABOUT THIS?!?
SKOWW
THEY HAD THEIR CHANCE.
TAKE CARE OF THE LASERS AND THE PEOPLE...
OH, AND COVER YOUR EYES.

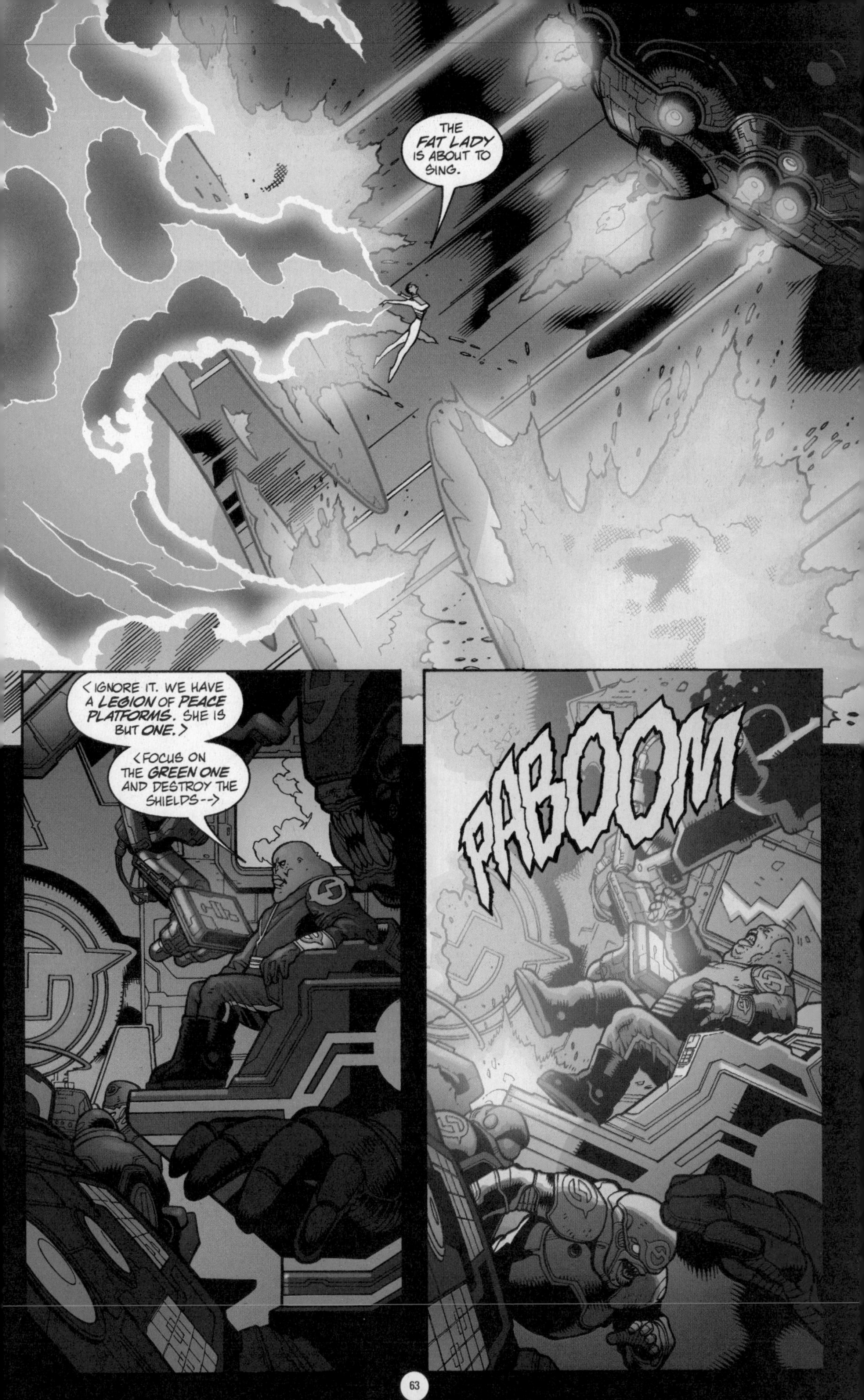
THE FAT LADY IS ABOUT TO SING.
< IGNORE IT. WE HAVE A LEGION OF PEACE PLATFORMS. SHE IS BUT ONE. >
< FOCUS ON THE GREEN ONE AND DESTROY THE SHIELDS-- >
PABOOM

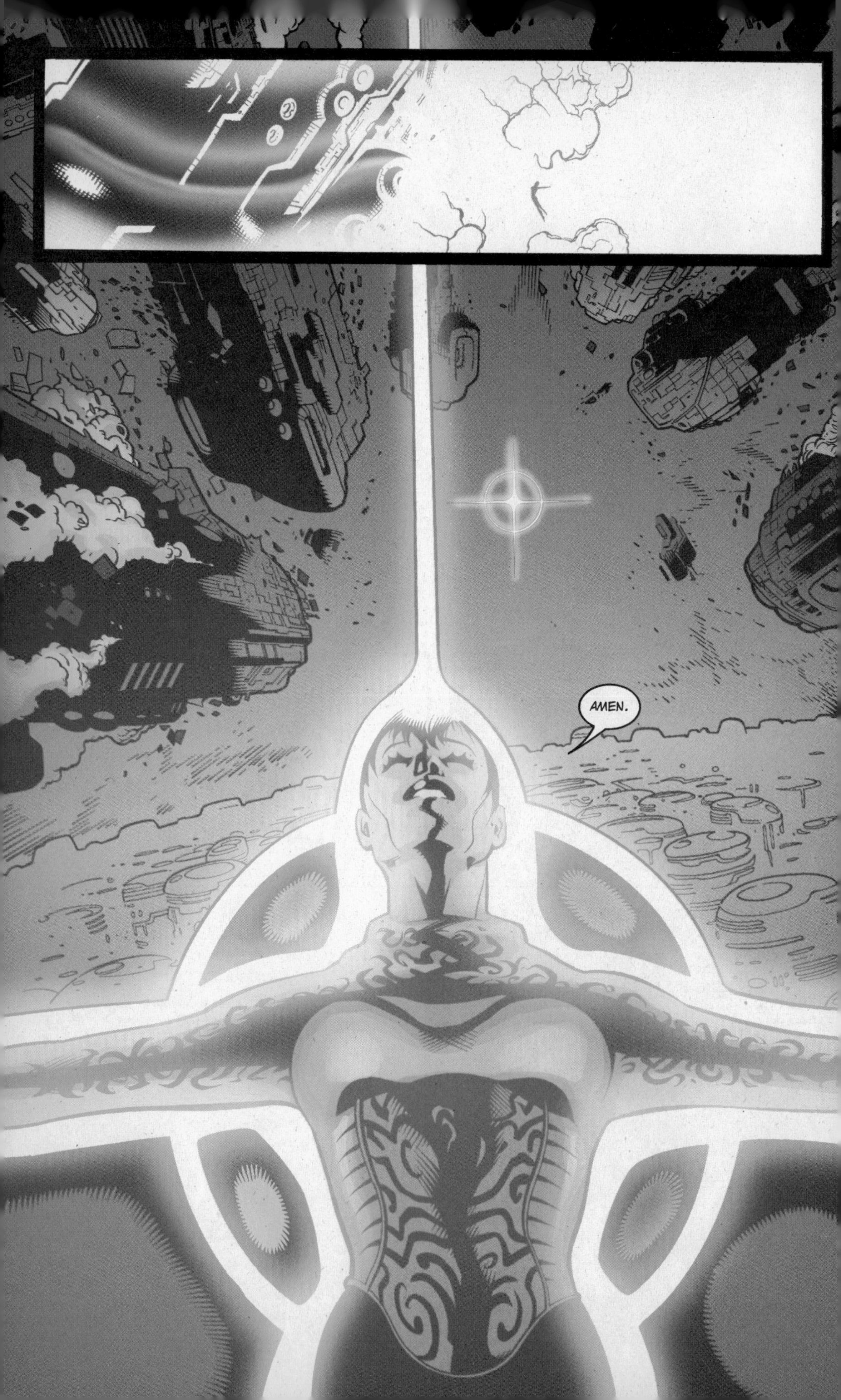
AMEN.

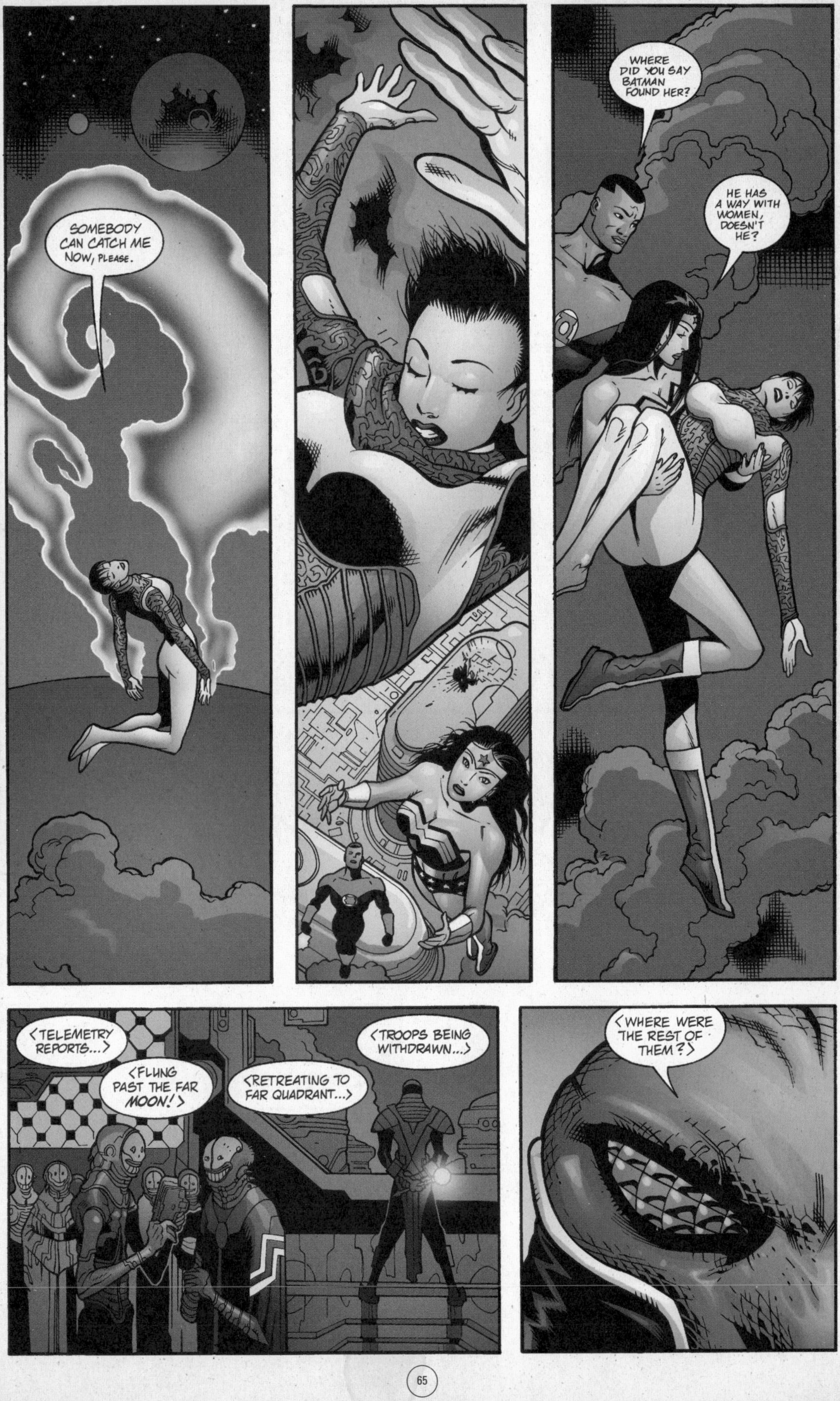
SOMEBODY CAN CATCH ME NOW, PLEASE.
WHERE DID YOU SAY BATMAN FOUND HER?
HE HAS A WAY WITH WOMEN, DOESN'T HE?
<TELEMETRY REPORTS...>
<FLUNG PAST THE FAR MOON!>
<RETREATING TO FAR QUADRANT...>
<TROOPS BEING WITHDRAWN...>
<WHERE WERE THE REST OF THEM?>

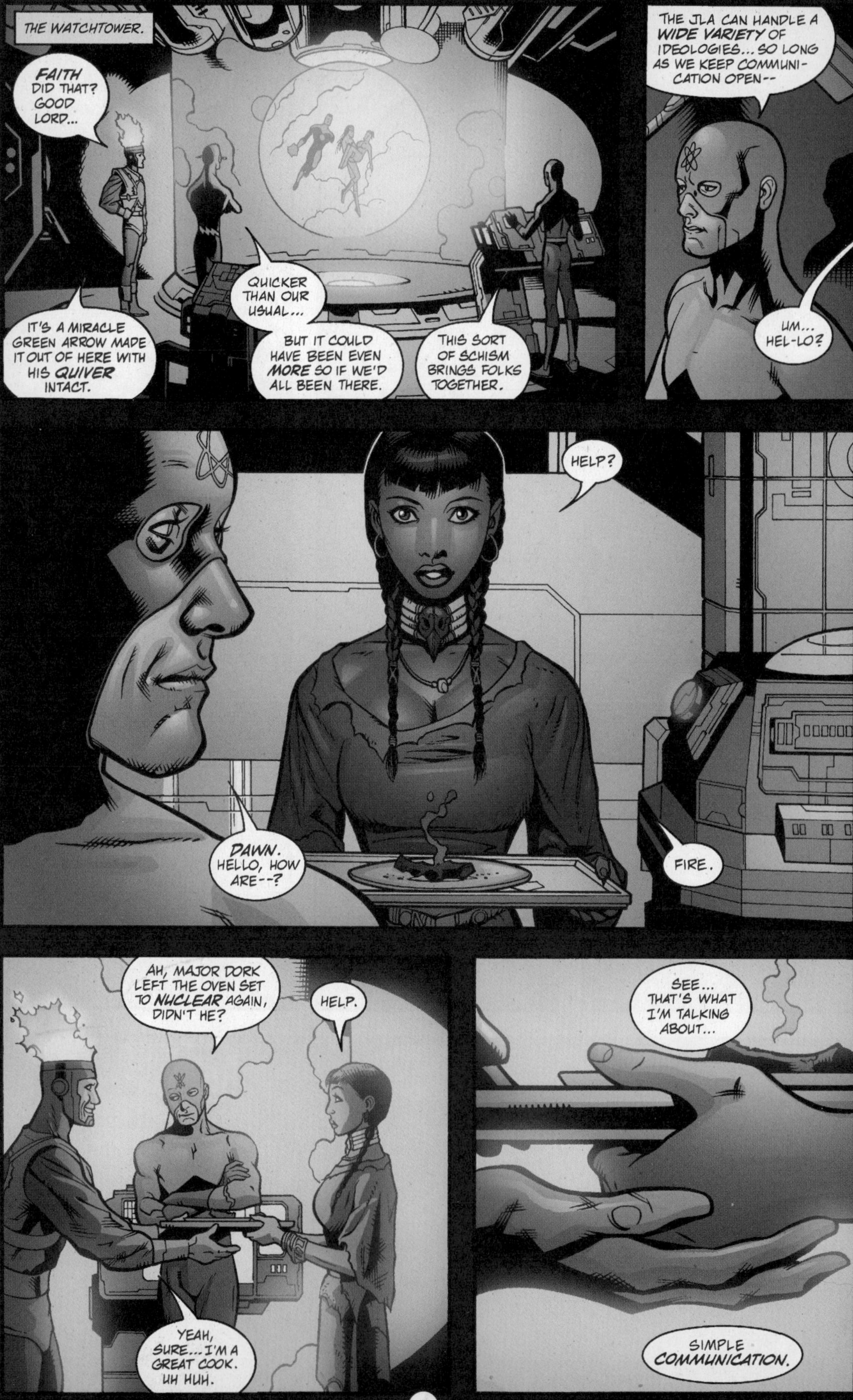
THE WATCHTOWER.
FAITH DID THAT? GOOD LORD...
IT'S A MIRACLE GREEN ARROW MADE IT OUT OF HERE WITH HIS QUIVER INTACT.
QUICKER THAN OUR USUAL...
BUT IT COULD HAVE BEEN EVEN MORE SO IF WE'D ALL BEEN THERE.
THIS SORT OF SCHISM BRINGS FOLKS TOGETHER.
THE JLA CAN HANDLE A WIDE VARIETY OF IDEOLOGIES... SO LONG AS WE KEEP COMMUNI-CATION OPEN--
UM... HEL-LO?
HELP?
DAWN. HELLO, HOW ARE--?
FIRE.
AH, MAJOR DORK LEFT THE OVEN SET TO NUCLEAR AGAIN, DIDN'T HE?
HELP.
YEAH, SURE... I'M A GREAT COOK. UH HUH.
SEE... THAT'S WHAT I'M TALKING ABOUT...
SIMPLE COMMUNICATION.

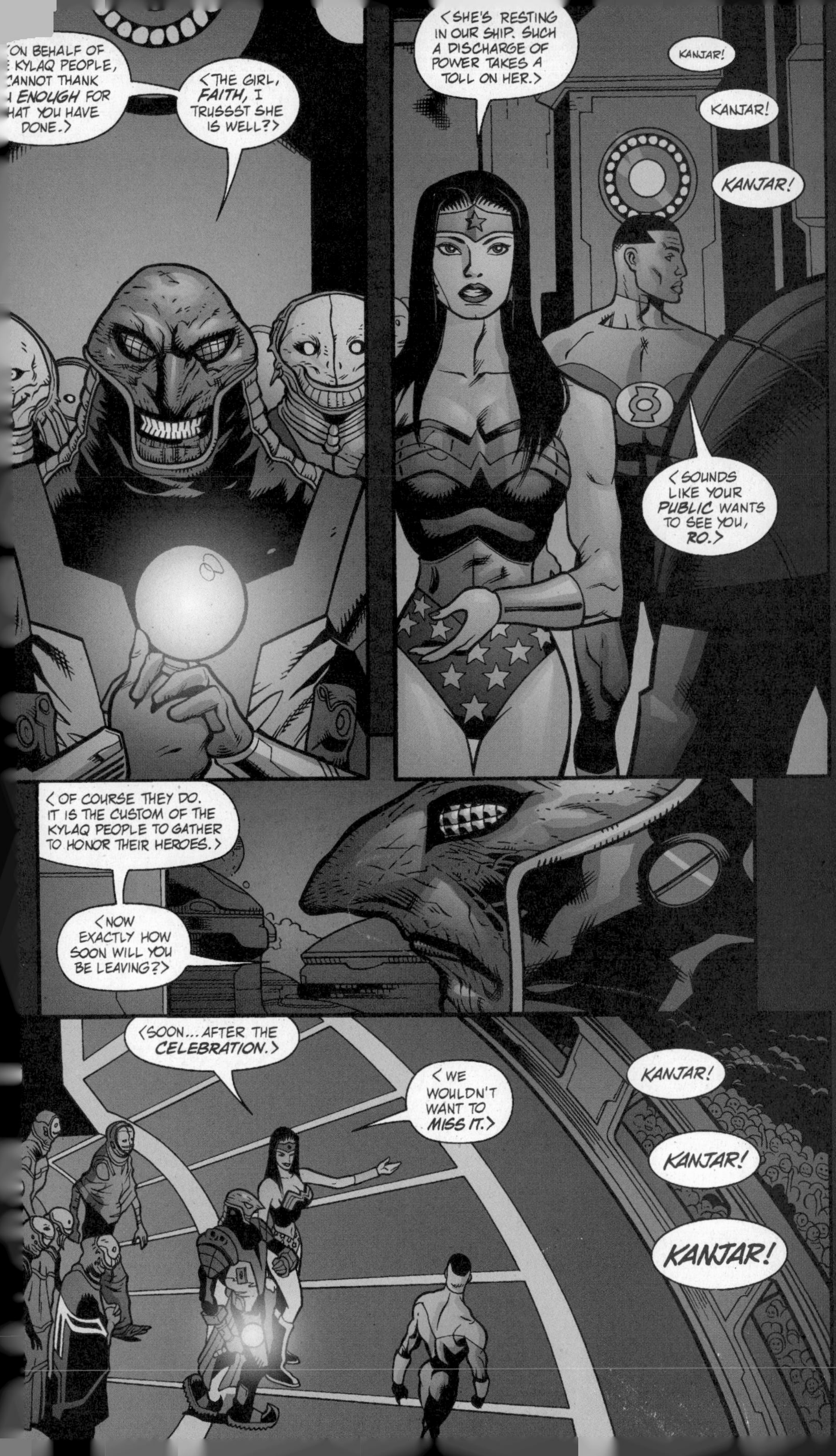

ON BEHALF OF E KYLAQ PEOPLE, CANNOT THANK ENOUGH FOR HAT YOU HAVE DONE.>
<THE GIRL, FAITH, I TRUSSST SHE IS WELL?>
<SHE'S RESTING IN OUR SHIP. SUCH A DISCHARGE OF POWER TAKES A TOLL ON HER.>
KANJAR!
KANJAR!
KANJAR!
<SOUNDS LIKE YOUR PUBLIC WANTS TO SEE YOU, RO.>
<OF COURSE THEY DO. IT IS THE CUSTOM OF THE KYLAQ PEOPLE TO GATHER TO HONOR THEIR HEROES.>
<NOW EXACTLY HOW SOON WILL YOU BE LEAVING?>
<SOON... AFTER THE CELEBRATION.>
<WE WOULDN'T WANT TO MISS IT.>
KANJAR!
KANJAR!
KANJAR!

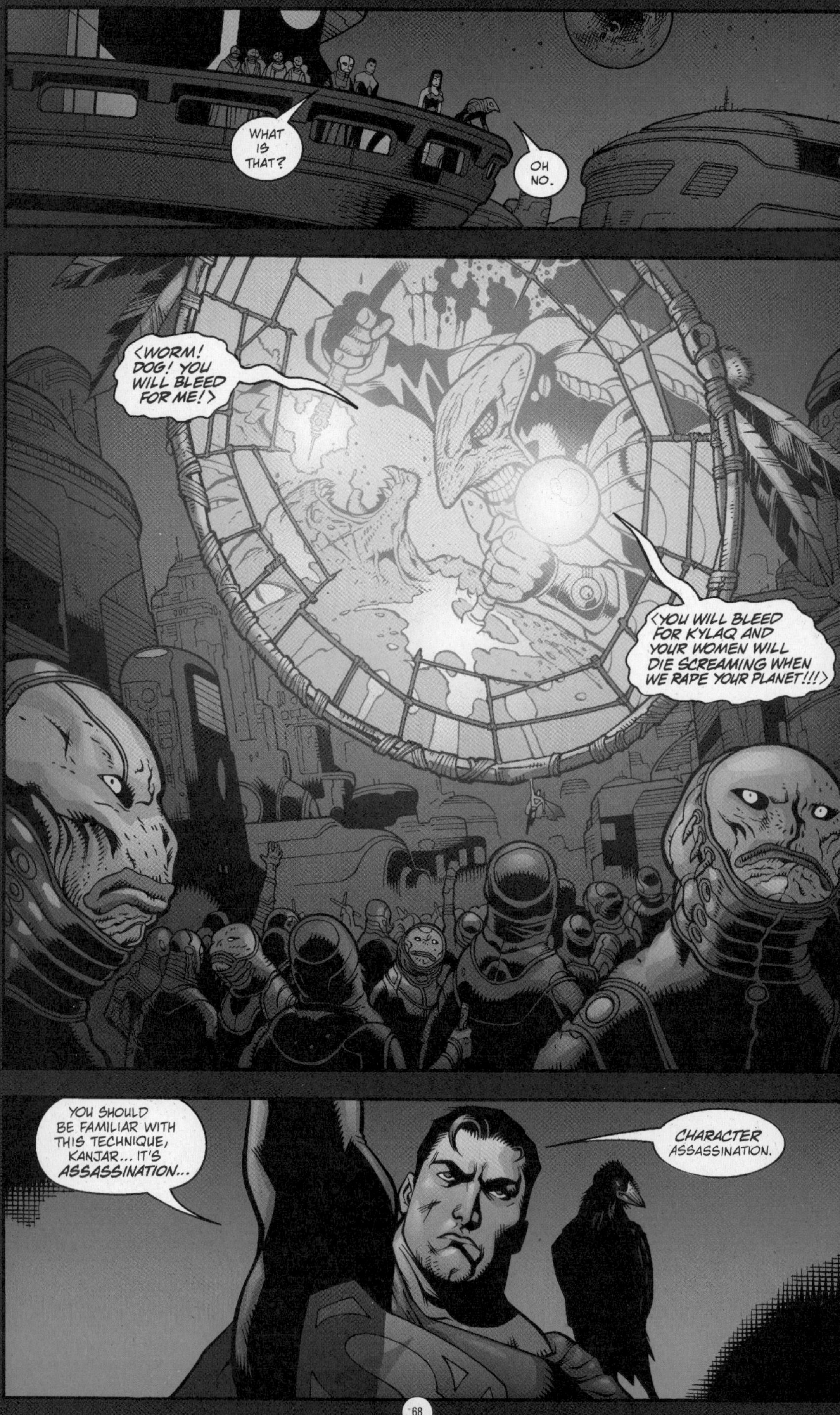
WHAT IS THAT?
OH NO.
<WORM! DOG! YOU WILL BLEED FOR ME!>
<YOU WILL BLEED FOR KYLAQ AND YOUR WOMEN WILL DIE SCREAMING WHEN WE RAPE YOUR PLANET!!!>
YOU SHOULD BE FAMILIAR WITH THIS TECHNIQUE, KANJAR... IT'S ASSASSINATION...
CHARACTER ASSASSINATION.

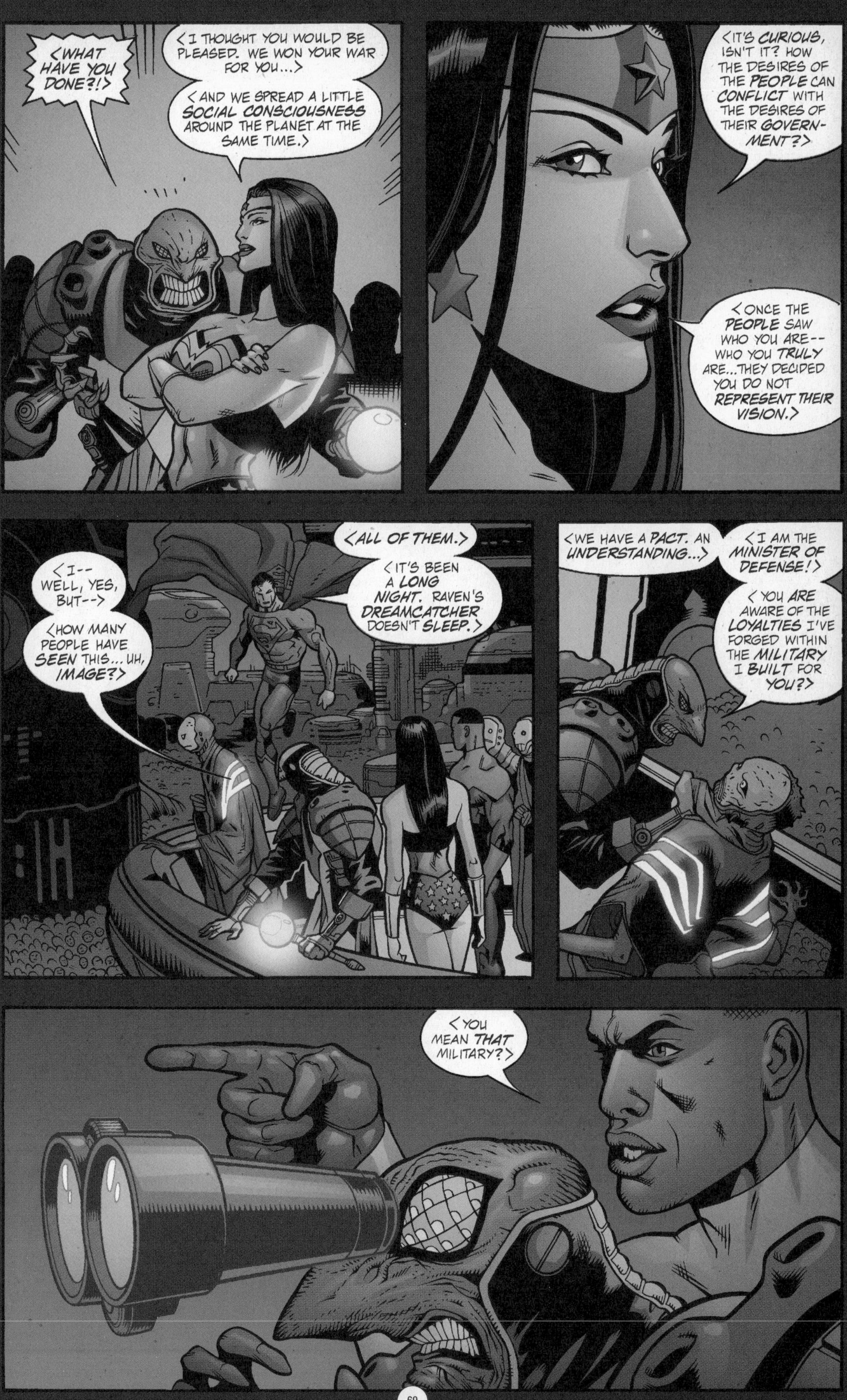
<WHAT HAVE YOU DONE?!>
<I THOUGHT YOU WOULD BE PLEASED. WE WON YOUR WAR FOR YOU...>
<AND WE SPREAD A LITTLE SOCIAL CONSCIOUSNESS AROUND THE PLANET AT THE SAME TIME.>
<IT'S CURIOUS, ISN'T IT? HOW THE DESIRES OF THE PEOPLE CAN CONFLICT WITH THE DESIRES OF THEIR GOVERNMENT?>
<ONCE THE PEOPLE SAW WHO YOU ARE-- WHO YOU TRULY ARE...THEY DECIDED YOU DO NOT REPRESENT THEIR VISION.>
<I-- WELL, YES, BUT-->
<HOW MANY PEOPLE HAVE SEEN THIS... UH, IMAGE?>
<ALL OF THEM.>
<IT'S BEEN A LONG NIGHT. RAVEN'S DREAMCATCHER DOESN'T SLEEP.>
<WE HAVE A PACT. AN UNDERSTANDING...>
<I AM THE MINISTER OF DEFENSE!>
<YOU ARE AWARE OF THE LOYALTIES I'VE FORGED WITHIN THE MILITARY I BUILT FOR YOU?>
<YOU MEAN THAT MILITARY?>

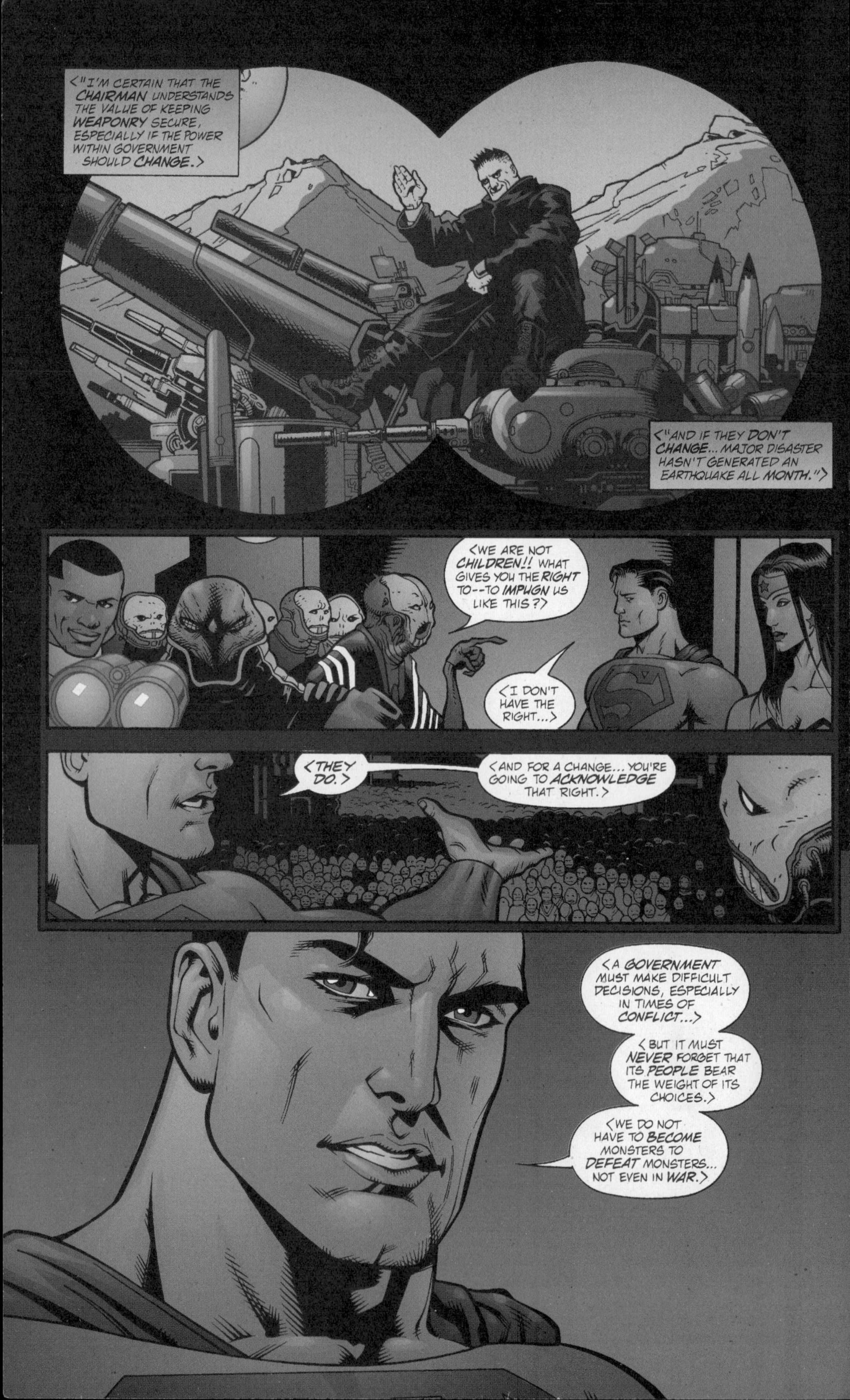

<"I'M CERTAIN THAT THE CHAIRMAN UNDERSTANDS THE VALUE OF KEEPING WEAPONRY SECURE, ESPECIALLY IF THE POWER WITHIN GOVERNMENT SHOULD CHANGE.>
<"AND IF THEY DON'T CHANGE... MAJOR DISASTER HASN'T GENERATED AN EARTHQUAKE ALL MONTH.">
<WE ARE NOT CHILDREN!! WHAT GIVES YOU THE RIGHT TO--TO IMPUGN US LIKE THIS?>
<I DON'T HAVE THE RIGHT...>
<THEY DO.>
<AND FOR A CHANGE... YOU'RE GOING TO ACKNOWLEDGE THAT RIGHT.>
<A GOVERNMENT MUST MAKE DIFFICULT DECISIONS, ESPECIALLY IN TIMES OF CONFLICT...>
<BUT IT MUST NEVER FORGET THAT ITS PEOPLE BEAR THE WEIGHT OF ITS CHOICES.>
<WE DO NOT HAVE TO BECOME MONSTERS TO DEFEAT MONSTERS... NOT EVEN IN WAR.>

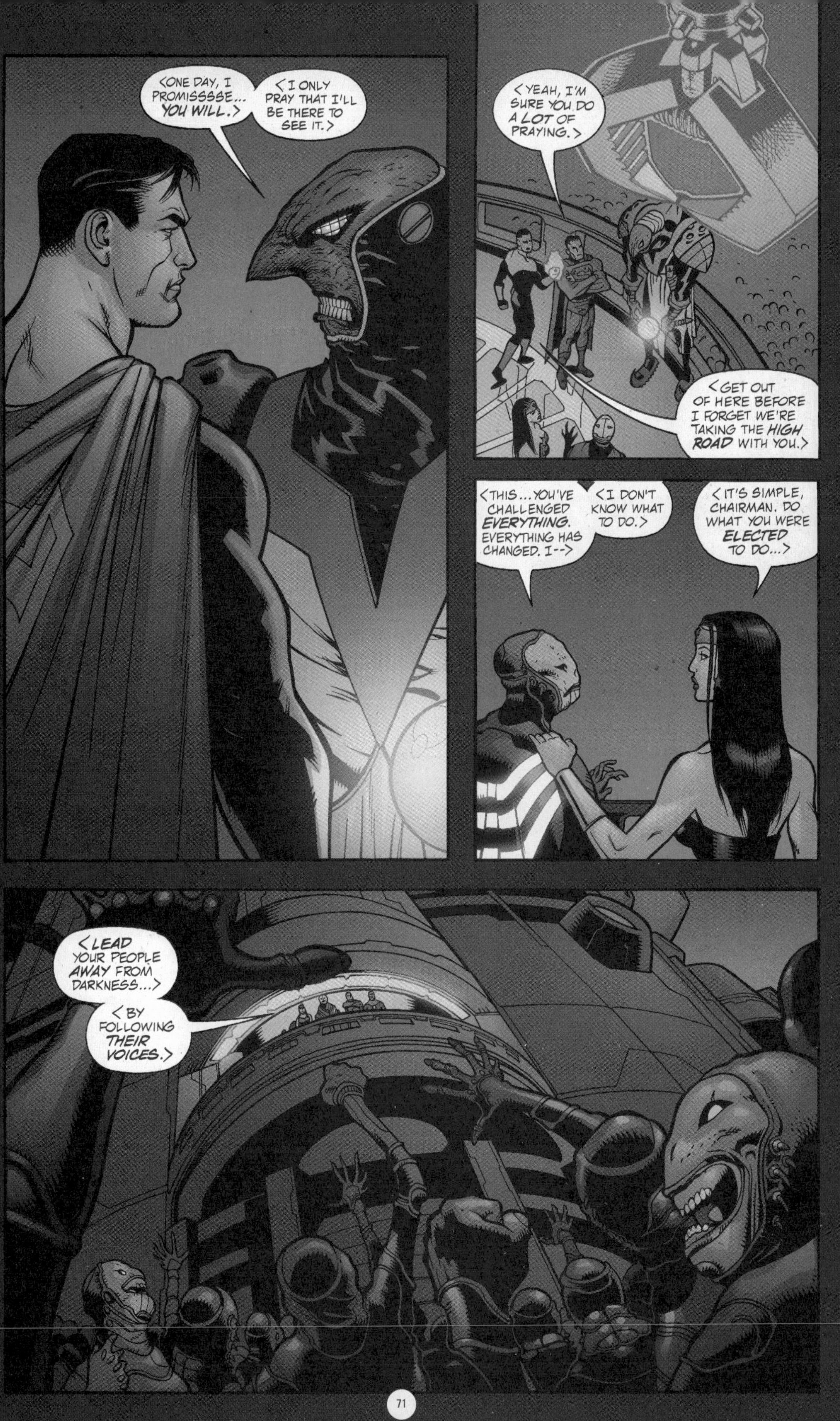
<ONE DAY, I PROMISSSSE... YOU WILL.>
<I ONLY PRAY THAT I'LL BE THERE TO SEE IT.>
<YEAH, I'M SURE YOU DO A LOT OF PRAYING.>
<GET OUT OF HERE BEFORE I FORGET WE'RE TAKING THE HIGH ROAD WITH YOU.>
<THIS... YOU'VE CHALLENGED EVERYTHING. EVERYTHING HAS CHANGED. I-->
<I DON'T KNOW WHAT TO DO.>
<IT'S SIMPLE, CHAIRMAN. DO WHAT YOU WERE ELECTED TO DO...>
<LEAD YOUR PEOPLE AWAY FROM DARKNESS...>
<BY FOLLOWING THEIR VOICES.>

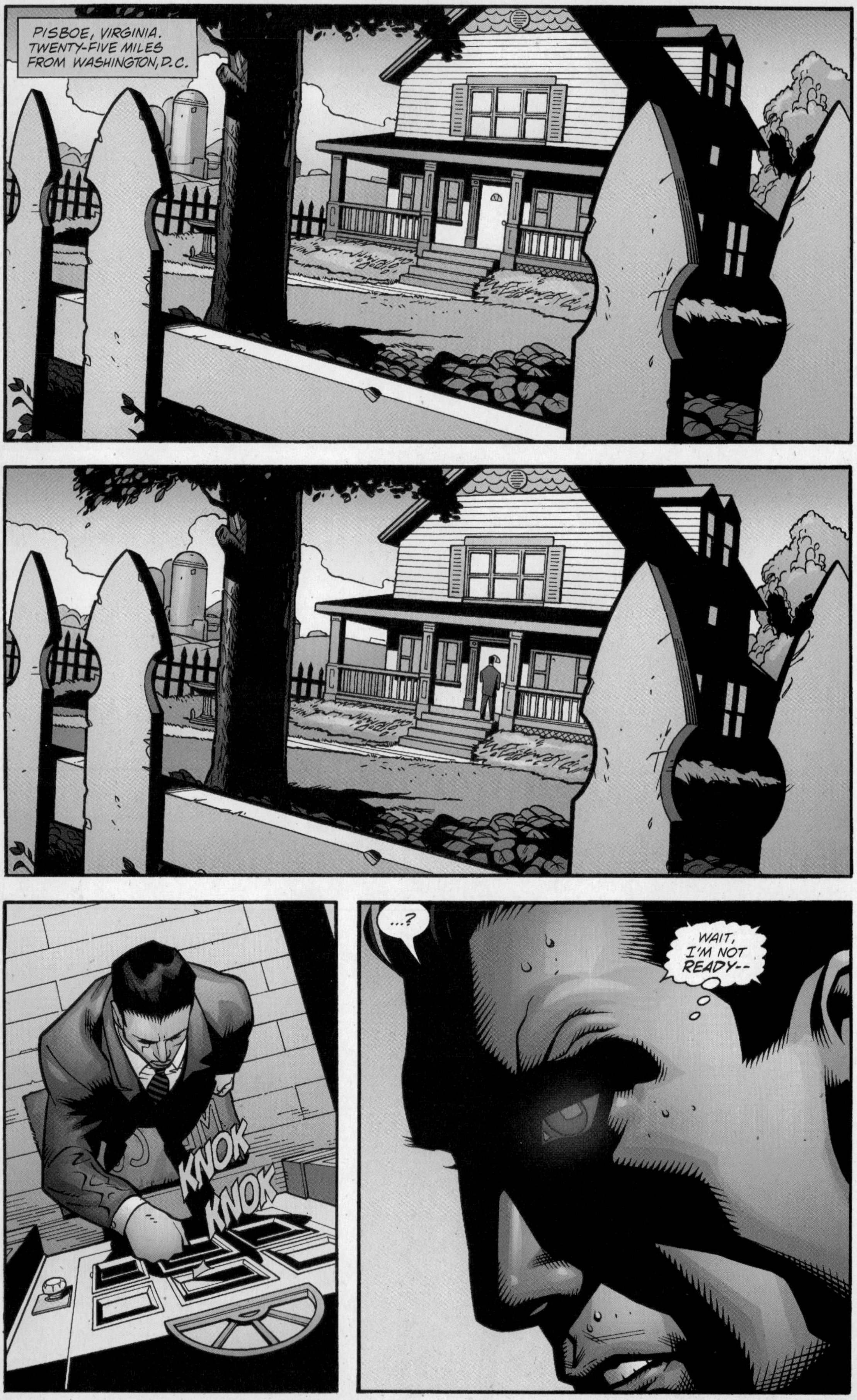
PISBOE, VIRGINIA. TWENTY-FIVE MILES FROM WASHINGTON, D.C.
KNOK
KNOK
...?
WAIT, I'M NOT READY--

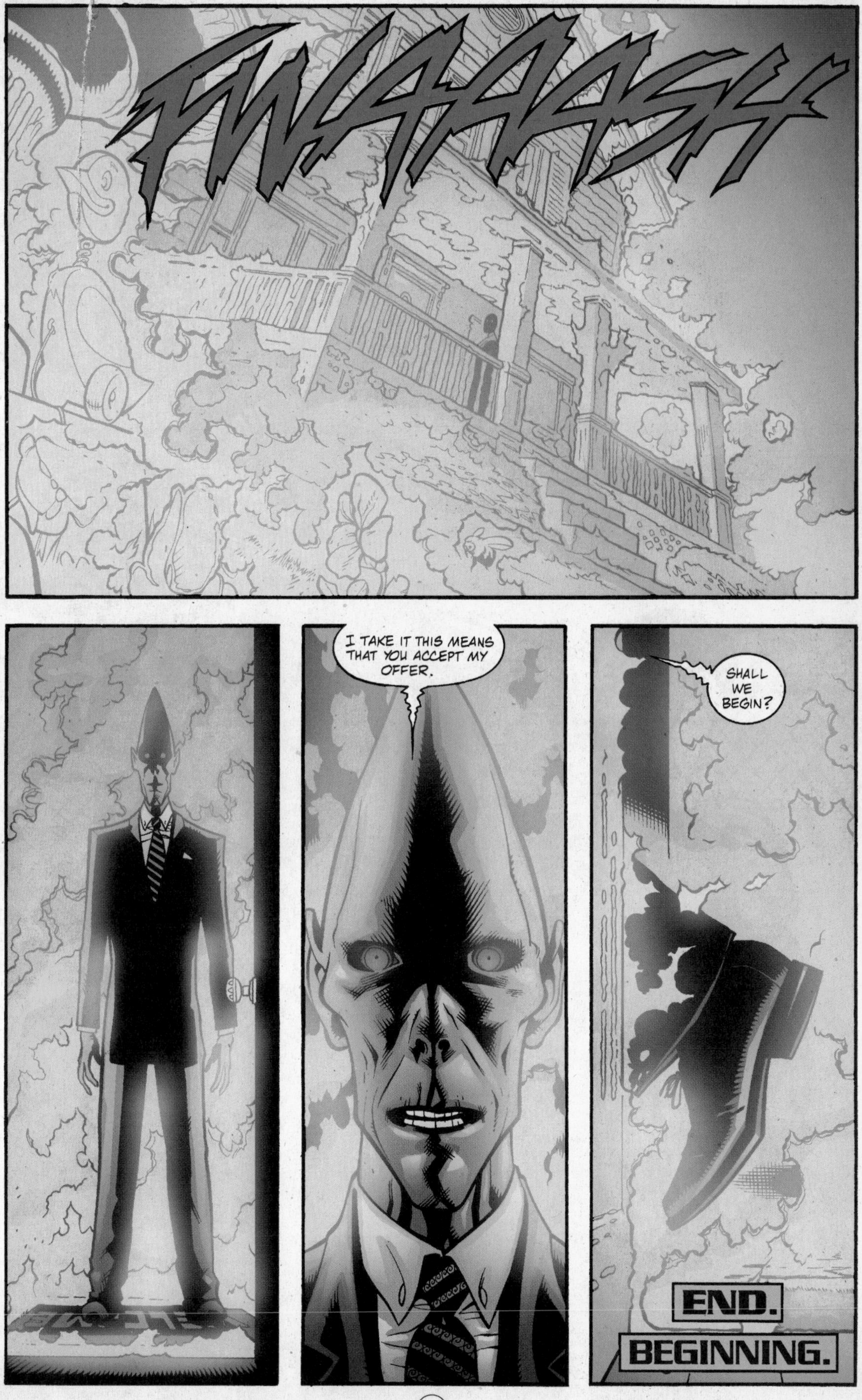
FWAAASH
I TAKE IT THIS MEANS THAT YOU ACCEPT MY OFFER.
SHALL WE BEGIN?
END.
BEGINNING.

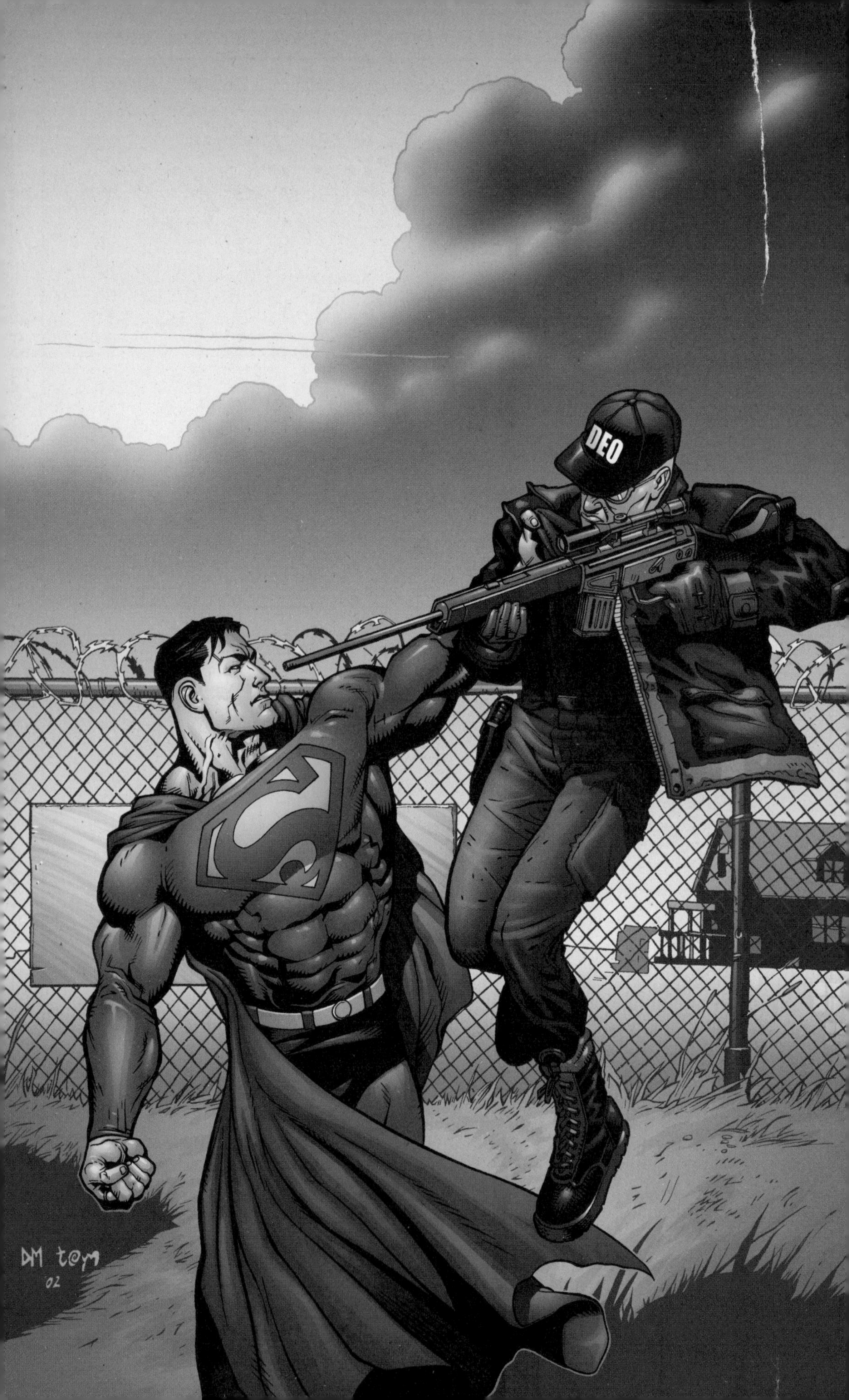
DEO
DM t@m
'02

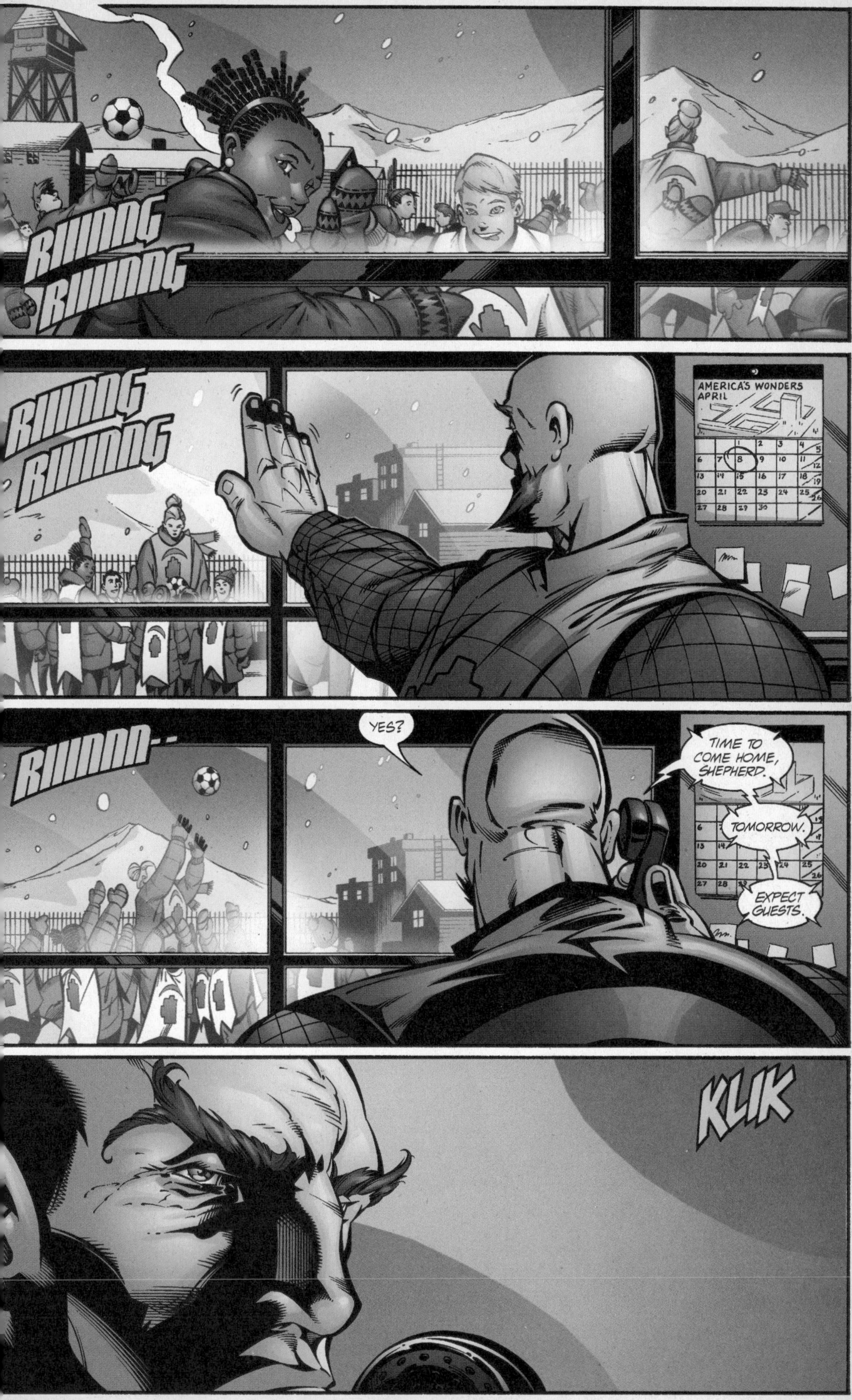

RIIINNG RIIINNG
RIIINNG RIIINNG
AMERICA'S WONDERS
APRIL
RIIINNN--
YES?
TIME TO COME HOME, SHEPHERD.
TOMORROW.
EXPECT GUESTS.
KLIK

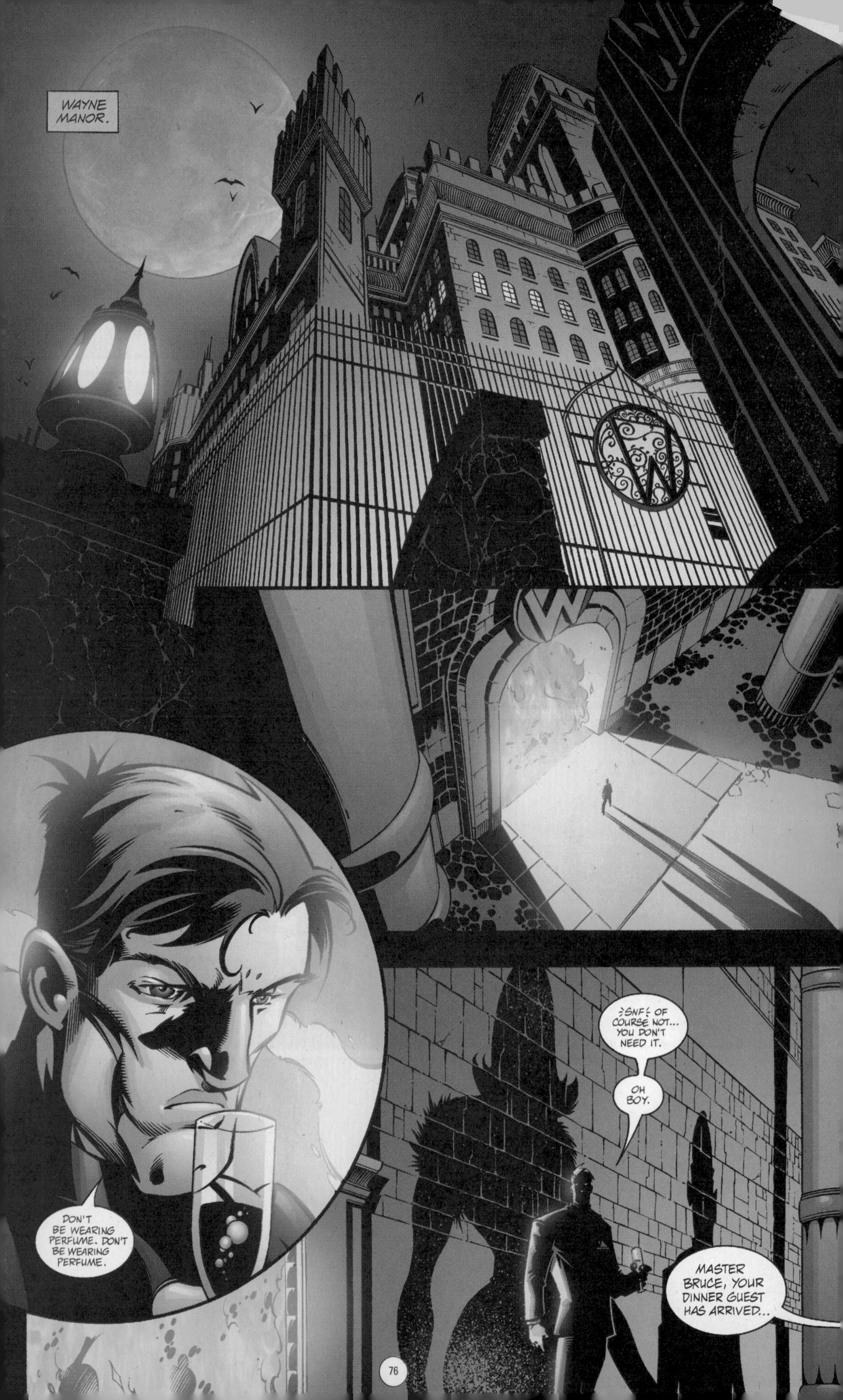
WAYNE MANOR.
DON'T BE WEARING PERFUME. DON'T BE WEARING PERFUME.
⸗SNF⸗ OF COURSE NOT... YOU DON'T NEED IT.
OH BOY.
MASTER BRUCE, YOUR DINNER GUEST HAS ARRIVED...

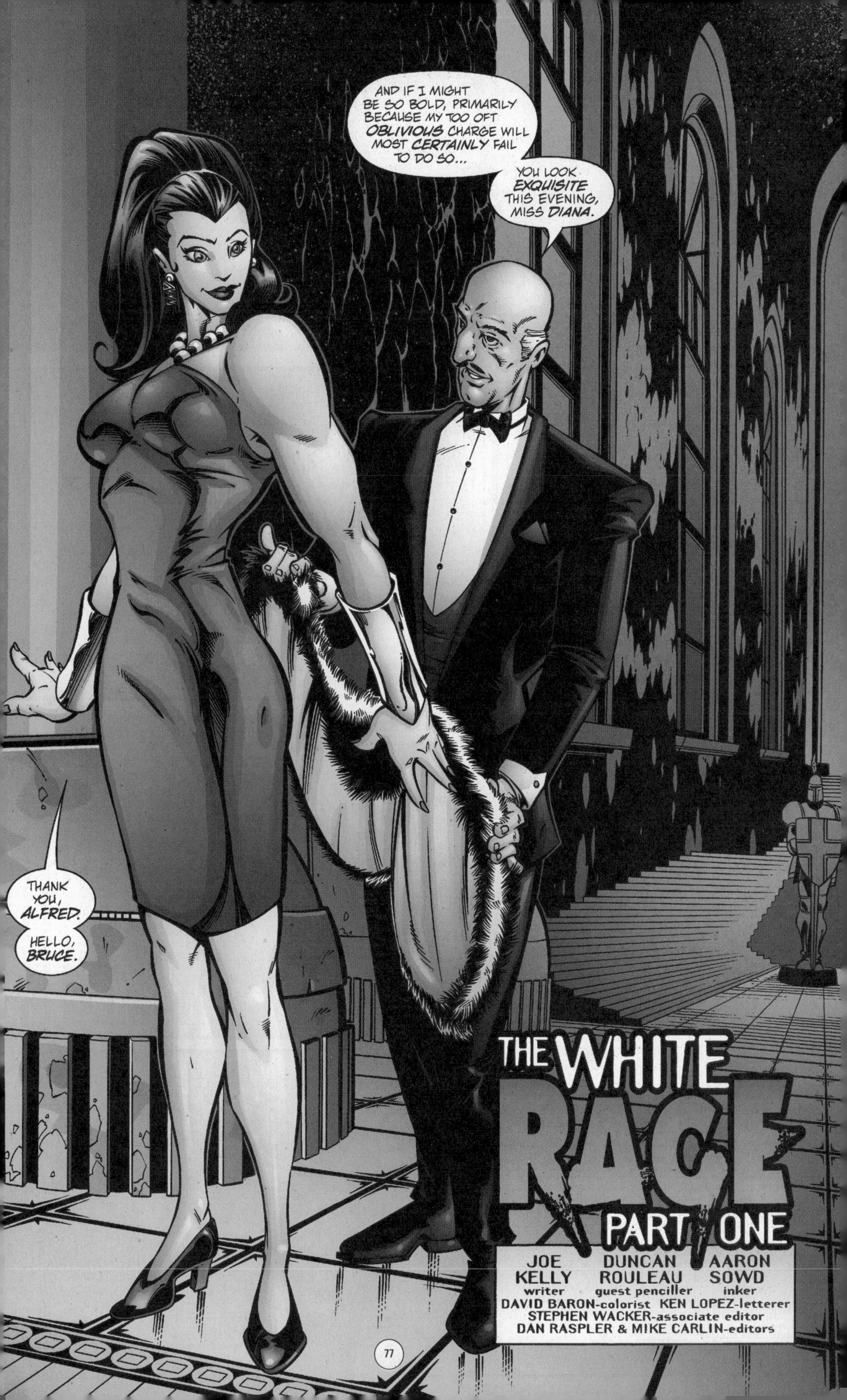

AND IF I MIGHT BE SO BOLD, PRIMARILY BECAUSE MY TOO OFT OBLIVIOUS CHARGE WILL MOST CERTAINLY FAIL TO DO SO...
YOU LOOK EXQUISITE THIS EVENING, MISS DIANA.
THANK YOU, ALFRED.
HELLO, BRUCE.
THE WHITE RACE
PART ONE
JOE KELLY writer
DUNCAN ROULEAU guest penciller
AARON SOWD inker
DAVID BARON-colorist KEN LOPEZ-letterer
STEPHEN WACKER-associate editor
DAN RASPLER & MIKE CARLIN-editors

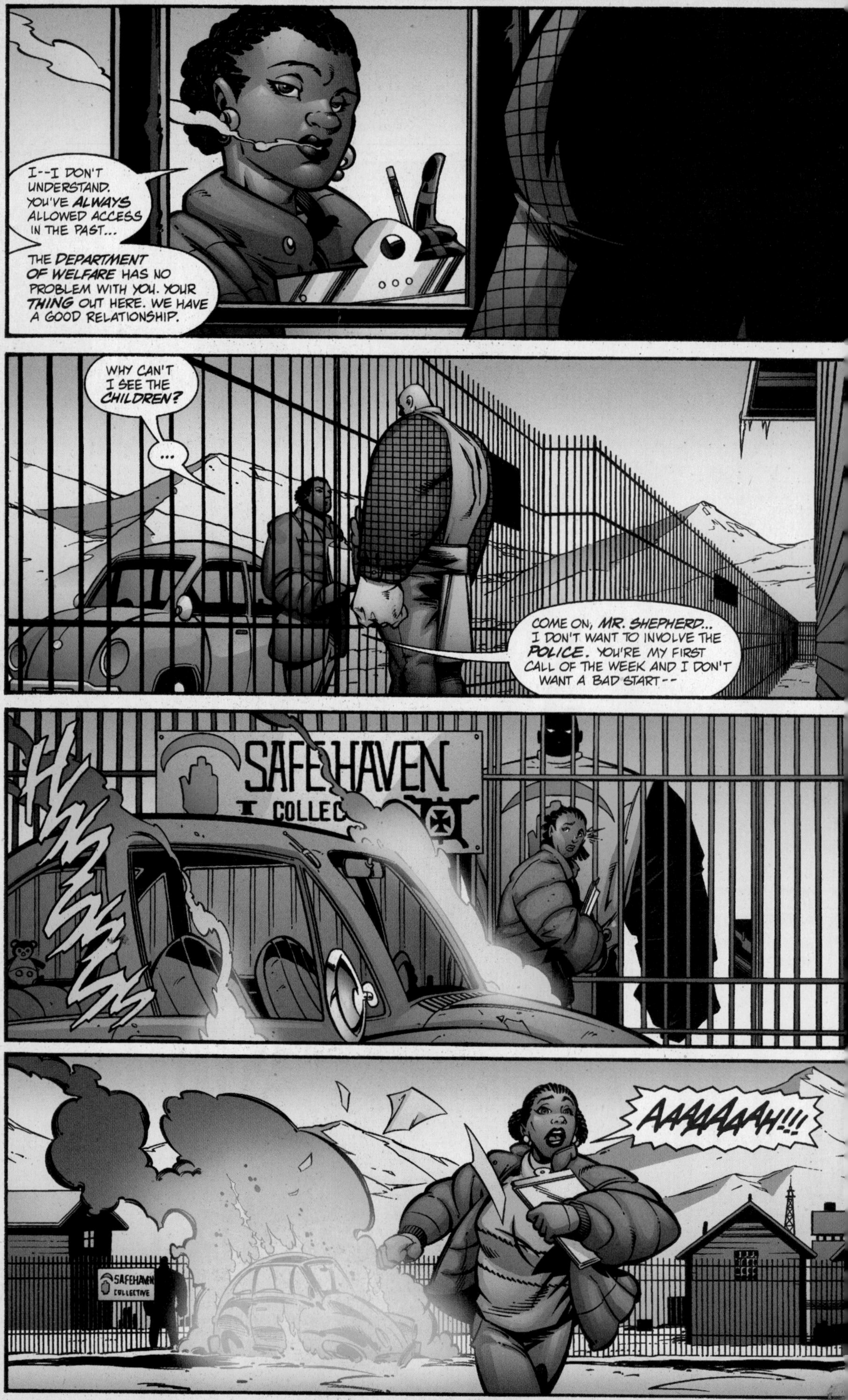

I--I DON'T UNDERSTAND. YOU'VE ALWAYS ALLOWED ACCESS IN THE PAST...
THE DEPARTMENT OF WELFARE HAS NO PROBLEM WITH YOU. YOUR THING OUT HERE. WE HAVE A GOOD RELATIONSHIP.
WHY CAN'T I SEE THE CHILDREN?
...
COME ON, MR. SHEPHERD... I DON'T WANT TO INVOLVE THE POLICE. YOU'RE MY FIRST CALL OF THE WEEK AND I DON'T WANT A BAD START--
SAFEHAVEN
COLLEC
HWMMMM
AAAAAAAH!!!
SAFEHAVEN
COLLECTIVE

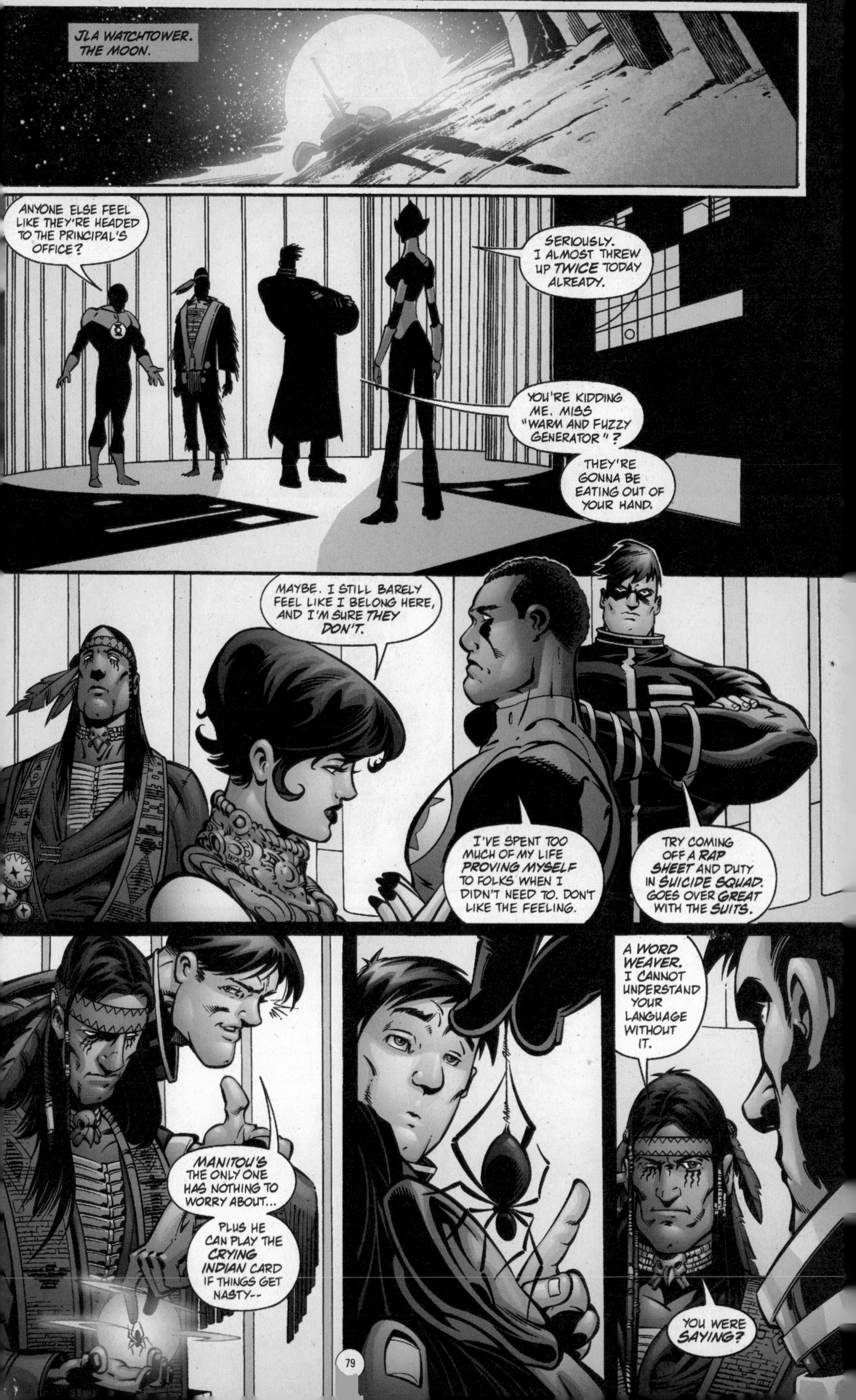

JLA WATCHTOWER. THE MOON.
ANYONE ELSE FEEL LIKE THEY'RE HEADED TO THE PRINCIPAL'S OFFICE?
SERIOUSLY. I ALMOST THREW UP TWICE TODAY ALREADY.
YOU'RE KIDDING ME. MISS "WARM AND FUZZY GENERATOR"?
THEY'RE GONNA BE EATING OUT OF YOUR HAND.
MAYBE. I STILL BARELY FEEL LIKE I BELONG HERE, AND I'M SURE THEY DON'T.
I'VE SPENT TOO MUCH OF MY LIFE PROVING MYSELF TO FOLKS WHEN I DIDN'T NEED TO. DON'T LIKE THE FEELING.
TRY COMING OFF A RAP SHEET AND DUTY IN SUICIDE SQUAD. GOES OVER GREAT WITH THE SUITS.
MANITOU'S THE ONLY ONE HAS NOTHING TO WORRY ABOUT...
PLUS HE CAN PLAY THE CRYING INDIAN CARD IF THINGS GET NASTY--
A WORD WEAVER. I CANNOT UNDERSTAND YOUR LANGUAGE WITHOUT IT.
YOU WERE SAYING?

THE JUSTICE LEAGUE IS AN *ORGANIC* THING.

IT EXISTS TO *COPE* WITH THE EVER-CHANGING FACE OF *TERROR* BESIEGING THE EARTH... AND IN THAT WAY, IT TOO, MUST SOMETIMES *EVOLVE*.

OUR CORE ROSTER HAS BEEN *EXPANDED* WITH *PROBATIONARY* MEMBERS.

FAITH, MANITOU RAVEN, AND *MAJOR DISASTER* WERE INSTRUMENTAL IN ENDING THE *OBSIDIAN AGE* CRISIS --

AND OUR NEW *GREEN LANTERN* IS NOT ONLY A HERO IN HIS OWN RIGHT, BUT A TRUSTED FRIEND AS WELL.

TODAY IS AN OPPORTUNITY FOR THE *WORLD COUNCIL* TO MEET THEM, ASK QUESTIONS, AND CONTINUE THE *OPEN RELATIONSHIP* THE JLA HAS ENJOYED WITH THE WORLD'S LEADERS.

I'LL START, SUPERMAN...

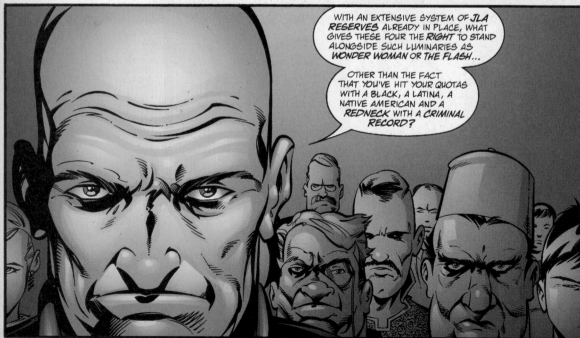

WITH AN EXTENSIVE SYSTEM OF *JLA RESERVES* ALREADY IN PLACE, WHAT GIVES THESE FOUR THE *RIGHT* TO STAND ALONGSIDE SUCH LUMINARIES AS *WONDER WOMAN* OR *THE FLASH*...

OTHER THAN THE FACT THAT YOU'VE HIT YOUR QUOTAS WITH A *BLACK*, A *LATINA*, A *NATIVE AMERICAN* AND A *REDNECK* WITH A *CRIMINAL RECORD*?

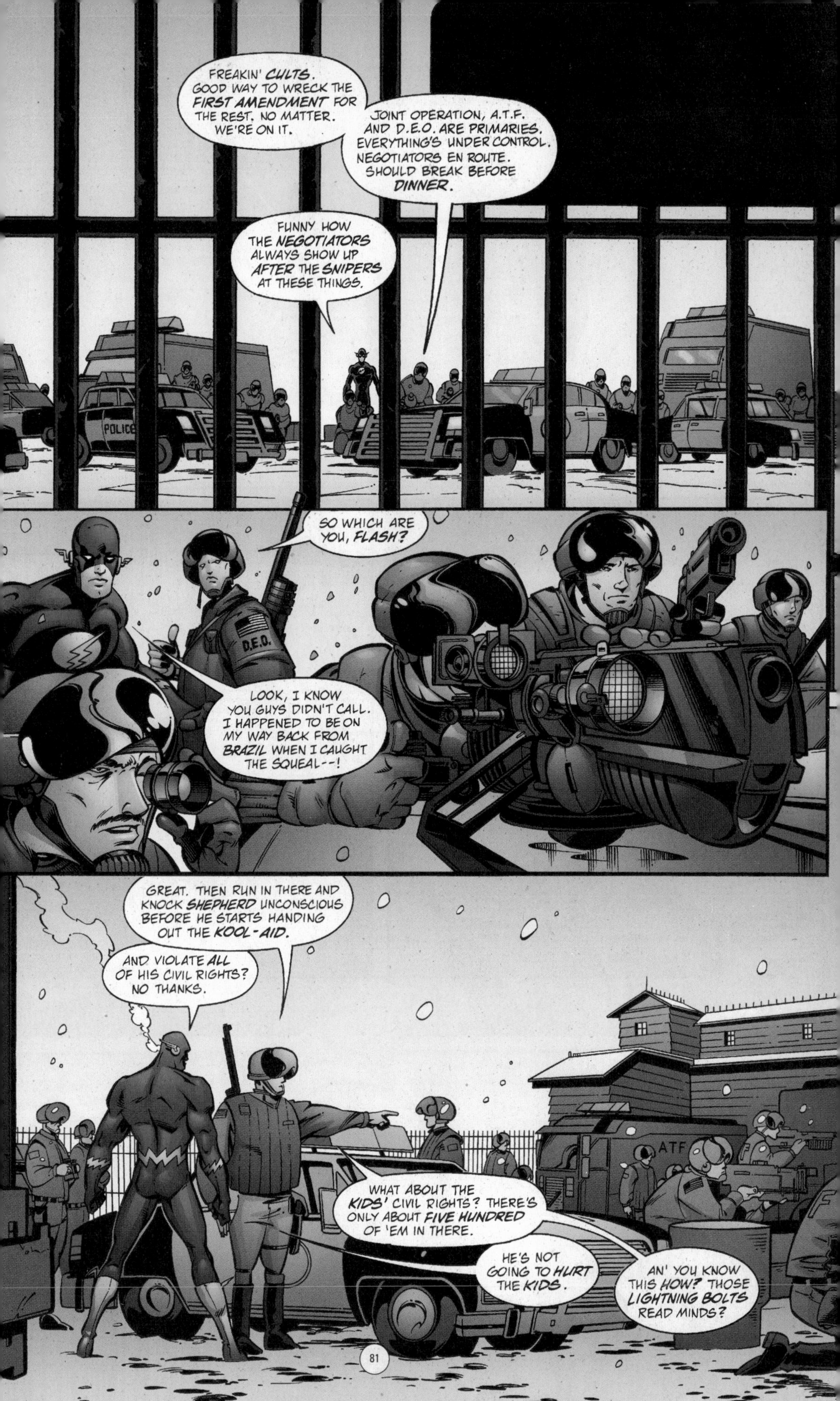
FREAKIN' CULTS. GOOD WAY TO WRECK THE FIRST AMENDMENT FOR THE REST. NO MATTER. WE'RE ON IT.
JOINT OPERATION, A.T.F. AND D.E.O. ARE PRIMARIES. EVERYTHING'S UNDER CONTROL. NEGOTIATORS EN ROUTE. SHOULD BREAK BEFORE DINNER.
FUNNY HOW THE NEGOTIATORS ALWAYS SHOW UP AFTER THE SNIPERS AT THESE THINGS.
POLICE
SO WHICH ARE YOU, FLASH?
D.E.O.
LOOK, I KNOW YOU GUYS DIDN'T CALL. I HAPPENED TO BE ON MY WAY BACK FROM BRAZIL WHEN I CAUGHT THE SQUEAL--!
GREAT. THEN RUN IN THERE AND KNOCK SHEPHERD UNCONSCIOUS BEFORE HE STARTS HANDING OUT THE KOOL-AID.
AND VIOLATE ALL OF HIS CIVIL RIGHTS? NO THANKS.
ATF
WHAT ABOUT THE KIDS' CIVIL RIGHTS? THERE'S ONLY ABOUT FIVE HUNDRED OF 'EM IN THERE.
HE'S NOT GOING TO HURT THE KIDS.
AN' YOU KNOW THIS HOW? THOSE LIGHTNING BOLTS READ MINDS?

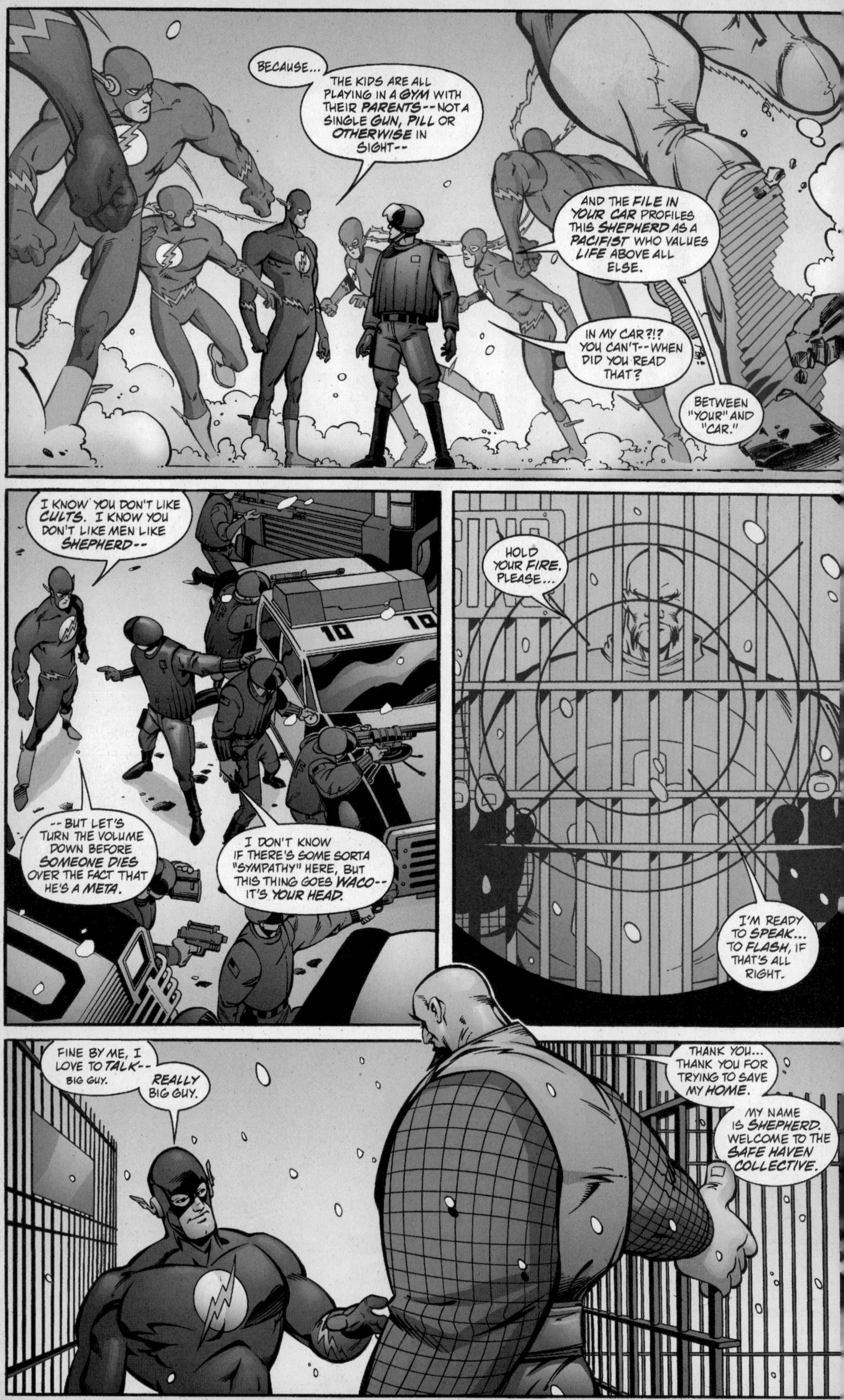
BECAUSE...
THE KIDS ARE ALL PLAYING IN A GYM WITH THEIR PARENTS--NOT A SINGLE GUN, PILL OR OTHERWISE IN SIGHT--
AND THE FILE IN YOUR CAR PROFILES THIS SHEPHERD AS A PACIFIST WHO VALUES LIFE ABOVE ALL ELSE.
IN MY CAR?!? YOU CAN'T--WHEN DID YOU READ THAT?
BETWEEN "YOUR" AND "CAR."
I KNOW YOU DON'T LIKE CULTS. I KNOW YOU DON'T LIKE MEN LIKE SHEPHERD--
--BUT LET'S TURN THE VOLUME DOWN BEFORE SOMEONE DIES OVER THE FACT THAT HE'S A META.
I DON'T KNOW IF THERE'S SOME SORTA "SYMPATHY" HERE, BUT THIS THING GOES WACO--IT'S YOUR HEAD.
10
10
HOLD YOUR FIRE. PLEASE...
I'M READY TO SPEAK... TO FLASH, IF THAT'S ALL RIGHT.
FINE BY ME, I LOVE TO TALK-- BIG GUY.
REALLY BIG GUY.
THANK YOU... THANK YOU FOR TRYING TO SAVE MY HOME.
MY NAME IS SHEPHERD. WELCOME TO THE SAFE HAVEN COLLECTIVE.

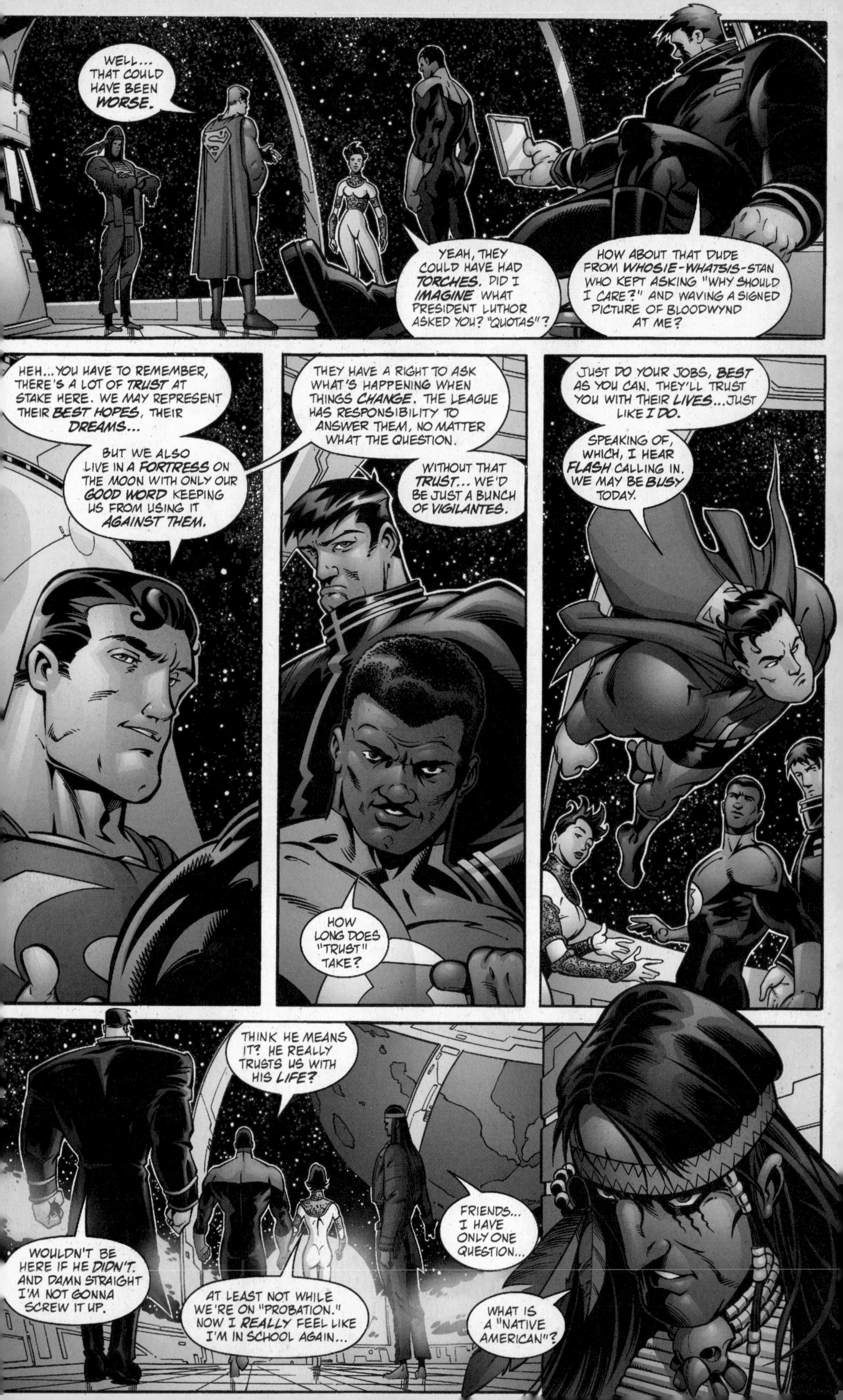
WELL... THAT COULD HAVE BEEN WORSE.
YEAH, THEY COULD HAVE HAD TORCHES. DID I IMAGINE WHAT PRESIDENT LUTHOR ASKED YOU? "QUOTAS"?
HOW ABOUT THAT DUDE FROM WHOSIE-WHATSIS-STAN WHO KEPT ASKING "WHY SHOULD I CARE?" AND WAVING A SIGNED PICTURE OF BLOODWYND AT ME?
HEH... YOU HAVE TO REMEMBER, THERE'S A LOT OF TRUST AT STAKE HERE. WE MAY REPRESENT THEIR BEST HOPES, THEIR DREAMS...
BUT WE ALSO LIVE IN A FORTRESS ON THE MOON WITH ONLY OUR GOOD WORD KEEPING US FROM USING IT AGAINST THEM.
THEY HAVE A RIGHT TO ASK WHAT'S HAPPENING WHEN THINGS CHANGE. THE LEAGUE HAS RESPONSIBILITY TO ANSWER THEM, NO MATTER WHAT THE QUESTION.
WITHOUT THAT TRUST... WE'D BE JUST A BUNCH OF VIGILANTES.
HOW LONG DOES "TRUST" TAKE?
JUST DO YOUR JOBS, BEST AS YOU CAN. THEY'LL TRUST YOU WITH THEIR LIVES... JUST LIKE I DO.
SPEAKING OF, WHICH, I HEAR FLASH CALLING IN. WE MAY BE BUSY TODAY.
THINK HE MEANS IT? HE REALLY TRUSTS US WITH HIS LIFE?
WOULDN'T BE HERE IF HE DIDN'T. AND DAMN STRAIGHT I'M NOT GONNA SCREW IT UP.
AT LEAST NOT WHILE WE'RE ON "PROBATION." NOW I REALLY FEEL LIKE I'M IN SCHOOL AGAIN...
FRIENDS... I HAVE ONLY ONE QUESTION...
WHAT IS A "NATIVE AMERICAN"?

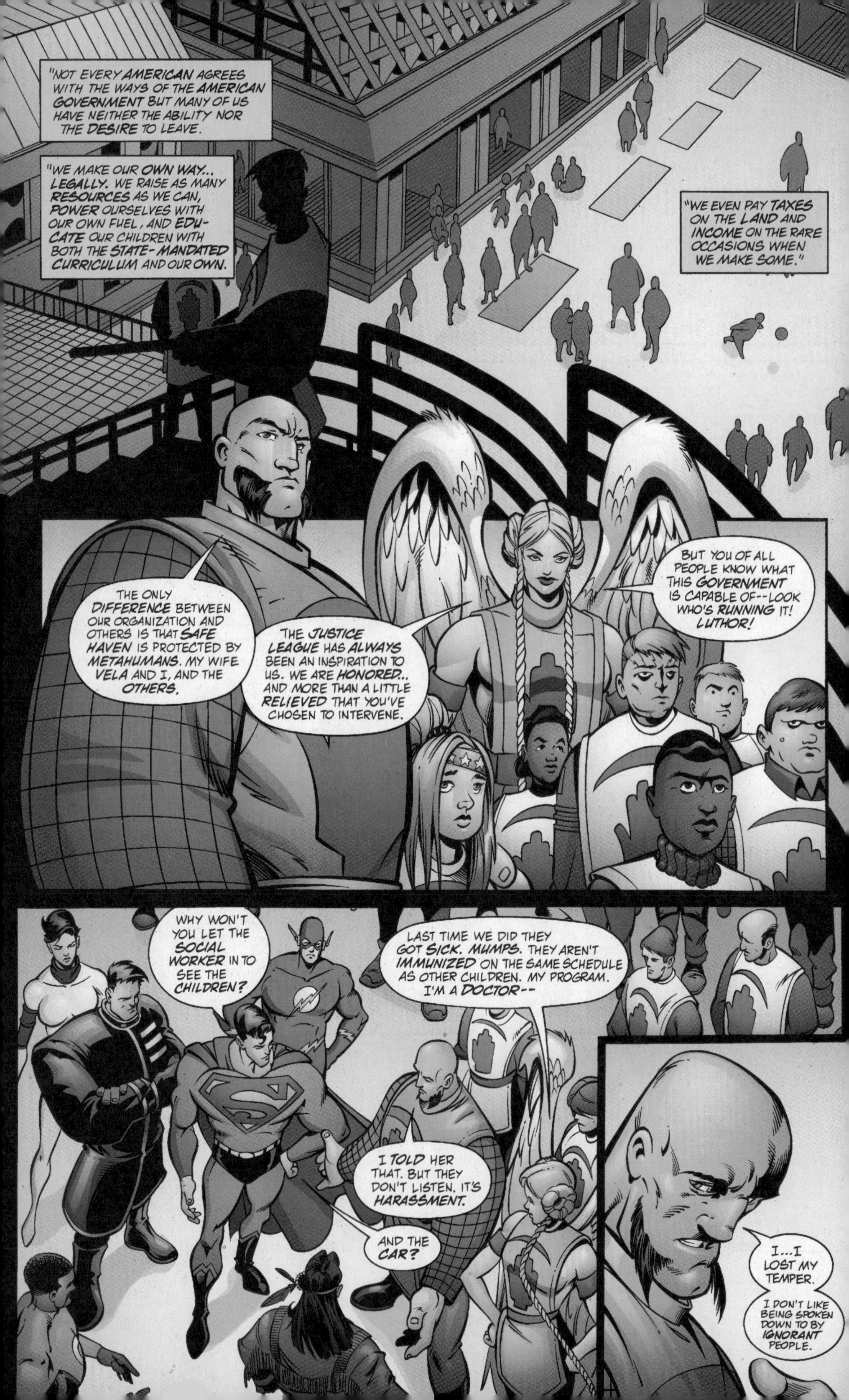
"NOT EVERY AMERICAN AGREES WITH THE WAYS OF THE AMERICAN GOVERNMENT BUT MANY OF US HAVE NEITHER THE ABILITY NOR THE DESIRE TO LEAVE.
"WE MAKE OUR OWN WAY... LEGALLY. WE RAISE AS MANY RESOURCES AS WE CAN, POWER OURSELVES WITH OUR OWN FUEL, AND EDUCATE OUR CHILDREN WITH BOTH THE STATE-MANDATED CURRICULUM AND OUR OWN.
"WE EVEN PAY TAXES ON THE LAND AND INCOME ON THE RARE OCCASIONS WHEN WE MAKE SOME."
THE ONLY DIFFERENCE BETWEEN OUR ORGANIZATION AND OTHERS IS THAT SAFE HAVEN IS PROTECTED BY METAHUMANS. MY WIFE VELA AND I, AND THE OTHERS.
THE JUSTICE LEAGUE HAS ALWAYS BEEN AN INSPIRATION TO US. WE ARE HONORED... AND MORE THAN A LITTLE RELIEVED THAT YOU'VE CHOSEN TO INTERVENE.
BUT YOU OF ALL PEOPLE KNOW WHAT THIS GOVERNMENT IS CAPABLE OF--LOOK WHO'S RUNNING IT! LUTHOR!
WHY WON'T YOU LET THE SOCIAL WORKER IN TO SEE THE CHILDREN?
LAST TIME WE DID THEY GOT SICK. MUMPS. THEY AREN'T IMMUNIZED ON THE SAME SCHEDULE AS OTHER CHILDREN. MY PROGRAM. I'M A DOCTOR--
I TOLD HER THAT. BUT THEY DON'T LISTEN. IT'S HARASSMENT.
AND THE CAR?
I...I LOST MY TEMPER.
I DON'T LIKE BEING SPOKEN DOWN TO BY IGNORANT PEOPLE.

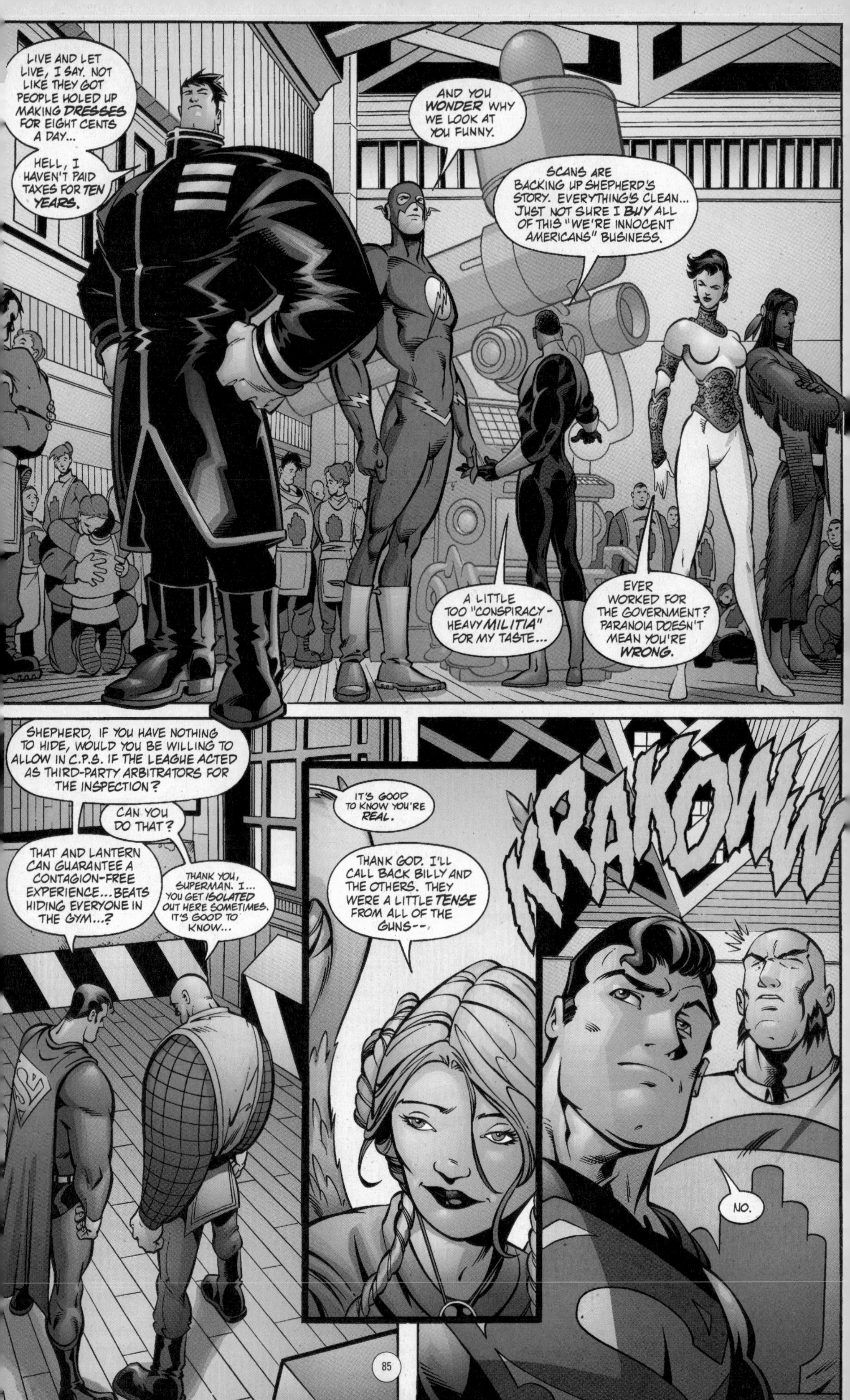

LIVE AND LET LIVE, I SAY. NOT LIKE THEY GOT PEOPLE HOLED UP MAKING DRESSES FOR EIGHT CENTS A DAY...
HELL, I HAVEN'T PAID TAXES FOR TEN YEARS.
AND YOU WONDER WHY WE LOOK AT YOU FUNNY.
SCANS ARE BACKING UP SHEPHERD'S STORY. EVERYTHING'S CLEAN... JUST NOT SURE I BUY ALL OF THIS "WE'RE INNOCENT AMERICANS" BUSINESS.
A LITTLE TOO "CONSPIRACY-HEAVY MILITIA" FOR MY TASTE...
EVER WORKED FOR THE GOVERNMENT? PARANOIA DOESN'T MEAN YOU'RE WRONG.
SHEPHERD, IF YOU HAVE NOTHING TO HIDE, WOULD YOU BE WILLING TO ALLOW IN C.P.S. IF THE LEAGUE ACTED AS THIRD-PARTY ARBITRATORS FOR THE INSPECTION?
CAN YOU DO THAT?
THAT AND LANTERN CAN GUARANTEE A CONTAGION-FREE EXPERIENCE...BEATS HIDING EVERYONE IN THE GYM...?
THANK YOU, SUPERMAN. I... YOU GET ISOLATED OUT HERE SOMETIMES. IT'S GOOD TO KNOW...
IT'S GOOD TO KNOW YOU'RE REAL.
THANK GOD. I'LL CALL BACK BILLY AND THE OTHERS. THEY WERE A LITTLE TENSE FROM ALL OF THE GUNS--
KRAKOWW
NO.

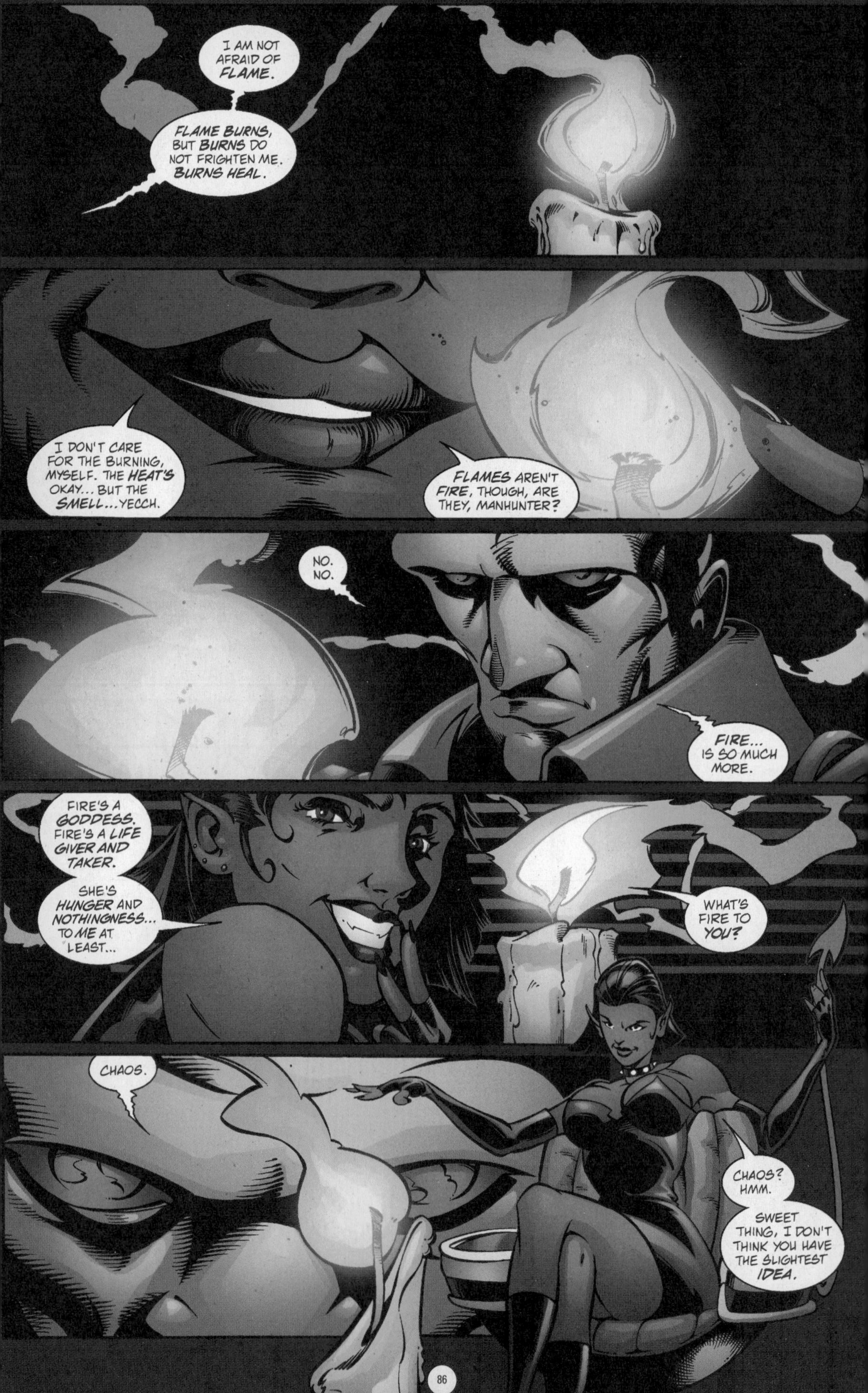
I AM NOT AFRAID OF FLAME.
FLAME BURNS, BUT BURNS DO NOT FRIGHTEN ME. BURNS HEAL.
I DON'T CARE FOR THE BURNING, MYSELF. THE HEAT'S OKAY... BUT THE SMELL... YECCH.
FLAMES AREN'T FIRE, THOUGH, ARE THEY, MANHUNTER?
NO. NO.
FIRE... IS SO MUCH MORE.
FIRE'S A GODDESS. FIRE'S A LIFE GIVER AND TAKER.
SHE'S HUNGER AND NOTHINGNESS... TO ME AT LEAST...
WHAT'S FIRE TO YOU?
CHAOS.
CHAOS? HMM.
SWEET THING, I DON'T THINK YOU HAVE THE SLIGHTEST IDEA.

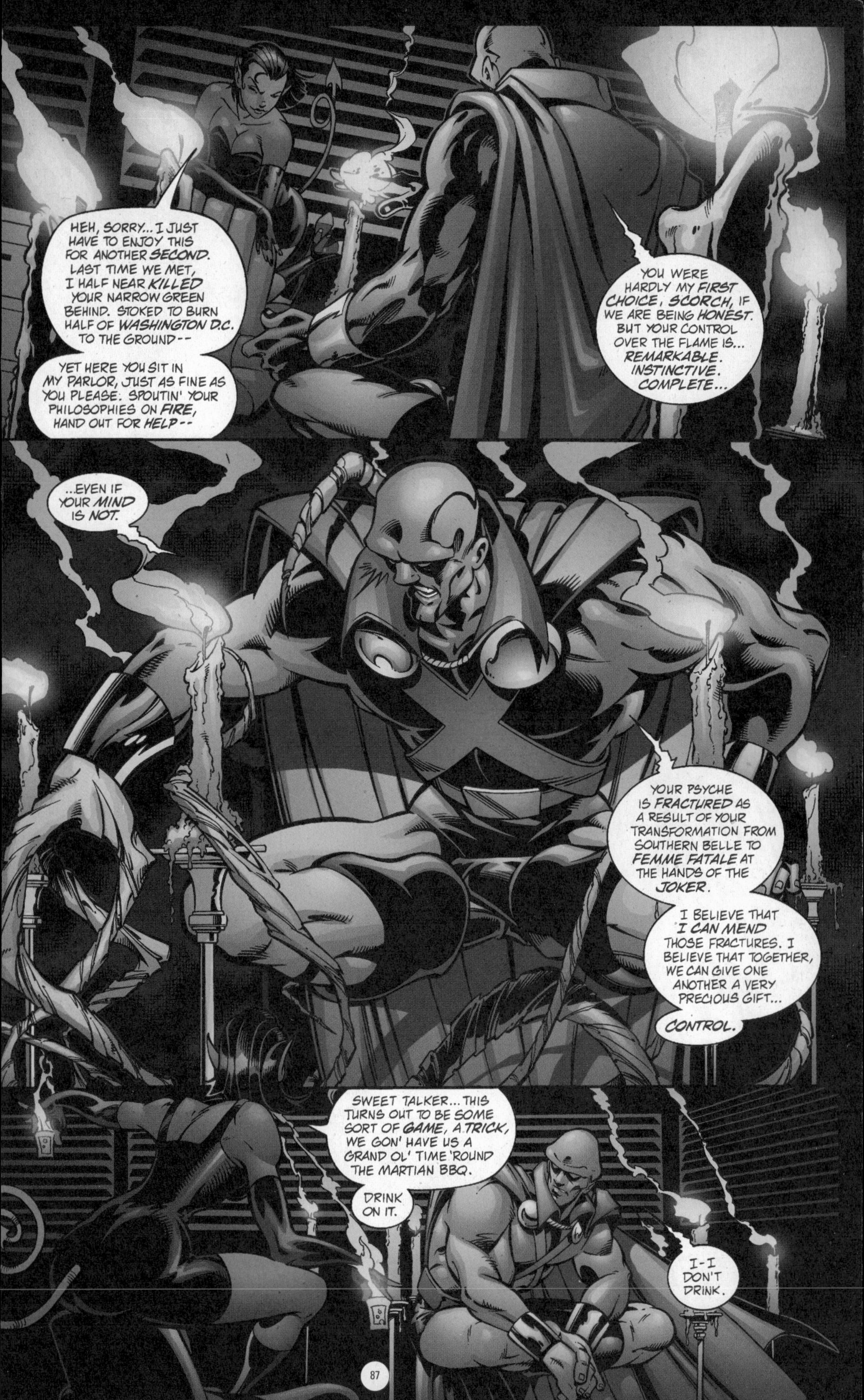
HEH, SORRY... I JUST HAVE TO ENJOY THIS FOR ANOTHER SECOND. LAST TIME WE MET, I HALF NEAR KILLED YOUR NARROW GREEN BEHIND. STOKED TO BURN HALF OF WASHINGTON D.C. TO THE GROUND--
YET HERE YOU SIT IN MY PARLOR, JUST AS FINE AS YOU PLEASE: SPOUTIN' YOUR PHILOSOPHIES ON FIRE, HAND OUT FOR HELP--
YOU WERE HARDLY MY FIRST CHOICE, SCORCH, IF WE ARE BEING HONEST. BUT YOUR CONTROL OVER THE FLAME IS... REMARKABLE. INSTINCTIVE. COMPLETE...
...EVEN IF YOUR MIND IS NOT.
YOUR PSYCHE IS FRACTURED AS A RESULT OF YOUR TRANSFORMATION FROM SOUTHERN BELLE TO FEMME FATALE AT THE HANDS OF THE JOKER.
I BELIEVE THAT I CAN MEND THOSE FRACTURES. I BELIEVE THAT TOGETHER, WE CAN GIVE ONE ANOTHER A VERY PRECIOUS GIFT...
CONTROL.
SWEET TALKER... THIS TURNS OUT TO BE SOME SORT OF GAME, A TRICK, WE GON' HAVE US A GRAND OL' TIME 'ROUND THE MARTIAN BBQ.
DRINK ON IT.
I-I DON'T DRINK.

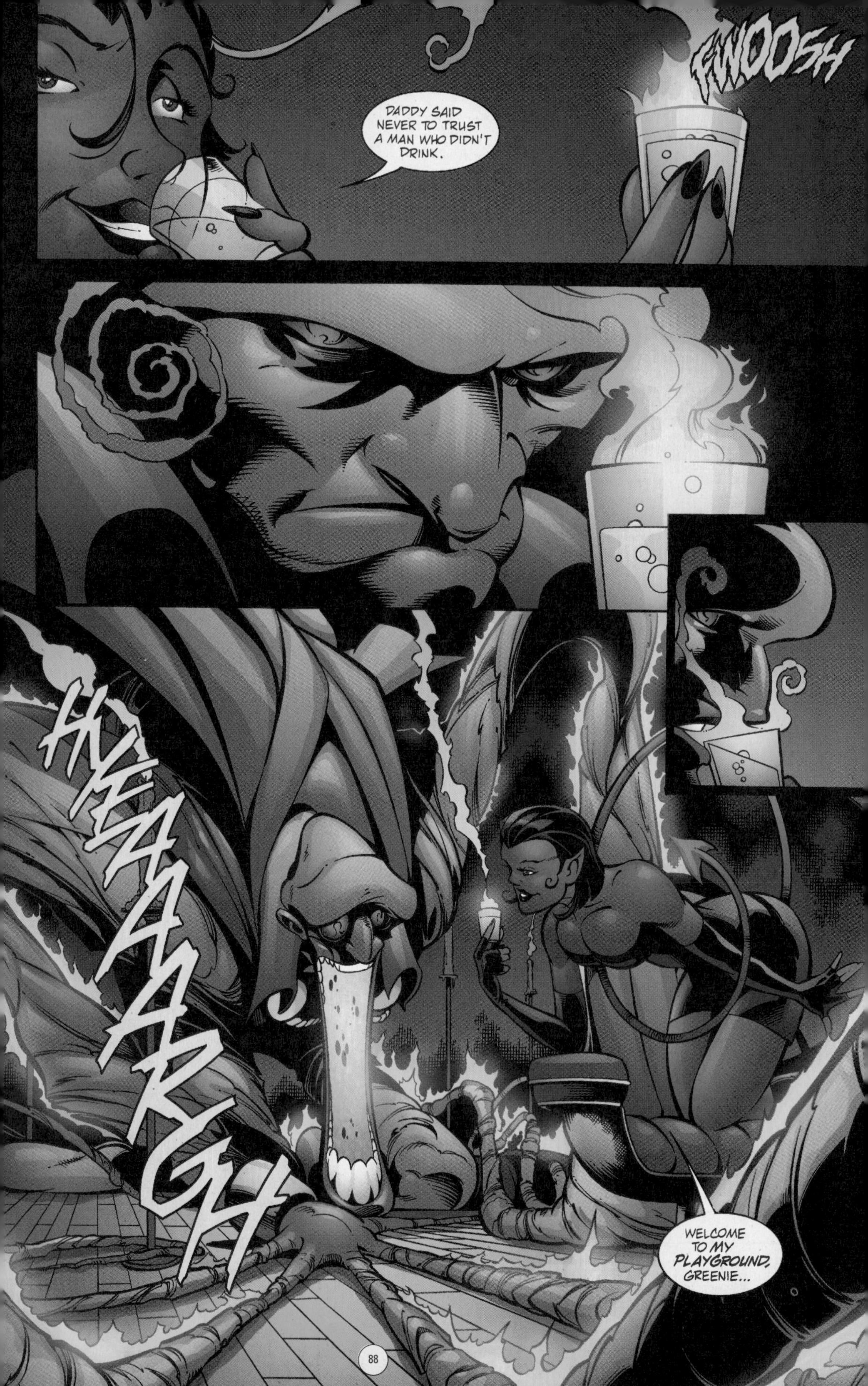
FWOOSH
DADDY SAID NEVER TO TRUST A MAN WHO DIDN'T DRINK.
HWAAARGH
WELCOME TO MY PLAYGROUND, GREENIE...

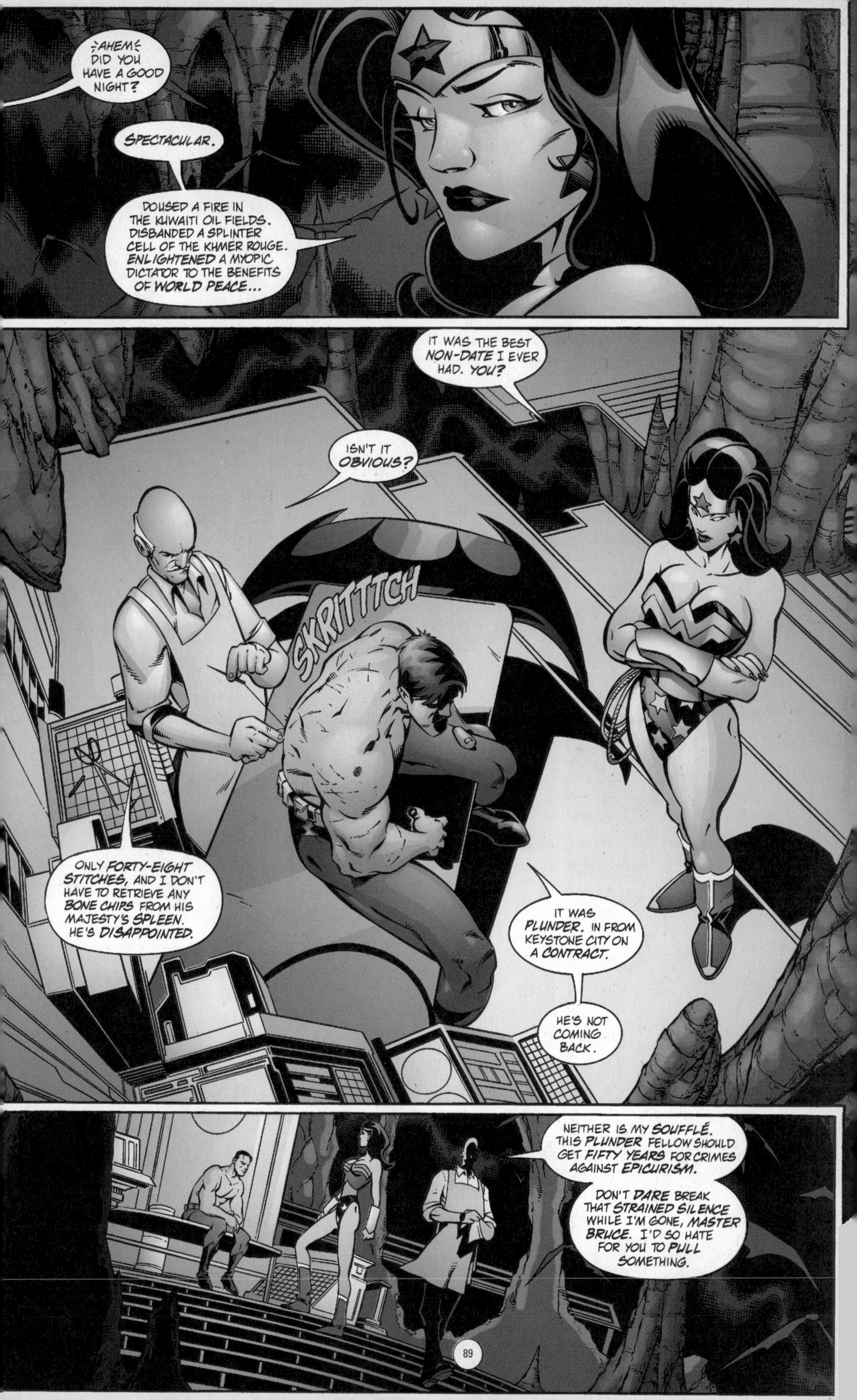

-AHEM- DID YOU HAVE A GOOD NIGHT?
SPECTACULAR.
DOUSED A FIRE IN THE KUWAITI OIL FIELDS. DISBANDED A SPLINTER CELL OF THE KHMER ROUGE. ENLIGHTENED A MYOPIC DICTATOR TO THE BENEFITS OF WORLD PEACE...
IT WAS THE BEST NON-DATE I EVER HAD. YOU?
ISN'T IT OBVIOUS?
SKRITTTCH
ONLY FORTY-EIGHT STITCHES, AND I DON'T HAVE TO RETRIEVE ANY BONE CHIPS FROM HIS MAJESTY'S SPLEEN. HE'S DISAPPOINTED.
IT WAS PLUNDER. IN FROM KEYSTONE CITY ON A CONTRACT.
HE'S NOT COMING BACK.
NEITHER IS MY SOUFFLÉ. THIS PLUNDER FELLOW SHOULD GET FIFTY YEARS FOR CRIMES AGAINST EPICURISM.
DON'T DARE BREAK THAT STRAINED SILENCE WHILE I'M GONE, MASTER BRUCE. I'D SO HATE FOR YOU TO PULL SOMETHING.

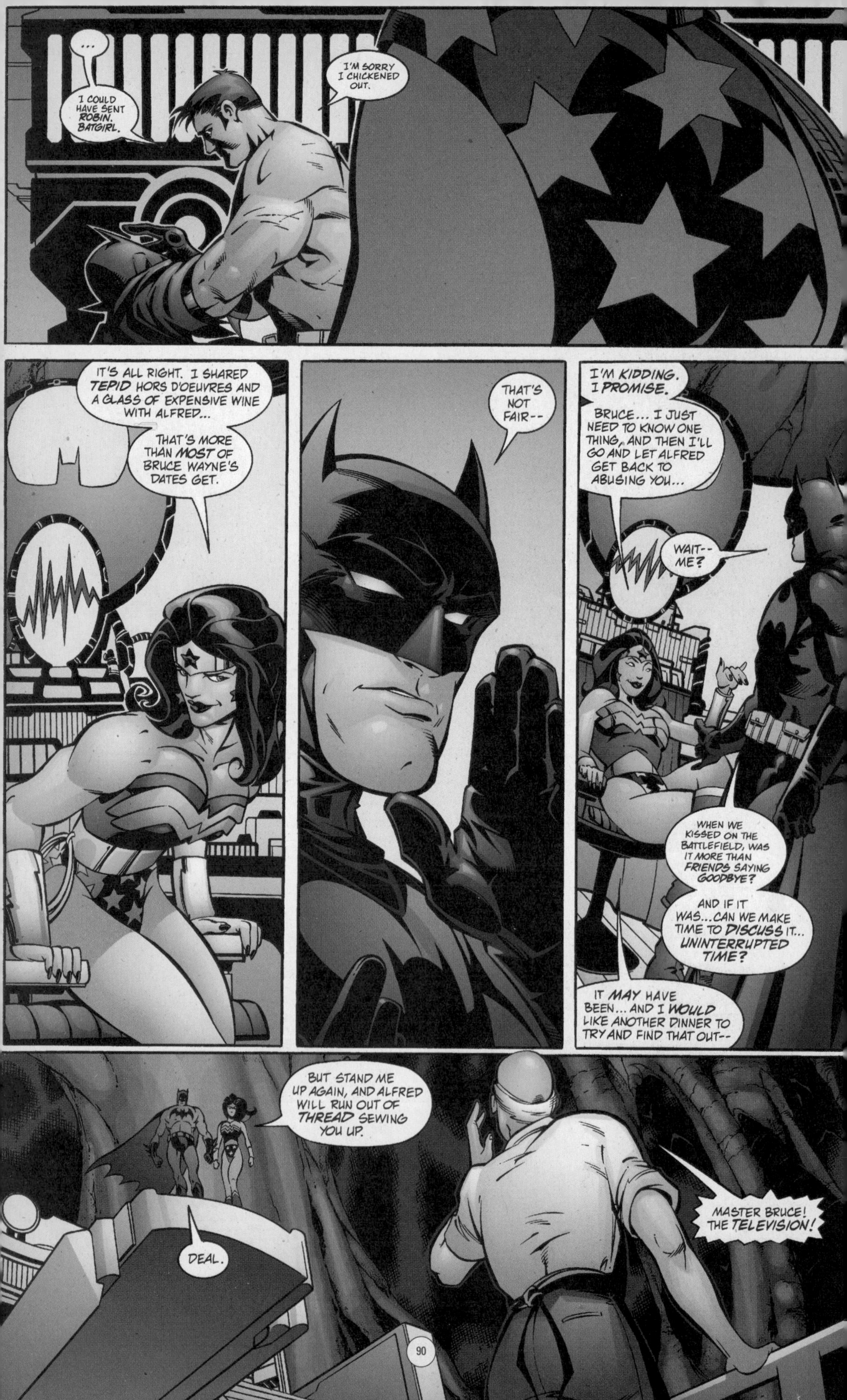
...
I COULD HAVE SENT ROBIN. BATGIRL.
I'M SORRY I CHICKENED OUT.
IT'S ALL RIGHT. I SHARED TEPID HORS D'OEUVRES AND A GLASS OF EXPENSIVE WINE WITH ALFRED...
THAT'S MORE THAN MOST OF BRUCE WAYNE'S DATES GET.
THAT'S NOT FAIR--
I'M KIDDING. I PROMISE.
BRUCE... I JUST NEED TO KNOW ONE THING, AND THEN I'LL GO AND LET ALFRED GET BACK TO ABUSING YOU...
WAIT-- ME?
WHEN WE KISSED ON THE BATTLEFIELD, WAS IT MORE THAN FRIENDS SAYING GOODBYE?
AND IF IT WAS... CAN WE MAKE TIME TO DISCUSS IT... UNINTERRUPTED TIME?
IT MAY HAVE BEEN... AND I WOULD LIKE ANOTHER DINNER TO TRY AND FIND THAT OUT--
BUT STAND ME UP AGAIN, AND ALFRED WILL RUN OUT OF THREAD SEWING YOU UP.
DEAL.
MASTER BRUCE! THE TELEVISION!

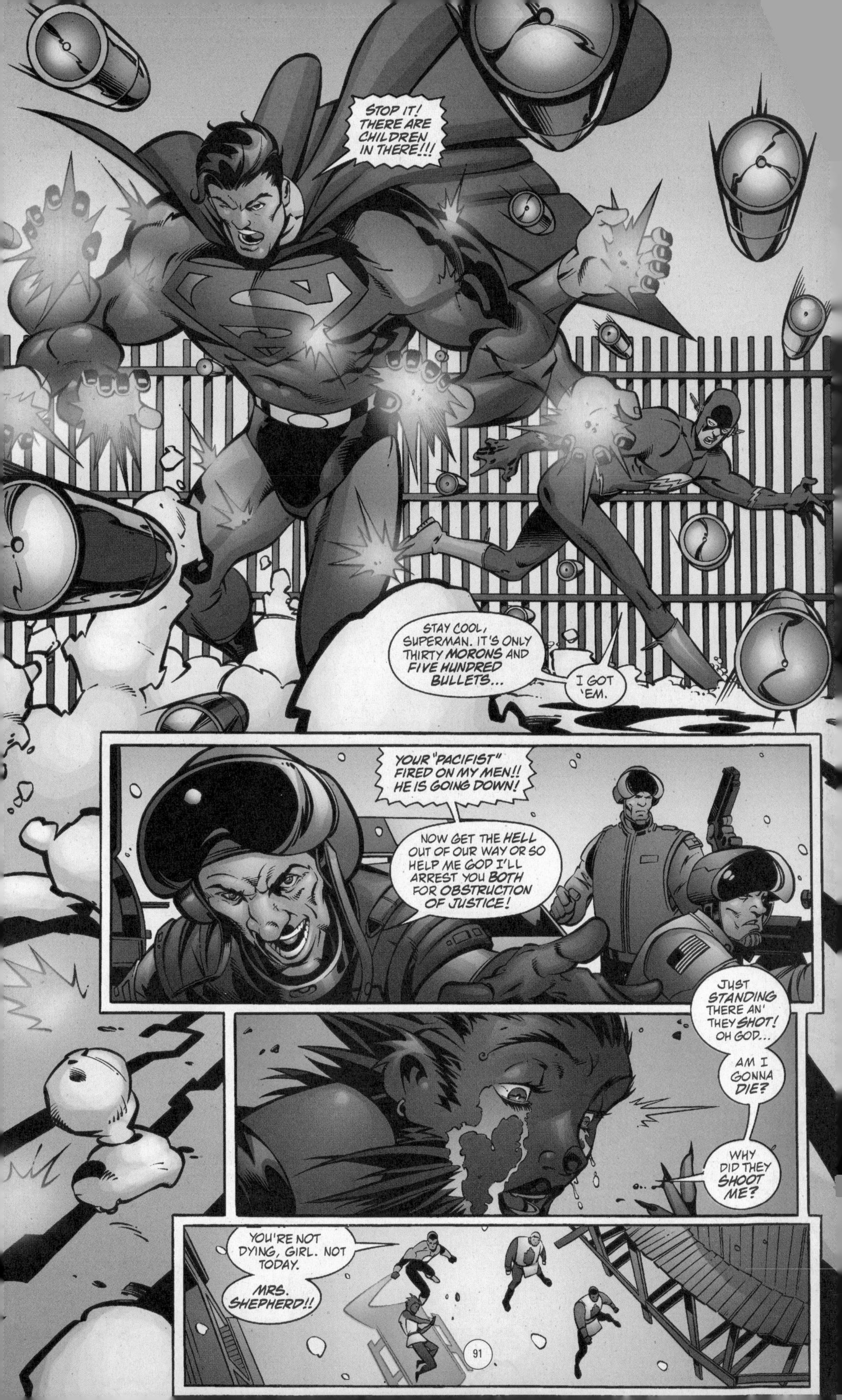
STOP IT! THERE ARE CHILDREN IN THERE!!!
STAY COOL, SUPERMAN. IT'S ONLY THIRTY MORONS AND FIVE HUNDRED BULLETS...
I GOT 'EM.
YOUR "PACIFIST" FIRED ON MY MEN!! HE IS GOING DOWN!
NOW GET THE HELL OUT OF OUR WAY OR SO HELP ME GOD I'LL ARREST YOU BOTH FOR OBSTRUCTION OF JUSTICE!
JUST STANDING THERE AN' THEY SHOT! OH GOD...
AM I GONNA DIE?
WHY DID THEY SHOOT ME?
YOU'RE NOT DYING, GIRL. NOT TODAY.
MRS. SHEPHERD!!

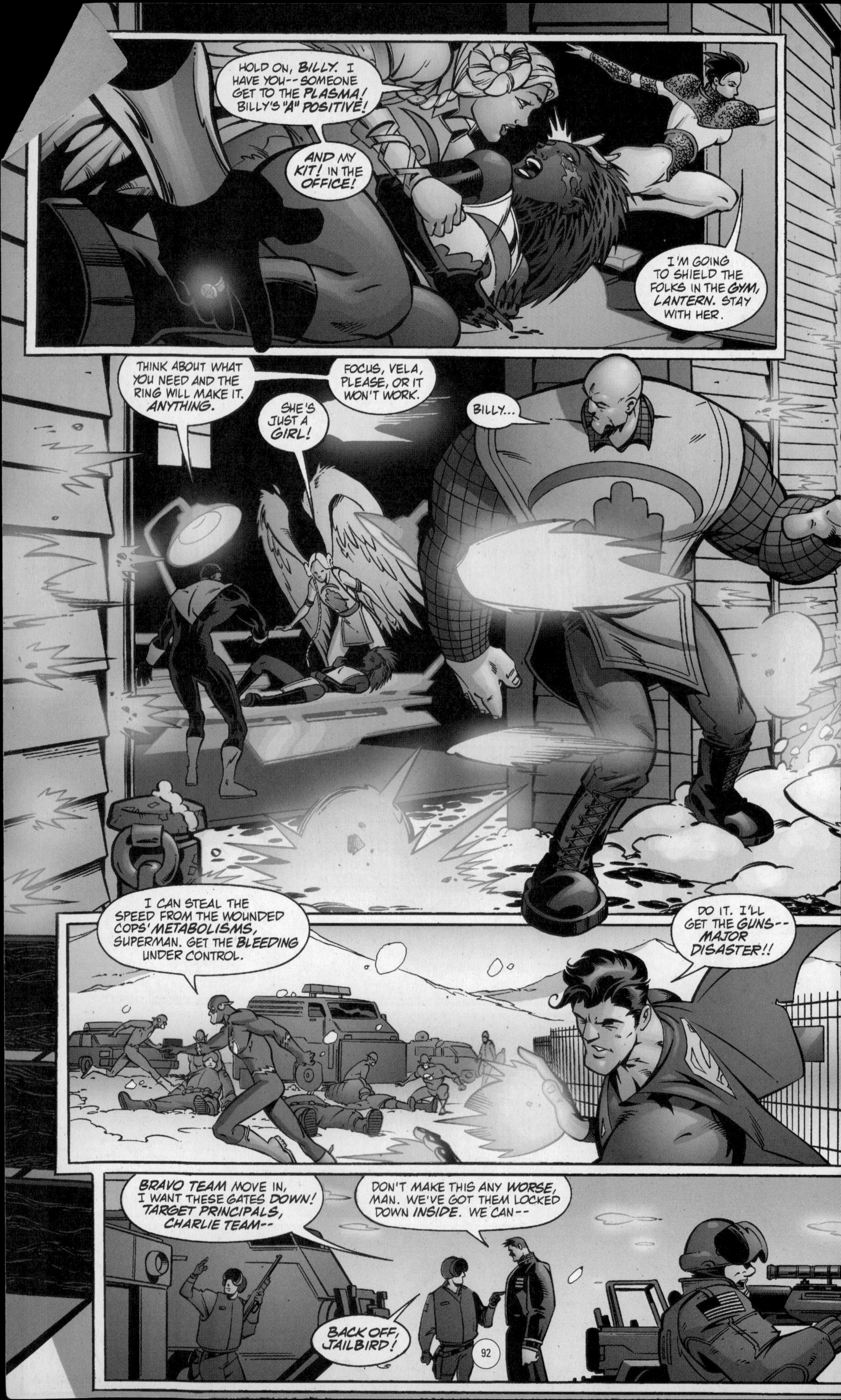
HOLD ON, BILLY. I HAVE YOU--SOMEONE GET TO THE PLASMA! BILLY'S "A" POSITIVE!
AND MY KIT! IN THE OFFICE!
I'M GOING TO SHIELD THE FOLKS IN THE GYM, LANTERN. STAY WITH HER.
THINK ABOUT WHAT YOU NEED AND THE RING WILL MAKE IT. ANYTHING.
FOCUS, VELA, PLEASE, OR IT WON'T WORK.
SHE'S JUST A GIRL!
BILLY...
I CAN STEAL THE SPEED FROM THE WOUNDED COPS' METABOLISMS, SUPERMAN. GET THE BLEEDING UNDER CONTROL.
DO IT. I'LL GET THE GUNS--MAJOR DISASTER!!
BRAVO TEAM MOVE IN, I WANT THESE GATES DOWN! TARGET PRINCIPALS, CHARLIE TEAM--
DON'T MAKE THIS ANY WORSE, MAN. WE'VE GOT THEM LOCKED DOWN INSIDE. WE CAN--
BACK OFF, JAILBIRD!

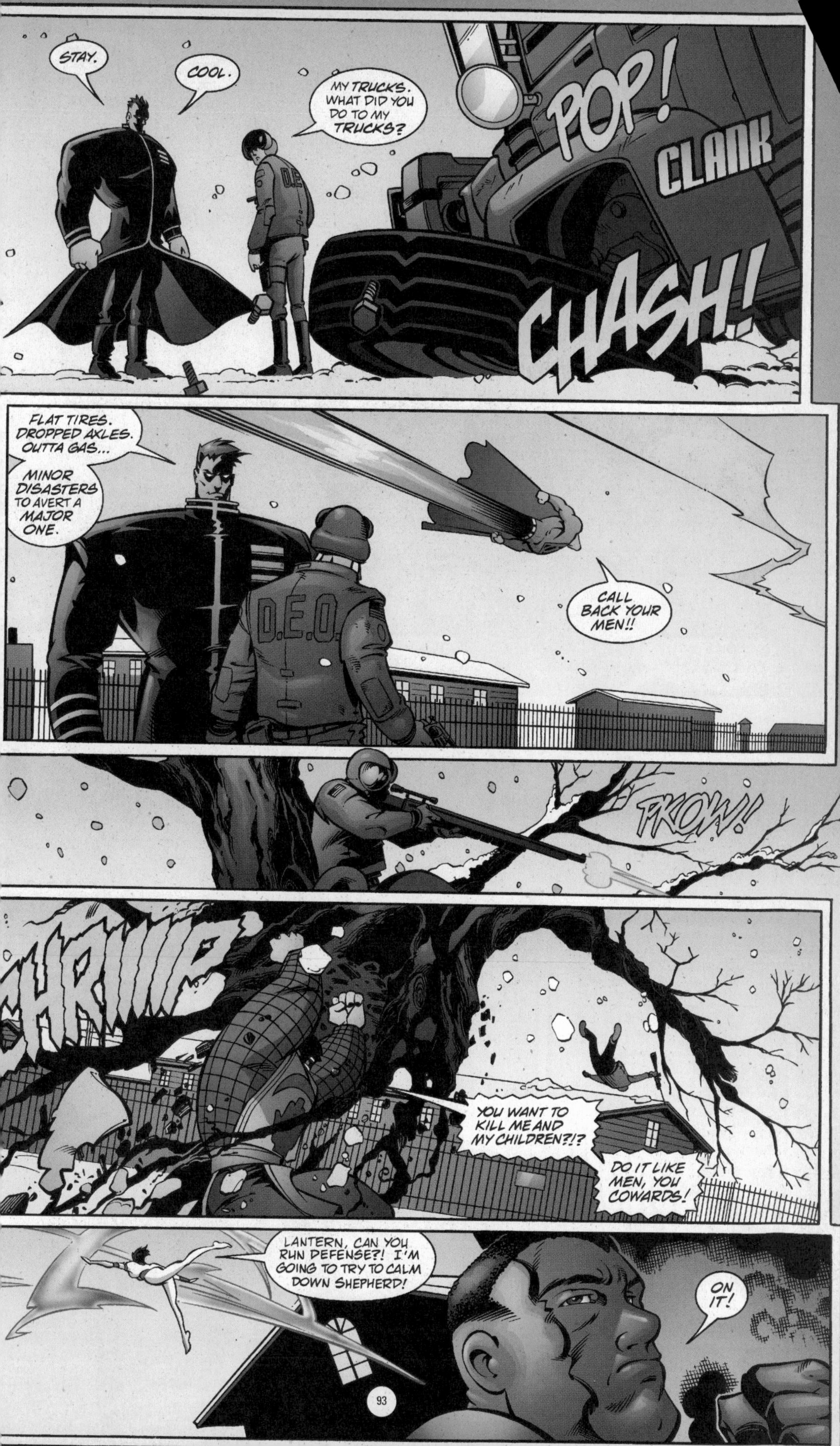
STAY.
COOL.
MY TRUCKS. WHAT DID YOU DO TO MY TRUCKS?
POP!
CLANK
CHASH!
FLAT TIRES. DROPPED AXLES. OUTTA GAS...
MINOR DISASTERS TO AVERT A MAJOR ONE.
D.E.O.
CALL BACK YOUR MEN!!
PKOW!
SHRUUP
YOU WANT TO KILL ME AND MY CHILDREN?!?
DO IT LIKE MEN, YOU COWARDS!
LANTERN, CAN YOU RUN DEFENSE?! I'M GOING TO TRY TO CALM DOWN SHEPHERD!
ON IT!

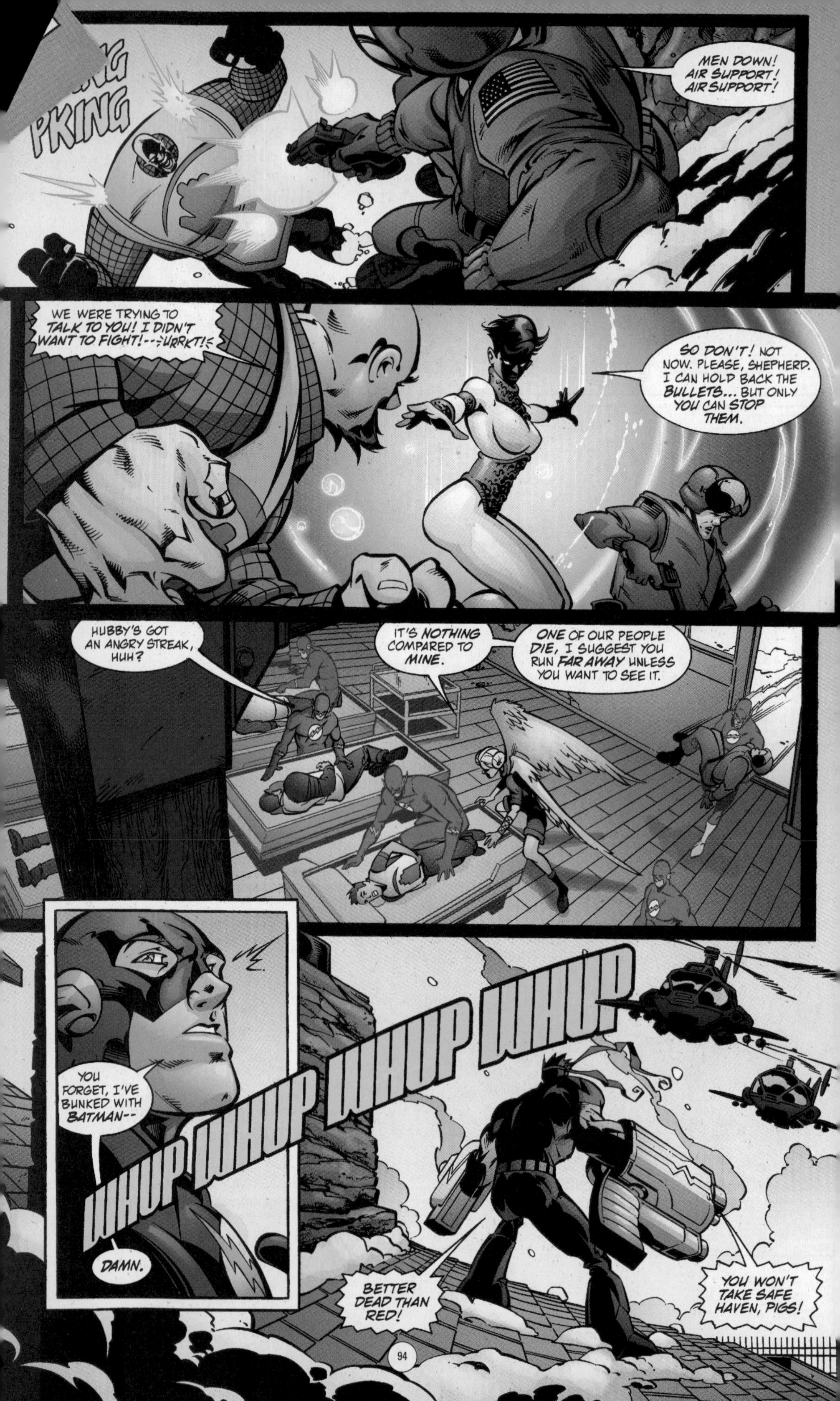
PKING
MEN DOWN! AIR SUPPORT! AIR SUPPORT!
WE WERE TRYING TO TALK TO YOU! I DIDN'T WANT TO FIGHT!--URRKT!
SO DON'T! NOT NOW. PLEASE, SHEPHERD. I CAN HOLD BACK THE BULLETS... BUT ONLY YOU CAN STOP THEM.
HUBBY'S GOT AN ANGRY STREAK, HUH?
IT'S NOTHING COMPARED TO MINE.
ONE OF OUR PEOPLE DIE, I SUGGEST YOU RUN FAR AWAY UNLESS YOU WANT TO SEE IT.
YOU FORGET, I'VE BUNKED WITH BATMAN--
DAMN.
WHUP WHUP WHUP WHUP
BETTER DEAD THAN RED!
YOU WON'T TAKE SAFE HAVEN, PIGS!

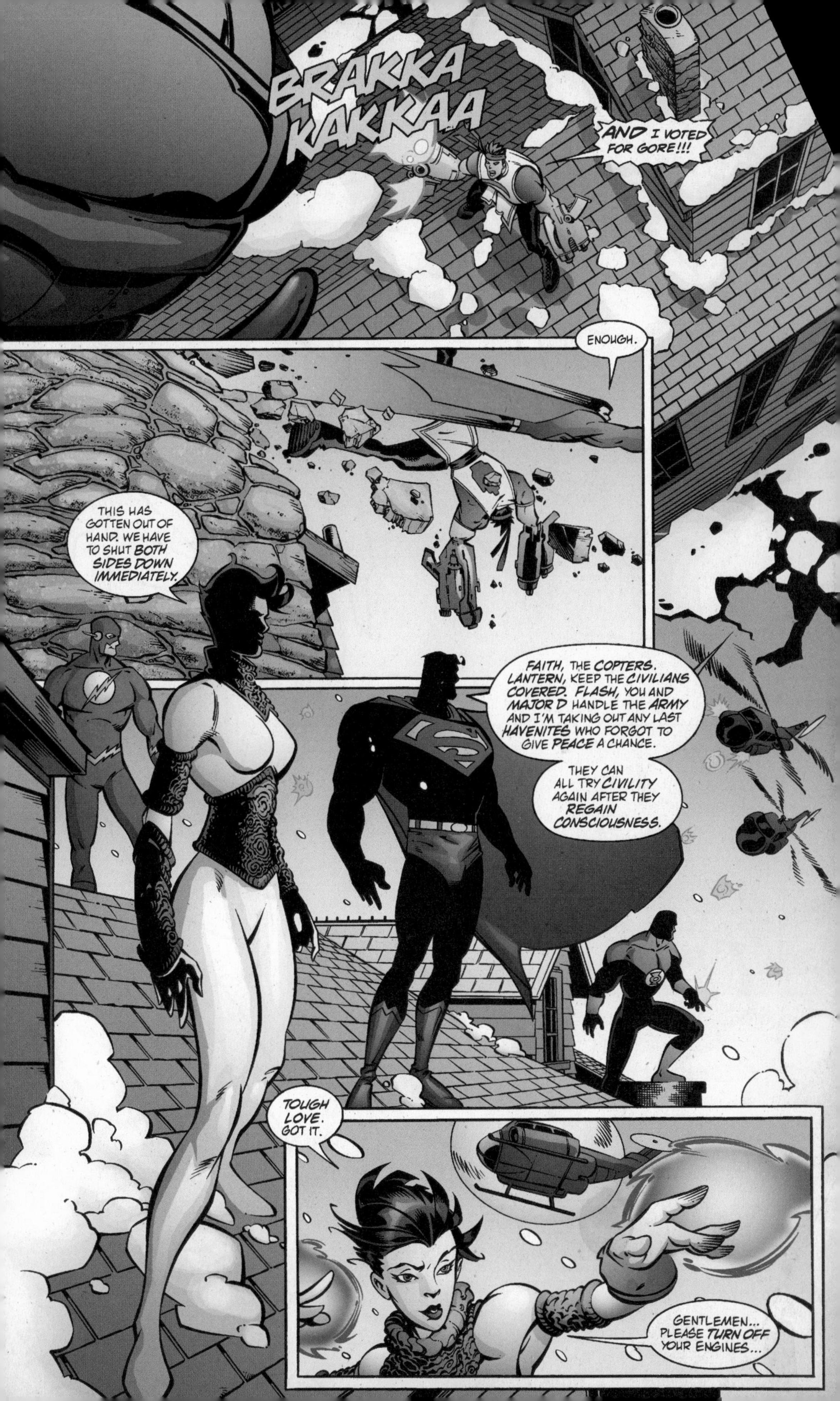
BRAKKA KAKKAA
AND I VOTED FOR GORE!!!
ENOUGH.
THIS HAS GOTTEN OUT OF HAND. WE HAVE TO SHUT BOTH SIDES DOWN IMMEDIATELY.
FAITH, THE COPTERS. LANTERN, KEEP THE CIVILIANS COVERED. FLASH, YOU AND MAJOR D HANDLE THE ARMY AND I'M TAKING OUT ANY LAST HAVENITES WHO FORGOT TO GIVE PEACE A CHANCE.
THEY CAN ALL TRY CIVILITY AGAIN AFTER THEY REGAIN CONSCIOUSNESS.
TOUGH LOVE. GOT IT.
GENTLEMEN... PLEASE TURN OFF YOUR ENGINES...

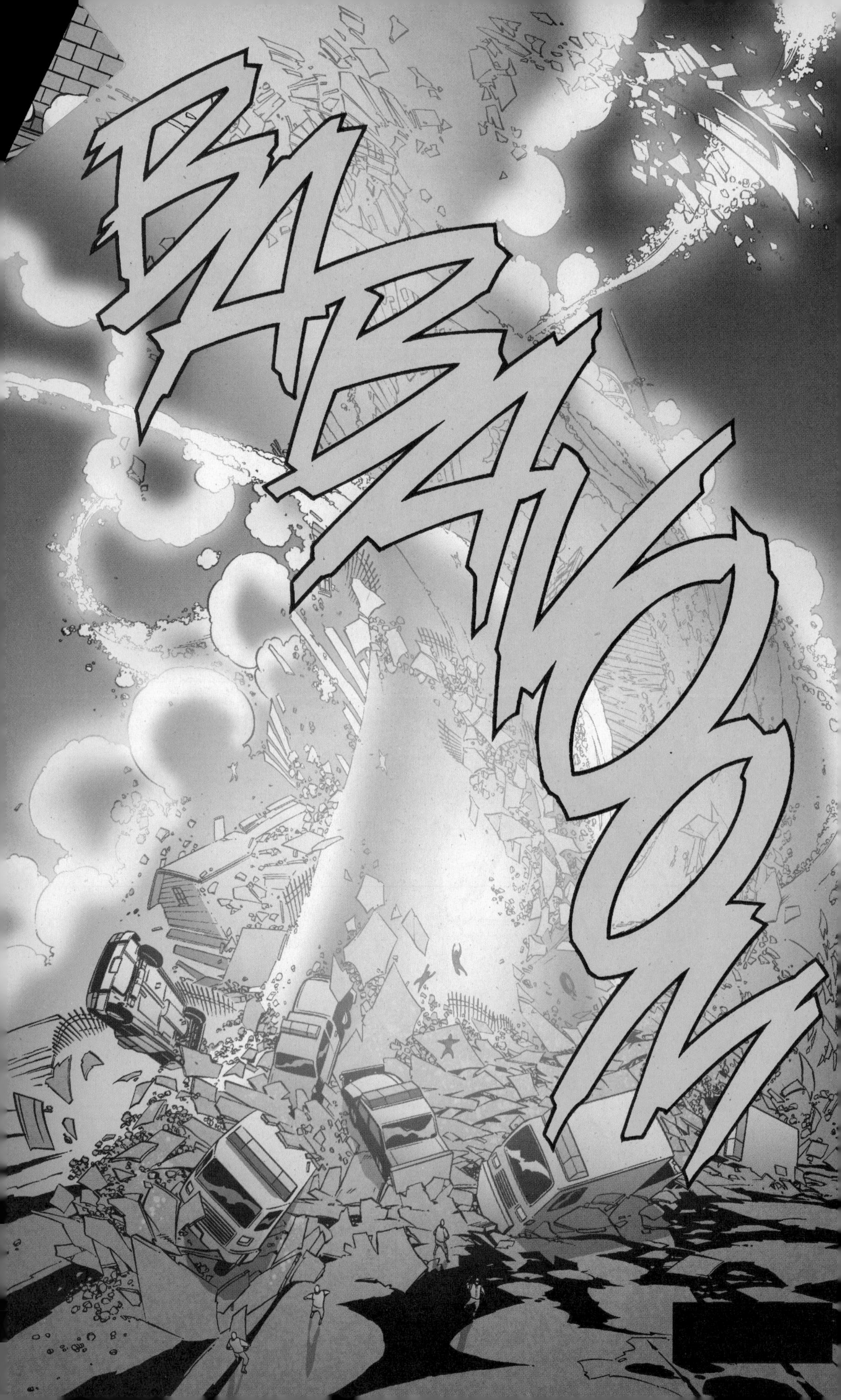
BABANOOM

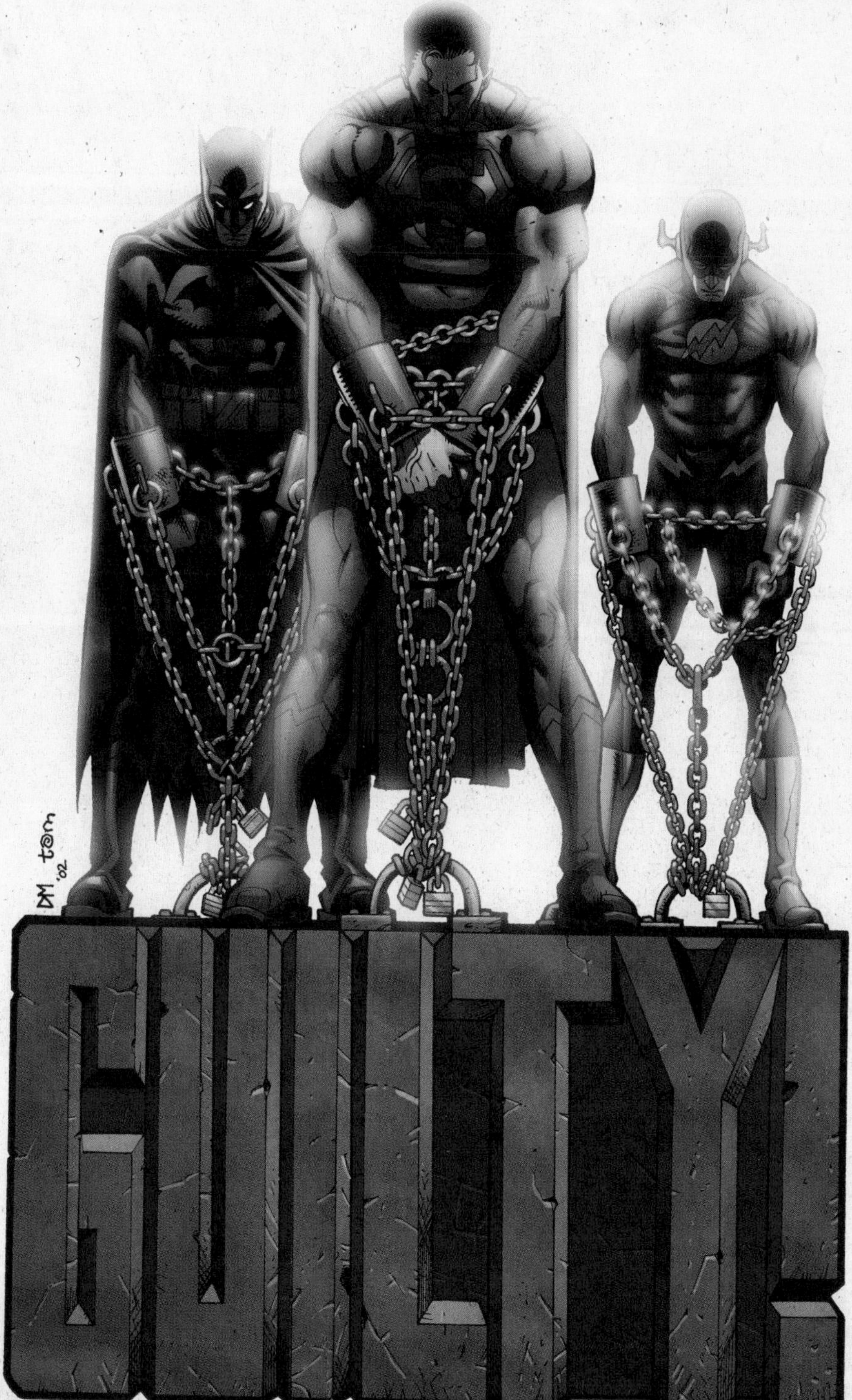
GUILTY!

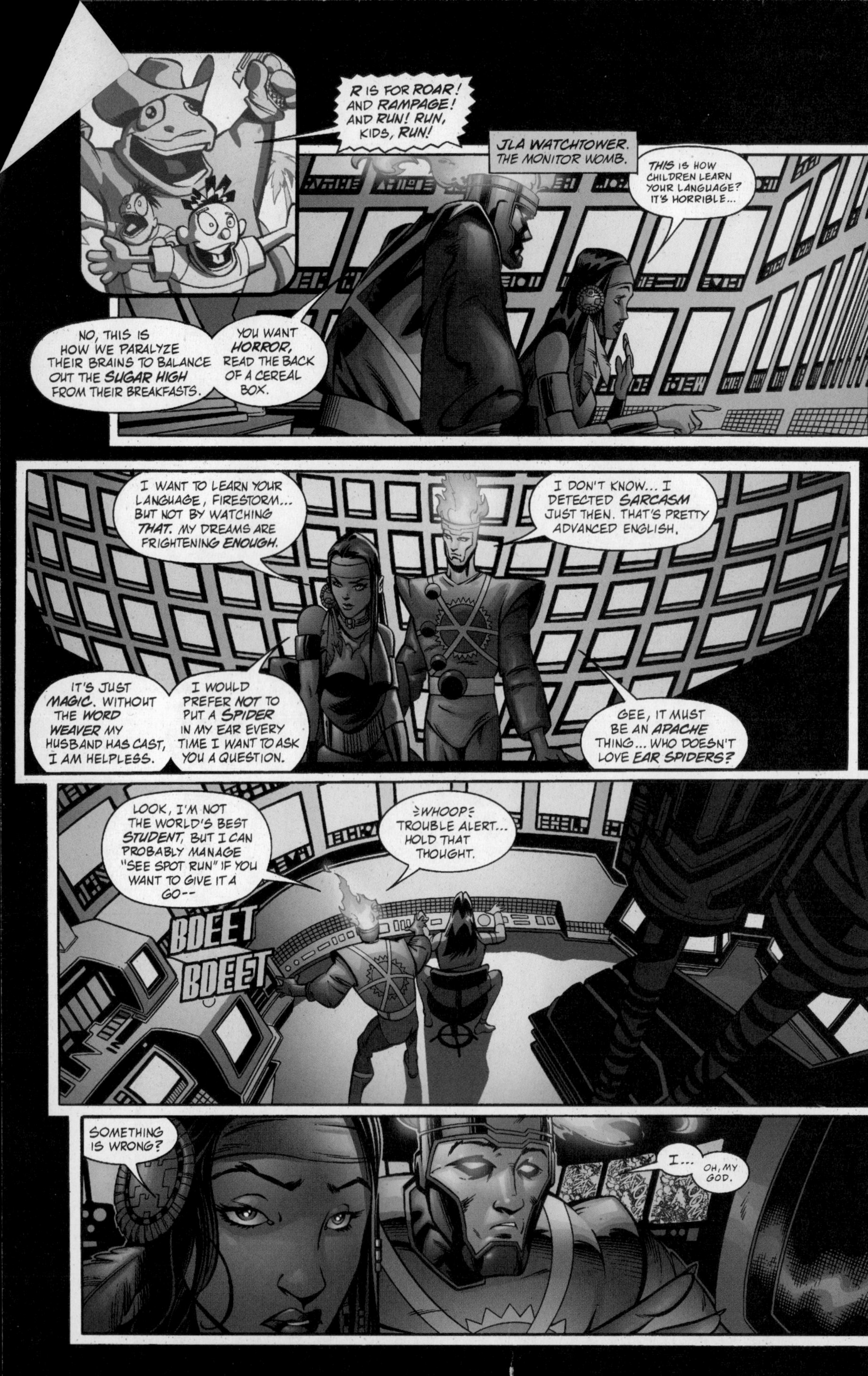
R IS FOR ROAR! AND RAMPAGE! AND RUN! RUN, KIDS, RUN!
JLA WATCHTOWER. THE MONITOR WOMB.
THIS IS HOW CHILDREN LEARN YOUR LANGUAGE? IT'S HORRIBLE...
YOU WANT HORROR, READ THE BACK OF A CEREAL BOX.
NO, THIS IS HOW WE PARALYZE THEIR BRAINS TO BALANCE OUT THE SUGAR HIGH FROM THEIR BREAKFASTS.
I WANT TO LEARN YOUR LANGUAGE, FIRESTORM... BUT NOT BY WATCHING THAT. MY DREAMS ARE FRIGHTENING ENOUGH.
I DON'T KNOW... I DETECTED SARCASM JUST THEN. THAT'S PRETTY ADVANCED ENGLISH.
IT'S JUST MAGIC. WITHOUT THE WORD WEAVER MY HUSBAND HAS CAST, I AM HELPLESS.
I WOULD PREFER NOT TO PUT A SPIDER IN MY EAR EVERY TIME I WANT TO ASK YOU A QUESTION.
GEE, IT MUST BE AN APACHE THING... WHO DOESN'T LOVE EAR SPIDERS?
LOOK, I'M NOT THE WORLD'S BEST STUDENT, BUT I CAN PROBABLY MANAGE "SEE SPOT RUN" IF YOU WANT TO GIVE IT A GO--
WHOOP TROUBLE ALERT... HOLD THAT THOUGHT.
BDEET
BDEET
SOMETHING IS WRONG?
I... OH, MY GOD.

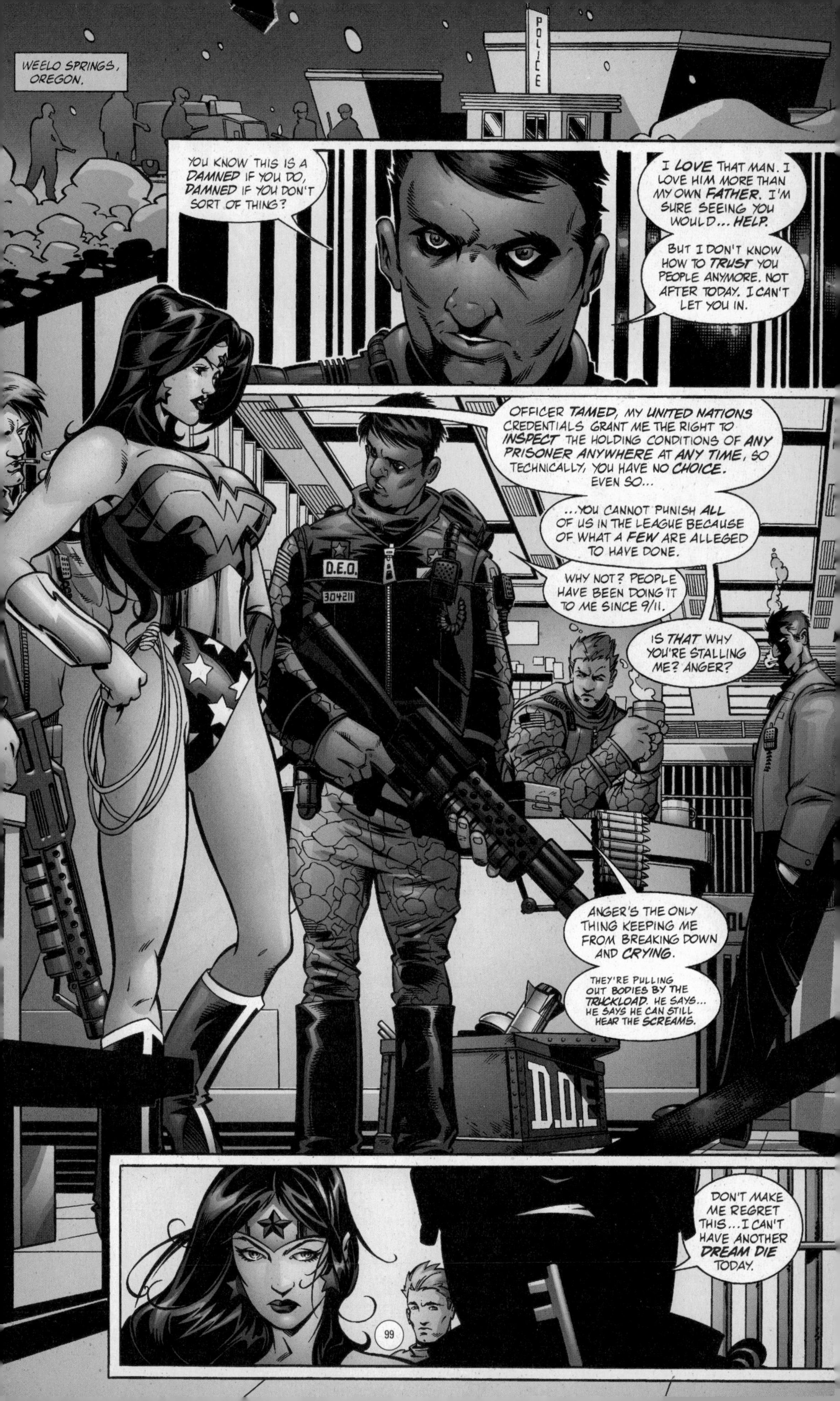
WEELO SPRINGS, OREGON.
POLICE
YOU KNOW THIS IS A DAMNED IF YOU DO, DAMNED IF YOU DON'T SORT OF THING?
I LOVE THAT MAN. I LOVE HIM MORE THAN MY OWN FATHER. I'M SURE SEEING YOU WOULD... HELP.
BUT I DON'T KNOW HOW TO TRUST YOU PEOPLE ANYMORE. NOT AFTER TODAY. I CAN'T LET YOU IN.
OFFICER TAMED, MY UNITED NATIONS CREDENTIALS GRANT ME THE RIGHT TO INSPECT THE HOLDING CONDITIONS OF ANY PRISONER ANYWHERE AT ANY TIME, SO TECHNICALLY, YOU HAVE NO CHOICE. EVEN SO...
...YOU CANNOT PUNISH ALL OF US IN THE LEAGUE BECAUSE OF WHAT A FEW ARE ALLEGED TO HAVE DONE.
WHY NOT? PEOPLE HAVE BEEN DOING IT TO ME SINCE 9/11.
IS THAT WHY YOU'RE STALLING ME? ANGER?
D.E.O.
304211
ANGER'S THE ONLY THING KEEPING ME FROM BREAKING DOWN AND CRYING.
THEY'RE PULLING OUT BODIES BY THE TRUCKLOAD. HE SAYS... HE SAYS HE CAN STILL HEAR THE SCREAMS.
D.O.E
DON'T MAKE ME REGRET THIS... I CAN'T HAVE ANOTHER DREAM DIE TODAY.

THE WHITE RAGE
PART TWO

JOE	DUNCAN	AARON		DAVID BARON	KEN LOPEZ
KELLY	ROULEAU	SOWD		colorist	letterer
				VALERIE D'ORAZIO	MIKE CARLIN
writer	guest penciller	inker		assistant editor	editor

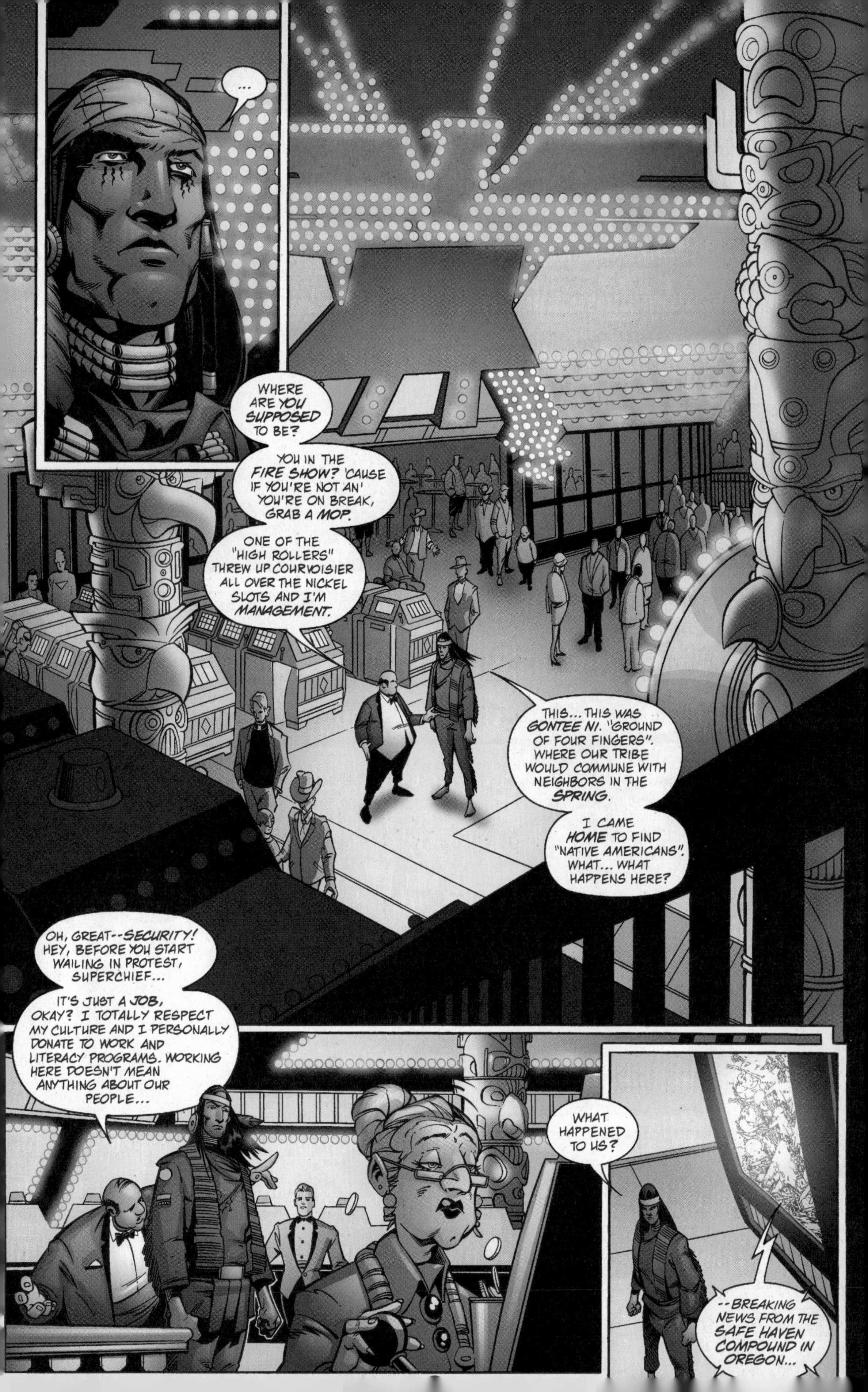
...
WHERE ARE YOU SUPPOSED TO BE?
YOU IN THE FIRE SHOW? 'CAUSE IF YOU'RE NOT AN' YOU'RE ON BREAK, GRAB A MOP.
ONE OF THE "HIGH ROLLERS" THREW UP COURVOISIER ALL OVER THE NICKEL SLOTS AND I'M MANAGEMENT.
THIS... THIS WAS GONTEE NI. "GROUND OF FOUR FINGERS". WHERE OUR TRIBE WOULD COMMUNE WITH NEIGHBORS IN THE SPRING.
I CAME HOME TO FIND "NATIVE AMERICANS". WHAT... WHAT HAPPENS HERE?
OH, GREAT--SECURITY! HEY, BEFORE YOU START WAILING IN PROTEST, SUPERCHIEF...
IT'S JUST A JOB, OKAY? I TOTALLY RESPECT MY CULTURE AND I PERSONALLY DONATE TO WORK AND LITERACY PROGRAMS. WORKING HERE DOESN'T MEAN ANYTHING ABOUT OUR PEOPLE...
WHAT HAPPENED TO US?
--BREAKING NEWS FROM THE SAFE HAVEN COMPOUND IN OREGON...

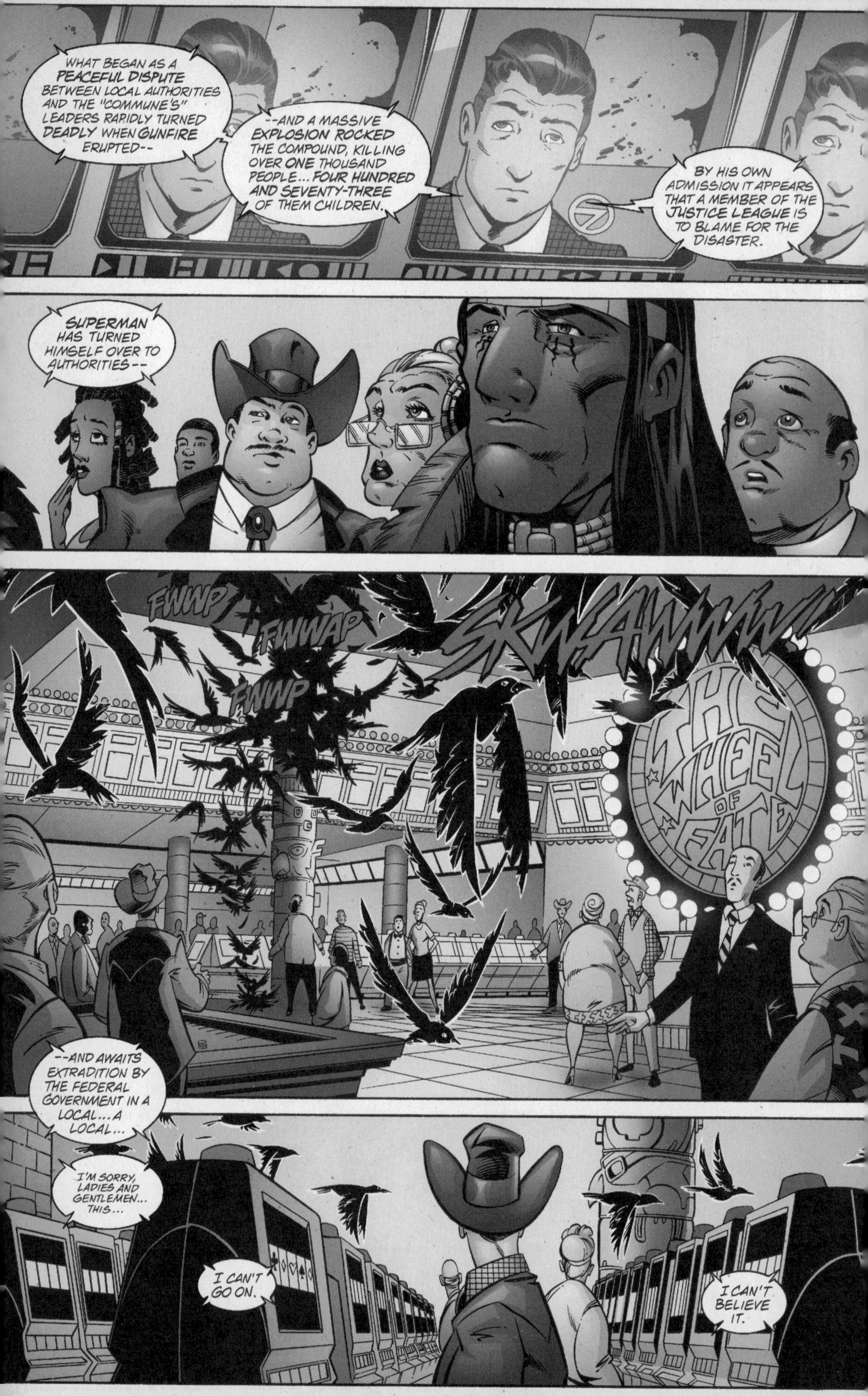
WHAT BEGAN AS A PEACEFUL DISPUTE BETWEEN LOCAL AUTHORITIES AND THE "COMMUNE'S" LEADERS RAPIDLY TURNED DEADLY WHEN GUNFIRE ERUPTED--
--AND A MASSIVE EXPLOSION ROCKED THE COMPOUND, KILLING OVER ONE THOUSAND PEOPLE... FOUR HUNDRED AND SEVENTY-THREE OF THEM CHILDREN.
BY HIS OWN ADMISSION IT APPEARS THAT A MEMBER OF THE JUSTICE LEAGUE IS TO BLAME FOR THE DISASTER.
SUPERMAN HAS TURNED HIMSELF OVER TO AUTHORITIES--
FWWP
FWWAP
SKWAWWW!
FWWP
THE WHEEL OF FATE
--AND AWAITS EXTRADITION BY THE FEDERAL GOVERNMENT IN A LOCAL... A LOCAL...
I'M SORRY, LADIES AND GENTLEMEN... THIS...
I CAN'T GO ON.
I CAN'T BELIEVE IT.

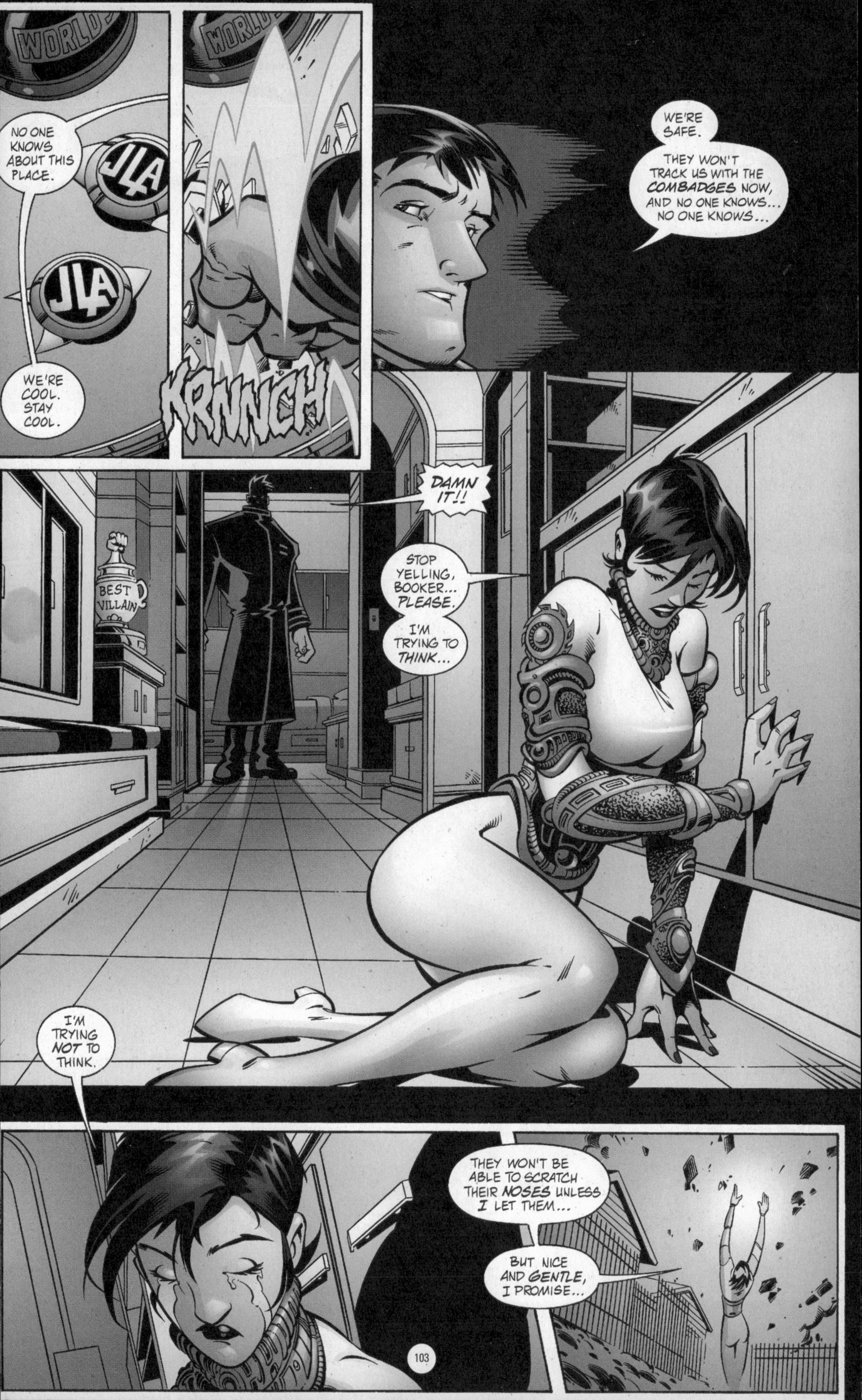
WORLD'S
NO ONE KNOWS ABOUT THIS PLACE.
WE'RE COOL. STAY COOL.
KRNNCH
WE'RE SAFE.
THEY WON'T TRACK US WITH THE COMBADGES NOW, AND NO ONE KNOWS... NO ONE KNOWS...
DAMN IT!!
BEST VILLAIN
STOP YELLING, BOOKER... PLEASE.
I'M TRYING TO THINK...
I'M TRYING NOT TO THINK.
THEY WON'T BE ABLE TO SCRATCH THEIR NOSES UNLESS I LET THEM...
BUT NICE AND GENTLE, I PROMISE...

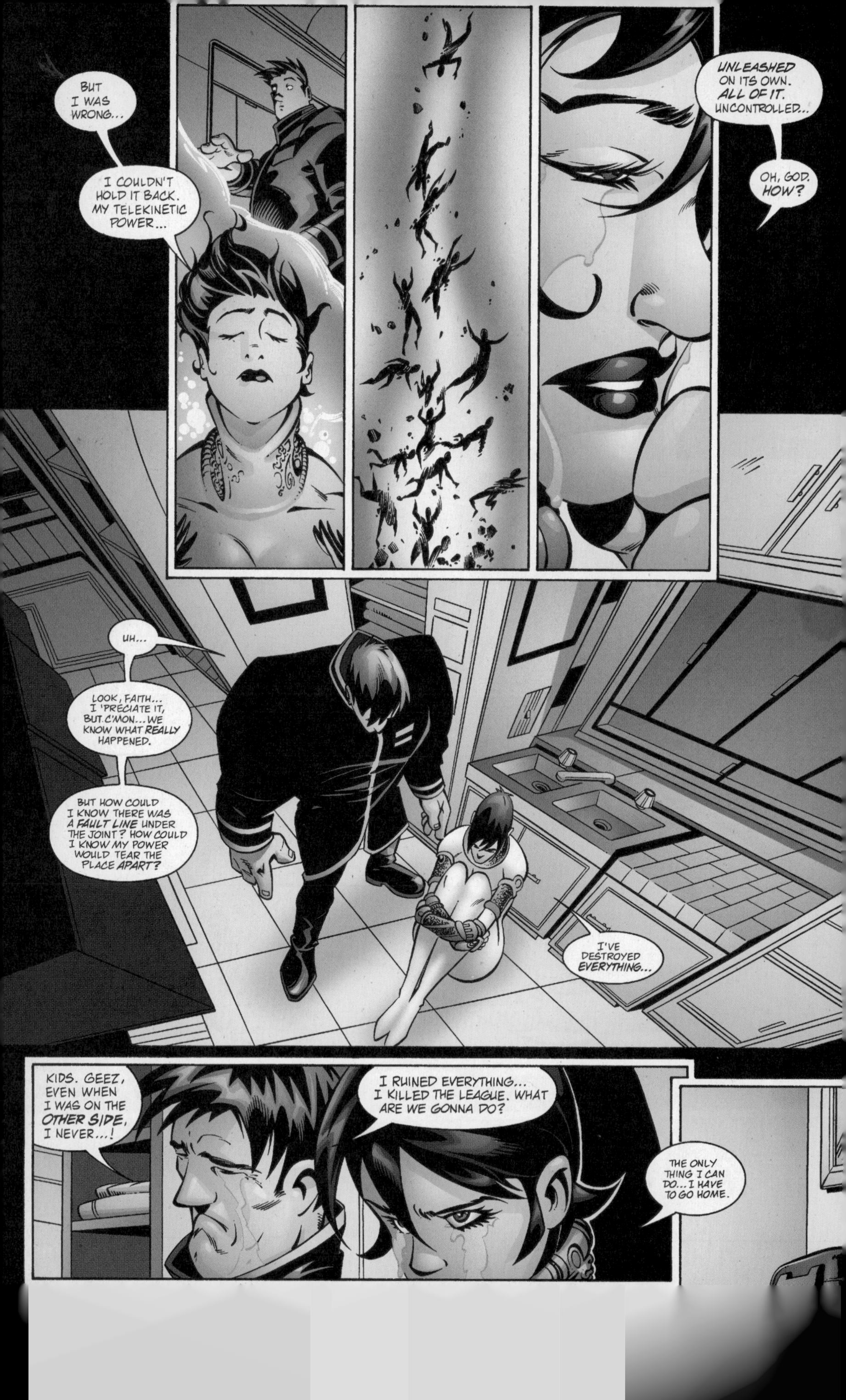

BUT I WAS WRONG...
I COULDN'T HOLD IT BACK. MY TELEKINETIC POWER...
UNLEASHED ON ITS OWN. ALL OF IT. UNCONTROLLED...
OH, GOD. HOW?
UH...
LOOK, FAITH... I 'PRECIATE IT, BUT, C'MON... WE KNOW WHAT REALLY HAPPENED.
BUT HOW COULD I KNOW THERE WAS A FAULT LINE UNDER THE JOINT? HOW COULD I KNOW MY POWER WOULD TEAR THE PLACE APART?
I'VE DESTROYED EVERYTHING...
KIDS. GEEZ, EVEN WHEN I WAS ON THE OTHER SIDE, I NEVER...!
I RUINED EVERYTHING... I KILLED THE LEAGUE. WHAT ARE WE GONNA DO?
THE ONLY THING I CAN DO... I HAVE TO GO HOME.

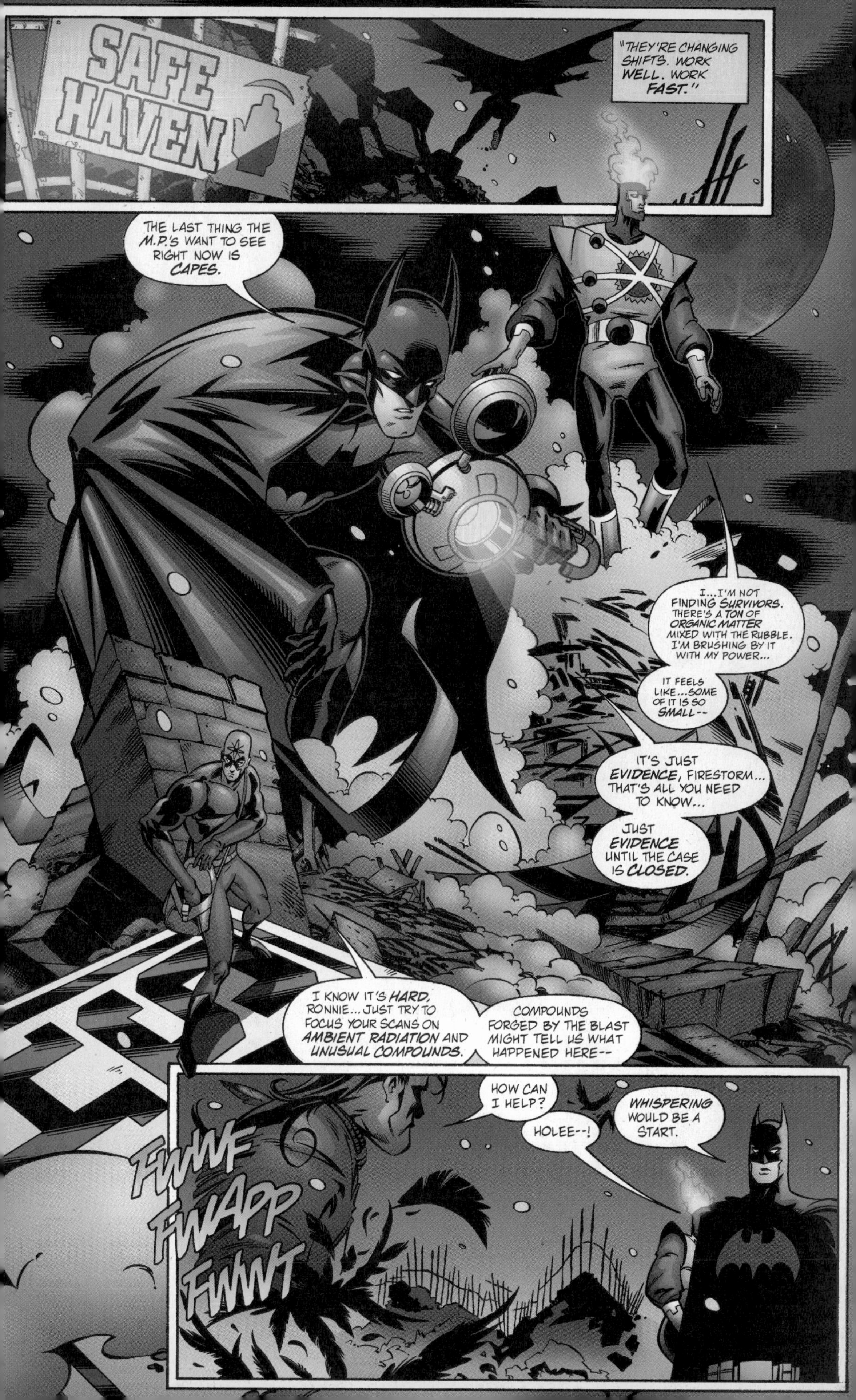
SAFE HAVEN
"THEY'RE CHANGING SHIFTS. WORK WELL. WORK FAST."
THE LAST THING THE M.P.'S WANT TO SEE RIGHT NOW IS CAPES.
I...I'M NOT FINDING SURVIVORS. THERE'S A TON OF ORGANIC MATTER MIXED WITH THE RUBBLE. I'M BRUSHING BY IT WITH MY POWER...
IT FEELS LIKE...SOME OF IT IS SO SMALL--
IT'S JUST EVIDENCE, FIRESTORM... THAT'S ALL YOU NEED TO KNOW...
JUST EVIDENCE UNTIL THE CASE IS CLOSED.
I KNOW IT'S HARD, RONNIE... JUST TRY TO FOCUS YOUR SCANS ON AMBIENT RADIATION AND UNUSUAL COMPOUNDS.
COMPOUNDS FORGED BY THE BLAST MIGHT TELL US WHAT HAPPENED HERE--
FWWF FWAPP FWWT
HOW CAN I HELP?
HOLEE--!
WHISPERING WOULD BE A START.

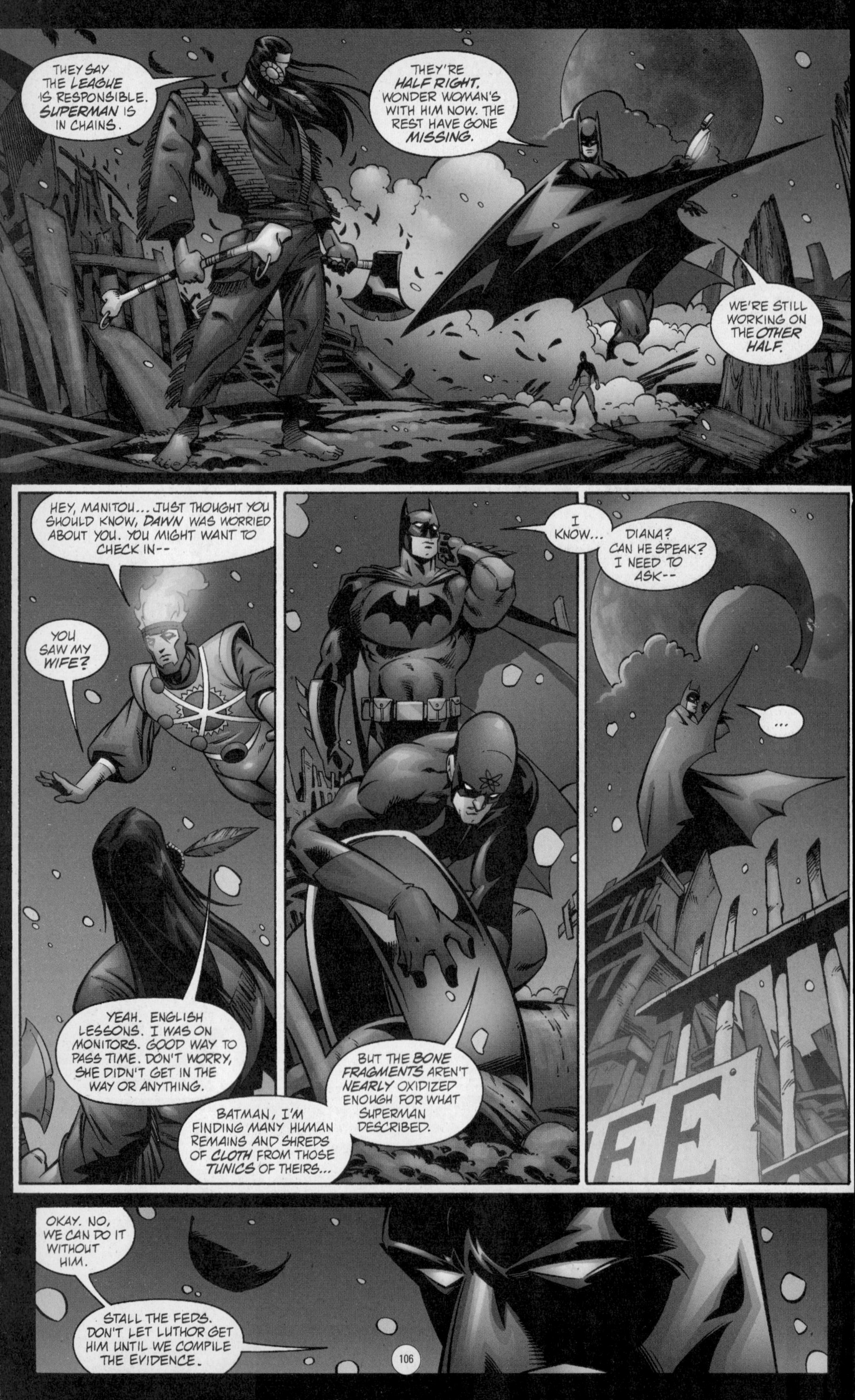

THEY SAY THE LEAGUE IS RESPONSIBLE. SUPERMAN IS IN CHAINS.
THEY'RE HALF RIGHT. WONDER WOMAN'S WITH HIM NOW. THE REST HAVE GONE MISSING.
WE'RE STILL WORKING ON THE OTHER HALF.
HEY, MANITOU... JUST THOUGHT YOU SHOULD KNOW, DAWN WAS WORRIED ABOUT YOU. YOU MIGHT WANT TO CHECK IN--
YOU SAW MY WIFE?
YEAH. ENGLISH LESSONS. I WAS ON MONITORS. GOOD WAY TO PASS TIME. DON'T WORRY, SHE DIDN'T GET IN THE WAY OR ANYTHING.
I KNOW...
BATMAN, I'M FINDING MANY HUMAN REMAINS AND SHREDS OF CLOTH FROM THOSE TUNICS OF THEIRS...
BUT THE BONE FRAGMENTS AREN'T NEARLY OXIDIZED ENOUGH FOR WHAT SUPERMAN DESCRIBED.
DIANA? CAN HE SPEAK? I NEED TO ASK--
...
OKAY. NO, WE CAN DO IT WITHOUT HIM.
STALL THE FEDS. DON'T LET LUTHOR GET HIM UNTIL WE COMPILE THE EVIDENCE.

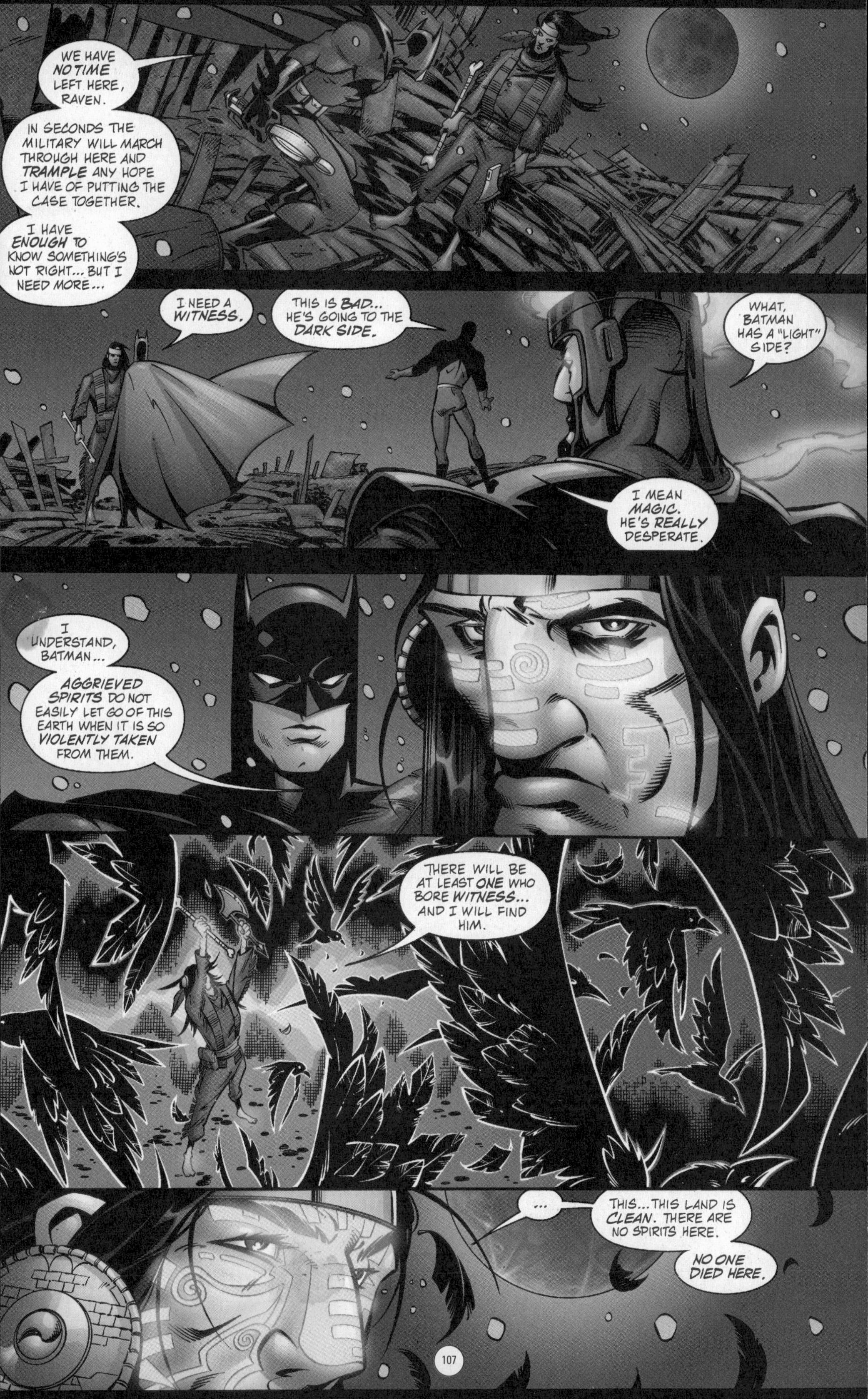

WE HAVE NO TIME LEFT HERE, RAVEN.
IN SECONDS THE MILITARY WILL MARCH THROUGH HERE AND TRAMPLE ANY HOPE I HAVE OF PUTTING THE CASE TOGETHER.
I HAVE ENOUGH TO KNOW SOMETHING'S NOT RIGHT... BUT I NEED MORE...
I NEED A WITNESS.
THIS IS BAD... HE'S GOING TO THE DARK SIDE.
WHAT, BATMAN HAS A "LIGHT" SIDE?
I MEAN MAGIC. HE'S REALLY DESPERATE.
I UNDERSTAND, BATMAN...
AGGRIEVED SPIRITS DO NOT EASILY LET GO OF THIS EARTH WHEN IT IS SO VIOLENTLY TAKEN FROM THEM.
THERE WILL BE AT LEAST ONE WHO BORE WITNESS... AND I WILL FIND HIM.
...
THIS... THIS LAND IS CLEAN. THERE ARE NO SPIRITS HERE.
NO ONE DIED HERE.

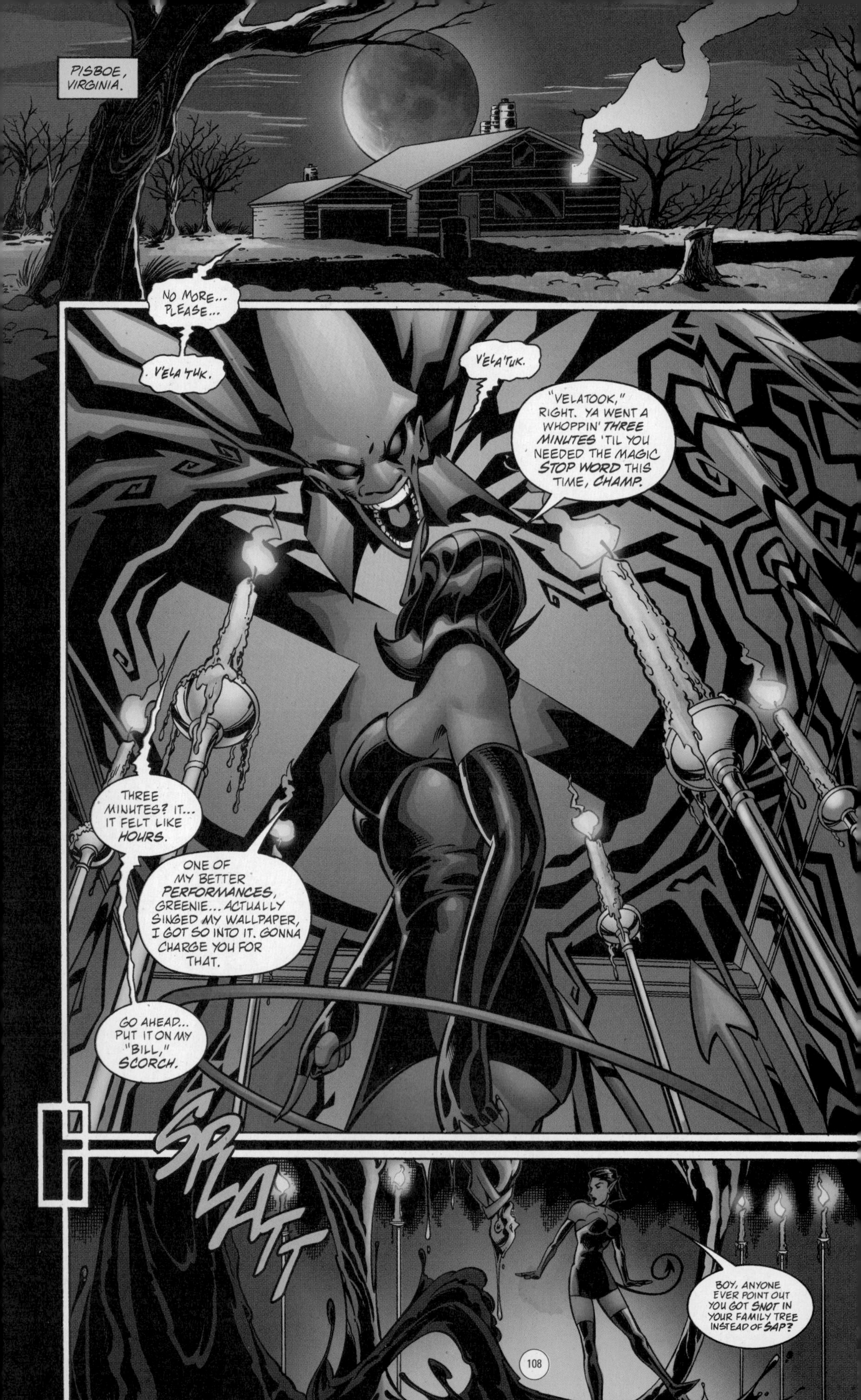
PISBOE, VIRGINIA.
NO MORE... PLEASE...
V'ELA'TUK.
V'ELA'TUK.
"VELATOOK," RIGHT. YA WENT A WHOPPIN' THREE MINUTES 'TIL YOU NEEDED THE MAGIC STOP WORD THIS TIME, CHAMP.
THREE MINUTES? IT... IT FELT LIKE HOURS.
ONE OF MY BETTER PERFORMANCES, GREENIE... ACTUALLY SINGED MY WALLPAPER, I GOT SO INTO IT. GONNA CHARGE YOU FOR THAT.
GO AHEAD... PUT IT ON MY "BILL," SCORCH.
SPLATT
BOY, ANYONE EVER POINT OUT YOU GOT SNOT IN YOUR FAMILY TREE INSTEAD OF SAP?

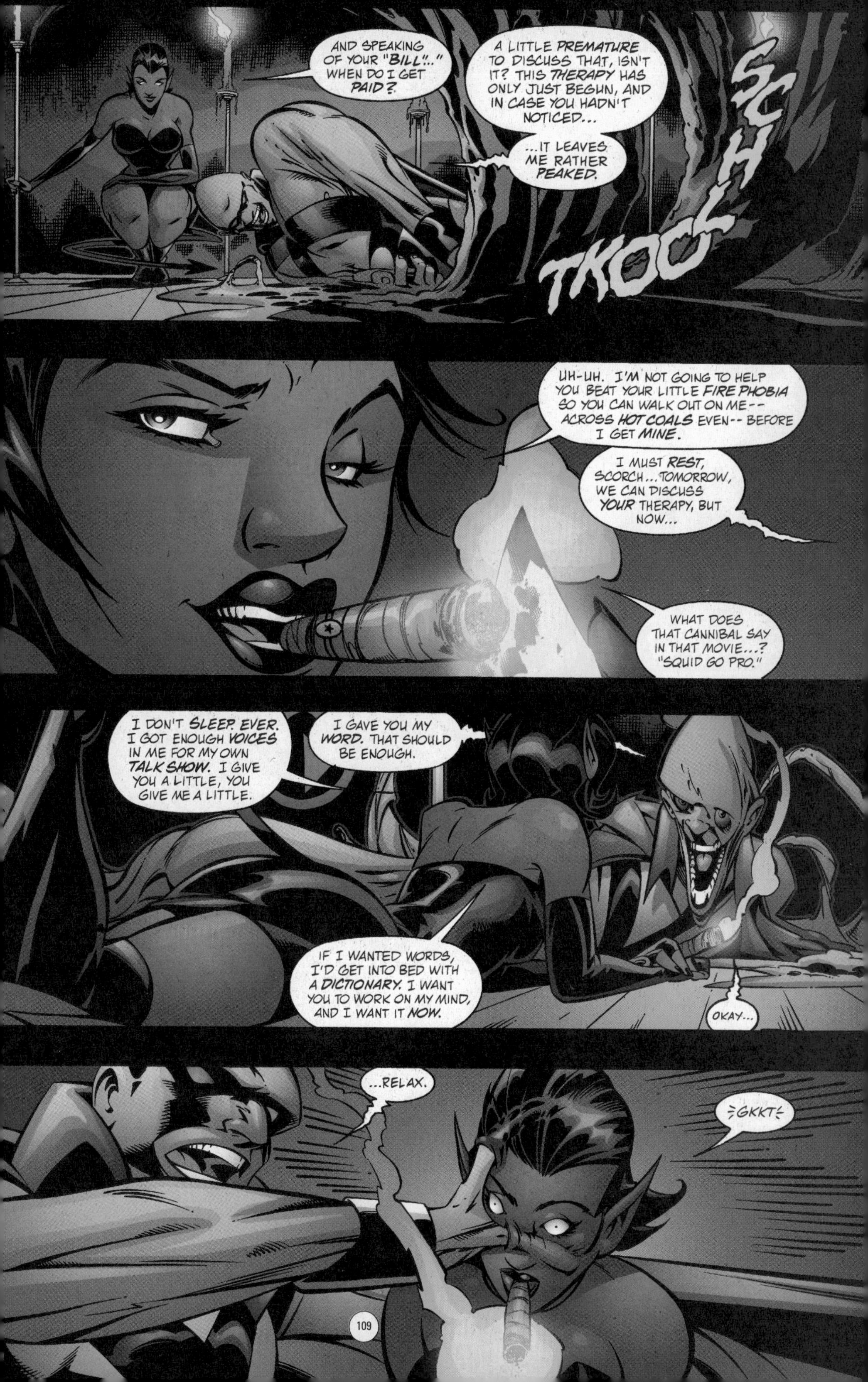

AND SPEAKING OF YOUR "BILL"..." WHEN DO I GET PAID?
A LITTLE PREMATURE TO DISCUSS THAT, ISN'T IT? THIS THERAPY HAS ONLY JUST BEGUN, AND IN CASE YOU HADN'T NOTICED...
...IT LEAVES ME RATHER PEAKED.
SCHLTKOOL
UH-UH. I'M NOT GOING TO HELP YOU BEAT YOUR LITTLE FIRE PHOBIA SO YOU CAN WALK OUT ON ME-- ACROSS HOT COALS EVEN-- BEFORE I GET MINE.
I MUST REST, SCORCH... TOMORROW, WE CAN DISCUSS YOUR THERAPY, BUT NOW...
WHAT DOES THAT CANNIBAL SAY IN THAT MOVIE...? "SQUID GO PRO."
I DON'T SLEEP. EVER. I GOT ENOUGH VOICES IN ME FOR MY OWN TALK SHOW. I GIVE YOU A LITTLE, YOU GIVE ME A LITTLE.
I GAVE YOU MY WORD. THAT SHOULD BE ENOUGH.
IF I WANTED WORDS, I'D GET INTO BED WITH A DICTIONARY. I WANT YOU TO WORK ON MY MIND, AND I WANT IT NOW.
OKAY...
...RELAX.
GKKT

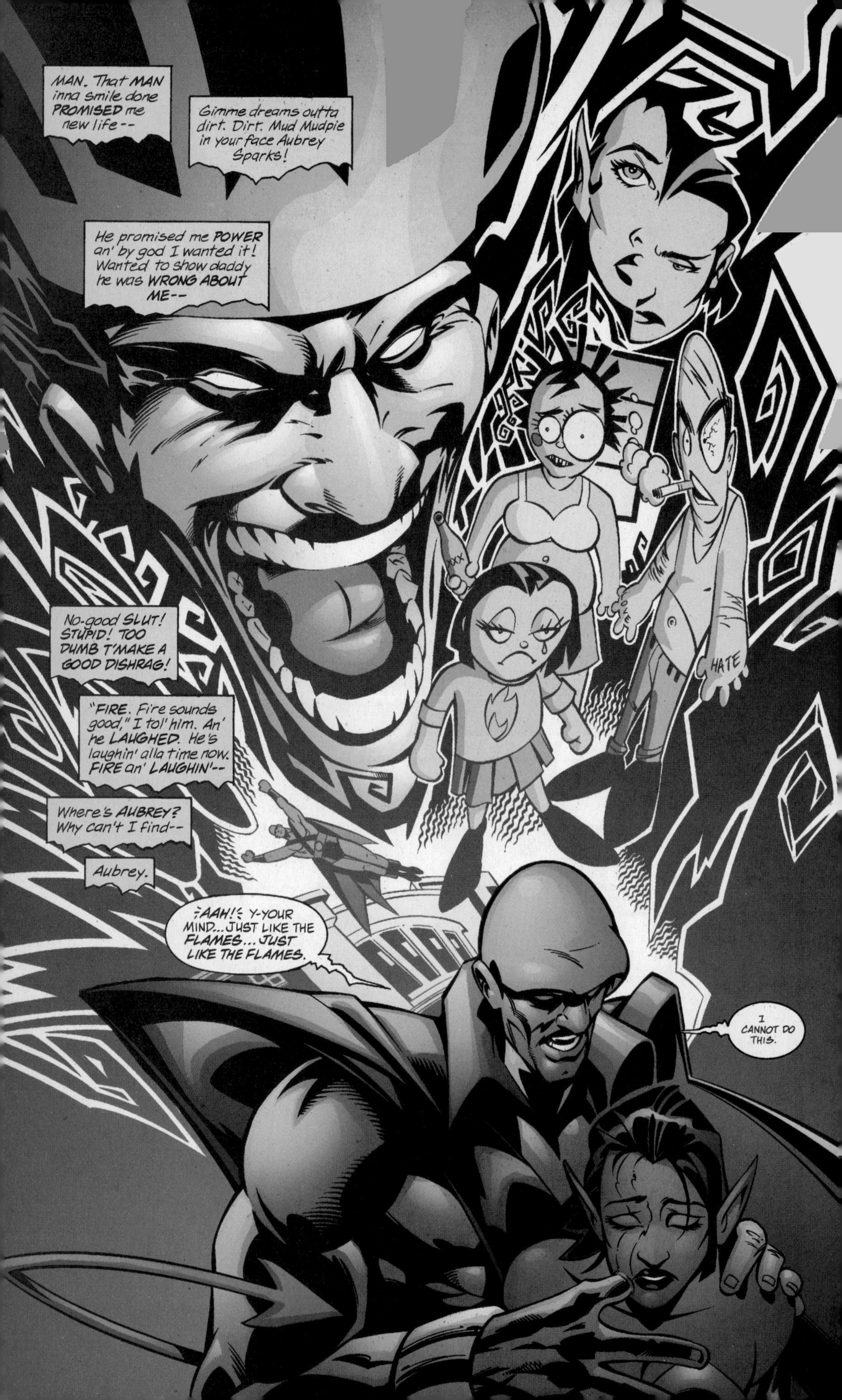
MAN. That MAN inna smile done PROMISED me new life--
Gimme dreams outta dirt. Dirt. Mud Mudpie in your face Aubrey Sparks!
He promised me POWER an' by god I wanted it! Wanted to show daddy he was WRONG ABOUT ME--
No-good SLUT! STUPID! TOO DUMB T'MAKE A GOOD DISHRAG!
"FIRE. Fire sounds good," I tol' him. An' he LAUGHED. He's laughin' alla time now. FIRE an' LAUGHIN'--
Where's AUBREY? Why can't I find--
Aubrey.
AAH! Y-YOUR MIND... JUST LIKE THE FLAMES... JUST LIKE THE FLAMES.
I CANNOT DO THIS.
HATE

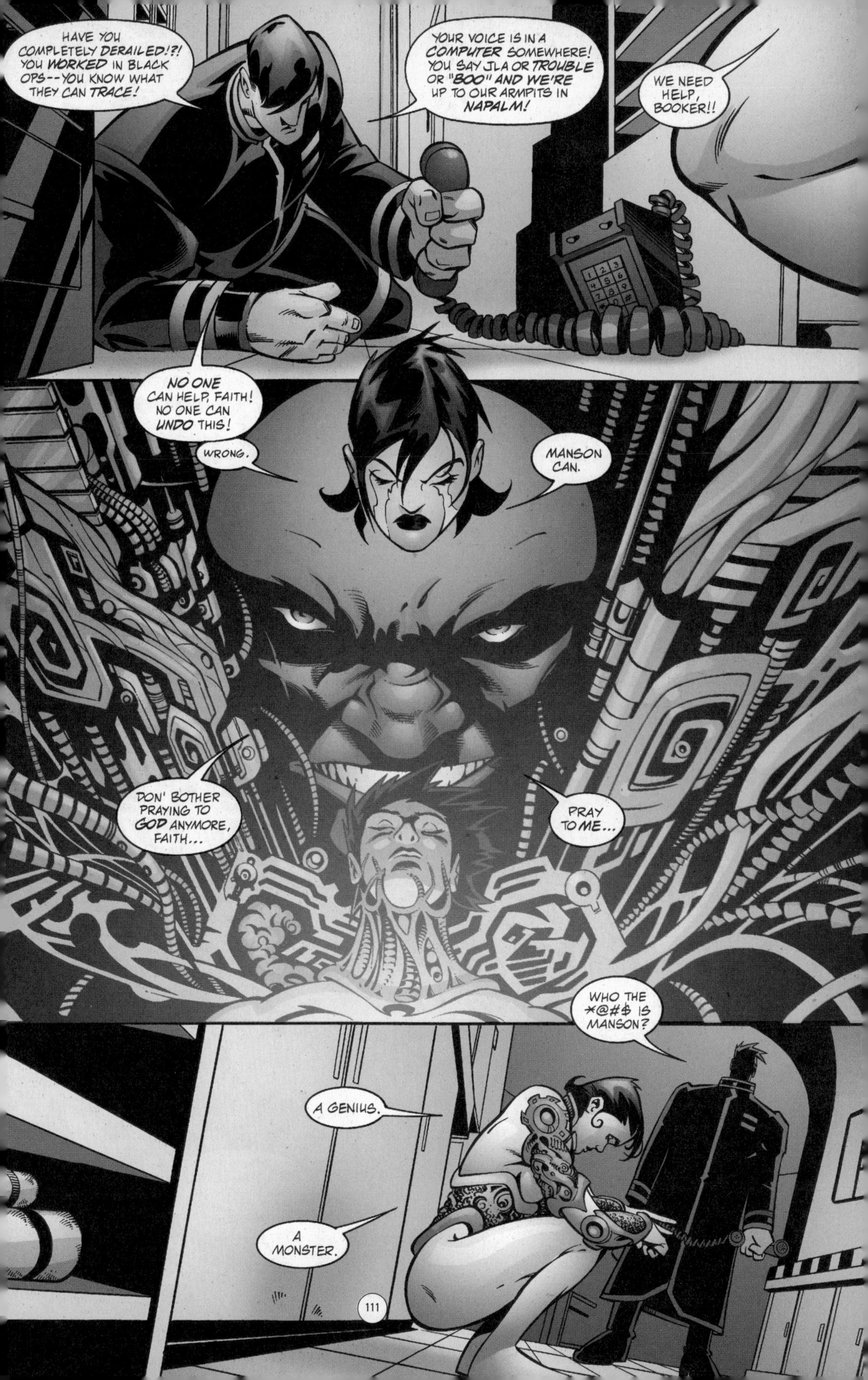

HAVE YOU COMPLETELY DERAILED!?! YOU WORKED IN BLACK OPS--YOU KNOW WHAT THEY CAN TRACE!
YOUR VOICE IS IN A COMPUTER SOMEWHERE! YOU SAY JLA OR TROUBLE OR "BOO" AND WE'RE UP TO OUR ARMPITS IN NAPALM!
WE NEED HELP, BOOKER!!
NO ONE CAN HELP, FAITH! NO ONE CAN UNDO THIS!
WRONG.
MANSON CAN.
DON' BOTHER PRAYING TO GOD ANYMORE, FAITH...
PRAY TO ME...
WHO THE *@#$ IS MANSON?
A GENIUS.
A MONSTER.

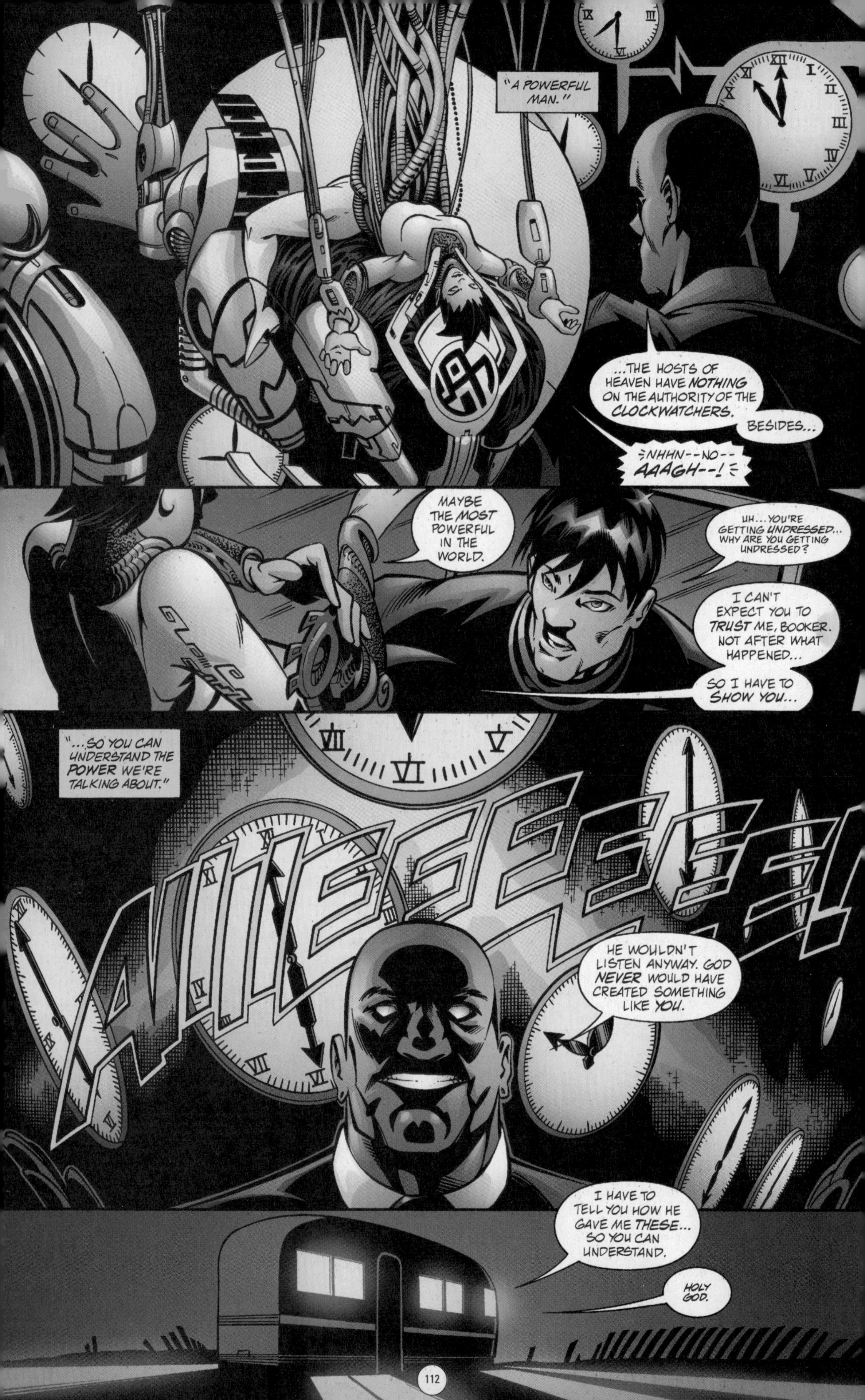
"A POWERFUL MAN."
...THE HOSTS OF HEAVEN HAVE NOTHING ON THE AUTHORITY OF THE CLOCKWATCHERS.
BESIDES...
NHHN--NO-- AAAGH--!
MAYBE THE MOST POWERFUL IN THE WORLD.
UH... YOU'RE GETTING UNDRESSED... WHY ARE YOU GETTING UNDRESSED?
I CAN'T EXPECT YOU TO TRUST ME, BOOKER. NOT AFTER WHAT HAPPENED...
SO I HAVE TO SHOW YOU...
"...SO YOU CAN UNDERSTAND THE POWER WE'RE TALKING ABOUT."
WHEEEEE!
HE WOULDN'T LISTEN ANYWAY. GOD NEVER WOULD HAVE CREATED SOMETHING LIKE YOU.
I HAVE TO TELL YOU HOW HE GAVE ME THESE... SO YOU CAN UNDERSTAND.
HOLY GOD.

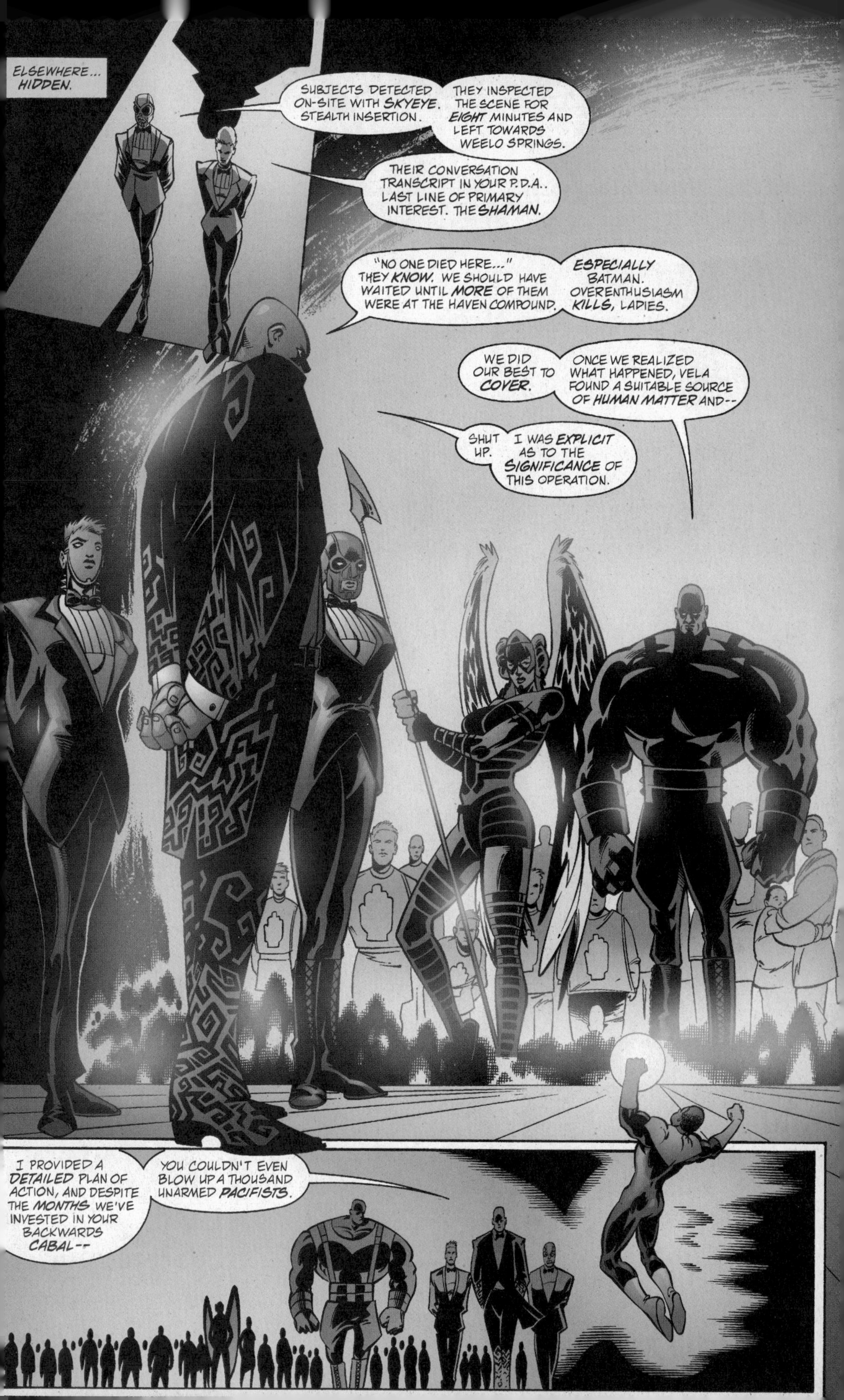
ELSEWHERE... HIDDEN.
SUBJECTS DETECTED ON-SITE WITH SKYEYE. STEALTH INSERTION.
THEY INSPECTED THE SCENE FOR EIGHT MINUTES AND LEFT TOWARDS WEELO SPRINGS.
THEIR CONVERSATION TRANSCRIPT IN YOUR P.D.A.. LAST LINE OF PRIMARY INTEREST. THE SHAMAN.
"NO ONE DIED HERE..." THEY KNOW. WE SHOULD HAVE WAITED UNTIL MORE OF THEM WERE AT THE HAVEN COMPOUND.
ESPECIALLY BATMAN. OVERENTHUSIASM KILLS, LADIES.
WE DID OUR BEST TO COVER.
ONCE WE REALIZED WHAT HAPPENED, VELA FOUND A SUITABLE SOURCE OF HUMAN MATTER AND--
SHUT UP.
I WAS EXPLICIT AS TO THE SIGNIFICANCE OF THIS OPERATION.
I PROVIDED A DETAILED PLAN OF ACTION, AND DESPITE THE MONTHS WE'VE INVESTED IN YOUR BACKWARDS CABAL--
YOU COULDN'T EVEN BLOW UP A THOUSAND UNARMED PACIFISTS.

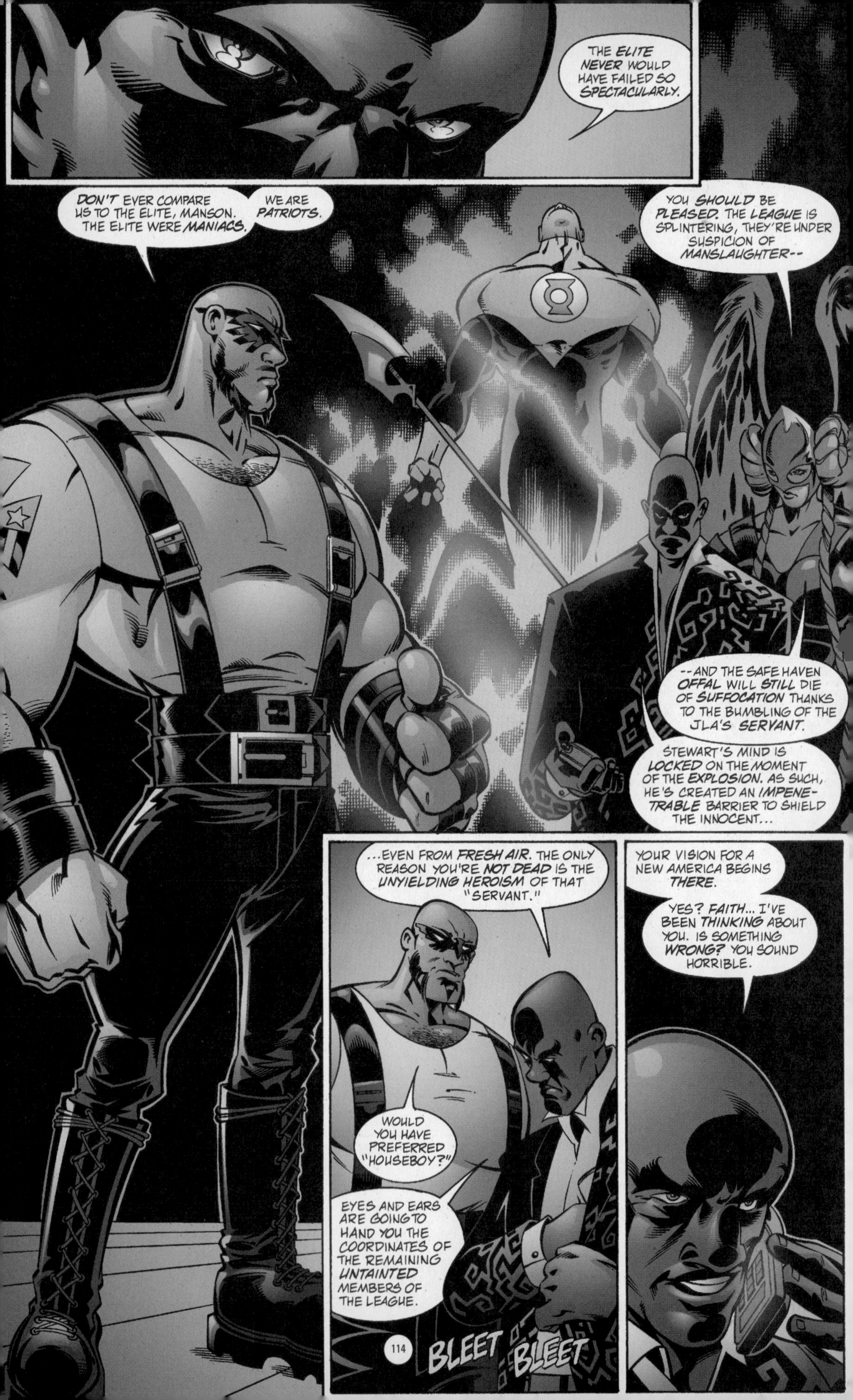
THE ELITE NEVER WOULD HAVE FAILED SO SPECTACULARLY.
DON'T EVER COMPARE US TO THE ELITE, MANSON. THE ELITE WERE MANIACS.
WE ARE PATRIOTS.
YOU SHOULD BE PLEASED. THE LEAGUE IS SPLINTERING, THEY'RE UNDER SUSPICION OF MANSLAUGHTER--
--AND THE SAFE HAVEN OFFAL WILL STILL DIE OF SUFFOCATION THANKS TO THE BUMBLING OF THE JLA'S SERVANT.
STEWART'S MIND IS LOCKED ON THE MOMENT OF THE EXPLOSION. AS SUCH, HE'S CREATED AN IMPENETRABLE BARRIER TO SHIELD THE INNOCENT...
...EVEN FROM FRESH AIR. THE ONLY REASON YOU'RE NOT DEAD IS THE UNYIELDING HEROISM OF THAT "SERVANT."
WOULD YOU HAVE PREFERRED "HOUSEBOY?"
EYES AND EARS ARE GOING TO HAND YOU THE COORDINATES OF THE REMAINING UNTAINTED MEMBERS OF THE LEAGUE.
BLEET BLEET
YOUR VISION FOR A NEW AMERICA BEGINS THERE.
YES? FAITH... I'VE BEEN THINKING ABOUT YOU. IS SOMETHING WRONG? YOU SOUND HORRIBLE.

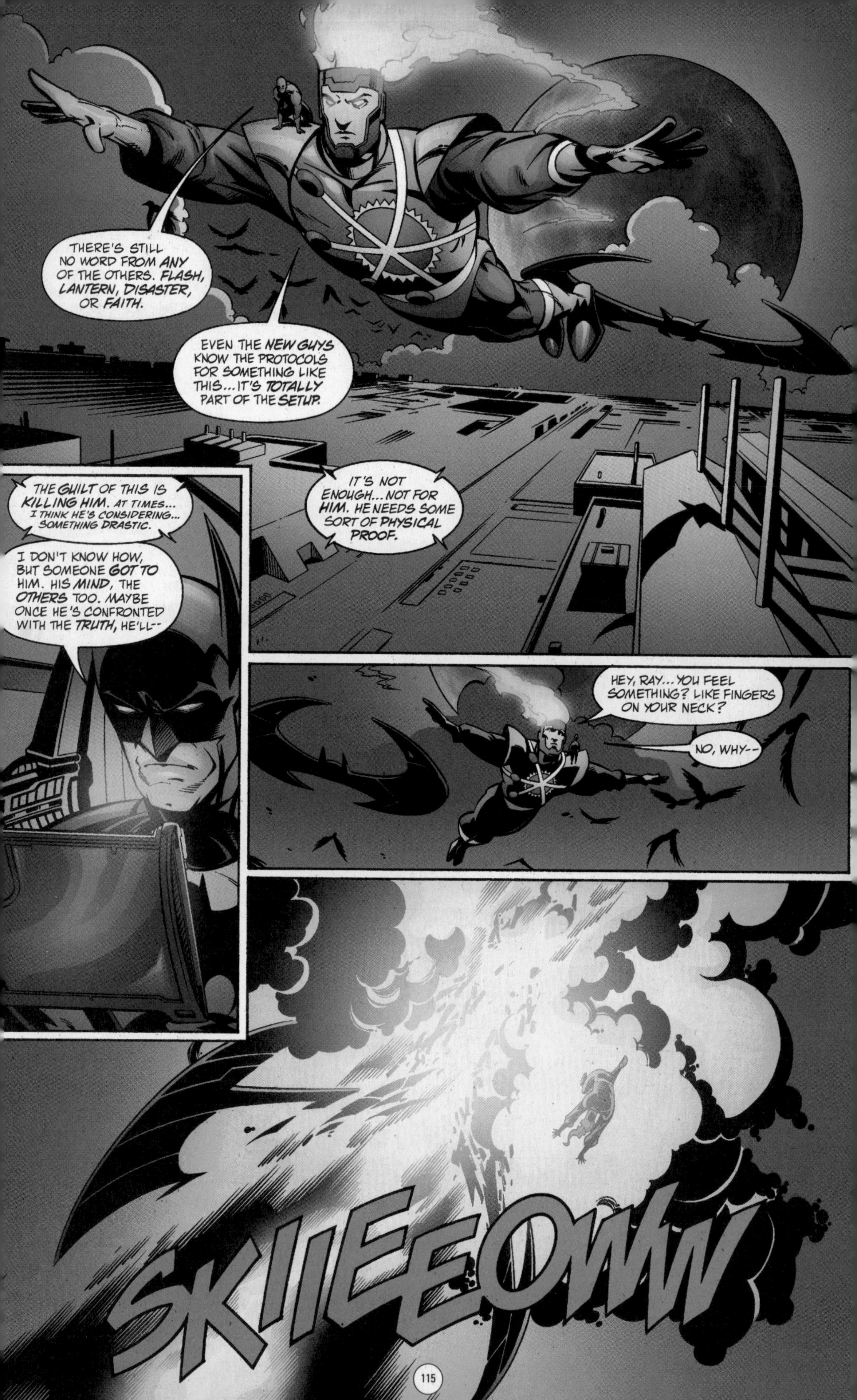
THERE'S STILL NO WORD FROM ANY OF THE OTHERS. FLASH, LANTERN, DISASTER, OR FAITH.
EVEN THE NEW GUYS KNOW THE PROTOCOLS FOR SOMETHING LIKE THIS...IT'S TOTALLY PART OF THE SETUP.
THE GUILT OF THIS IS KILLING HIM. AT TIMES... I THINK HE'S CONSIDERING... SOMETHING DRASTIC.
IT'S NOT ENOUGH...NOT FOR HIM. HE NEEDS SOME SORT OF PHYSICAL PROOF.
I DON'T KNOW HOW, BUT SOMEONE GOT TO HIM. HIS MIND, THE OTHERS TOO. MAYBE ONCE HE'S CONFRONTED WITH THE TRUTH, HE'LL--
HEY, RAY...YOU FEEL SOMETHING? LIKE FINGERS ON YOUR NECK?
NO, WHY--
SKIIEEOWW

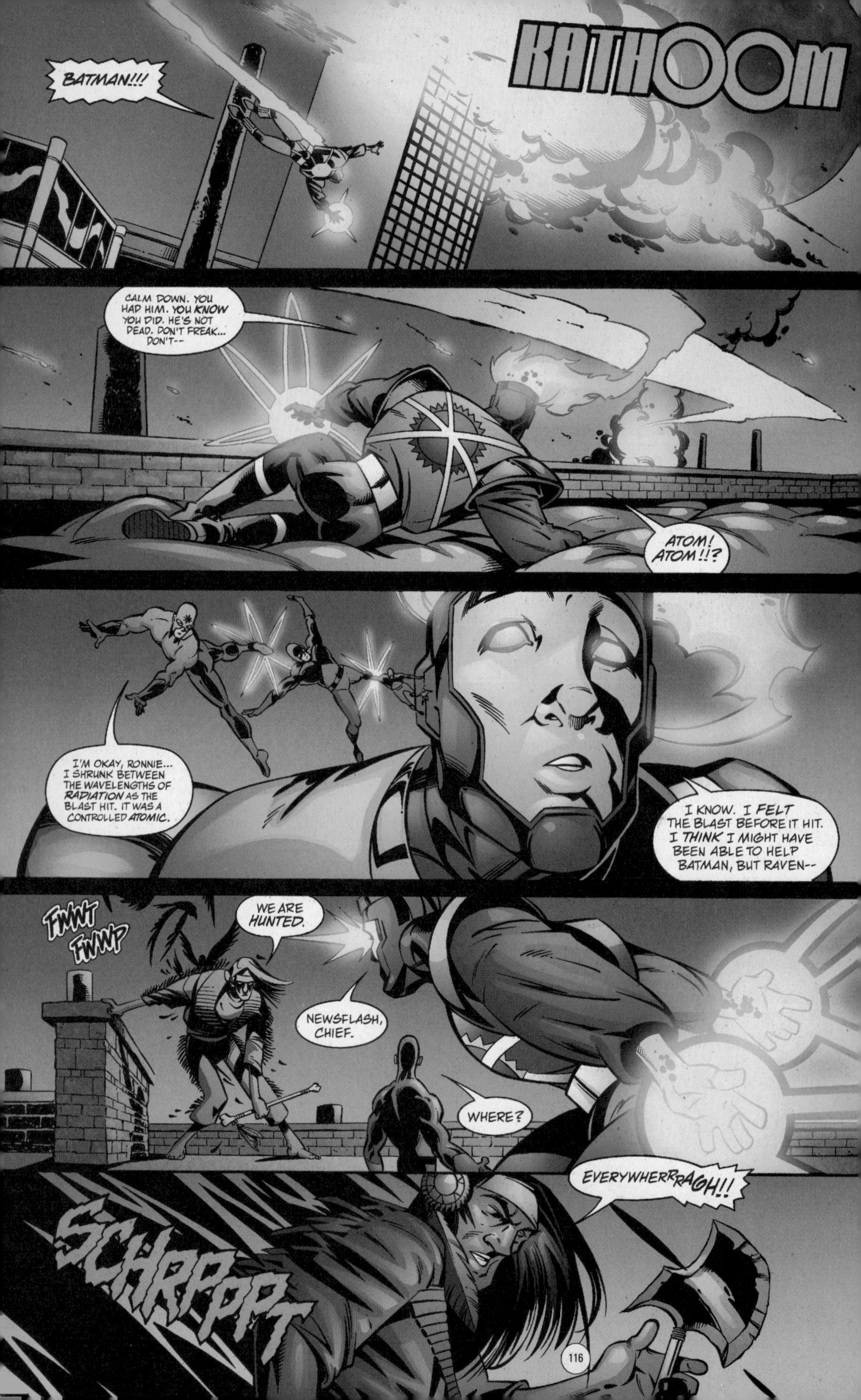

KATHOOM
BATMAN!!!
CALM DOWN. YOU HAD HIM. YOU KNOW YOU DID. HE'S NOT DEAD. DON'T FREAK... DON'T--
ATOM! ATOM!!?
I'M OKAY, RONNIE... I SHRUNK BETWEEN THE WAVELENGTHS OF RADIATION AS THE BLAST HIT. IT WAS A CONTROLLED ATOMIC.
I KNOW. I FELT THE BLAST BEFORE IT HIT. I THINK I MIGHT HAVE BEEN ABLE TO HELP BATMAN, BUT RAVEN--
FWWT FWWP
WE ARE HUNTED.
NEWSFLASH, CHIEF.
WHERE?
EVERYWHERRRAGH!!
SCHRPPPT

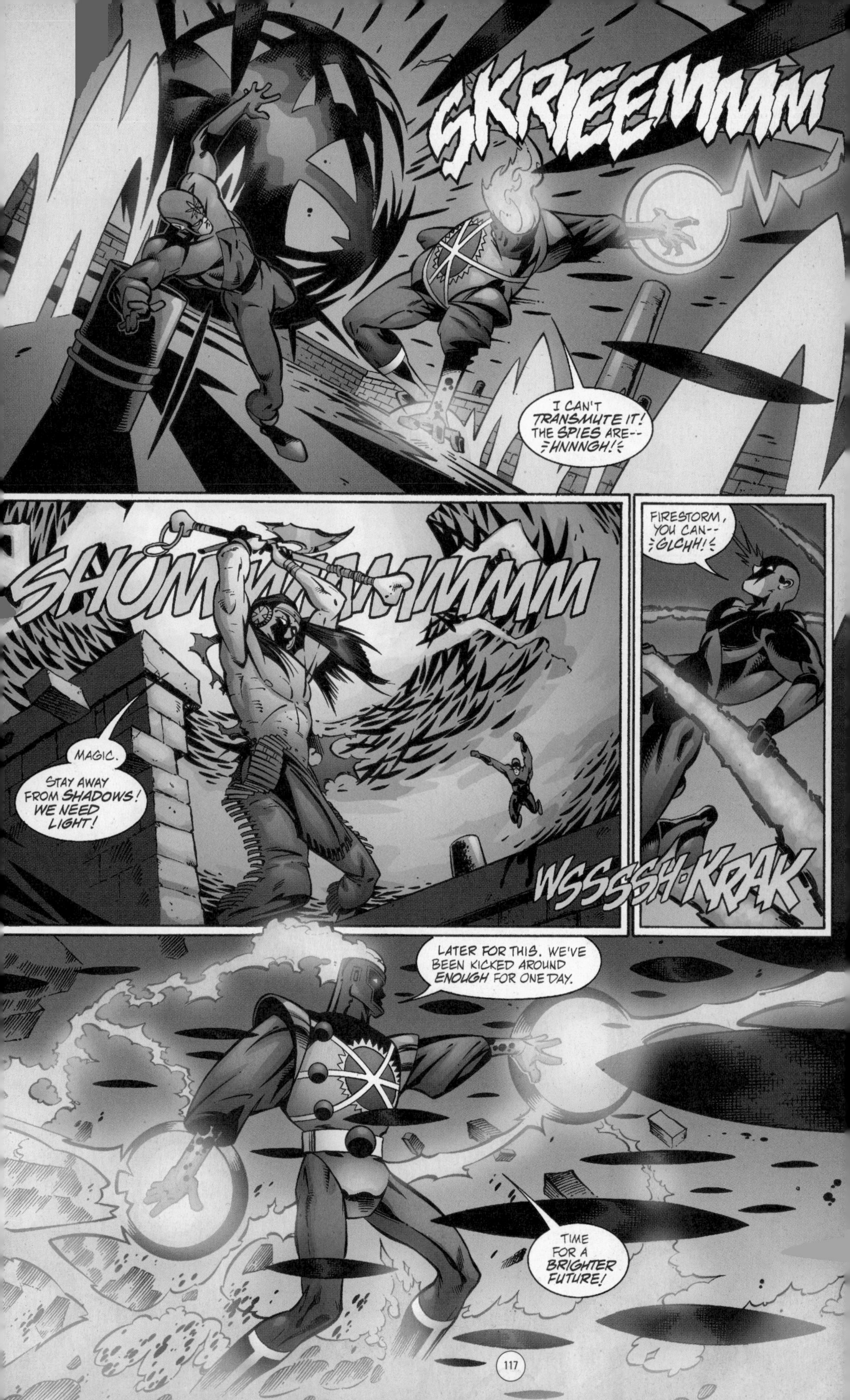
SKRIEEMMM
I CAN'T TRANSMUTE IT! THE SPIES ARE-- HNNNGH!
SHUMMMMMMMM
MAGIC.
STAY AWAY FROM SHADOWS! WE NEED LIGHT!
FIRESTORM, YOU CAN-- GLCHH!
WSSSSSH-KRAK
LATER FOR THIS. WE'VE BEEN KICKED AROUND ENOUGH FOR ONE DAY.
TIME FOR A BRIGHTER FUTURE!

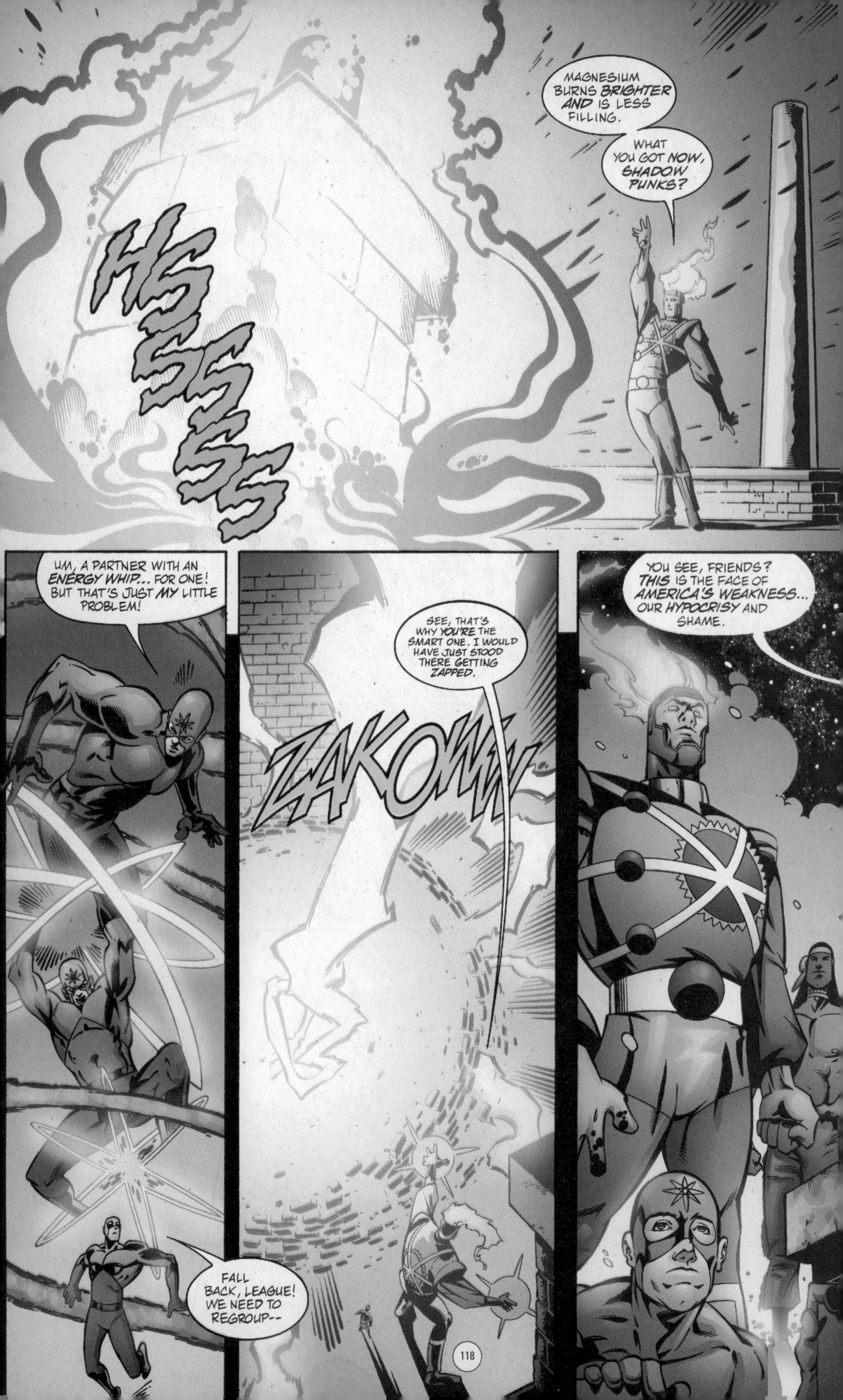
MAGNESIUM BURNS BRIGHTER AND IS LESS FILLING.
WHAT YOU GOT NOW, SHADOW PUNKS?
HSSSSS
UM, A PARTNER WITH AN ENERGY WHIP... FOR ONE! BUT THAT'S JUST MY LITTLE PROBLEM!
FALL BACK, LEAGUE! WE NEED TO REGROUP--
SEE, THAT'S WHY YOU'RE THE SMART ONE. I WOULD HAVE JUST STOOD THERE GETTING ZAPPED.
ZAKOWW
YOU SEE, FRIENDS? THIS IS THE FACE OF AMERICA'S WEAKNESS... OUR HYPOCRISY AND SHAME.

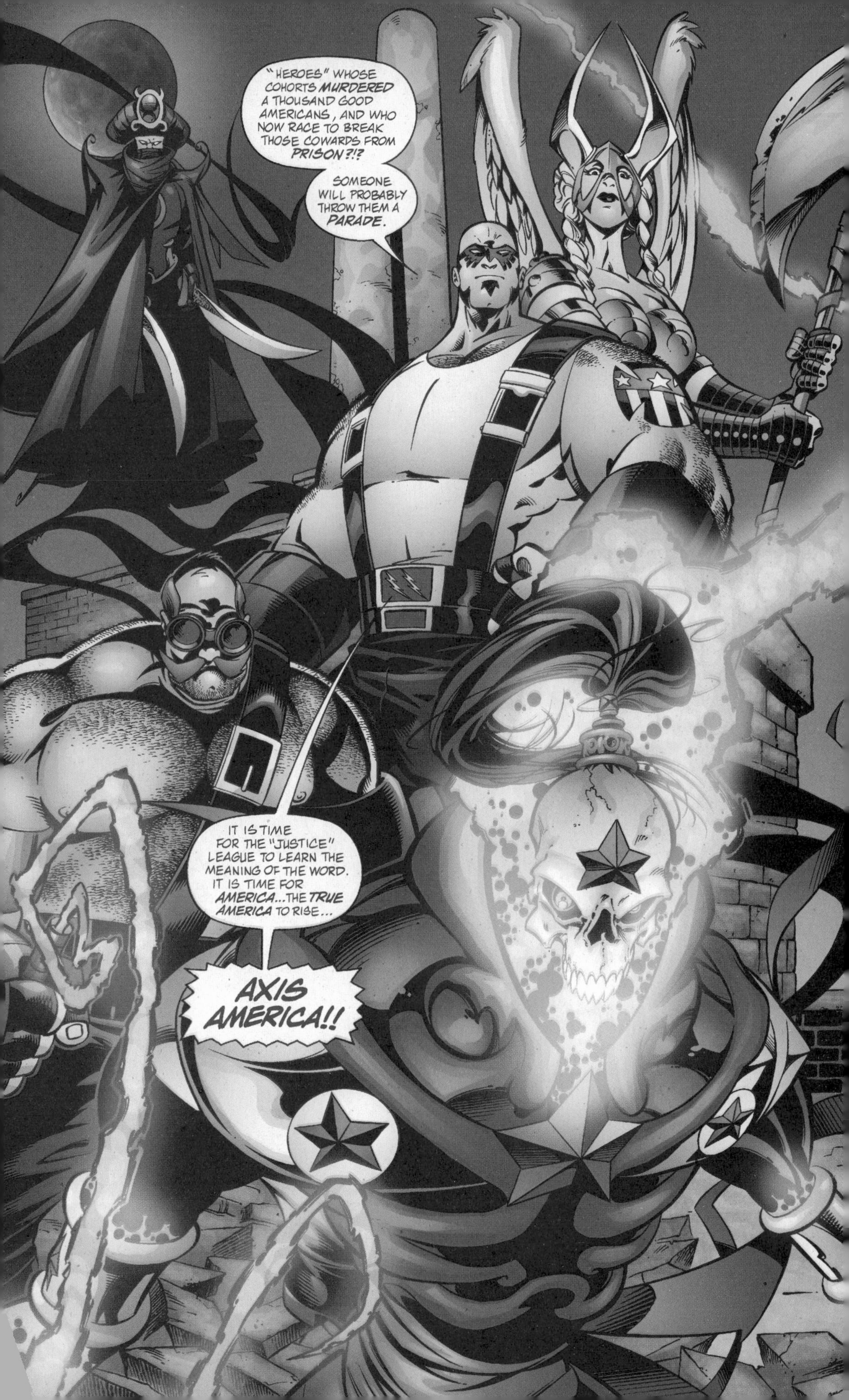

"HEROES" WHOSE COHORTS MURDERED A THOUSAND GOOD AMERICANS, AND WHO NOW RACE TO BREAK THOSE COWARDS FROM PRISON?!?
SOMEONE WILL PROBABLY THROW THEM A PARADE.
IT IS TIME FOR THE "JUSTICE" LEAGUE TO LEARN THE MEANING OF THE WORD. IT IS TIME FOR AMERICA...THE TRUE AMERICA TO RISE...
AXIS AMERICA!!

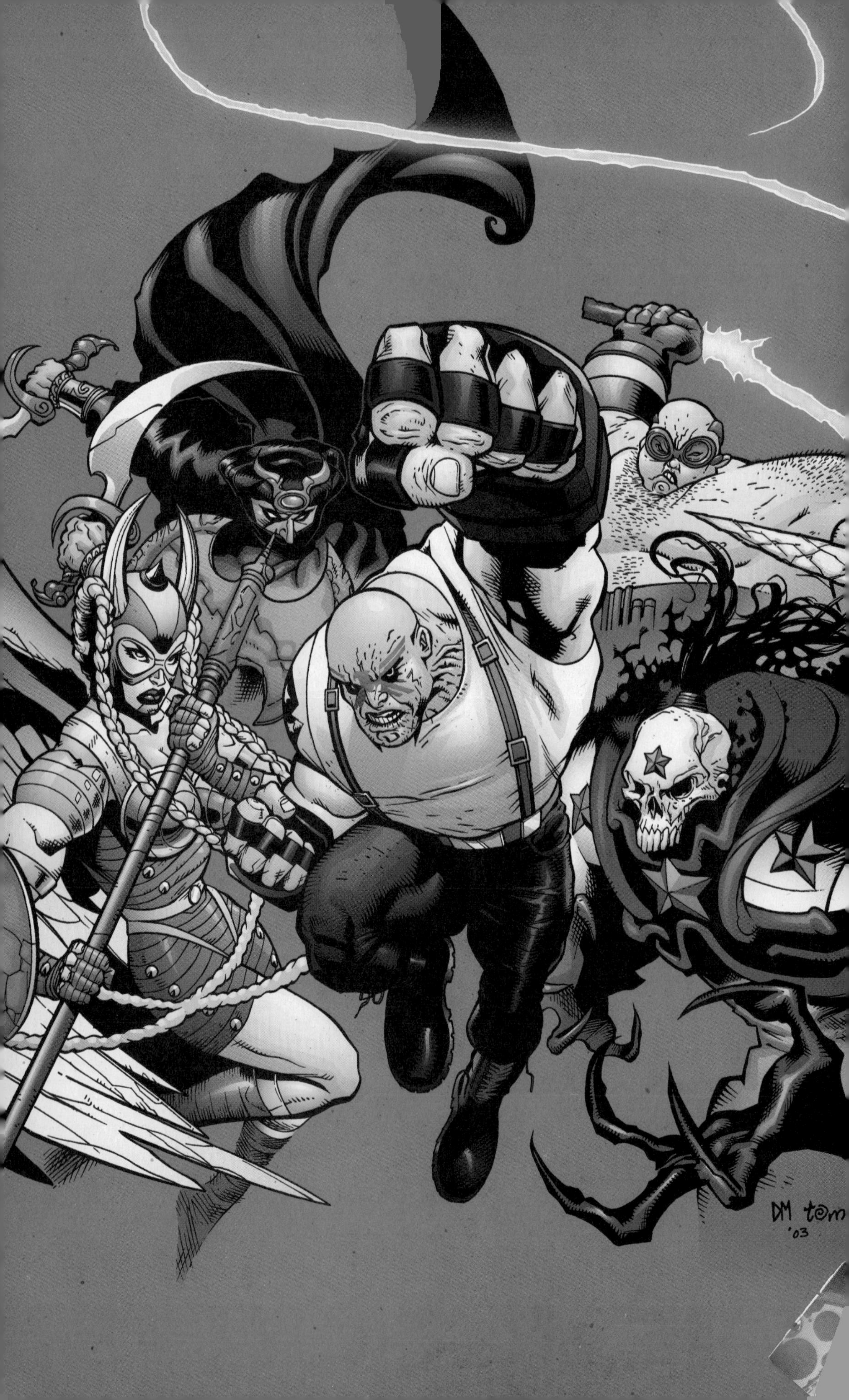
DM tom
'03

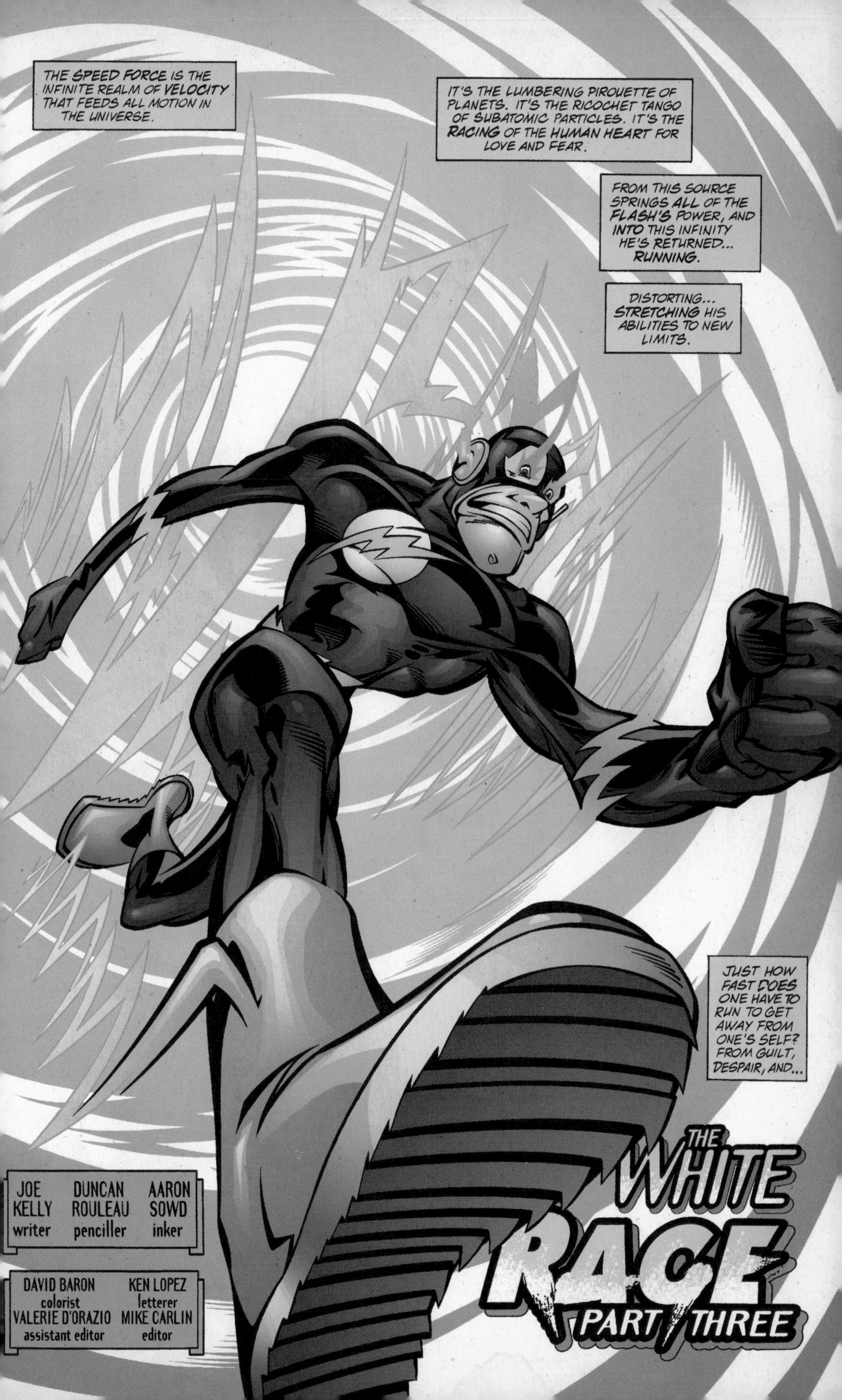

THE SPEED FORCE IS THE INFINITE REALM OF VELOCITY THAT FEEDS ALL MOTION IN THE UNIVERSE.
IT'S THE LUMBERING PIROUETTE OF PLANETS. IT'S THE RICOCHET TANGO OF SUBATOMIC PARTICLES. IT'S THE RACING OF THE HUMAN HEART FOR LOVE AND FEAR.
FROM THIS SOURCE SPRINGS ALL OF THE FLASH'S POWER, AND INTO THIS INFINITY HE'S RETURNED... RUNNING.
DISTORTING... STRETCHING HIS ABILITIES TO NEW LIMITS.
JUST HOW FAST DOES ONE HAVE TO RUN TO GET AWAY FROM ONE'S SELF? FROM GUILT, DESPAIR, AND...
THE WHITE RACE PART THREE
JOE KELLY writer DUNCAN ROULEAU penciller AARON SOWD inker
DAVID BARON colorist KEN LOPEZ letterer VALERIE D'ORAZIO assistant editor MIKE CARLIN editor

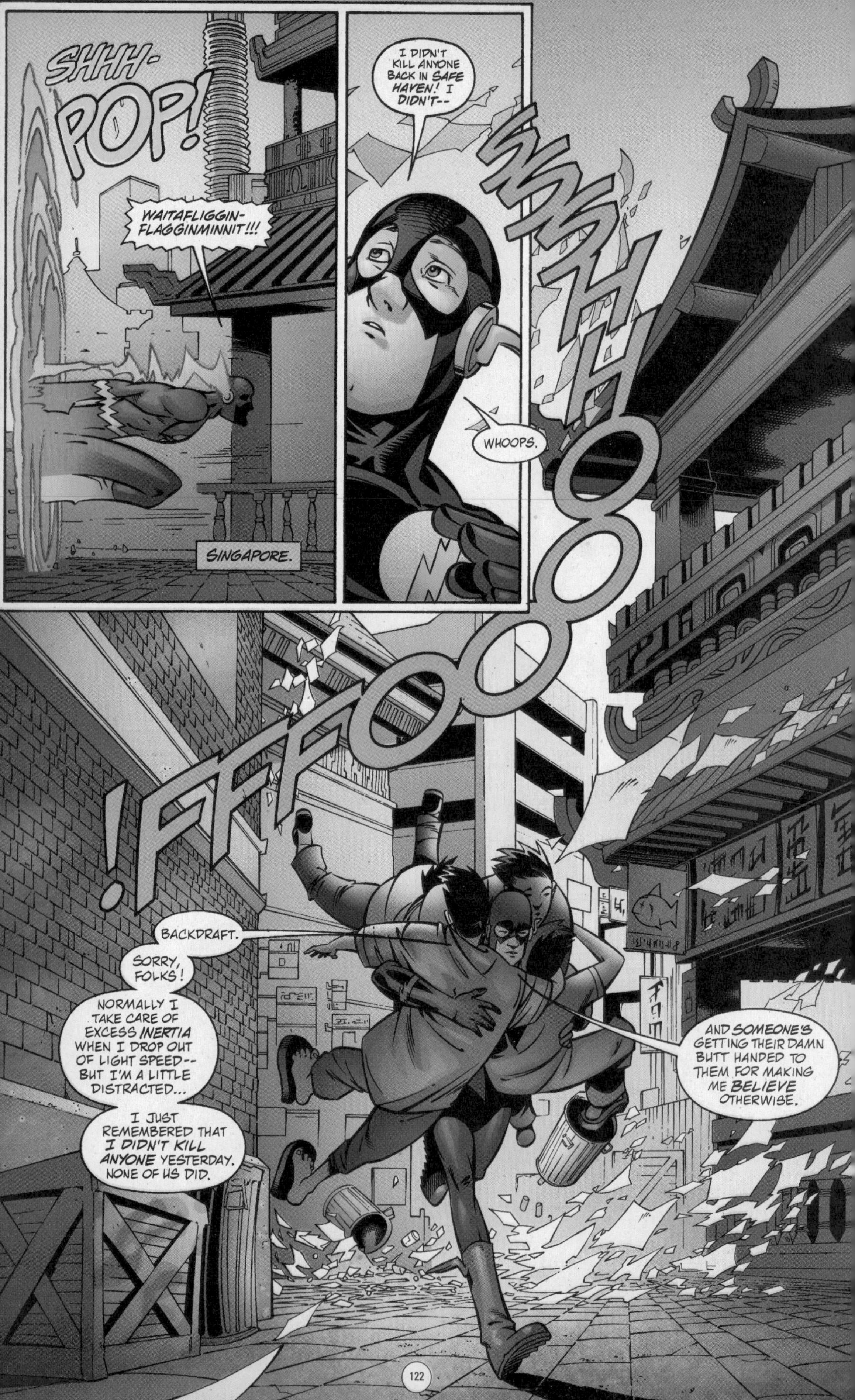
SHHH-
POP!
WAITAFLIGGIN-FLAGGINMINNIT!!!
SINGAPORE.
I DIDN'T KILL ANYONE BACK IN SAFE HAVEN! I DIDN'T--
WHOOPS.
WHOOSH!
BACKDRAFT.
SORRY, FOLKS!
NORMALLY I TAKE CARE OF EXCESS INERTIA WHEN I DROP OUT OF LIGHT SPEED--BUT I'M A LITTLE DISTRACTED...
I JUST REMEMBERED THAT I DIDN'T KILL ANYONE YESTERDAY. NONE OF US DID.
AND SOMEONE'S GETTING THEIR DAMN BUTT HANDED TO THEM FOR MAKING ME BELIEVE OTHERWISE.

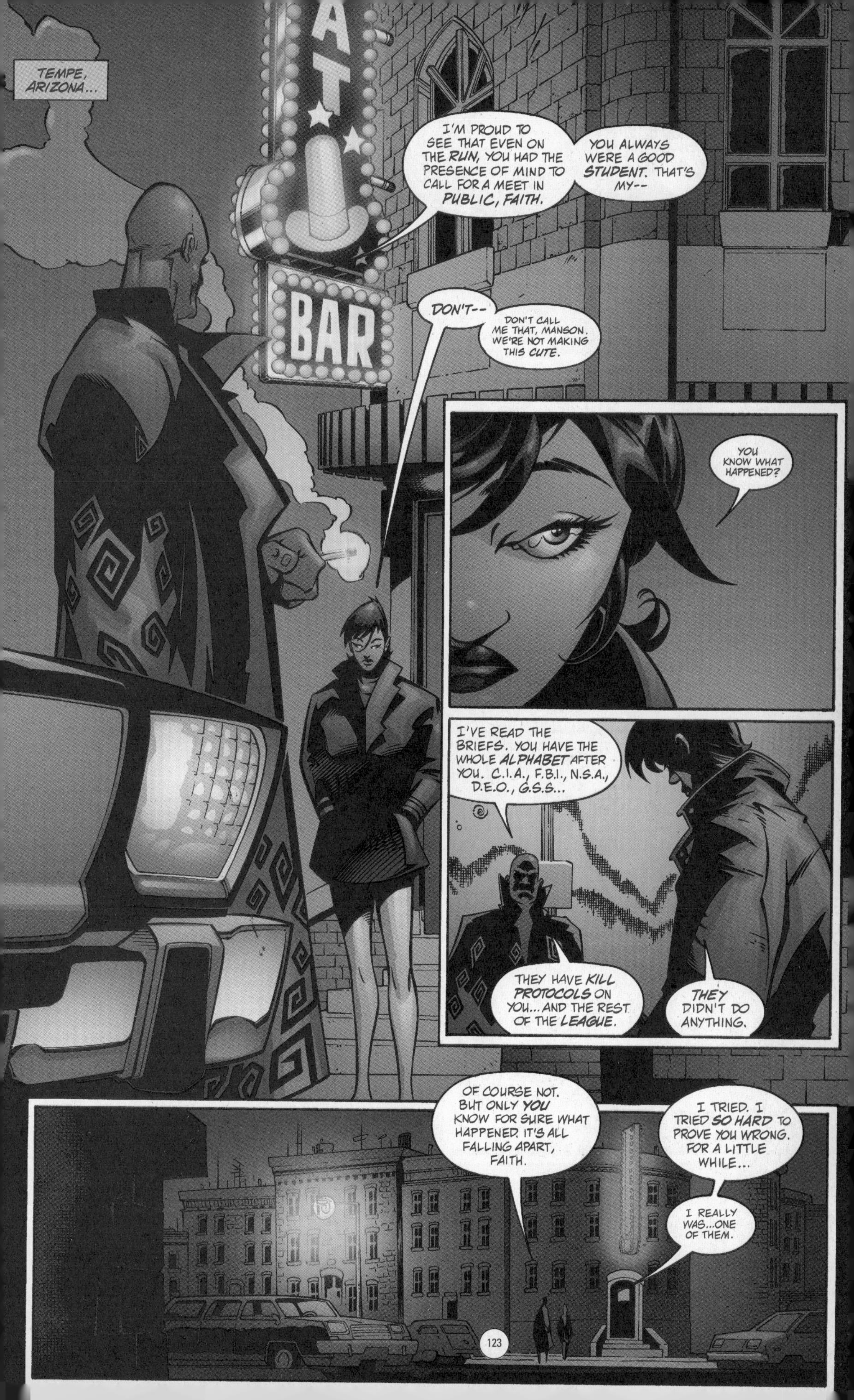
TEMPE, ARIZONA...
BAR
I'M PROUD TO SEE THAT EVEN ON THE RUN, YOU HAD THE PRESENCE OF MIND TO CALL FOR A MEET IN PUBLIC, FAITH.
YOU ALWAYS WERE A GOOD STUDENT. THAT'S MY--
DON'T--
DON'T CALL ME THAT, MANSON. WE'RE NOT MAKING THIS CUTE.
YOU KNOW WHAT HAPPENED?
I'VE READ THE BRIEFS. YOU HAVE THE WHOLE ALPHABET AFTER YOU. C.I.A., F.B.I., N.S.A., D.E.O., G.S.S...
THEY HAVE KILL PROTOCOLS ON YOU... AND THE REST OF THE LEAGUE.
THEY DIDN'T DO ANYTHING.
OF COURSE NOT. BUT ONLY YOU KNOW FOR SURE WHAT HAPPENED. IT'S ALL FALLING APART, FAITH.
I TRIED. I TRIED SO HARD TO PROVE YOU WRONG. FOR A LITTLE WHILE...
I REALLY WAS...ONE OF THEM.

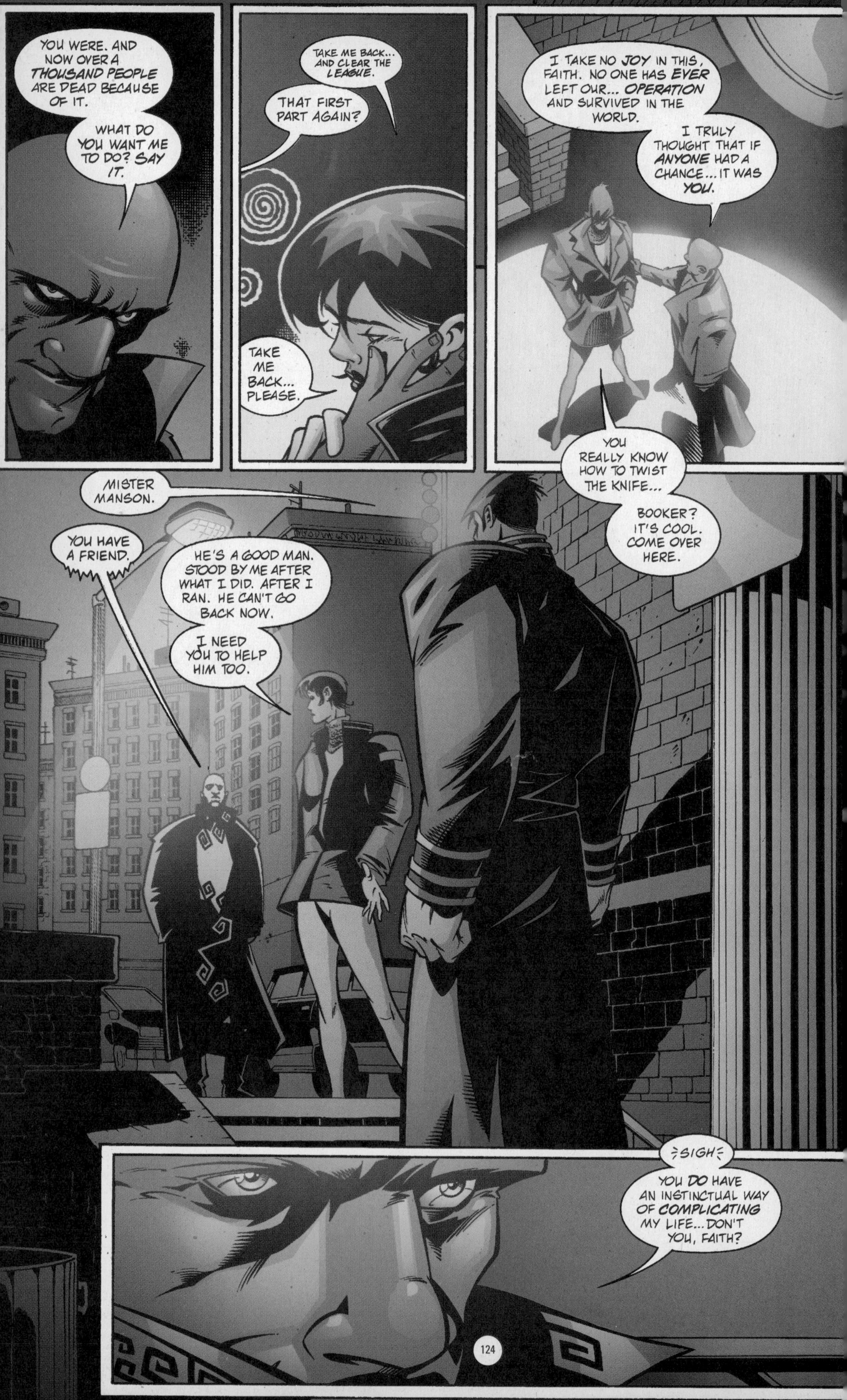

YOU WERE. AND NOW OVER A THOUSAND PEOPLE ARE DEAD BECAUSE OF IT.
WHAT DO YOU WANT ME TO DO? SAY IT.
TAKE ME BACK... AND CLEAR THE LEAGUE.
THAT FIRST PART AGAIN?
TAKE ME BACK... PLEASE.
I TAKE NO JOY IN THIS, FAITH. NO ONE HAS EVER LEFT OUR... OPERATION AND SURVIVED IN THE WORLD.
I TRULY THOUGHT THAT IF ANYONE HAD A CHANCE... IT WAS YOU.
YOU REALLY KNOW HOW TO TWIST THE KNIFE...
BOOKER? IT'S COOL. COME OVER HERE.
MISTER MANSON.
YOU HAVE A FRIEND.
HE'S A GOOD MAN. STOOD BY ME AFTER WHAT I DID. AFTER I RAN. HE CAN'T GO BACK NOW.
I NEED YOU TO HELP HIM TOO.
SIGH
YOU DO HAVE AN INSTINCTUAL WAY OF COMPLICATING MY LIFE... DON'T YOU, FAITH?

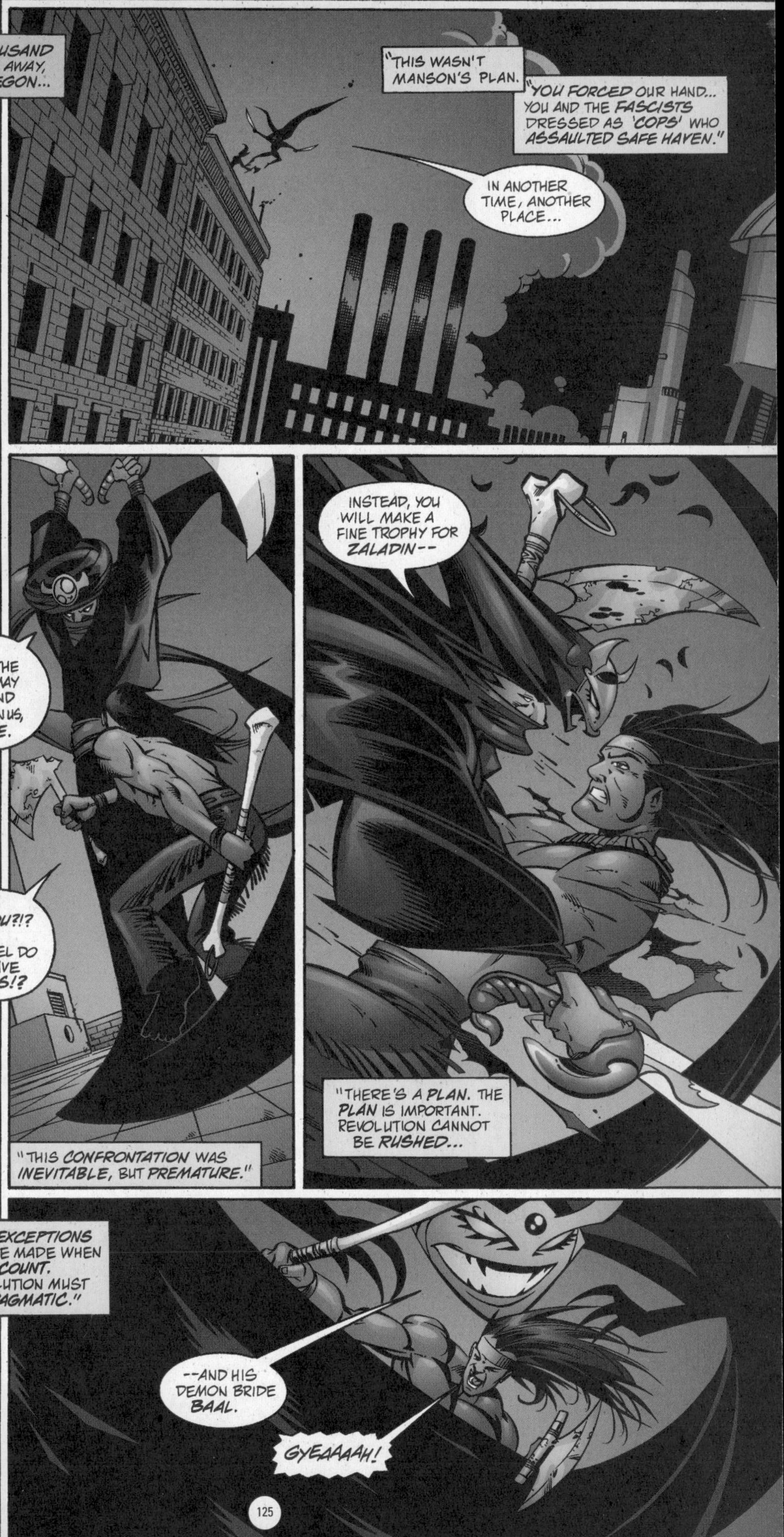

A THOUSAND MILES AWAY, IN OREGON...
"THIS WASN'T MANSON'S PLAN.
"YOU FORCED OUR HAND... YOU AND THE FASCISTS DRESSED AS 'COPS' WHO ASSAULTED SAFE HAVEN."
IN ANOTHER TIME, ANOTHER PLACE...
...YOU OF ALL THE LEAGUE MAY HAVE FOUND ALLIES IN US, APACHE.
WHO ARE YOU?!? WHAT QUARREL DO YOU HAVE WITH US!?
"THIS CONFRONTATION WAS INEVITABLE, BUT PREMATURE."
INSTEAD, YOU WILL MAKE A FINE TROPHY FOR ZALADIN--
"THERE'S A PLAN. THE PLAN IS IMPORTANT. REVOLUTION CANNOT BE RUSHED...
" BUT EXCEPTIONS CAN BE MADE WHEN THEY COUNT. REVOLUTION MUST BE PRAGMATIC."
--AND HIS DEMON BRIDE BAAL.
GYEAAAAH!

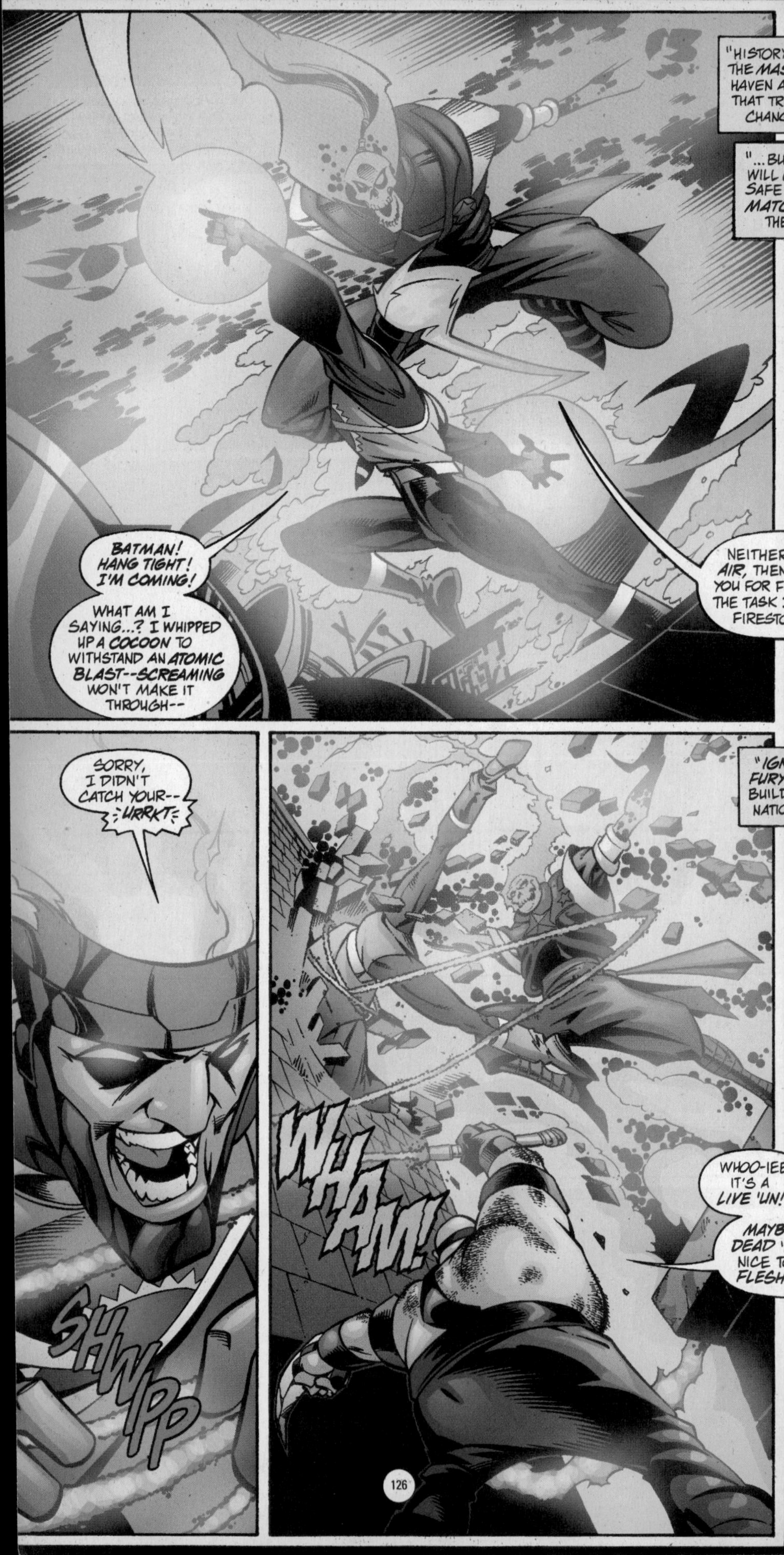

"HISTORY WILL REMEMBER THE MASSACRE AT SAFE HAVEN AS THE CATALYST THAT TRIGGERED THE CHANGE TO COME...
"...BUT KILLING YOU WILL GUARANTEE IT. SAFE HAVEN WAS THE MATCH... YOU'LL BE THE FLAME."
BATMAN! HANG TIGHT! I'M COMING!
WHAT AM I SAYING...? I WHIPPED UP A COCOON TO WITHSTAND AN ATOMIC BLAST--SCREAMING WON'T MAKE IT THROUGH--
NEITHER WILL AIR, THEN. THANK YOU FOR FINISHING THE TASK I STARTED, FIRESTORM.
SORRY, I DIDN'T CATCH YOUR-- URRKT!
SHWIPP
"IGNITING THE FURY THAT'S BEEN BUILDING IN THIS NATION FOR YEARS."
WHAM!
WHOO-IEE IT'S A LIVE 'UN!
MAYBE A DEAD 'UN, NOW! NICE TOSS, FLESHBURN!

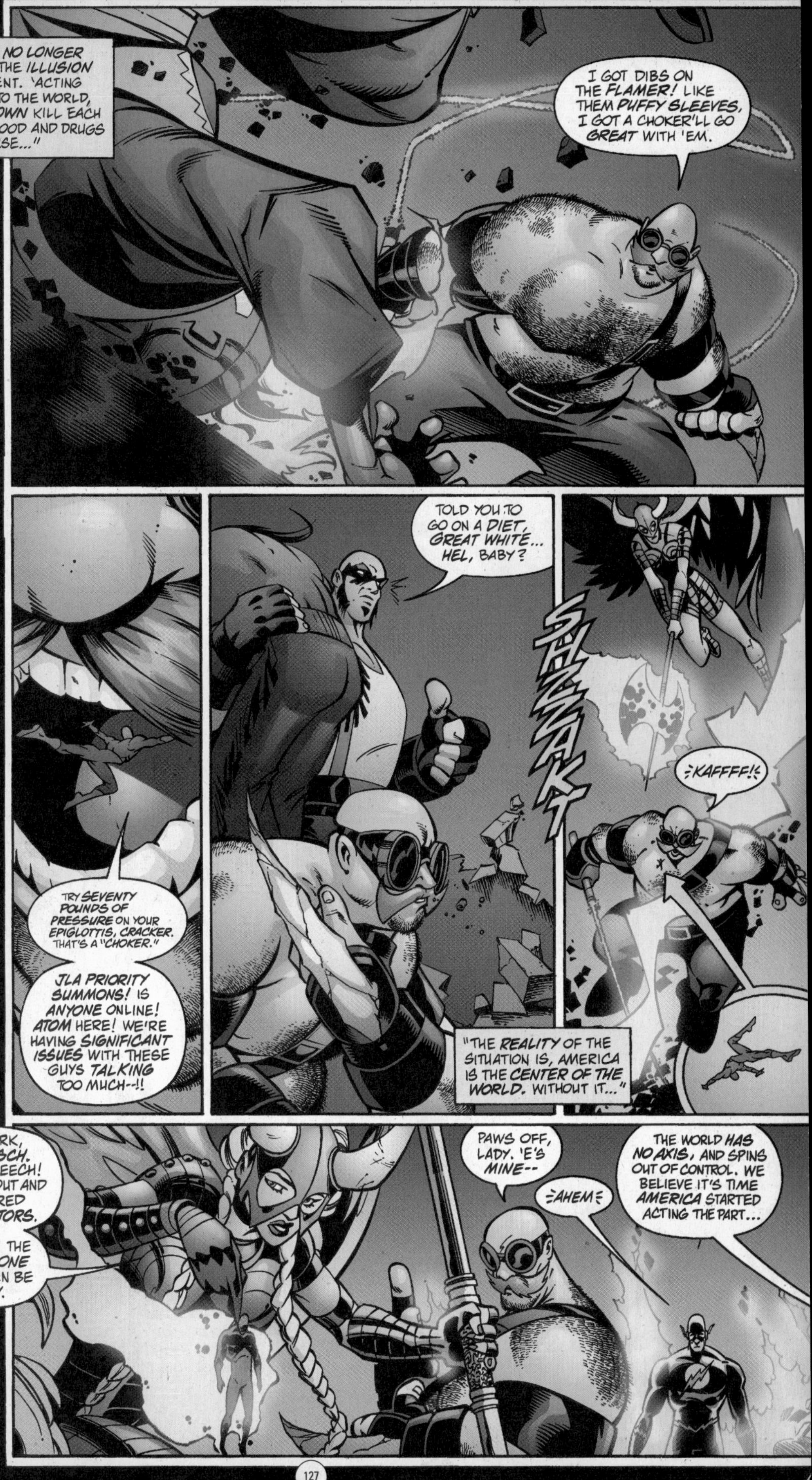
"AMERICANS NO LONGER BELIEVE IN THE ILLUSION YOU REPRESENT. 'ACTING POLICEMEN' TO THE WORLD, WHILE OUR OWN KILL EACH OTHER FOR FOOD AND DRUGS AND WORSE..."
I GOT DIBS ON THE FLAMER! LIKE THEM PUFFY SLEEVES, I GOT A CHOKER'LL GO GREAT WITH 'EM.
TRY SEVENTY POUNDS OF PRESSURE ON YOUR EPIGLOTTIS, CRACKER. THAT'S A "CHOKER."
JLA PRIORITY SUMMONS! IS ANYONE ONLINE! ATOM HERE! WE'RE HAVING SIGNIFICANT ISSUES WITH THESE GUYS TALKING TOO MUCH--!!
TOLD YOU TO GO ON A DIET, GREAT WHITE... HEL, BABY?
SHZAKT
KAFFFF!
"THE REALITY OF THE SITUATION IS, AMERICA IS THE CENTER OF THE WORLD. WITHOUT IT..."
NICE WORK, ÜBERMENSCH. AND NICE SPEECH! FIRST NIGHT OUT AND WE'VE SECURED THREE TRAITORS.
I THINK THE LITTLE ONE MAY EVEN BE A JEW.
PAWS OFF, LADY. 'E'S MINE--
AHEM
THE WORLD HAS NO AXIS, AND SPINS OUT OF CONTROL. WE BELIEVE IT'S TIME AMERICA STARTED ACTING THE PART...

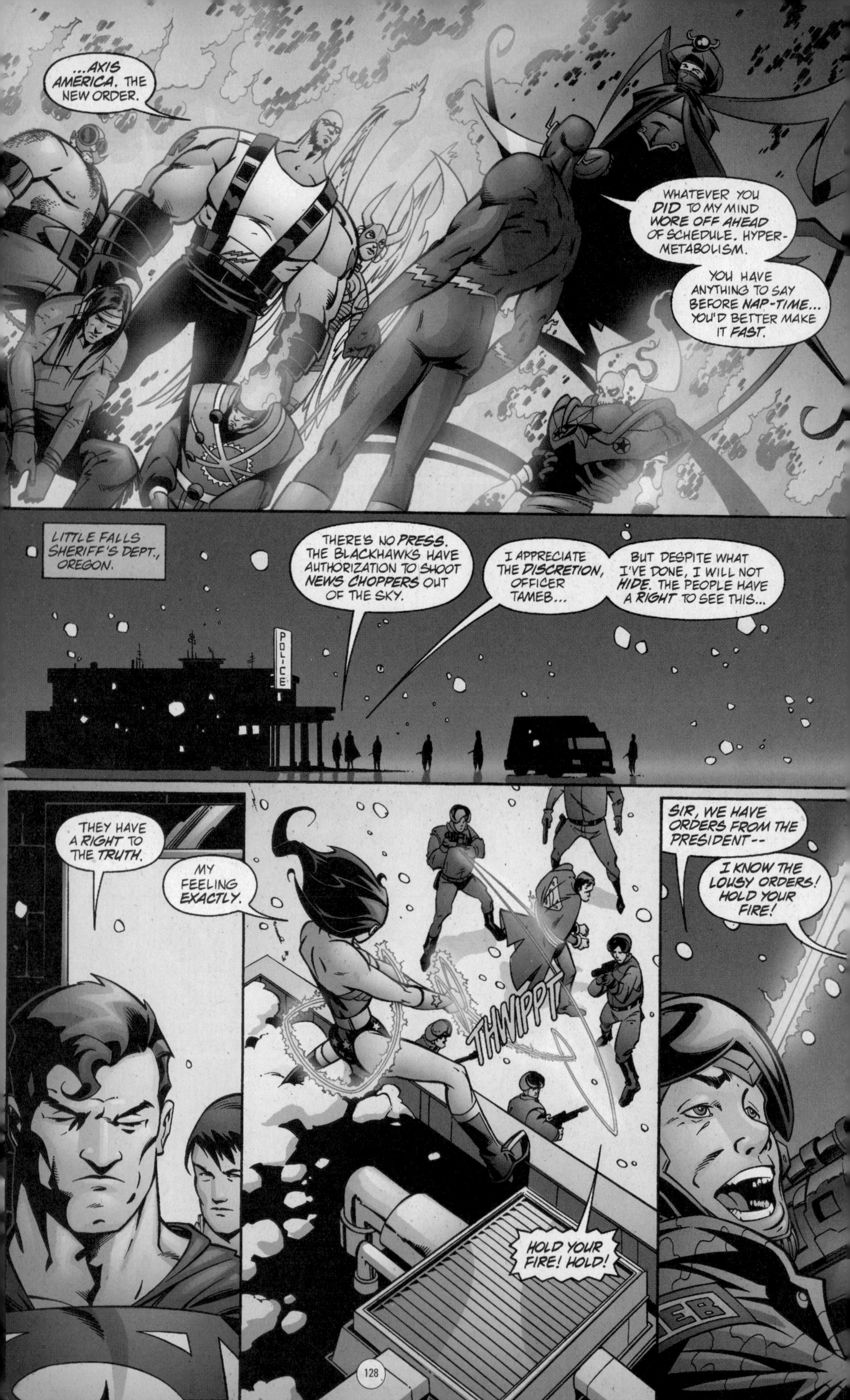
...AXIS AMERICA. THE NEW ORDER.
WHATEVER YOU DID TO MY MIND WORE OFF AHEAD OF SCHEDULE. HYPER-METABOLISM.
YOU HAVE ANYTHING TO SAY BEFORE NAP-TIME... YOU'D BETTER MAKE IT FAST.
LITTLE FALLS SHERIFF'S DEPT., OREGON.
THERE'S NO PRESS. THE BLACKHAWKS HAVE AUTHORIZATION TO SHOOT NEWS CHOPPERS OUT OF THE SKY.
I APPRECIATE THE DISCRETION, OFFICER TAMEB...
BUT DESPITE WHAT I'VE DONE, I WILL NOT HIDE. THE PEOPLE HAVE A RIGHT TO SEE THIS...
POLICE
THEY HAVE A RIGHT TO THE TRUTH.
MY FEELING EXACTLY.
THWIPPT
HOLD YOUR FIRE! HOLD!
SIR, WE HAVE ORDERS FROM THE PRESIDENT--
I KNOW THE LOUSY ORDERS! HOLD YOUR FIRE!

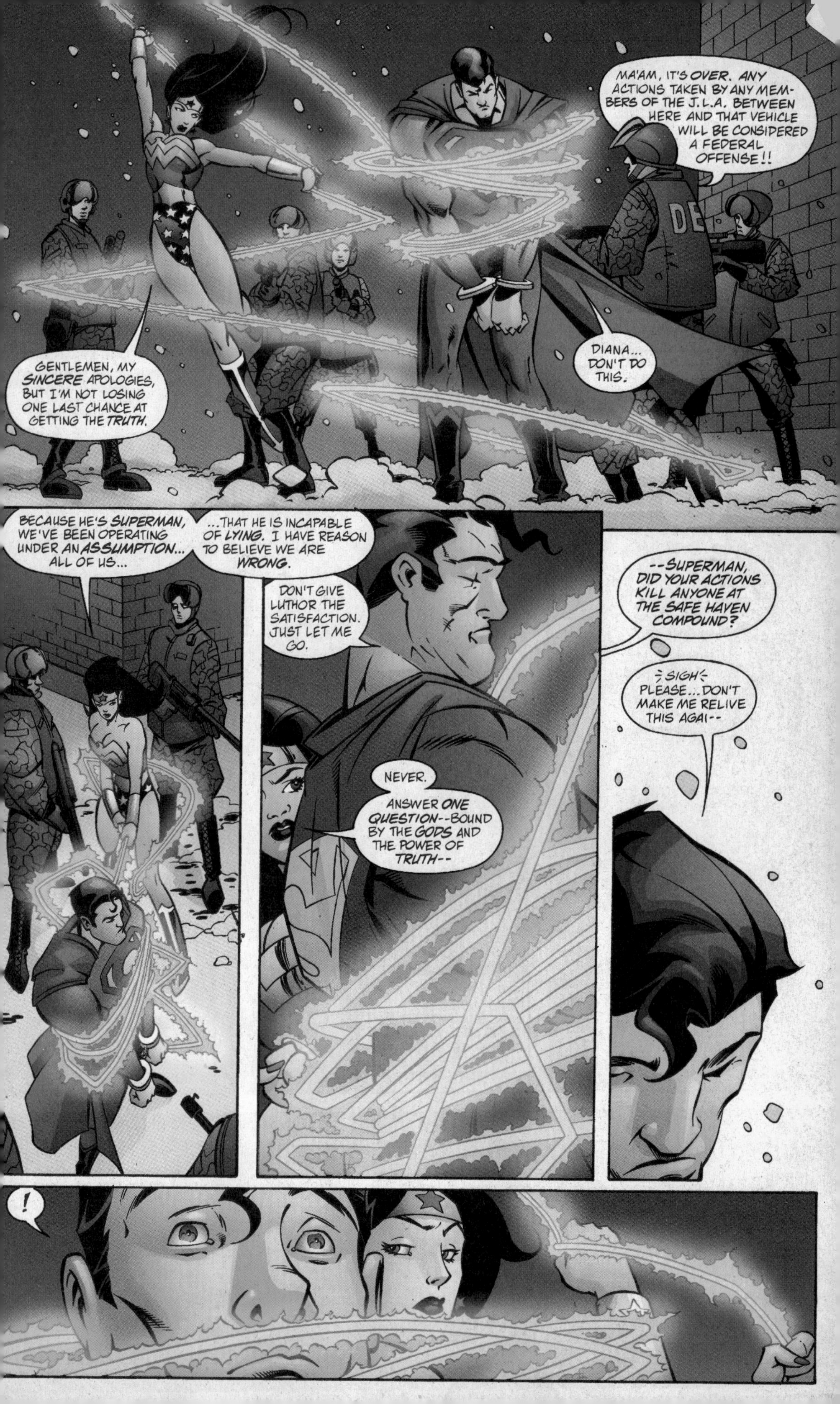
MA'AM, IT'S OVER. ANY ACTIONS TAKEN BY ANY MEMBERS OF THE J.L.A. BETWEEN HERE AND THAT VEHICLE WILL BE CONSIDERED A FEDERAL OFFENSE!!
GENTLEMEN, MY SINCERE APOLOGIES, BUT I'M NOT LOSING ONE LAST CHANCE AT GETTING THE TRUTH.
DIANA... DON'T DO THIS.
BECAUSE HE'S SUPERMAN, WE'VE BEEN OPERATING UNDER AN ASSUMPTION... ALL OF US...
...THAT HE IS INCAPABLE OF LYING. I HAVE REASON TO BELIEVE WE ARE WRONG.
DON'T GIVE LUTHOR THE SATISFACTION. JUST LET ME GO.
NEVER.
ANSWER ONE QUESTION--BOUND BY THE GODS AND THE POWER OF TRUTH--
--SUPERMAN, DID YOUR ACTIONS KILL ANYONE AT THE SAFE HAVEN COMPOUND?
SIGH
PLEASE... DON'T MAKE ME RELIVE THIS AGAI--
!

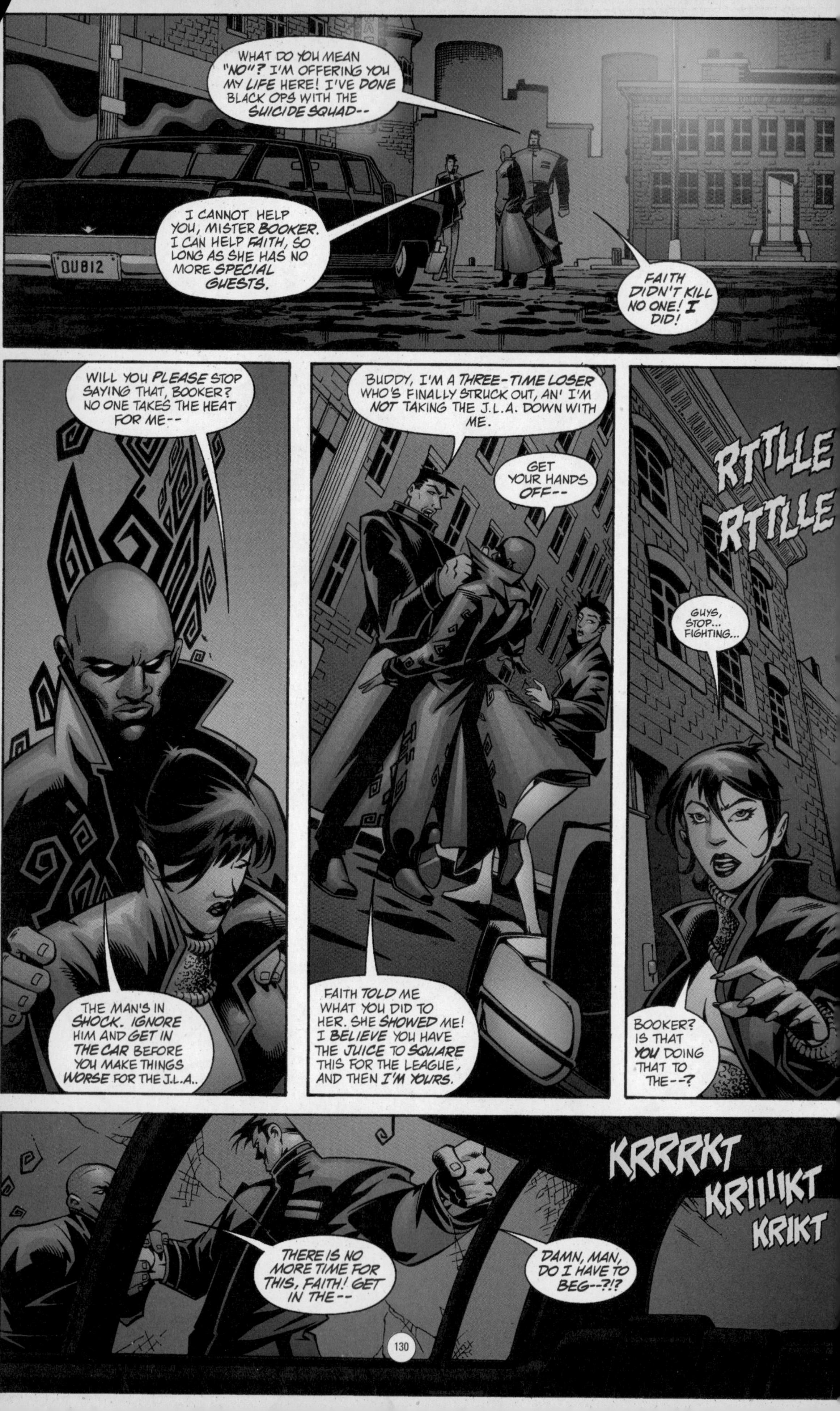
WHAT DO YOU MEAN "NO"? I'M OFFERING YOU MY LIFE HERE! I'VE DONE BLACK OPS WITH THE SUICIDE SQUAD--
QU812
I CANNOT HELP YOU, MISTER BOOKER. I CAN HELP FAITH, SO LONG AS SHE HAS NO MORE SPECIAL GUESTS.
FAITH DIDN'T KILL NO ONE! I DID!
WILL YOU PLEASE STOP SAYING THAT, BOOKER? NO ONE TAKES THE HEAT FOR ME--
THE MAN'S IN SHOCK. IGNORE HIM AND GET IN THE CAR BEFORE YOU MAKE THINGS WORSE FOR THE J.L.A..
BUDDY, I'M A THREE-TIME LOSER WHO'S FINALLY STRUCK OUT, AN' I'M NOT TAKING THE J.L.A. DOWN WITH ME.
GET YOUR HANDS OFF--
FAITH TOLD ME WHAT YOU DID TO HER. SHE SHOWED ME! I BELIEVE YOU HAVE THE JUICE TO SQUARE THIS FOR THE LEAGUE, AND THEN I'M YOURS.
RTTLLE
RTTLLE
GUYS, STOP... FIGHTING...
BOOKER? IS THAT YOU DOING THAT TO THE--?
KRRRKT
KRIIIIKT
KRIKT
THERE IS NO MORE TIME FOR THIS, FAITH! GET IN THE--
DAMN, MAN, DO I HAVE TO BEG--?!?

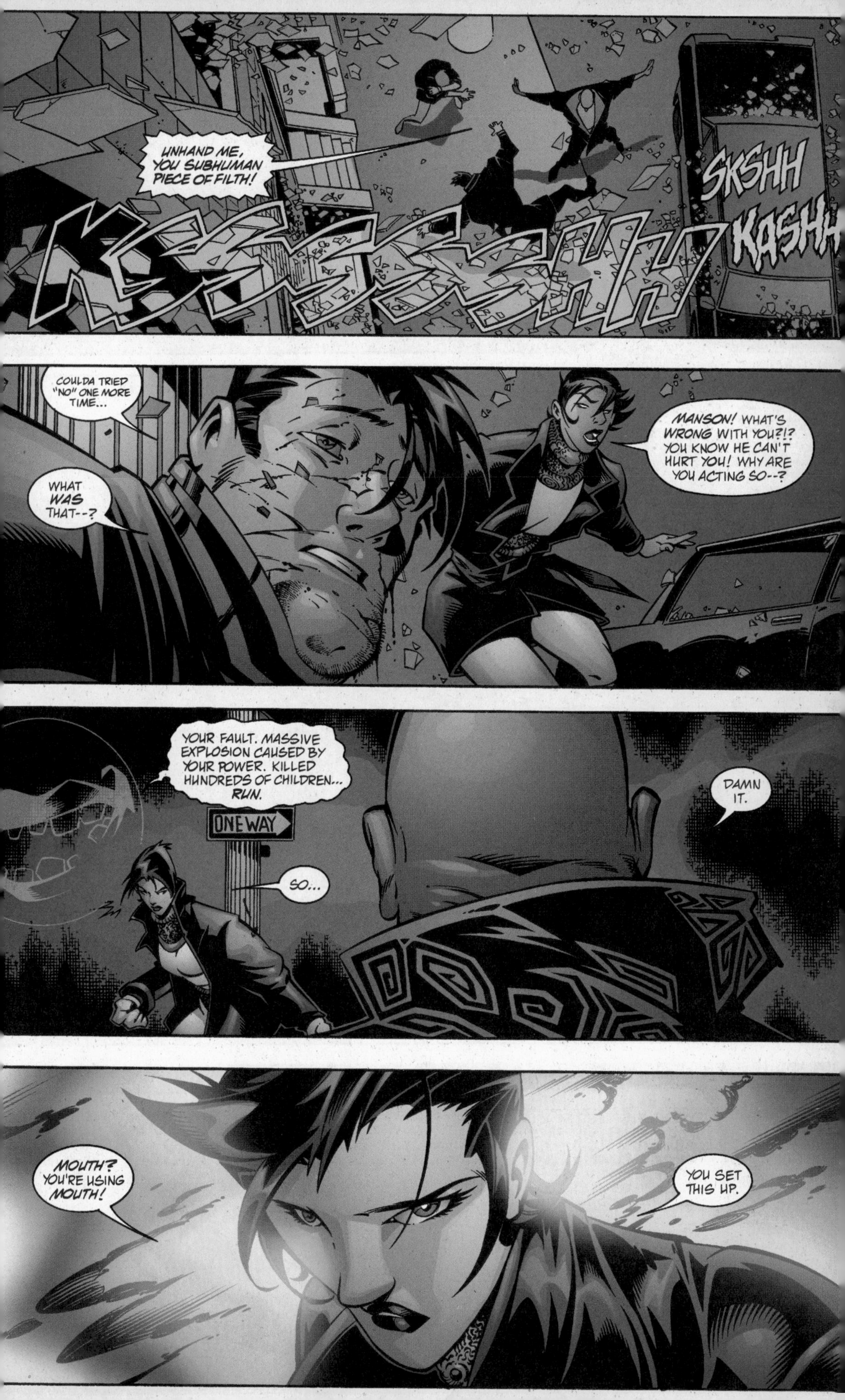
UNHAND ME, YOU SUBHUMAN PIECE OF FILTH!
SKSHH
KASHH
COULDA TRIED "NO" ONE MORE TIME...
WHAT WAS THAT--?
MANSON! WHAT'S WRONG WITH YOU?!? YOU KNOW HE CAN'T HURT YOU! WHY ARE YOU ACTING SO--?
YOUR FAULT. MASSIVE EXPLOSION CAUSED BY YOUR POWER. KILLED HUNDREDS OF CHILDREN... RUN.
ONE WAY
SO...
DAMN IT.
MOUTH? YOU'RE USING MOUTH!
YOU SET THIS UP.

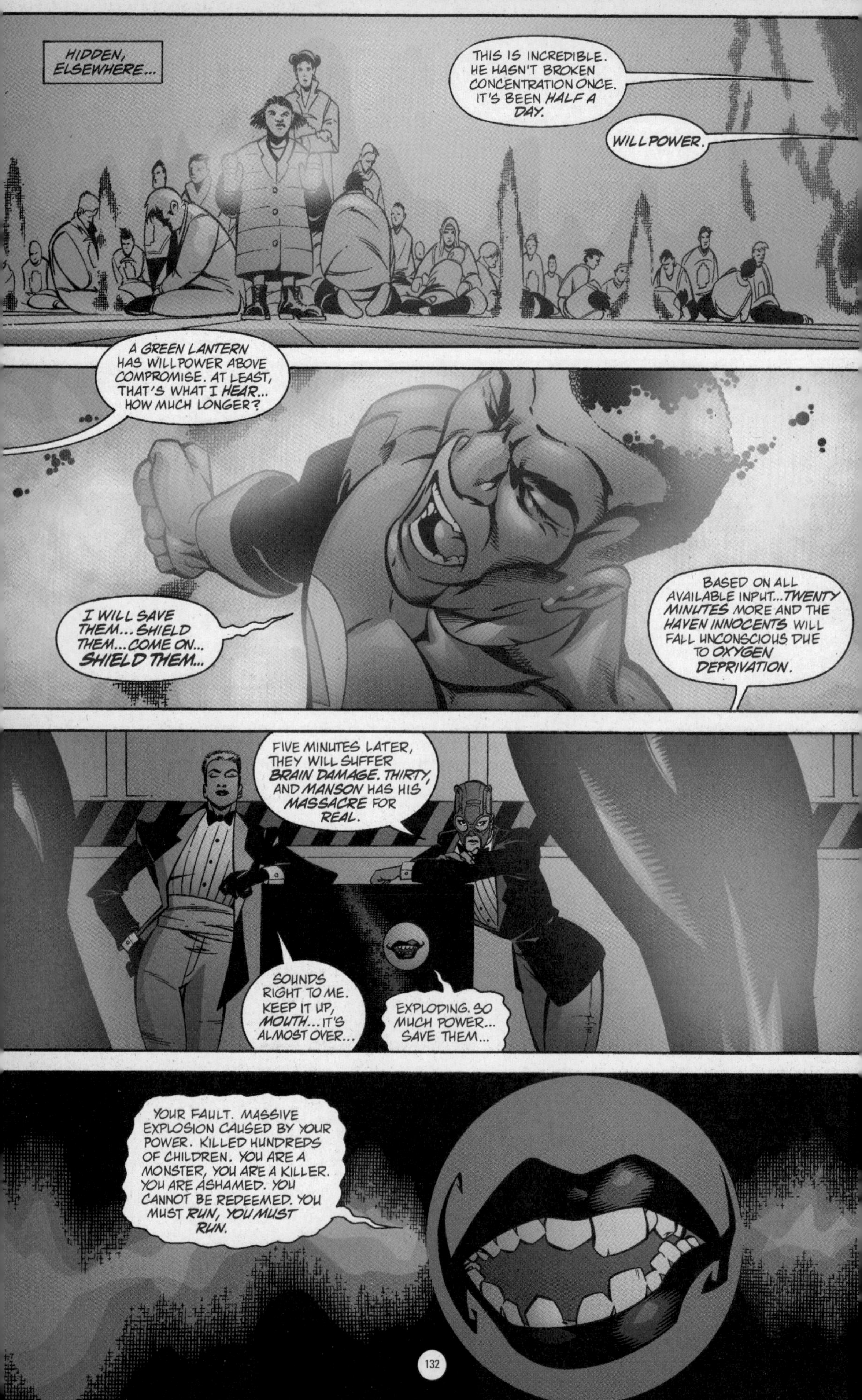
HIDDEN, ELSEWHERE...
THIS IS INCREDIBLE. HE HASN'T BROKEN CONCENTRATION ONCE. IT'S BEEN HALF A DAY.
WILLPOWER.
A GREEN LANTERN HAS WILLPOWER ABOVE COMPROMISE. AT LEAST, THAT'S WHAT I HEAR... HOW MUCH LONGER?
I WILL SAVE THEM... SHIELD THEM... COME ON... SHIELD THEM...
BASED ON ALL AVAILABLE INPUT... TWENTY MINUTES MORE AND THE HAVEN INNOCENTS WILL FALL UNCONSCIOUS DUE TO OXYGEN DEPRIVATION.
FIVE MINUTES LATER, THEY WILL SUFFER BRAIN DAMAGE. THIRTY, AND MANSON HAS HIS MASSACRE FOR REAL.
SOUNDS RIGHT TO ME. KEEP IT UP, MOUTH... IT'S ALMOST OVER...
EXPLODING. SO MUCH POWER... SAVE THEM...
YOUR FAULT. MASSIVE EXPLOSION CAUSED BY YOUR POWER. KILLED HUNDREDS OF CHILDREN. YOU ARE A MONSTER, YOU ARE A KILLER. YOU ARE ASHAMED. YOU CANNOT BE REDEEMED. YOU MUST RUN, YOU MUST RUN.

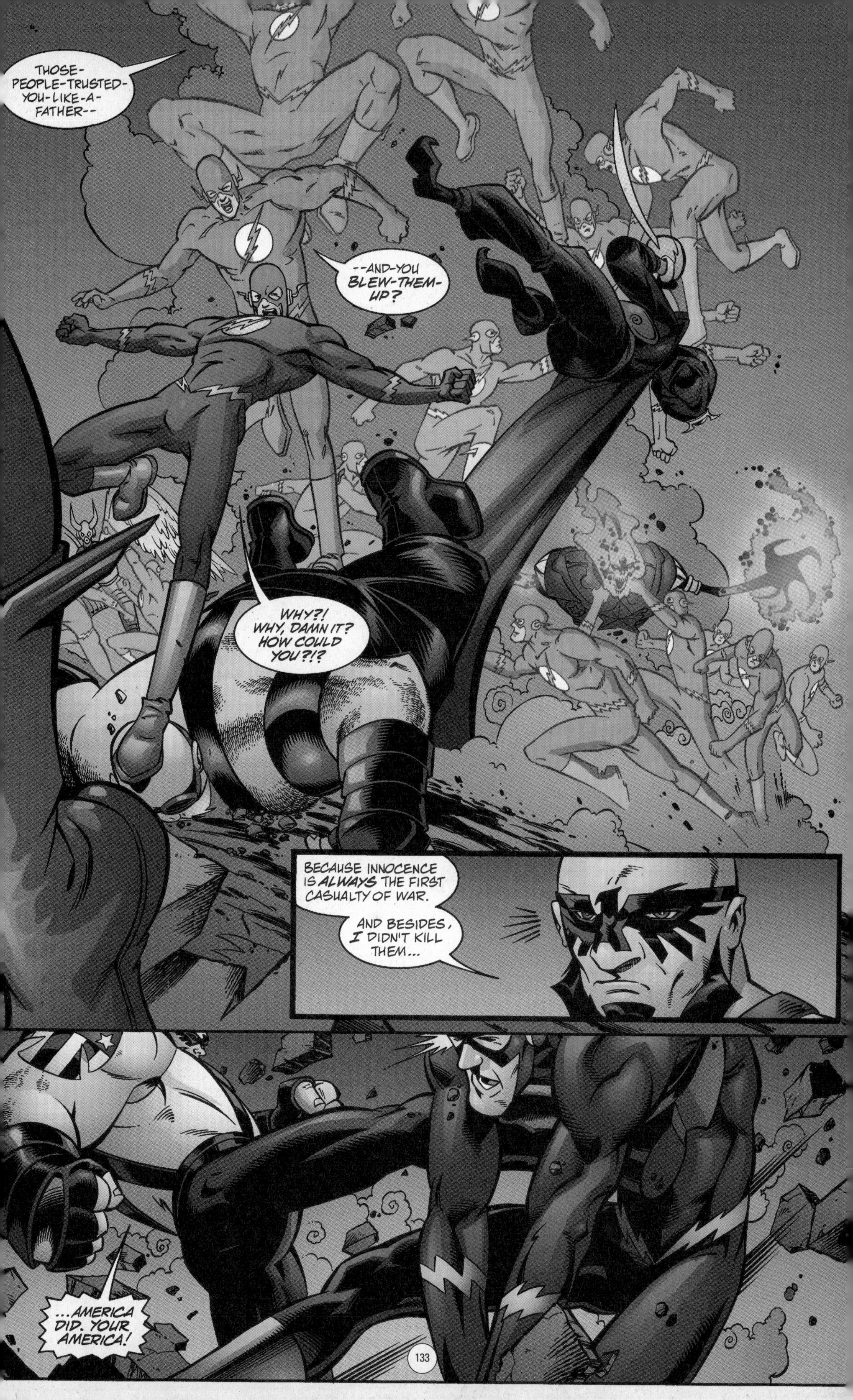
THOSE-PEOPLE-TRUSTED-YOU-LIKE-A-FATHER--
--AND-YOU BLEW-THEM-UP?
WHY?! WHY, DAMN IT? HOW COULD YOU?!?
BECAUSE INNOCENCE IS ALWAYS THE FIRST CASUALTY OF WAR.
AND BESIDES, I DIDN'T KILL THEM...
...AMERICA DID. YOUR AMERICA!

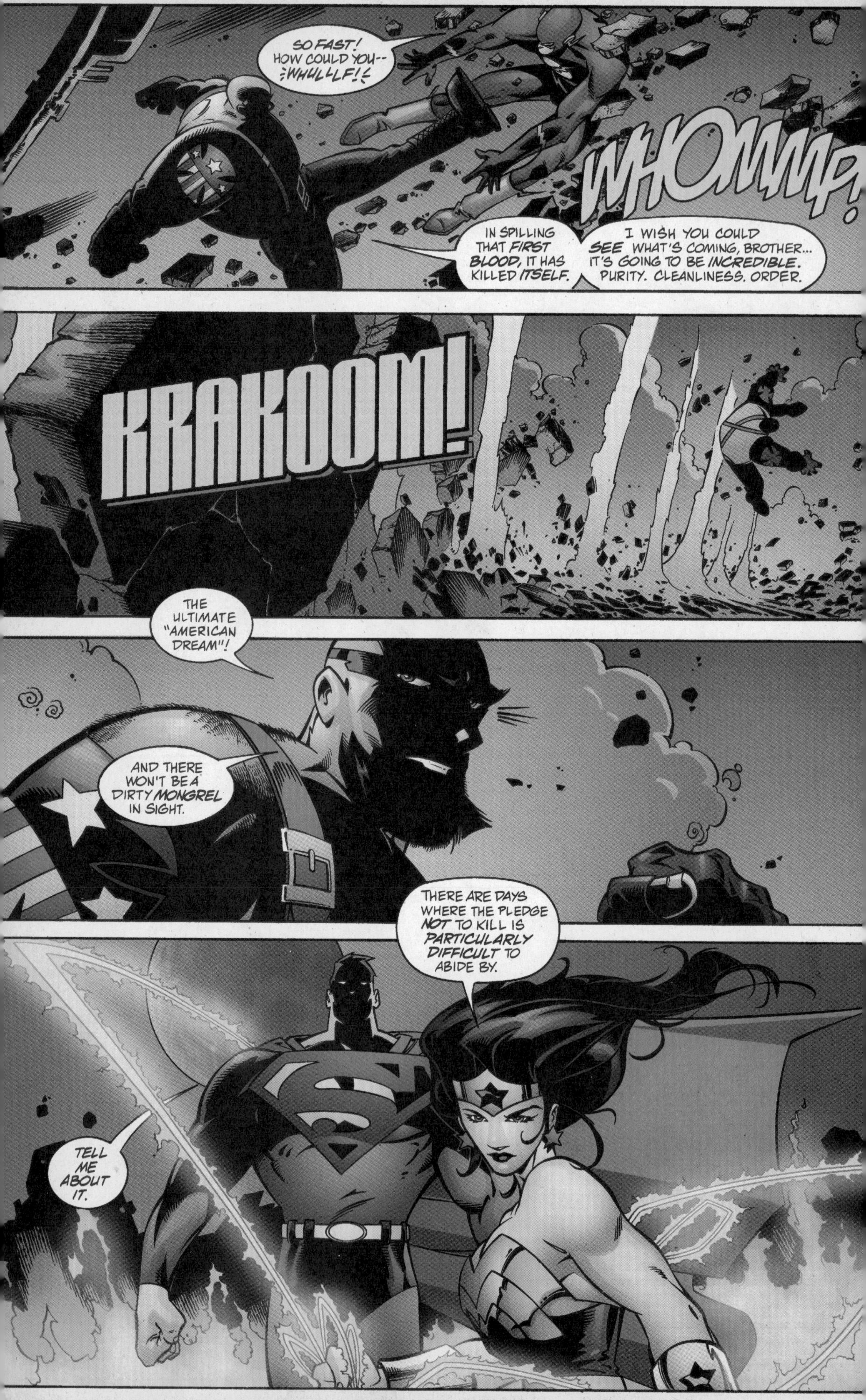
SO FAST! HOW COULD YOU-- ≒WHULLLF!≒
WHOMMP!
IN SPILLING THAT FIRST BLOOD, IT HAS KILLED ITSELF.
I WISH YOU COULD SEE WHAT'S COMING, BROTHER... IT'S GOING TO BE INCREDIBLE. PURITY. CLEANLINESS. ORDER.
KRAKOOM!
THE ULTIMATE "AMERICAN DREAM"!
AND THERE WON'T BE A DIRTY MONGREL IN SIGHT.
THERE ARE DAYS WHERE THE PLEDGE NOT TO KILL IS PARTICULARLY DIFFICULT TO ABIDE BY.
TELL ME ABOUT IT.

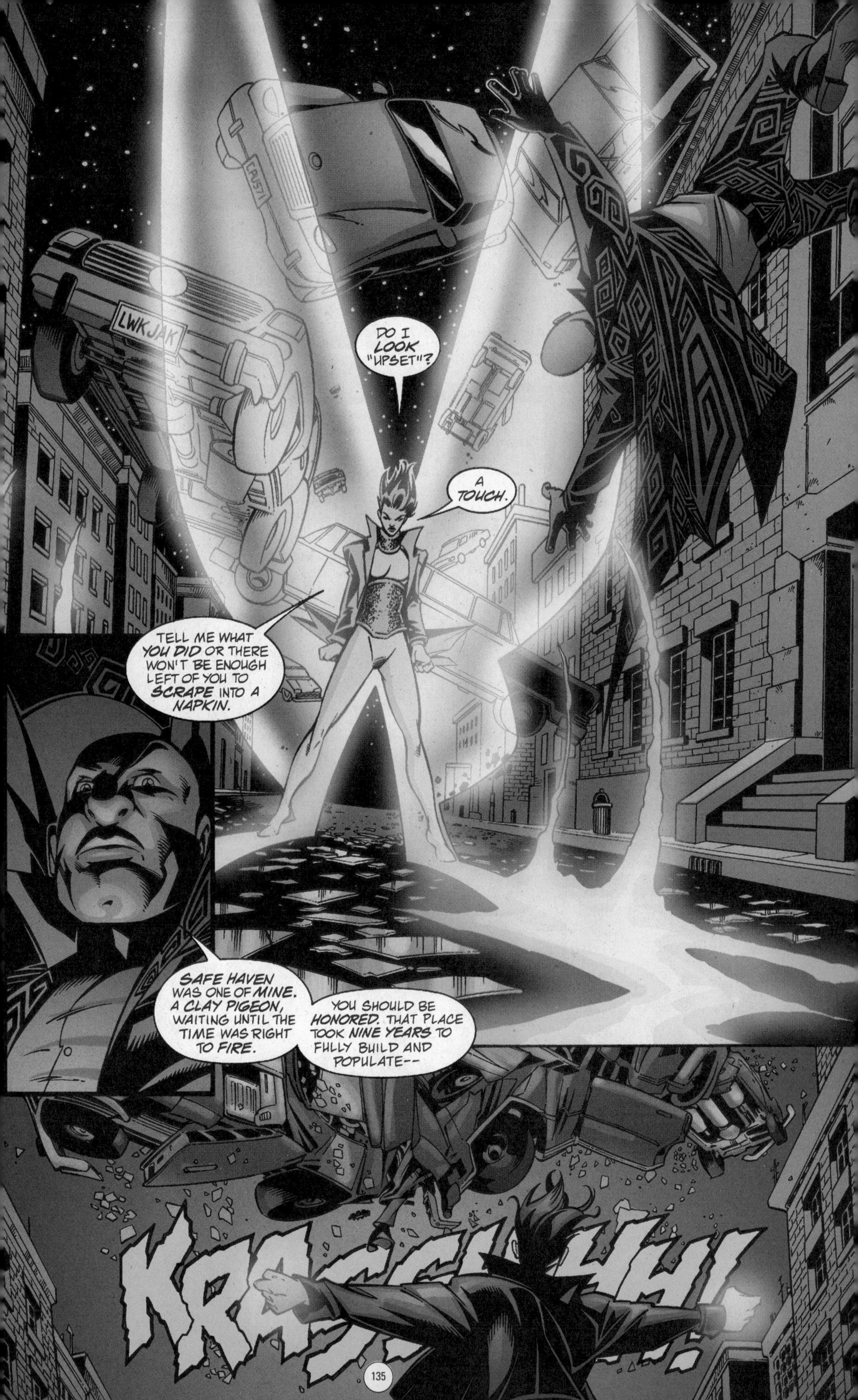
LWKJAK
DO I LOOK "UPSET"?
A TOUCH.
TELL ME WHAT YOU DID OR THERE WON'T BE ENOUGH LEFT OF YOU TO SCRAPE INTO A NAPKIN.
SAFE HAVEN WAS ONE OF MINE. A CLAY PIGEON, WAITING UNTIL THE TIME WAS RIGHT TO FIRE.
YOU SHOULD BE HONORED. THAT PLACE TOOK NINE YEARS TO FULLY BUILD AND POPULATE--

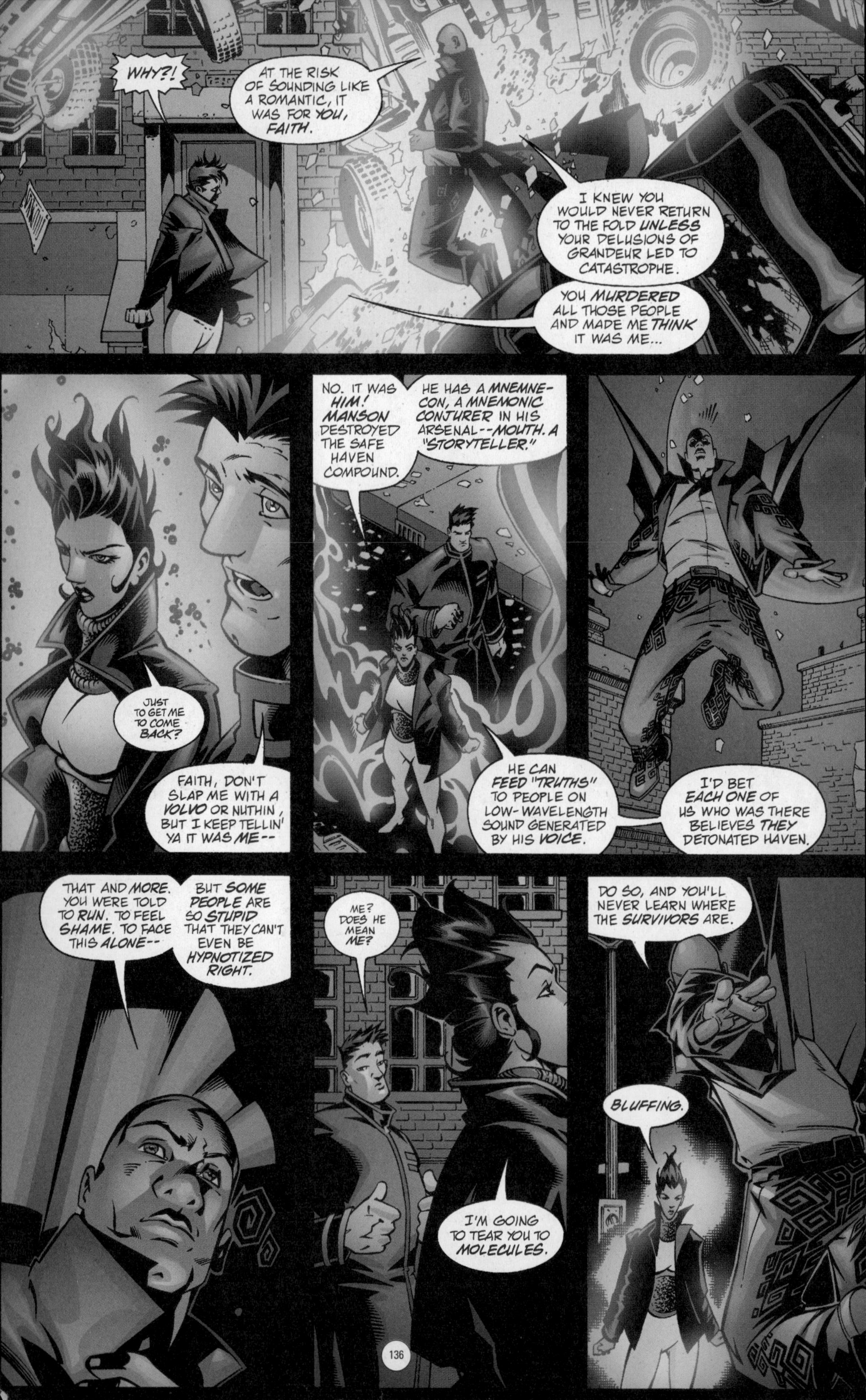
WHY?!
AT THE RISK OF SOUNDING LIKE A ROMANTIC, IT WAS FOR YOU, FAITH.
I KNEW YOU WOULD NEVER RETURN TO THE FOLD UNLESS YOUR DELUSIONS OF GRANDEUR LED TO CATASTROPHE.
YOU MURDERED ALL THOSE PEOPLE AND MADE ME THINK IT WAS ME...
JUST TO GET ME TO COME BACK?
FAITH, DON'T SLAP ME WITH A VOLVO OR NUTHIN, BUT I KEEP TELLIN' YA IT WAS ME--
NO. IT WAS HIM! MANSON DESTROYED THE SAFE HAVEN COMPOUND.
HE HAS A MNEMNECON, A MNEMONIC CONJURER IN HIS ARSENAL--MOUTH. A "STORYTELLER."
HE CAN FEED "TRUTHS" TO PEOPLE ON LOW-WAVELENGTH SOUND GENERATED BY HIS VOICE.
I'D BET EACH ONE OF US WHO WAS THERE BELIEVES THEY DETONATED HAVEN.
THAT AND MORE. YOU WERE TOLD TO RUN. TO FEEL SHAME. TO FACE THIS ALONE--
BUT SOME PEOPLE ARE SO STUPID THAT THEY CAN'T EVEN BE HYPNOTIZED RIGHT.
ME? DOES HE MEAN ME?
I'M GOING TO TEAR YOU TO MOLECULES.
DO SO, AND YOU'LL NEVER LEARN WHERE THE SURVIVORS ARE.
BLUFFING.

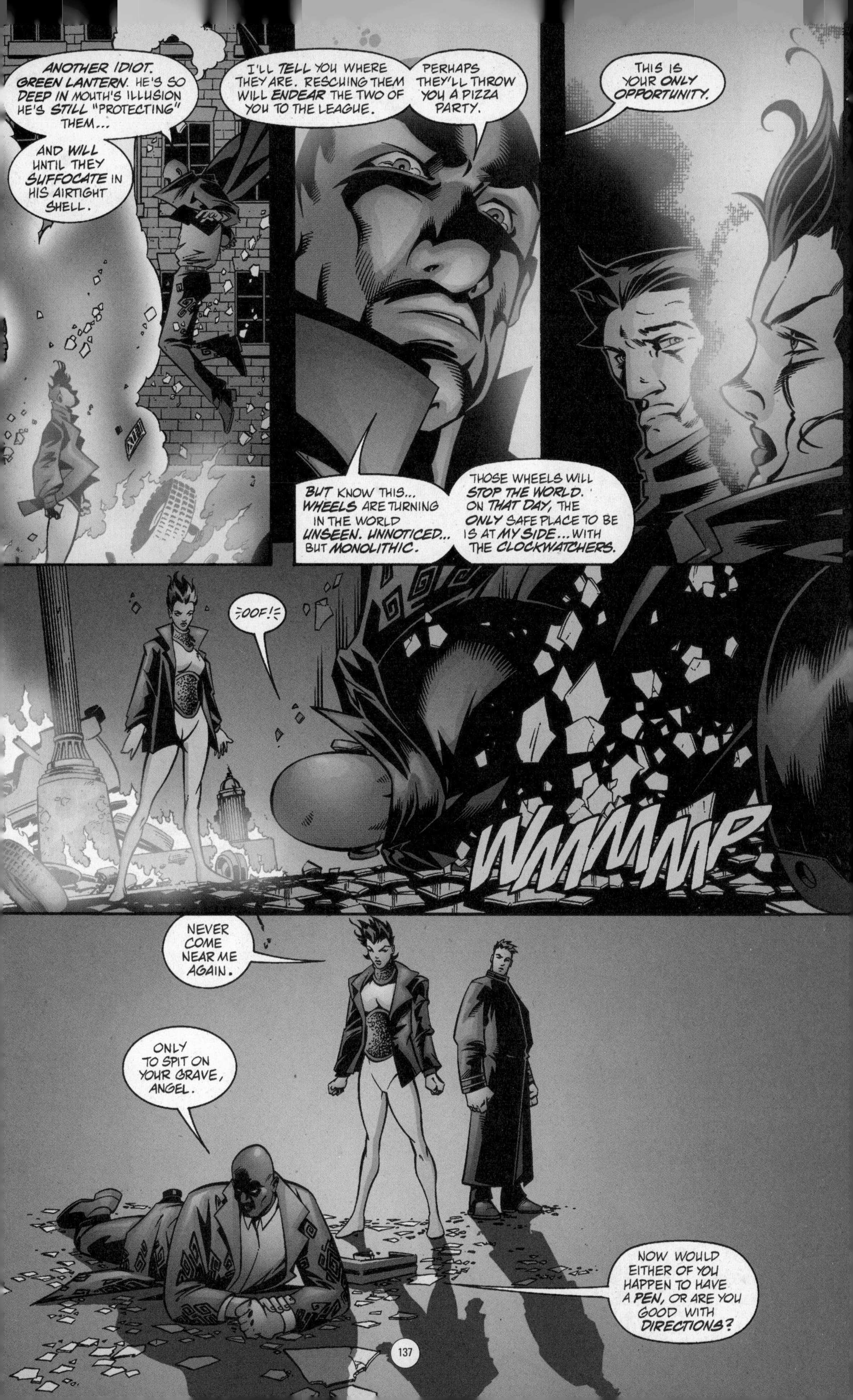
ANOTHER IDIOT. GREEN LANTERN. HE'S SO DEEP IN MOUTH'S ILLUSION HE'S STILL "PROTECTING" THEM...
AND WILL UNTIL THEY SUFFOCATE IN HIS AIRTIGHT SHELL.
I'LL TELL YOU WHERE THEY ARE. RESCUING THEM WILL ENDEAR THE TWO OF YOU TO THE LEAGUE.
PERHAPS THEY'LL THROW YOU A PIZZA PARTY.
THIS IS YOUR ONLY OPPORTUNITY.
BUT KNOW THIS... WHEELS ARE TURNING IN THE WORLD UNSEEN. UNNOTICED... BUT MONOLITHIC.
THOSE WHEELS WILL STOP THE WORLD. ON THAT DAY, THE ONLY SAFE PLACE TO BE IS AT MY SIDE... WITH THE CLOCKWATCHERS.
OOF!
WMMMP
NEVER COME NEAR ME AGAIN.
ONLY TO SPIT ON YOUR GRAVE, ANGEL.
NOW WOULD EITHER OF YOU HAPPEN TO HAVE A PEN, OR ARE YOU GOOD WITH DIRECTIONS?

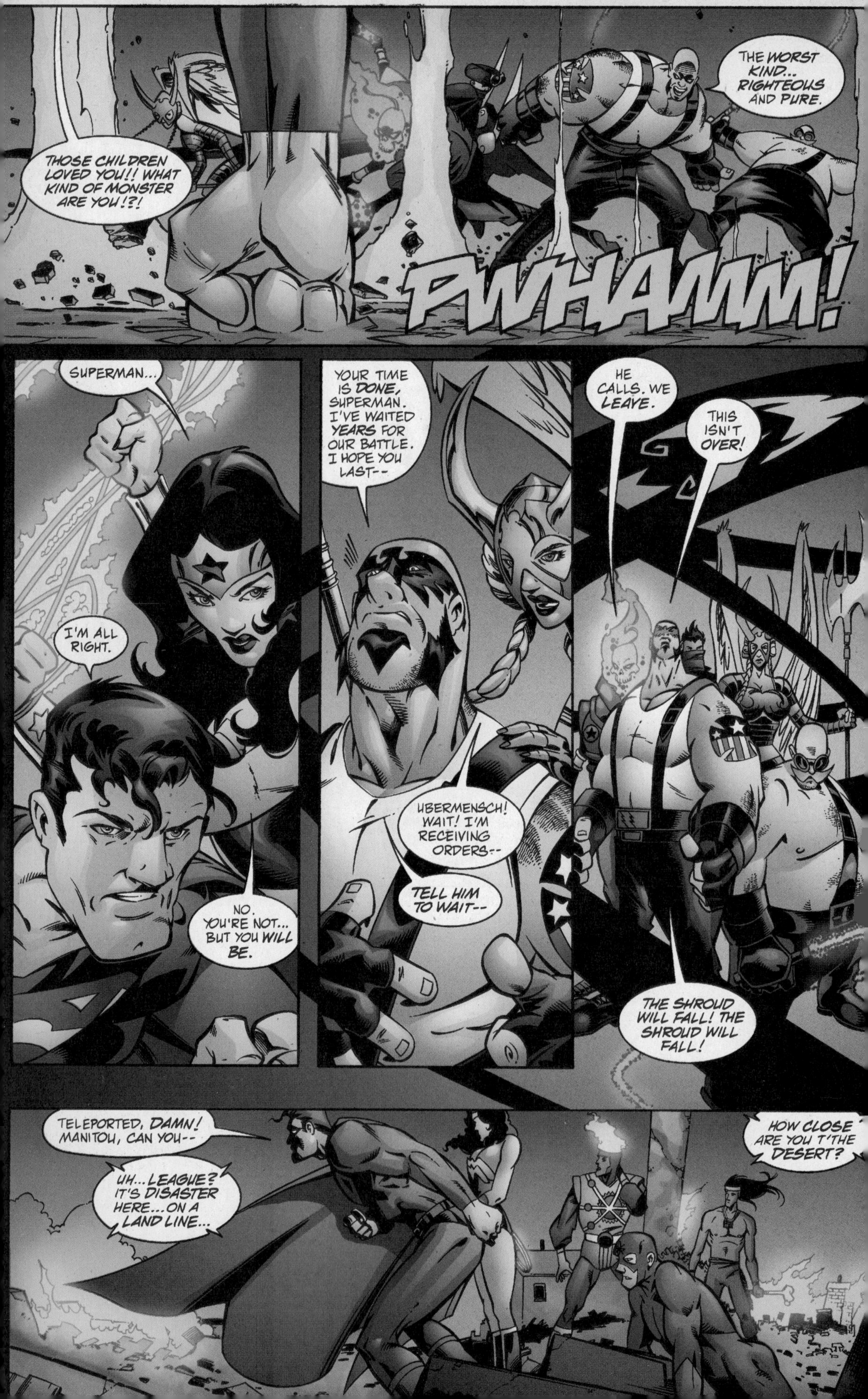
THOSE CHILDREN LOVED YOU!! WHAT KIND OF MONSTER ARE YOU!?!
THE WORST KIND... RIGHTEOUS AND PURE.
PWHAMMM!
SUPERMAN...
I'M ALL RIGHT.
NO. YOU'RE NOT... BUT YOU WILL BE.
YOUR TIME IS DONE, SUPERMAN. I'VE WAITED YEARS FOR OUR BATTLE. I HOPE YOU LAST--
UBERMENSCH! WAIT! I'M RECEIVING ORDERS--
TELL HIM TO WAIT--
HE CALLS. WE LEAVE.
THIS ISN'T OVER!
THE SHROUD WILL FALL! THE SHROUD WILL FALL!
TELEPORTED, DAMN! MANITOU, CAN YOU--
UH...LEAGUE? IT'S DISASTER HERE...ON A LAND LINE...
HOW CLOSE ARE YOU T'THE DESERT?

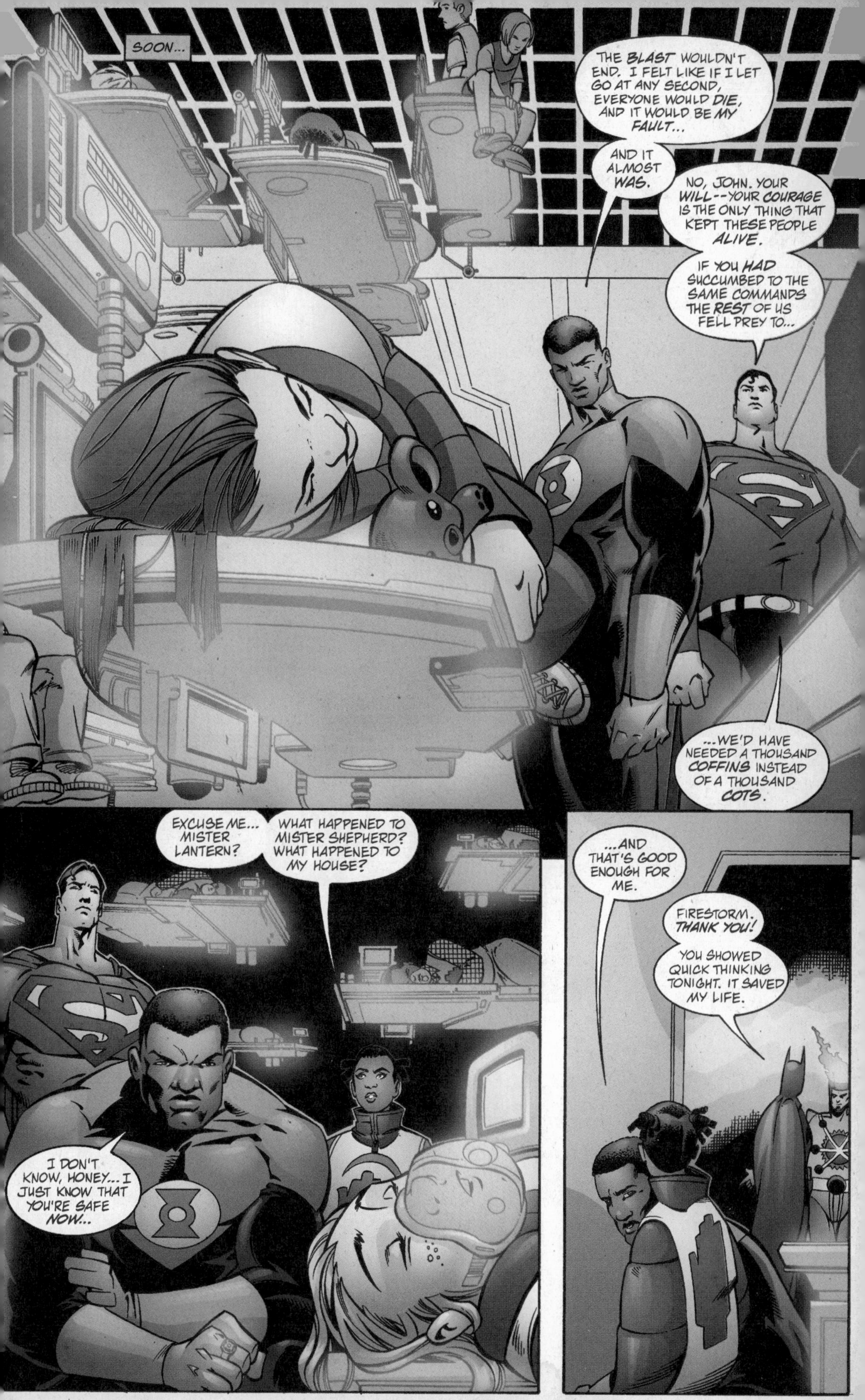
SOON...
THE BLAST WOULDN'T END. I FELT LIKE IF I LET GO AT ANY SECOND, EVERYONE WOULD DIE, AND IT WOULD BE MY FAULT...
AND IT ALMOST WAS.
NO, JOHN. YOUR WILL--YOUR COURAGE IS THE ONLY THING THAT KEPT THESE PEOPLE ALIVE.
IF YOU HAD SUCCUMBED TO THE SAME COMMANDS THE REST OF US FELL PREY TO...
...WE'D HAVE NEEDED A THOUSAND COFFINS INSTEAD OF A THOUSAND COTS.
EXCUSE ME... MISTER LANTERN?
WHAT HAPPENED TO MISTER SHEPHERD? WHAT HAPPENED TO MY HOUSE?
I DON'T KNOW, HONEY... I JUST KNOW THAT YOU'RE SAFE NOW...
...AND THAT'S GOOD ENOUGH FOR ME.
FIRESTORM. THANK YOU!
YOU SHOWED QUICK THINKING TONIGHT. IT SAVED MY LIFE.

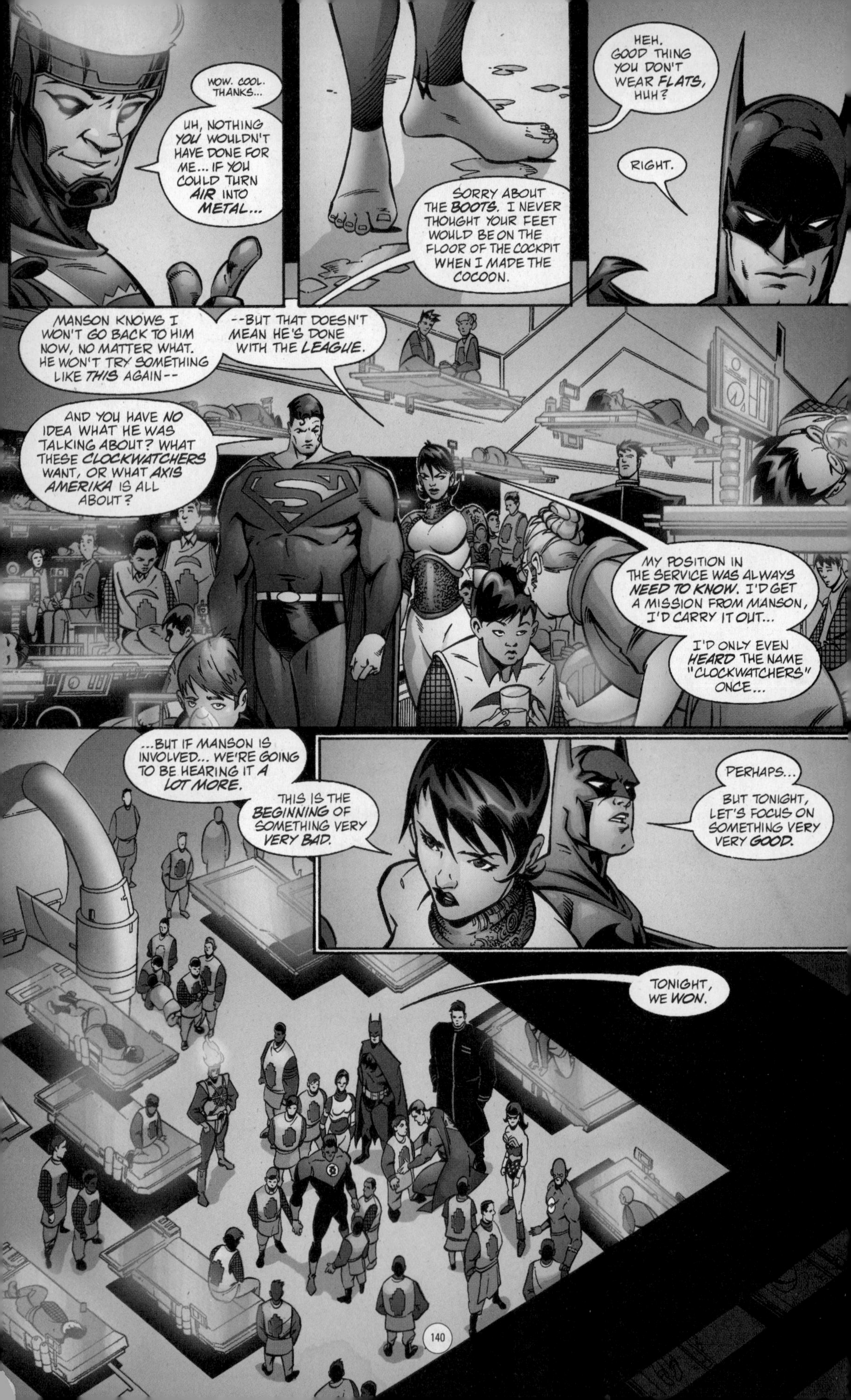
WOW. COOL. THANKS...
UH, NOTHING YOU WOULDN'T HAVE DONE FOR ME... IF YOU COULD TURN AIR INTO METAL...
SORRY ABOUT THE BOOTS. I NEVER THOUGHT YOUR FEET WOULD BE ON THE FLOOR OF THE COCKPIT WHEN I MADE THE COCOON.
HEH. GOOD THING YOU DON'T WEAR FLATS, HUH?
RIGHT.
MANSON KNOWS I WON'T GO BACK TO HIM NOW, NO MATTER WHAT. HE WON'T TRY SOMETHING LIKE THIS AGAIN--
--BUT THAT DOESN'T MEAN HE'S DONE WITH THE LEAGUE.
AND YOU HAVE NO IDEA WHAT HE WAS TALKING ABOUT? WHAT THESE CLOCKWATCHERS WANT, OR WHAT AXIS AMERIKA IS ALL ABOUT?
MY POSITION IN THE SERVICE WAS ALWAYS NEED TO KNOW. I'D GET A MISSION FROM MANSON, I'D CARRY IT OUT...
I'D ONLY EVEN HEARD THE NAME "CLOCKWATCHERS" ONCE...
...BUT IF MANSON IS INVOLVED... WE'RE GOING TO BE HEARING IT A LOT MORE.
THIS IS THE BEGINNING OF SOMETHING VERY VERY BAD.
PERHAPS...
BUT TONIGHT, LET'S FOCUS ON SOMETHING VERY VERY GOOD.
TONIGHT, WE WON.

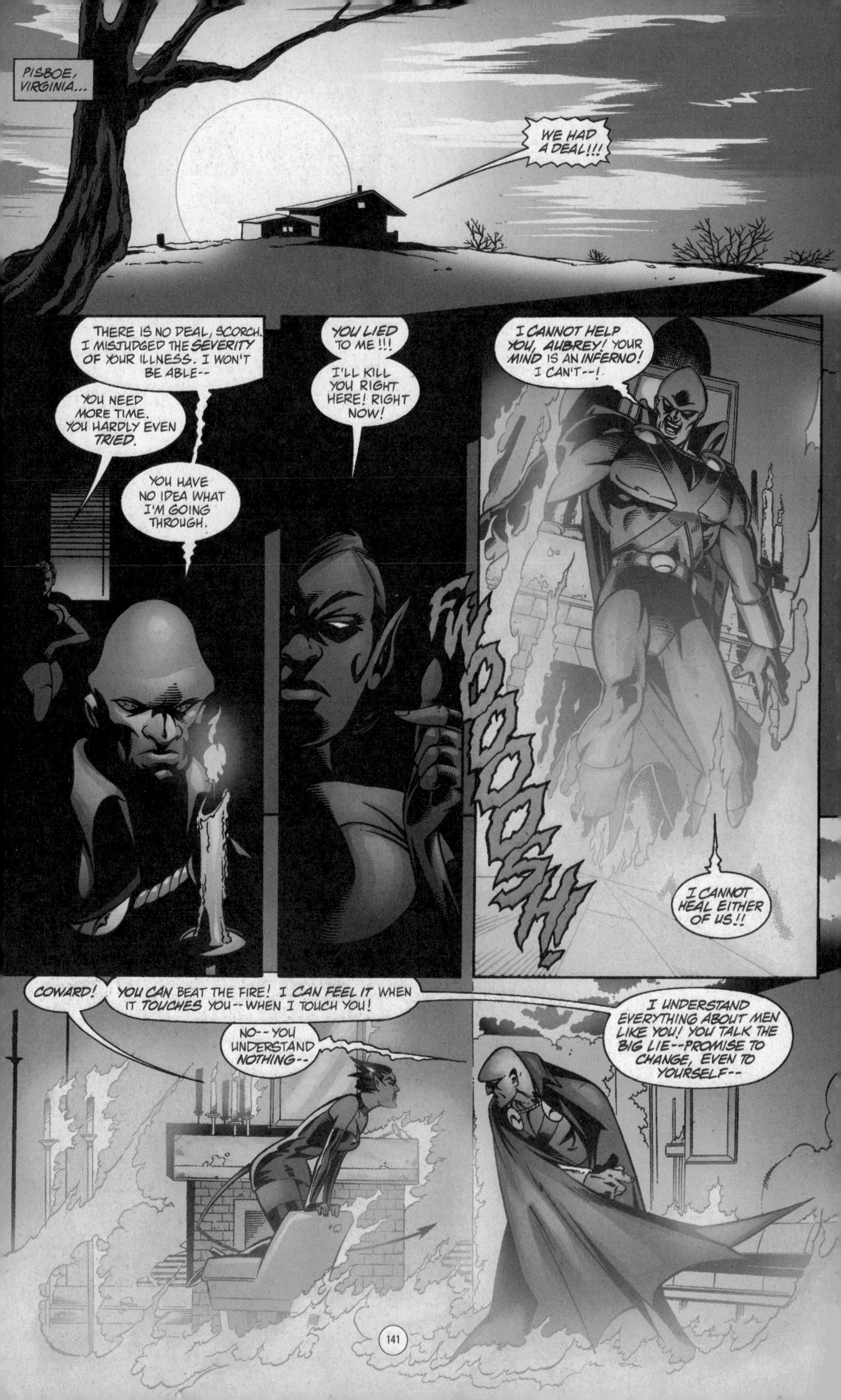

PISBOE, VIRGINIA...
WE HAD A DEAL!!!
THERE IS NO DEAL, SCORCH. I MISJUDGED THE SEVERITY OF YOUR ILLNESS. I WON'T BE ABLE--
YOU NEED MORE TIME. YOU HARDLY EVEN TRIED.
YOU HAVE NO IDEA WHAT I'M GOING THROUGH.
YOU LIED TO ME!!!
I'LL KILL YOU RIGHT HERE! RIGHT NOW!
I CANNOT HELP YOU, AUBREY! YOUR MIND IS AN INFERNO! I CAN'T--!
FWOOOOSH!
I CANNOT HEAL EITHER OF US!!
COWARD!
YOU CAN BEAT THE FIRE! I CAN FEEL IT WHEN IT TOUCHES YOU--WHEN I TOUCH YOU!
NO--YOU UNDERSTAND NOTHING--
I UNDERSTAND EVERYTHING ABOUT MEN LIKE YOU! YOU TALK THE BIG LIE--PROMISE TO CHANGE, EVEN TO YOURSELF--

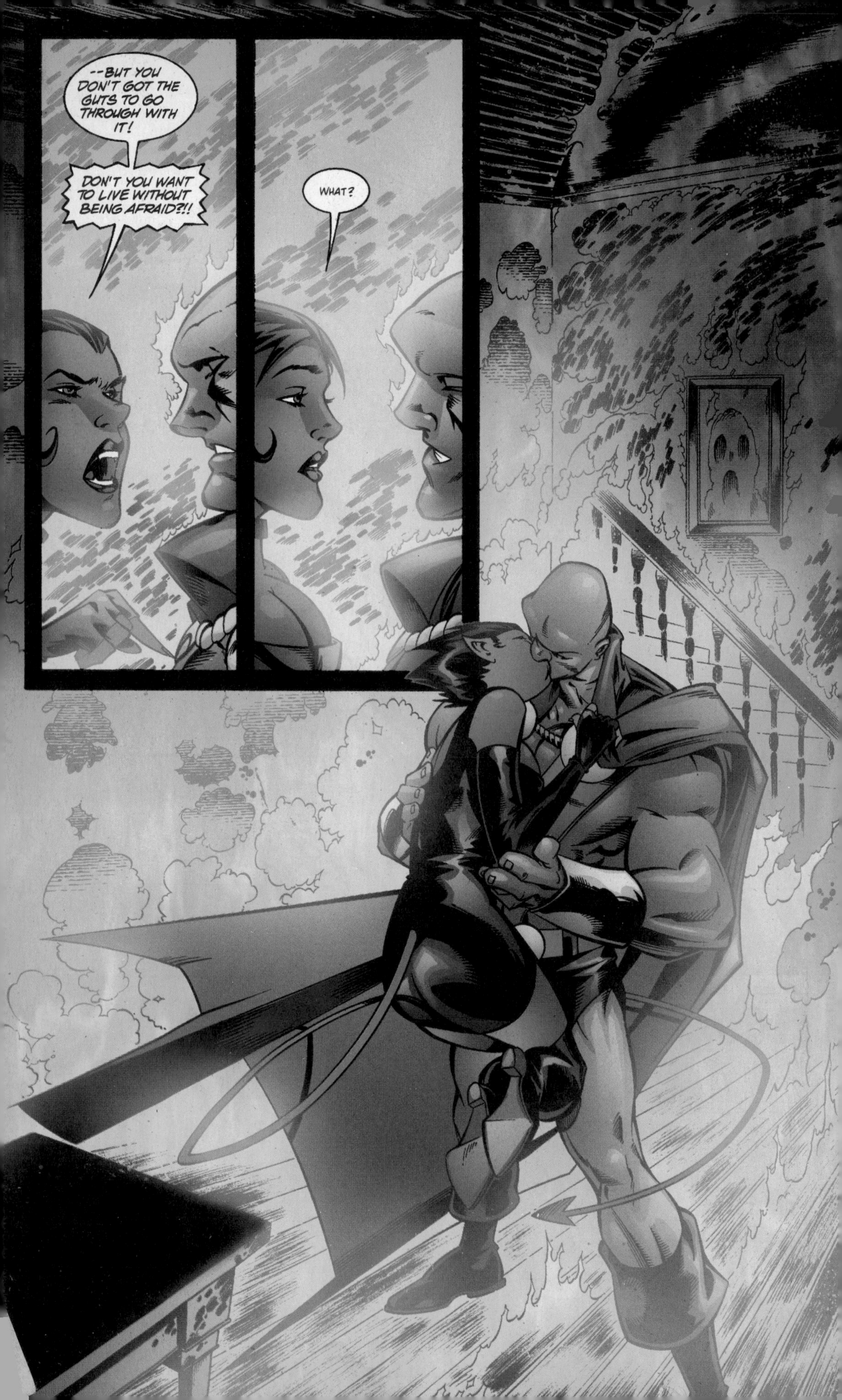
--BUT YOU DON'T GOT THE GUTS TO GO THROUGH WITH IT!
DON'T YOU WANT TO LIVE WITHOUT BEING AFRAID?!!
WHAT?

JLA DON'T MISS A SINGLE VOLUME FEATURING THE WORLD'S GREATEST SUPER-HEROES

VOLUME 1:
NEW WORLD ORDER
Morrison/Porter/Dell

VOLUME 2:
AMERICAN DREAMS
Morrison/Porter/Dell/various

VOLUME 3:
ROCK OF AGES
Morrison/Porter/Dell/various

VOLUME 4:
STRENGTH IN NUMBERS
Morrison/Porter/Dell/various

VOLUME 5:
JUSTICE FOR ALL
Morrison/Waid/Porter/various

VOLUME 6:
WORLD WAR III
Morrison/DeMatteis/Porter/
various

VOLUME 7:
TOWER OF BABEL
Waid/Porter/Dell/various

VOLUME 8:
DIVIDED WE FALL
Waid/Hitch/Neary/various

VOLUME 9:
TERROR INCOGNITA
Waid/Dixon/Beatty/Hitch/
various

VOLUME 10:
GOLDEN PERFECT
Kelly/Mahnke/Nguyen

VOLUME 11:
OBSIDIAN AGE BOOK 1
Kelly/Mahnke/Guichet/
Nguyen/Propst

VOLUME 12:
OBSIDIAN AGE BOOK 2
Kelly/Mahnke/Guichet/Larossa/
Nguyen/Propst/Milgrom

JLA: Earth 2
Morrison/Quitely

JLA: A League of One
Moeller

JLA: One Million
Morrison/Semeiks/various

JLA: Riddle of the Beast
A. Grant/various

**JLA: World Without
Grown-Ups**
Dezago/Ramos/Nauck/various

JLA: Year One
Waid/Augustyn/Kitson/Bair/various

JLA/JSA: Virtue & Vice
Goyer/Johns/Pacheco/Merino

**JLA/The Titans:
The Technis Imperative**
Grayson/Jimenez/Pelletier/various

**Justice League:
A Midsummer's Nightmare**
Waid/Nicieza/various

**Justice League of America:
The Nail**
Davis/Farmer

**Secret Origins
Featuring the JLA**
various

THE HEROES OF THE JUSTICE LEAGUE CAN ALSO BE FOUND IN THESE BOOKS FROM DC: